PRAISE FOR *SURROUNDED BY OTHERS AND YET SO ALONE*

"This book is a compilation of extraordinary stories told by a master storyteller. J. W. Freiberg has met some amazingly resilient survivors of a somewhat broken system and has told their tales with uncommon grace. His humanity, his compassion, and his love for the details of the law shine through his stories with clarity!"

—Jacqueline Olds, MD
Associate Professor of Child Psychiatry,
Harvard Medical School

"These surprising and moving stories draw us a vivid map of the many worlds of loneliness. J. W. Freiberg has so much to teach us about the causes of loneliness and what it's like to be trapped there. And he's a hell of a storyteller with some amazing tales to tell."

—Richard Schwartz, MD
Associate Professor of Adult Psychiatry,
Harvard Medical School

SURROUNDED BY OTHERS AND YET SO ALONE

SURROUNDED BY OTHERS AND YET SO ALONE

A LAWYER'S CASE STORIES OF LOVE, LONELINESS, AND LITIGATION

J. W. Freiberg

PHILIA BOOKS, LTD.

Published by Philia Books, Ltd., Boston, MA
www.thelonelinessbooks.com

Edited and designed by Girl Friday Productions
www.girlfridayproductions.com

Cover design: Kathleen Lynch

ISBN (paperback): 978-0-9975899-4-8
ISBN (ebook): 978-0-9975899-5-5

Library of Congress Control Number: 2020902646

For Joaquin
and
for Ama

The bright stars in the evening of my years

—

Distance is not the measure of remoteness. The wall of our own garden may enclose more secrets than the Great Wall of China, and the soul of a little girl may be more fully guarded by silence than are the Saharan oases by the density of the sands.

—Antoine de Saint-Exupéry, *Wind, Sand and Stars*

CONTENTS

PREFACE

BESSEL VAN DER KOLK, MD

Perhaps my favorite course in college was constitutional law. I think that was because it was there where I learned about how our lives are in part organized by the "rules of the game" that our laws and norms prescribe, and how these forces create the matrix that defines the social boundaries in which we live. These rules of the game are not abstractions: they impose dramatic and real-world effects on how well we live, determining, for example, to what degree we have access to quality schools and whether or not our particular neighborhood has access to clean water, safe food, and adequate protection of our persons and property. The idea that some people's profession is to help interpret the laws in order to define—and to constantly redefine—these rules, and to struggle to ensure that justice is done, was positively thrilling to me as a student. If I could have imagined myself an appellate judge or Supreme Court justice, I believe I would almost certainly have gone to law school.

But I didn't. I became a psychiatrist, a "shrink"—a person who helps people cope with overwhelming emotions, shameful impulses, and self-destructive behaviors inside the rules of the game that form the boundaries of their lives. Enclosed and entrapped in that context, I often wish I had the power to move around the chess pieces on the board—to alter the boundaries—in order to stack the cards more in my patients' favor. But mental health clinicians have no such power.

In my work, lawyers often play important roles. For instance, as a young psychiatrist, I served as the last superintendent of a large and outdated public mental hospital; I was thrilled to see it closed down. This updating in how we deal with the mentally ill was in significant part due to idealistic attorneys who, through appropriate litigation, brought about overall reform to the old state hospital system of which it was a part. From that point forward, provisions were made to help mental patients live better lives in community-based programs. Through the years, I have encountered other attorneys in particular law cases in which a psychiatry patient of mine was involved—or in which I served as an expert witness—who were deeply committed to helping find real-world solutions to the real-world issues that underlay the case. In doing this—in moving the chess pieces of the lives of my patients—they positively affected the mental health of my patients while resolving the particular legal issue in play. In several fiercely litigated, and very painful, custody disputes, for example, I worked alongside attorneys who exhibited commendable sensitivity as to how to handle the matter being litigated without destroying the relationships, and sometimes the lives, of the individuals involved. Occasionally, this sensitivity rose to the level of wisdom, where attorneys never lost sight of the fragility and vulnerability of the persons who had become entangled in the legal proceedings. I saw this play out, for example, when counsel had no choice but to call to the stand a victim-witness in a child molestation case, which was one type of case in which I would often serve as an expert witness.

Not surprisingly, in my capacity as an expert witness in criminal and civil law cases, especially in those cases arising from molestation of a child—whether by their own parents, or by adults in authority, like Roman Catholic priests—I also encountered defense attorneys who cared more about the money they were making than about the mental health of the litigants they deposed and questioned—including very young victim-witnesses. So, I became familiar with another aspect of the law—the cynical part. And, of course, this type of unscrupulous attorney was capable of causing great psychological harm, since all too often might makes right in our legal system, allowing those with the deepest pockets to prevail, independent of the merits of their case.

But then, the following day, I might find myself working with amazing public defenders. These lawyers earned only a fraction of the fees earned by the defense attorneys who had wealthy clients and large corporate accounts, but making money was not what they sought to do with their law degrees. And alongside these seldom-heralded heroes on the criminal law side of the legal system, I worked with and came to greatly admire other modestly paid attorneys who worked on the civil side, including those who provided legal services to the Southern Poverty Law Center, the Women's Law Project, and numerous other legal organizations—lawyers who often made all the difference in the lives of people in need of assistance who couldn't afford to pay for it on their own.

And then there is J. W. Freiberg. A former social-psychology professor, a gourmet cook, a blue water sailor, and a fluent French speaker (one of the fascinating stories in this book will keep you spellbound, and walk you through Paris), Freiberg served for over three decades as the go-to attorney in Boston for child protective social service organizations, adoption agencies, and scores of private practices of psychiatrists, psychologists, and clinical social workers. By drawing on his multiple skill sets, he played the role of a crucial intermediary between psychiatric medicine, family law, victim services, international adoption, and my particular specialty, "developmental psychopathology"—the study of everything that can go wrong with the minds and brains of children who have been abandoned, neglected, abused, or otherwise mistreated. As you will discover in Freiberg's case studies, interfacing between the law and the social-psychological stresses that litigants experience and inflict on one another in legal proceedings requires both professional expertise and insight—and it all works best when legal representation is delivered with wisdom, humor, compassion, and a keen discernment of what makes people tick. And that is just what Freiberg was able to give his clients, as I saw in years of professional interaction as we worked on particular cases together, and as you will learn about in this book.

As a psychiatrist, I listen to people in clinical sessions, prescribe medications, and suggest and provide a range of treatments to help my patients feel more at peace, and more like themselves—more like the way they were meant to be. But I surely cannot change around the chess pieces of their lives. That is what a good attorney can do for his clients, and what Freiberg did in his law practice, as reported in the pages that follow. At times, he tells us, he was presented with cases that could not be meaningfully resolved merely with legal maneuvers—cases where full and just resolution required real-world chess moves. And it was particularly these complex (i.e., part legal, part social-psychological) cases that fascinated and seemingly delighted him, and to which he brought his unique combination of legal skills and psychological insights—together with his willingness to . . . well . . . to move around those chess pieces. Boston is a very small city within any given sector, and the more Freiberg resolved law cases by working out solutions to the social-psychological underpinnings of the legal troubles that found their way to his clients, the more such cases he was referred by other attorneys. At times, as in the case story entitled "Three Souls Caught in a Spider's Web," you'll see Freiberg resolve a law case by actually forging a new life for his client, while making amends to those his client had harmed. The handling of the case reads like a Sherlock Holmes story, with Freiberg and his Dr. Watson, the skillful and colorful private eye "Longfellow," outworking and outwitting the opposition and finally finding the key that fit the lock—the chess move that resolved the entire matter, to the benefit of everyone involved.

***

What we have in Freiberg, I'm happy to say, is the Oliver Sacks of law. Freiberg's stories of law cases—like Sacks's clinical tales of his neurology patients—lead the reader through a fascinating accounting of the technical workings of their respective professions. But both writers do so much more for us than that, for both report to us how, by being forced to think outside the box, they worked to resolve the singular and fascinating cases that came their way. And Freiberg, like Sacks, has an unpretentious ease of expression in his flowing prose that sometimes brings a tear, sometimes a smile, and often an insight. Both writers manage to report their professional intervention in deadly serious real-world circumstances with a lightness of touch that seems almost ethereal. Freiberg never lectures his reader; on the contrary, his voice seems more like a whisper from the person sitting next to you as you both look out at the legal drama seemingly unfolding on its own in the pages you read.

Bessel van der Kolk, MD
Boston, 2019

PROLOGUE

My recent book *Four Seasons of Loneliness* presented four law-case stories that illustrated half of the story of chronic loneliness, depicting the tragically sad fates of clients who had a painful absence of significant others in their lives. *Surrounded by Others and Yet So Alone* is about the other half of the story: it is about those who live enmeshed in a network of connections with family, friends, neighbors, partners, teammates, and the like—but who nonetheless experience life as a terribly lonely venture. Their connections are misconnections, and their faulty linkages to others in their lives fail to provide the security, nurturing, and soothing care that others enjoy from their healthy connective networks.

Taken separately, each of the lives depicted in this book illuminates a different mode of misconnection, and is intended to demonstrate how that particular type of relational malfunction can generate the sensation of chronic loneliness. What we learn from these case histories when we take them together is that subjectively lonely persons can feel just as detached and alone as those who are objectively isolated.

Surrounded by Others and Yet So Alone is expressly *not* a study of how and why certain types of psychologically compromised individuals—depressives or paranoid persons, for example—can experience devastating loneliness even while involved in a stable network of interpersonal relationships. On the contrary, the cases presented in this

book chronicle the lives of clients who were psychologically sound—
so far as I ever knew. So what we are observing in these cases is the
impact of misconnection on psychologically capable individuals.

SO HOW DID A LAWYER GET
INVOLVED WITH THESE ISSUES?

In my first career, I was an assistant professor in the Sociology
Department of Boston University. For a decade, I taught social psychology and social theory—and then one day in my midthirties, almost
by chance, off I went to law school. After my initial legal training at
one of Boston's leading firms, I was recruited by a senior attorney at a
far smaller firm to become his partner, and to serve as general counsel
to Massachusetts's largest and oldest children's social services agency.
Additional large-scale agencies soon asked me to serve as their general counsel as well, as did numerous smaller agencies with varying
focuses, a dozen adoption agencies, and scores of private practices of
psychiatrists, psychologists, and clinical social workers. I had become
typecast as Boston's "psych lawyer"—whether I liked it or not—and
that was that for the remainder of my career.

Besides my handling of the routine legal matters that any general
counsel sees, it became progressively more common for the professional clinicians in these agencies to call me seeking case-specific legal
consultation. Under Massachusetts law, these mental health professionals were "mandated reporters"—meaning that they were legally
required to immediately report any suspicion of abuse or neglect of
a child to the child welfare authorities—just as they were compelled
by additional regulations to report both spousal and elder abuse. But
while their reporting responsibilities were clear, what wasn't at all clear
was whether something they had been told by a five-year-old, or something they thought they had observed in the behavior of an adult client,
constituted adequate cause to trigger their reporting responsibilities.
Could they get sued if their observations were in error? Was what they
had heard or observed in a counseling session adequate cause to call
the police in an elder abuse matter? Was there legal exposure if they
counseled a domestically abused client to confront or leave an abusive

spouse, and the client was assaulted or killed during their effort to break free? What was the risk to their professional licensure if they testified truthfully in a court hearing but against the interests of their client or patient? There were hundreds of such questions posed over the years, and for each one, I was presented a detailed description of the underlying fact pattern depicting the life of the clinician's client or patient.

In the end, these case consultations proved the most interesting aspect of my law practice. My job, of course, was to provide advice on whatever specific legal questions were raised in a particular case. But given my social-psychology training, I found no way to constrain myself from simultaneously considering the fact patterns I was hearing as de facto social scientific data. My detailed case notes from these consultations total well over a thousand such cases, and on top of these matters, I litigated scores of additional cases in the state and federal trial courts of Massachusetts. Now, largely retired from the active practice of law, I have time to review these notes, and to extract from them the lessons they tell us about why human social interactions can malfunction so profoundly.

So, you might wonder, why, among the myriad of differing social-psychological patterns I could discern in these cases, have I chosen to write these two books about clients who suffered from chronic loneliness? For two principal reasons. First, because chronic loneliness has become a public health crisis of the first order. An ever-increasing number of adult households in the United States are now single-person households: in 2018, the percentage of such homesteads stood at 28 percent.[1] In today's United States, 63 percent of adults have never married, whereas in 1960, only 28 percent of adults remained single.[2] Not surprisingly, this progressive demise of the nuclear family (following upon the quasi-extinction of the multigenerational family life typical of times past) has had a major impact on how people feel about the quality and certainty of their connections to their families. In 2010, over 35 percent of American adults reported that they considered themselves to be chronically lonely, up from 20 percent two decades

1.   Jonathan Vespa, Jamie M. Lewis, and Rose M. Kreider, *America's Families and Living Arrangements: 2012* (Washington, DC: US Census Bureau Report, 2013).
2.   Current Population Survey of the United States Census Bureau, 2018.

earlier.[3] Stop and think for a moment about this appalling statistic. We're literally falling apart, and the consequences are very substantial. The late John Cacioppo and his University of Chicago colleagues have long since documented that chronically lonely people suffer significantly increased morbidity and mortality rates.[4] Douglas Nemecek, MD, Cigna insurance's chief medical officer for behavioral health, has reported that the findings of the Cigna 2018 U.S. Loneliness Index suggest that the problem has reached "epidemic" proportions, rivaling the risks posed by heavy smoking and obesity.[5] And the future looks bleaker yet: the nation's 75 million millennials (aged twenty-three through thirty-seven) and Generation Z adults (eighteen to twenty-two) score as the loneliest US demographic, and on top of that, they report being in worse health than earlier generations were at their age.[6]

But there is a second reason for my interest in this subset of my law cases. Just as you cannot study hunger without researching and reporting about the food supply, you cannot study loneliness without thinking about the connections that people make—or fail to make—with one another. And when I read and reread my notes from the law cases that reintroduced to me the details of the lives of clients suffering from chronic loneliness, I came upon the finding that loneliness is not an emotion but is, instead, a sensation. Loneliness, I realized, is the sensation of inadequate connections to others, just as hunger is the sensation of inadequate nourishment and thirst is the sensation of inadequate hydration. In significant part, we share these sensations with other species in the animal kingdom, unlike our emotions, which are quintessentially human overlays.

This distinction has important consequences. Our sensations (except for audial input) are controlled and processed by the parietal lobe of our brain, while our emotions are controlled and processed in the temporal lobe by the limbic system, particularly the amygdala. This distinction is critical because while we can make conscious input into temporal lobe functioning, quite the opposite is the case with the

3. Brad Edmondson, "All the Lonely People," *AARP,* November/December 2010.
4. John T. Cacioppo and William Patrick, *Loneliness: Human Nature and the Need for Social Connection* (New York: W. W. Norton, 2008).
5. *CIGNA 2018 U.S. Loneliness Index,* Cigna, 2018, https://www.cigna.com/assets/docs/newsroom/loneliness-survey-2018-fact-sheet.pdf.
6. *CIGNA 2018 U.S. Loneliness Index.*

parietal lobe, or "old brain," functions. This is why you can talk yourself out of being angry (an emotion) but you cannot talk yourself out of being hungry or thirsty—or lonely (three of the sensations).

MISCONNECTION AND LONELY LIVES

When I searched through my notes from cases involving clients who were plagued with subjective chronic loneliness generated by their defective connections with others in their lives, I found that they fell out into five principal *modes of misconnection*. In other words, at least for the several hundred individuals whose files I was reviewing, there seemed to be five basic ways in which they misconnected with people around them. Accordingly, I searched for a case in each category of misconnection that would typify—or at least do a good job of exhibiting—each of these modes of faulty connection. My method, if it even deserves such a term, is simply to allow each of these case histories to speak for itself—and for its genre. Later, in a brief epilogue, we can take a look at the overall topography of the subjective chronic loneliness that is induced by misconnection. In the meantime, permit me just a few additional paragraphs to briefly introduce you to the cast of characters you will meet in the case studies that follow.

Tenuous Connections

In some of the law cases I reviewed, the connections between my clients and others in their lives were defective in that they were uncertain, tentative, or unreliable. The nature of the uncertainty varied from case to case, but the effect of the ambiguity was the same: individuals who could not trust the solidity and certainty of their interpersonal relationships often experienced themselves as chronically disconnected. In my dealings with this subset of clients, some characterized their relationships as problematic, and others described their links to those around them as conditional, equivocal, or erratic. Most reported living with an ever-present fear that their connections to those they cared most about could vanish at any moment, and many reported horrifically frightening repetitive nightmares in which they could no longer locate or make contact with the key persons in their lives.

But there was one tenuous connection story that stood head and shoulders above the rest, and that's the case I want to share with you in detail. It is the case of Victoria, a beautiful little six-year-old girl with boundless charm. Victoria's mother, an operating-room nurse at a Boston hospital, became pregnant through an affair with a visiting French postdoctoral student. Her lover returned to France before her discovery of the pregnancy, and she determined to never tell him. Not long thereafter, she met a surgeon who had recently joined the hospital staff. The couple fell in love and decided to raise the child together— but they failed to take the step of marrying each other. When Victoria's mother died unexpectedly of a stroke six years later, the only "father" that Victoria had ever known learned that he had no legal relation- ship whatsoever with his child. None, that is, unless I could somehow devise a strategy that would convince a Massachusetts Probate and Family Court judge to overlook the legal precedent that cut strongly against us and refrain from removing from my client's life the single person on the face of the earth he cared most about.

One-Way Connections

One-way connections, I learned, can cause excruciating pain to those who suffer them. Unrequited love is the classic example of this mode of misconnection, and this is something we all know: Could there be anyone reading these words who passed through their adolescence without falling head over heels in love with someone who couldn't have cared less about them? And, of course, unrequited love does not spare adults: it certainly is not rare for a love story to end for one partner in a relationship, while the other remains blissfully unaware, as enamored as ever. Numerous divorce clients came to my office distraught with the recent withdrawal of love and the severance of connection by the very person they cared most about. And several times it was the other way around: the person seeking legal counsel was preparing to jettison someone whom they had promised to stay connected with until "death do [them] part." One among this latter group even sought advice from me about how best to break the devastating news to his unsuspecting, no-longer-so-significant other who was, as my client phrased it, "completely blind about my being already gone." As if I knew.

The one-directional faulty connection case I want you to think about concerns a criminal defense attorney whom I was asked to represent in disbarment proceedings brought against him and heard before the Supreme Judicial Court of Massachusetts. The allegations filed by the Office of the Bar Counsel set forth a troubling fact pattern: in a decade of court-appointed criminal defense work, with very few exceptions, the attorney had never settled a case. Given that well over 95 percent of all such cases are resolved with plea bargains, it was aberrant and puzzling that this singular public defender took essentially all his cases to trial—and proceeded to lose almost every single one of them. You will meet three of his past clients—each in their respective prison cell—and hear from their perspectives how their lives were profoundly degraded by their attorney's aberrant definition of what they understood to be a professional relationship.

Fraudulent Connections

A rarer but particularly pernicious mode of misconnection occurs when a relationship is based on material false representations by one party. Erving Goffman, in his seminal book *The Presentation of Self in Everyday Life*, initiated the study of face-to-face interactions from a dramaturgical perspective.[7] Goffman believed that when two individuals meet, they each try to control the initial impression they give the other by managing their facial expressions, controlling their posture, editing what they say, and so on. This is something that we all do to a certain extent, and arguably it's the norm—*until the picture we present of who we actually are becomes so distorted that it amounts to relational fraud.* My fraudulent misconnection cases had a consistent pattern: the underlying deceit constituted an Achilles' heel to the relationship, and remained as explosively armed through time as does an

---

7.   Erving Goffman, *The Presentation of Self in Everyday Life* (New York: Doubleday, 1959).

undetonated ordnance that digs itself into the mud during wartime, waiting patiently to be triggered years later.

The singular case of a client named Shi Pei-Pu illustrates this mode of misconnection better than any other. Mr. Shi (pronounced "she," which is the family name) was the Chinese opera singer whose life story was depicted in the Tony Award–winning Broadway play *M. Butterfly*, as well as in the magnificent film of the same name starring Jeremy Irons.[8] Mr. Shi, I was to learn, was a master of deceit, and this is the tale of how he conned his male French lover into believing that he was a woman—for nearly thirty years. Mr. Shi's deception and manipulation knew no bounds: he went so far as to adopt a child, as its mother, and later to misrepresent his gender to the French authorities and emigrate with the child to France as a woman. Shi's true gender was revealed only after he and his French lover were arrested in Paris and subsequently convicted of international espionage and sentenced to long prison terms.

Obstructed Connections

My task in representing a ten-year-old cancer patient named "Billy" was to get at least one of his parents free and clear of the obstructions that rendered them emotionally incapable of allowing him, as Billy phrased it, to "feel their love." It was almost immediately clear that getting his hedge-fund-addicted father to clear his channel was hopeless, so my efforts became concentrated on Billy's mother. It wasn't that his mother didn't love the boy, I learned, it was just, again as Billy put it, "that she does love the way a flashlight shines light when its batteries have just about died. It's just a glow: it doesn't help you see in the dark." What was entirely astonishing about the case was how it ballooned from what at first seemed like a simple matter for a family therapy clinician into dealings with a Rhode Island Mafia don, the principal assistant district attorney for Los Angeles County, and the Offices of the United States Attorney for Southern California. Billy's case began so

---

8.   Jeremy Irons's remarkable performance of Shi Pei-Pu is readily available on YouTube. I highly recommend you view at least the suicide scene before reading my case study.

innocently, but in the end, it tipped over the first in a line of dominoes that led to the resignation in disgrace of a United States congressman.

Dangerous Connections

Finally, we need to take a look at the fact that some defective connections are dangerous, and some are even life threatening. Over the years, quite a few such cases brought me into contact with clients whose links to their closest companions brought them as much pain and suffering as they brought shelter and nourishment. Healthy connections, in contrast, provide each of us with sanctuary—with safety and with the soothing touch of those who love us.

The dangerous connection story I want to share with you wasn't actually a law case.

Somewhat over a year before this non-case took shape, the most perfect French bakery shop you can imagine opened in my neighborhood. Its arrival was like manna from heaven: beautiful, traditional French baking went on *in front of your eyes* in the back two-thirds of the bakery, while the front third of the space was given over to the retail shop where bread and pastries were alluringly displayed on antique French bread racks. It all seemed too good to be true, and, unfortunately, it was. When I finally perceived that my favorite baker was in grave danger, I saddled up my briefcase as if it were Rocinante, and rode off to her rescue like a dime-store Don Quixote. Alas, I had no more idea of the labyrinth of adventures that lay ahead for me than did the original Knight of the Woeful Countenance.

A NOTE ON THE ORIGIN OF THE LAW CASE STORIES

Those who have read early drafts of these stories have inquired, almost to a person, if they are fact or fiction. These stories come from the files of law cases on which I worked, and they contain a myriad of details about the lives of clients whom I counseled and represented. That being said, limits imposed by privilege and confidentiality requirements oblige me to modify identifying specifics of the cases from which these stories are drawn. I do this by changing names, altering identifying details, shifting locations, integrating elements from related law cases, and modifying some components of the actual cases I litigated, negotiated, and consulted on. But rest assured: the lessons about loneliness and connection that speak out from these stories come from very real law cases.

J. W. Freiberg
Paris, 2019

THE GIRL WHO
INHERITED FRANCE

I half walked, half jogged back to my office from the new federal courthouse on Boston Harbor. I was trying with all my heart and soul to avoid arriving late for the initial meeting with a new client named Victoria Bergeron: the last thing I wanted was to start a new attorney-client relationship with a disappointment. But alas, as soon as I popped out of the elevator the receptionist—barely able to suppress a grin for some reason—let me know in no uncertain terms that I was too late: "Ms. Bergeron is waiting for you in your office, and the gentleman who accompanied her is using the washroom." I nodded, cursed under my breath, and kept right on moving. Twenty steps later, I knocked on my own slightly ajar office door. No one answered, so I opened it fully to find—no one. Or so I thought at first. It was only on second glance that I saw a child's head barely sticking up above the back of one of the two client chairs that faced my desk. It was not until I rounded the desk that I first laid eyes on Victoria Bergeron—one of the cutest little girls you can imagine. She was petite by any standard, and graced with long, silky-looking brunette hair made up of a score of subtly different shades of brown. And then there were her eyes: they were so startlingly green that they seemed to be made of Imperial jade, and they were positively radiant when she flashed me her six-year-old's toothless smile.

We had just greeted each other when Jonathan Freeman, MD, knocked and entered. I assumed he was Victoria's father—they certainly treated each other as father and child. But I would soon learn that their relationship was far more complex than that and that the legal challenge facing me would be to do whatever I could to preserve the parent-child connection that Victoria had known all her life but which her changed circumstances had now rendered so entirely tenuous.

Dr. Freeman explained that Victoria was the daughter of his late significant other, Sandrine Bergeron, who had succumbed to a sudden and unexpected stroke just two months earlier. She was the daughter of a deceased French father and an American mother who had long since divorced. Her mother had remarried and currently lived with her second husband, a revival-tent minister, in a small town in a small town outside Fort Worth, Texas. Sandrine Bergeron and her mother, Dr. Freeman revealed, had been estranged for over a decade.

Dr. Freeman went on to describe how Bergeron had worked in Boston for many years as a surgical nurse practitioner at Beth Israel Deaconess Medical Center. That, it turned out, was the source of the referral to me: I had served on the hospital's board of overseers for many years. The hospital was also the source of Dr. Freeman's relationship with Bergeron: he had moved to Boston for his residency in orthopedic surgery, and within six weeks of first spotting Bergeron's eyes peering at him above her surgical mask as she handed him a scalpel, he asked her out on a first date.

Victoria was beginning to squirm a bit in her chair, so I asked if she might have any interest in a cup of hot chocolate; just a few minutes later, she was off to the coffee room, hand in hand with the office librarian. This freed up Dr. Freeman to describe in detail what brought him to my office, and the story he told me was as follows.

About seven years before our meeting, Sandrine Bergeron had attended a two-week training session at the hospital where she met and had an affair with another attendee—a young Parisian orthopedic surgeon. Within six weeks of the Frenchman's return to France, Bergeron had discovered that she was pregnant, and within another six weeks, Bergeron and Dr. Freeman first spotted each other in that operating room.

Not more than a fortnight later, Bergeron had sat Freeman down for a serious—and no doubt worrisome—conversation to announce that she was pregnant, and also that it was by a previous lover. She was also clear that she had no intention of terminating the pregnancy.

Dr. Freeman, ever more animated as he told me this story, said that he had visibly dazed Bergeron with his twofold response. First, he had assured her that her private life before they met was her business, and second, he explained to her that the pregnancy was actually wonderful news to him—great news, in fact—because he, too, had something he needed to share with her—he was irreversibly infertile. So, as Dr. Freeman phrased it, "We were in love, she was pregnant, and I was infertile—everything was copacetic." They pooled their money, bought a little house on "Pill Hill"—a popular neighborhood for doctors, walking distance from the hospital—and set up their life together.

Bergeron, reportedly, had hoped that the news of her settling down with Dr. Freeman would help patch up the relationship with her mother, but her efforts at rapprochement led only to a single and entirely perfunctory three-day visit just after Victoria's birth. There was not the slightest uptick in warmth or connection, and subsequently the relationship amounted to nothing more than an occasional exchange of Hallmark cards.

The couple, Dr. Freeman continued, were wonderfully happy together. They had, however, never gotten around to actually marrying—partly because of a baseless hope that somehow time and a grandchild would help heal Bergeron's relationship with her mother, but mostly because both Bergeron and Dr. Freeman had incredibly hectic work and childcare schedules.

My heart sank when Dr. Freeman told me this, and even more so when I learned what I feared might be the case: they had never approached an attorney to investigate "stepparent adoption." I described the easy pathway to permanency planning that they had missed. All they would have had to do, given that Bergeron had had sole legal and physical custody of Victoria, was to marry, file a petition for a stepparent adoption, and place legal notice of their intention in an appropriate newspaper for a few weeks. With this simple procedure, the adoption by Dr. Freeman would have permanently terminated Victoria's legal relationship to her birth father, whose name would have been replaced by Dr. Freeman's on Victoria's birth certificate.

Now, I explained, the circumstances were radically different. Dr. Freeman had no legal relationship whatsoever with the child—unless they had taken some liberties with the truth and put Dr. Freeman's name on the birth certificate as the child's father. They had not.

There was, of course, one further hope: disinterest on the part of the grandmother in taking on the very considerable work of raising a young child. At least the answer to this question was not yet known by Dr. Freeman, although perhaps there was a hint in that Victoria's grandmother had opted not to attend Bergeron's memorial services, and had been openly cold, even rude, to Dr. Freeman when he had called to tell her of her daughter's sudden and unexpected passing. Apparently, the stepfather had called out something like "Serves her right" in the background—loud enough to be heard.

Just at this point in the story, Victoria came skipping back into the room, her lips bearing admissible evidence that she had indeed enjoyed a hot chocolate. Clearly, we were done for the day, so Dr. Freeman and I arranged to meet soon for another appointment, sans Victoria. I asked Dr. Freeman to make a list of every doctor, every teacher, every friend—everyone he could think of—who would talk to me and potentially testify about the role he had played in Victoria's life. I also asked him to think about what strategy might work best with respect to the "g-r-a-n-d-m-o-t-h-e-r," spelling out the word.

As they prepared to leave, I received a very nice smile from Miss Victoria just before she leapt up into Dr. Freeman's arms and immediately fell asleep with her forehead pressed into the crook of his neck. The bond between them was perfectly obvious, and I couldn't imagine a more worthwhile legal task than doing everything I could to keep the two connected. Dr. Freeman—like most clients—asked for a preliminary assessment of his chances of prevailing. All I could answer in good faith, however, was "One step at a time" before a very worried-looking Dr. Freeman carried his little treasure out of my office.

***

It was crystal clear that, above and beyond Dr. Freeman's list of fact witnesses who would attest to the constancy of his co-parenting, I would need an expert witness who could opine about the psychological trauma that could befall Victoria if she were removed from her father's loving care so soon after losing her mother. I had in mind Dr. Evan Newsom—the chief of pediatrics at Boston Children's Hospital, whose entire career had been devoted to protecting and treating children in crisis. There was a problem with the case, however, that even a truckload of helpful fact witnesses and a world-class expert witness could not resolve: the last time I had researched controlling legal precedent on these issues, I had found that the law cut sharply against us. Unless some new appellate case had changed matters, if the grandmother pressed her rights, she would prevail *as a matter of law.*

The first step, accordingly, was legal research, which, in the days before computer-aided case law inquiry, meant rolling up your sleeves and spending most of the night in the firm's law library. I recruited an associate to help me, but after hours and hours of poring over the casebooks, neither of us could come up with anything helpful. Every which way we looked, controlling precedent blocked us: there was no way we could overcome the grandmother's claim if she wanted to take legal and physical custody of the child—unless, we thought, we could find some newsworthy dirt on her or her husband. But this pipe dream only led to our finding another precedent-setting line of cases that thwarted even that possibility. They held that if we found and introduced evidence that the grandmother was demonstrably unfit to raise the child, the court would have no choice but to grant legal custody of the child to the Massachusetts Department of Social Services. If that happened, Victoria would slide into the machinations of the Massachusetts foster care system, and in that scenario, Dr. Freeman's only chance of re-obtaining custody would be to sign up at an adoption agency behind a line of preapproved couples who had waited for years with the hope and dream of finding a child to adopt. Neither the associate nor I was a happy camper when we dragged our sorry selves out of the firm to each go home for a few hours' sleep. And when I shared our findings with my client the next day, Dr. Freeman went silent for quite a while as he absorbed the bad news, and then phrased his response succinctly. "So, is it checkmate?"

I thought for a moment, and stumbled upon one final possible solution to our problem: What if we set out to recruit the help of the one player in the world who could trump the grandmother? That, of course, would be Victoria's biological father. But even if we could locate him in France, what would we say to him? What exactly would we ask for? And how would we go about this? After a good half minute of silence thinking this through, I broke out of my musings to describe to Dr. Freeman my far-fetched idea. Then, before he could even respond, I asked him if Victoria by any chance spoke French—we might need that language capacity to attract the father's attention. "Perfect French," he replied. "Victoria is entirely bilingual—for a six-year-old." This was the first positive piece of news in the case.

My next question was far more practical. I asked the doctor if he was willing and able to spend the tidy sum of money it would cost to fund a full-court press in France to locate the father and try to convince him to come to Victoria's rescue. Dr. Freeman's response was immediate: "Anything." I thought for another moment, and then explained that this strategy brought with it an unavoidable risk. If Victoria's father filed an appearance, and the court indeed granted him legal custody, he could decide to take the child back to raise her in France, and there would be nothing we could do to stop him. I've never forgotten Dr. Freeman's response to my warning: "If I can't raise Victoria, I'd sure as hell rather see her raised in Paris, France, than in Paris, Texas."

I remember that even while I was laughing at his quip, I was asking myself, *Oh boy, just how deeply do you want to get involved in this case?* Complex custody cases are not merely time consuming to the max— they are also emotionally taxing. Think about it: if a commercial lease negotiation falls through, you call up your client and say, "Sorry, it just didn't work out; they won't pay to renovate the space . . . Looks like you'll need to locate another building . . ." It's much harder to call your client and tell them you just received notice from the court, and they had permanently lost custody of their child. Much harder.

***

And so I dove in. To the best of Dr. Freeman's knowledge, Dr. Henri Dagnaud had never been told that his two-week-long dalliance with

Sandrine Bergeron had resulted in a pregnancy. Clearly, I warned my client, the odds were that Dr. Dagnaud would not be particularly delighted by the news, and given that we would be asking him for an enormous favor, we would need to be very strategic in how we approached the gentleman. Two things, I announced, were clear to me from the start. The discussion needed to be held in person—not on the phone—and it needed to happen simultaneously with showing him photographs of his beautiful child.

Dr. Freeman had no hesitancy whatsoever about my proposed strategy: if we needed to travel to France to enhance our odds, then so be it. Whatever it took. The final thing I asked Dr. Freeman that evening was whether he had a problem with my meeting with and trying to delicately discuss these matters with Victoria. He responded that he thought my speaking directly with her about the entire upcoming process would be helpful, perhaps even important.

***

And so, as I drove to Dr. Freeman's house the following Saturday afternoon for my meeting with Victoria, a strategy for the case began to formulate in my mind. Assuming we could rally Dr. Dagnaud to our cause, the next—and even greater—challenge would be to convince a Massachusetts Probate and Family Court judge about the soundness of our two-father plan. This proposed custodial arrangement, I realized, was entirely dependent upon Victoria being bilingual.

I determined to speak in French with Victoria that afternoon. My thinking was—above and beyond confirming whether or not I could argue to the judge that the child would be able to relate to her French father—that perhaps I could establish a subliminal connection with Victoria by using the language in which she had communicated with her mother. My idea was that if I spoke to her in the tongue in which she had been soothed and nurtured, she might feel comfortable and more quickly trust me as an ally as we all set out together on an endeavor that would be as psychologically complex as it was legally byzantine.

And that's exactly what happened. In fact, at one point in our conversation, Victoria actually said to me, "You sound like my mommy." Anyway, about twenty minutes into our meeting, I approached the sensitive and complicated custody campaign that brought us together. While I didn't think much of the content of what I had to say got through to the child, I did feel that she came to trust me more than she otherwise would have—for a reason she was nowhere near being able to perceive. My plan, of course, was that this language linkup would also carry over to Dr. Dagnaud—if we ever succeeded in convincing him to join our struggle and appear at the custody trial. I'll never know for certain whether the trust Victoria showed in me toward the end of our meeting that day was boosted by our conversation having taken place in French, but she did pose two questions—back-to-back—that seemed to indicate that perhaps it had played a role. First, she asked, "Why did my mommy go away?" which she immediately followed up with, "Will my daddy go away too?"

My mind wandered for a brief moment as I thought through how to respond. There must be no greater blow to a human being's sense of connection than when a young child experiences the sudden and per-manent disappearance of a parent—particularly their mother. I would think that, to a six-year-old, the lesson to be garnered from the abrupt and definitive departure of their mother would be that anybody on whom you rely for your nurturing and safety might up and leave you at any time. And while there is, of course, some existential truth in this conclusion, that's basically not how human connection operates. In our era, on average, most of us have the opportunity to stay con-nected to our parents for roughly half a century, and to our siblings for the better part of three-quarters of a century. And then consider our friendships. Some of us are lucky enough to have friendships that date back to our school days, and all but the most reclusive of us have formed more recent friendships at work, or in our neighborhoods, or through our special interests. So, most of us, although certainly not all, experience some considerable degree of average relative constancy in our connections to those we care most about. But how does one responsibly reassure a six-year-old who had just lost her mother that her personal experience with the loss of connection was the exception, not the rule—especially in the context of a custody battle where the wrong outcome would lead to her separation from the man whom she understood to be her father?

Victoria kept staring at me, waiting for my answers to her two questions. Somehow, speaking to her in the language she had used exclusively with her mother seemed to have granted me entry into a sphere of psychological space where the child sought solace and comforting—despite the fact that this was only the second time we had ever met. The problem was that I knew no words—in French, in English, or in any other language—that would adequately respond to "Why did my mommy go away?" The pain of such a loss is a feeling, a sensation—not a concept, not a thought. That's why we comfort victims of great loss with somatic reassurance—we hold and hug them. That's why trauma psychiatrists treat trauma victims with somatically based modalities—not with talk therapy.

And then, just when I could see Victoria giving up on my articulating a magically soothing response to her unanswerable questions, exactly what needed to happen dawned on me like a revelation. I proposed a milk-and-cookie break in our meeting, and three minutes later, while Victoria was absorbed in the not-so-easy-at-age-six task of dividing the two halves of her Oreos without breaking either cookie, I found a moment to whisper my idea to Dr. Freeman. He just smiled and nodded.

Forty-five minutes later, the three of us walked into the local pet store, and an hour after that, we left with the softest, most huggable puppy it had for sale. And about fifty pounds of dog-care paraphernalia that set the good doctor back a small fortune. My idea was, it would be this tiny little love-seeking puppy who could best soothe Victoria's need for somatic reassurance. In mothering the puppy, she would mother herself. In reassuring the puppy that it was okay for it to leave its littermates, she would reassure herself that it was okay for her to move on in life beyond her loss. And in the thousands of hugs and kisses she would lavish on her new best friend—and in the two million puppy licks she would receive in exchange—she would find some of the somatic connection she had lost in the disappearance of her mother. Phew.

***

It was time to plot out the strategic details as to how we might meet Dr. Henri Dagnaud at a time, in a place, and in a manner that maximized the odds that he would at least listen to our proposal. I asked my office's private eye, Reginald Brooke—"Longfellow," as he was always called—to make use of his European contacts to come up with a Paris-based investigator who could discover as much as possible, as quickly as possible, about Dr. Dagnaud's personal and professional circumstances. Within three days, Longfellow called back to say he had located a private eye named Laurent Fauvet who was fully licensed and who had appreciable experience. It took just a week after I retained this gentleman's services to receive initial feedback from him. Dr. Henri Dagnaud practiced orthopedic surgery at Hôpital Cochin, just off Boulevard du Montparnasse in central Paris. He was a respected professional who also taught classes in surgery at the École de médecine of the Université de Paris, and he had recently published a book with two colleagues about new techniques in arthroscopic hip replacement. And—no surprise here—his résumé mentioned that he had once attended a two-week-long training at Beth Israel Deaconess Medical Center/Harvard Medical School. As far as Fauvet could ascertain, that was the only time Dr. Dagnaud had ever traveled to the United States. He was married, and the father of a young daughter. (I remember wincing at hearing this.) He was a member of a tennis club in Paris, and in winter he favored skiing; actually, he was a skier of some appreciable capacity, having been a competitive racer in college. He and his wife, Sophie Bernard, owned a flat in a fashionable neighborhood of Paris near the Parc Monceau, and they also owned a small ski cabin in the Haute-Savoie not far from Annecy. Bernard was an attorney by training but worked as a journalist specializing in reporting on legal matters. Her articles appeared often in *Libération*, an intelligent center-left daily paper that was born during the student movement of May 1968. There was nothing whatsoever on the negative side of the ledger: no lawsuits, no criminal matters, no financial troubles.

While the information obtained by the private eye certainly backed up the general concept we were trying to sell—that Victoria's biological father was an admirable gentleman who would make a superb co-father for the child—I garnered no useful suggestion from Mr. Fauvet about the strategic approach I might use to plead our case to

Dr. Dagnaud. The one and only idea I could think of was to somehow exploit my membership on the board of overseers of the hospital where Dr. Dagnaud had met Sandrine Bergeron. After a fruitless week spent trying to devise an approach that didn't take advantage of my position, I gave in and called Dr. Freeman. I shared with him my reluctance to play this card but asked nonetheless if there was a lecture series, or some equivalent forum, to which Dr. Dagnaud could possibly be invited. Dr. Freeman confirmed the following day that Dr. Dagnaud's recent book was of significant interest to several of his colleagues, and that he would be entirely welcome to give a talk in the Department of Orthopedics—if the hospital administration was in accord, and if I would translate. His first condition, of course, was precisely what my board membership allowed me to arrange for—so we had an approach.

***

It took several calls, but I finally succeeded in reaching the administrative office of the orthopedic department at Hôpital Cochin. I did my best to explain that I was a board member at the Boston hospital where Dr. Dagnaud had attended a training session about seven years earlier, and that I wished to propose an offer to him. Ten minutes into the conversation it became abundantly clear that while I was making headway, it was only because the administrator with whom I was speaking had mistaken me for a person of some considerable importance at the hospital—which I certainly was not. So I moved along quickly to avoid lingering on the moral quandary her misconception presented—and ended by saying that I would very much like to plan a trip to Paris to meet with Dr. Dagnaud in order to make him "quite an extraordinary offer." Somehow, I managed to convince her that I was only at liberty to discuss the offer directly with Dr. Dagnaud, and that I would be pleased to do so at a lunch or dinner, on whatever day was most convenient for the doctor.

***

And so it came to pass that, just shy of two weeks later, I landed at Paris-Charles De Gaulle Airport and headed for a small boutique hotel in the heart of the Latin Quarter—walking distance from Hôpital Cochin. It was a typical Paris winter day: gray, with the cobblestones underfoot seeming permanently damp, recent rain or not. Our luncheon meeting had been arranged for the following day, and the more I thought about it, the more I became convinced that Dr. Dagnaud would probably be awaiting an offer of a visiting professorship at Harvard Medical School, or some such equivalent, given the amount of confusion I had sowed in his administrative staff. And all I had to offer was a talk in the Department of Orthopedics at Beth Israel Deaconess Medical Center with airfare and a mighty $500 honorarium. Oh yes: and a very dear little child.

***

I had arranged to dine the evening of my arrival with close French friends of many decades. My goal in arranging the evening was far from purely social: the wife of this couple was Jeanne Clement, a brilliant professor of social psychology, with extensive research experience in family matters. Her husband, Francis, was a research professor specializing in medical economics, and a man of quite considerable insight. We met at Le Select on Boulevard du Montparnasse, a traditional brasserie that had not changed in well over a hundred years—it still hasn't. I almost immediately laid out precisely what I was in town to accomplish. Clement thought silently for quite a while before responding, and then in a voice ringing with certainty, she announced: "Nope, it's not going to work. You'd have to talk his wife into it. And she'll see this as an invasion of her family and unwelcome competition for her two-year-old. There's no way they could explain this to their child. So it's not going to work, definitely not."

The adamancy of his wife's position took Francis by surprise. The very nature of French conversation left him no choice but to "*discuter*" with his wife: "Slow down, Jeanne. Let's think of this from a negotiating point of view." Once she nodded her reluctant consent, Francis turned toward me and asked what I had to offer in exchange.

"Okay," I responded, delighted to be drawn out. "Only three things—no, possibly four. First, Victoria. This is a healthy, beautiful, charming, bilingual child—she's an asset, not a liability. Second, she *is* his biological child. Third, there would be no financial cost to him: my client will gladly cover all the expenses of raising the child. And fourth, who knows—perhaps there is some interest on the doctor's part about future linkage to the Harvard Medical School hospital group. That could conceivably be a by-product of all this . . . perhaps. I guess. I don't really know that, actually."

"Impossible," Jeanne repeated. "It's not going to work."

"Hang on, dear," Francis interjected again. "We're here to advise about the best approach, given where things are at."

"I think it should begin with the photographs," I broke in. "I'll start with a stunning photograph of the deceased mother from the era of their affair. The woman was gorgeous. The photo has got to grab his attention—hell, they were young, and involved in a very sexy two-week affair. He'll want to know her history since he last saw her, and about the pregnancy she never told him about. And, of course, I'll tell him about her sudden death, and about how this exposes his daughter to an almost certain loss of Dr. Freeman if he doesn't come to the rescue. And during all this talking, I'll be showing him photographs of the child—a whole pile of them so that he gets to know her visually, and to know her life space. Now what do you think?"

"You might have to pick this guy up off the floor," Francis replied.

"Or he'll just get up and walk out," Jeanne added.

"No, I don't think so," I came back. "I think he'll be too stunned by the photograph of his lover to just get up and leave. It won't just be his mind at work: his entire body will remember what she felt like, what she smelled like, what she sounded like—it could be very deep emotionally for him. And while he is in this mind/body state, I'll be introducing him to *their* absolutely beautiful six-year-old daughter. I've got a briefcase full of photographs, but there are two that matter most—one of Victoria's face, and one of Dr. Dagnaud's own face a few years back that my private eye located. Both have identical eyes—of Imperial jade. I've never seen eyes that color before."

"The eyes are identical?" both friends called out.

"Exactly," I added. "That's our hook."

"Anything else?" Jeanne wanted to know, still looking entirely dubious about the venture.

"Well," I added, "like I said, I have about another hundred photos of the child at play, at school, at her house, in her room, in the neighborhood where she lives, and so on. And I also brought along a certified DNA test kit with the child's DNA already in it, so the doctor can quickly have it matched with his own. There'll be no question here as to paternity, I'm assuming."

"Okay," Francis broke in. "Okay. Those are your props. But what's your argument?"

Such a good question. It shut me up for at least half a minute. Finally I just let it rip. "Okay, let's start with what's *not* in my argument," I began. "My research shows that in France there are paternal responsibilities that cannot be avoided. So, Dr. Dagnaud is financially liable for Victoria under French law—if only for very modest child support payments. But if I have it right—and this is a question for you two— paternal responsibility is part of French culture above and beyond the financial responsibility. Unless you two tell me otherwise, from what I understand, Dagnaud has a *moral* duty to fulfill his paternal responsibilities—no?" This garnered two positive nods. "Good. So I'm going to assume that he and I share that understanding. So now let's look at what I *am* going to argue. I think it's very simple, it's just: 'Dr. Dagnaud, you have a beautiful, healthy daughter, and she desperately needs your help. Period.'"

Jeanne broke in. "That's all fine, and it might appeal to him as the right thing to do. But how do you slow it down, how do you make it reasonable for them to help out? I mean, it's one thing if there's a get-to-know-you period, and then gradually, over time, as things develop, there's a mutual working out of the child's schedule. A six-year-old is a very different visitor than a high school student coming to spend a year abroad."

"Exactly," I added. "That has to be part of the plan. And I'm sure my expert pediatrician will be able to testify that, given how young the child is, it would be better for her if her introduction to the co-parenting plan begins very gradually. The child has just lost her mother, for God's sake: what the child clearly needs is a period of stability for the time being. Then, as the years roll by, the parties can work together to figure out what educational opportunities in France or what physical custody arrangements would be in her best interest. So, what makes sense psychologically also makes sense for my approach to the doctor—and to his wife. Am I making any sense here? Jeanne, are you still so certain I don't have a chance?"

Silence reigned. So I threw in the obvious next question: "So, what would you two do if you were confronted with the same circumstance?"

Now, there was even deeper silence. It was Jeanne who spoke first—slowly and thoughtfully. "You may have a stronger position than I appreciated. In the first place, the doctor's lawyer wife will know about the legal framework you described. But more important than that is the reputation issue. That's a big deal among medical doctors in France, and she's got to see how potentially embarrassing this whole thing could be if it played out poorly. And you're right about the responsibility element—it's not at all just about the financial support—not here in France. It's a closer call than I thought. What's your take, Francis? What would you have wanted to do?"

Francis didn't hesitate for a moment. "I think Jeanne's right. I don't think the doctor can just ignore this child; if that came out publicly, he'd look heartless. And why should he do that? I wouldn't. But his reaction may only be thirty percent of what matters. I mean, I don't know this guy's marriage, but I know mine: I think it will all turn on his wife's reaction. Your problem, Terry," Francis added, using my life-long nickname, "is that Victoria is definitely not *her* child. And, by the way, don't forget the inheritance law issue. In France, you can't cut any of your children out of your inheritance, and you can't treat them unequally. So the presence of this second child cuts their daughter's inheritance in half. You might want to handle this issue up front—have your guy leave his estate to both children."

I was so excited about the reduction in Jeanne's pessimism hat I actually thought for a moment about ordering a bottle of champagne. But that might have jinxed everything.

***

The following day, the morning seemed endless. I had absolutely no way to predict Dr. Dagnaud's reaction, and I had to ready myself for the very real possibility that he might indeed just get up and leave the table. Denial, after all, is not the rarest reaction to being confronted with a problem. And, of course, he could easily feel that he was being ambushed under false pretenses. Who could blame him?

Predictably, I failed to walk as slowly as I had promised myself I would, so I had been seated a good fifteen minutes before Dr. Dagnaud joined me in Le Languedoc—a humble but reliable small bistro on Boulevard du Montparnasse. At forty, Dr. Dagnaud had the tall, strong-chested build of a downhill skier, coupled with an open, very attractive face with—best of all—a pair of huge jade-green eyes! As soon as we had finished with a minimum of pleasantries, I opened my folder of photographs and slipped out the strikingly beautiful photograph of Sandrine Bergeron, his lover of seven years ago.

I'm not sure if Dr. Dagnaud even heard my admission and apology about misrepresenting the circumstances under which we were meeting, because the photograph had an even more powerful, somatic effect on him than I had dared hope for. Frozen, he sat perfectly still, making small, involuntary "uhm" sounds deep in his throat, lost in what must have been deliciously beautiful memories. I waited just as long as it took for Dr. Dagnaud to glance up at me on his own initiative, and only then did I begin describing what had befallen Bergeron. I explained how he would have never heard about what had come to pass but for her unexpected death and Dr. Freeman's desperate need for his help. During my entire monologue, I slipped across the table photograph after photograph of beautiful little Victoria—one by one. He was completely absorbed in them.

It was only when he'd been through the entire pile of pictures—twice—that Dr. Dagnaud finally looked up. I asked if he and Bergeron had remained in touch after his return to France, and he answered that they had, indeed, for several weeks—with a profusion of potential follow-up plans. But then, quite suddenly, the correspondence had ended. "Now I understand why; it was the pregnancy. God, I wish she'd told me," Dr. Dagnaud lamented in a tone of voice that didn't at all try to mask the power of the connection the two had shared.

I paused and let him collect his thoughts. "My idea," I said, breaking the silence, "is that, with your help, I think I can convince a judge that this child is far better off being raised by Dr. Freeman in Boston while young, and later—as you, your wife, and Dr. Freeman would work out between you—perhaps partly in Paris, so she could benefit from both languages and both cultures. She is completely bilingual. Depending on what you thought best, if you and your wife wanted, we could all recommend to the court that in the early years, your involvement would be just an occasional visit—or whatever worked best for you and your family. And please, please note, Doctor, Dr. Freeman does not want this to be a financial burden on you and your family in any way. He intends to pay all the expenses of raising the child. He doesn't care about the money at all. He only cares about being able to continue raising this child whom he adores. He'll never have another child—he's completely infertile. If he loses this child to Sandrine's mother—who lives in some little lost town in Texas—his life will be a car wreck. More importantly, this beautiful half-French child will grow up in an empty little ghost town outside of a mediocre city."

If truth be told, I'm not even sure Dr. Dagnaud heard much of what I had said. He was staring again, and entirely lost in the very first photograph of Victoria that I'd shown him—which he'd saved apart, off to the side. "She definitely has my crazy green eyes, doesn't she?" He repeated this three or four times.

I jumped on his remark, to set the hook, but I did so far too enthusiastically. "Aren't they remarkable? It was the first thing I noticed about her. I can't tell you how lovely this child is, Doctor. I spent half a day with her last week talking about how I was going to go meet another daddy for her, and how, if everything worked out right, she would have two daddies to keep her safe. She would be a jewel in your life, and a big sister to your little girl."

Dr. Dagnaud furled his brow at my having carelessly divulged personal information about his family that he knew he hadn't shared with me. While I couldn't tell what he made of my slipup, he certainly made it clear that he was about to get up and leave the table—and we hadn't even ordered yet. Just before he did so, Dr. Dagnaud leaned across the table and stared me squarely in the eyes, and stunned me with what he said. "Look, Counselor, it seems to me that this little girl is coming into my life whether I do it with grace and an open heart or whether I struggle around trying not to deal with it. Assuming the DNA test you brought confirms what seems obvious to me from the photos, I'm pretty much convinced this is the direction in which I'd like to head. Frankly, what else would be the right thing to do? But let me be clear with you: the issue will be my wife. Give me a day to think through how we introduce all this to her." He paused, taking a moment to plot his approach. "I assume I can take the photos to show her, no?" I nodded yes, although I pulled back the one of Sandrine, commenting, "You might want to think twice about taking this one."

"Good point," he replied. "And I'll need your help, for certain, in introducing this. And you should understand one thing: I have never been able to talk Sophie into anything. Ever. She has to get there on her own. Always. Call me at my office in the morning—eight a.m., sharp."

"I'll do just that. By the way," I added, "Dr. Freeman arrives tomorrow morning. My hope is that we can all get together and talk about where this could possibly head. You're a remarkable man, Doctor. I mean, for letting me present the situation with such . . . calm. Thank you."

Dr. Dagnaud called back over his shoulder as he left me behind at the table, "There are a number of gates to get through, Counselor; we'll see if you and I are still skiing on the same slope in a day or two." As I watched the doctor recede through the crowded restaurant, a new, dark worry bubbled up in my mind: hopefully the Dagnauds had met each other *after* Dr. Dagnaud's attendance at the Boston medical seminar. If not, if Dr. Dagnaud's affair with Sandrine was seen by his wife as infidelity on his part, we were almost certainly headed for trouble.

***

As the clock struck eight the following morning, I had Dr. Dagnaud's phone ringing. In my mind, I envisioned reaching a scratchy-voiced, disheveled, sleepless man in need of a shave, his coffee-spotted tie loosened at the collar. He'd been crying on and off during the night, and numerous drinks had been required to survive one of the toughest nights of his life.

While I couldn't confirm my melodramatic visual image from the phone call that ensued, the report from Dr. Dagnaud was not entirely inconsistent with what I had imagined. He confirmed that they had indeed been up all night, and he described how his wife had gone through, as he phrased it, "every known emotion in the human psyche; some repeatedly." The tone and tenor of the doctor's description of the night that seemed to me to signal that he was increasingly uncertain about the wisdom of supporting our effort, with all its complexities. "You might think of my wife as a journalist, but she was trained as an attorney. She's making an appointment today with a classmate of hers who does family law. We'll see how that plays out. Let's speak later in the day." My takeaway from the call confirmed everybody's suspicion: it would be Sophie Bernard who would decide matters on this side of the Atlantic.

Back at my hotel, there was a knock on my door, and I was handed a very formal message—almost as if it were a subpoena. I was to appear at Sophie Bernard's attorney's office at four p.m. that afternoon. The message said nothing further. Ten minutes later, my room phone rang. Dr. Freeman had arrived and was now in his room down the hall. Given that he was jet-lagged, we agreed to meet at seven that evening in the lobby: in the interim, he would nap, while I would plot.

My fear, as you might imagine, was that the attorney intended to ask me to back off. My legal research had shown how extremely little leverage was available to a Massachusetts probate court to enforce anything on an international basis. On top of this, Dr. Freeman arguably had no legal standing whatsoever—in Massachusetts or in Paris—to even seek judicial redress, precisely because he had no legal relationship to the child. Clearly, our best and only hope was a moral argument, and I now had confirmation that this was actually a stronger argument in French culture than in the United States. In France, Jeanne and Francis had confirmed, acting in *bonne foi* (good faith) satisfies both a secular norm and a moral duty. In its French context, the issue our case raised wasn't so much about what Dr. Dagnaud and Sophie Bernard *had* to do; it was more about what they *ought* to do in order to act in good faith. My strategy, accordingly, had to be aimed at enticing them to join the campaign—I had no meaningful way to force them to do anything.

***

The law office of Christine Dupont was not at all the pretentious affair I was expecting. On the contrary, it was a stately, wood-paneled, law-book-lined room in her private apartments. Maître

Dupont, who seemed about forty—the same age as both doctors—was trim and stylish looking. But she was not the formal, cold, bourgeois attorney I had expected. She had a far more open presence, and our conversation began with her charming, even disarming, inquiry that is translated rather accurately by its English equivalent: "So, what the fuck is this all about?"

And so I relayed to Maître Dupont everything I knew about the love affair, the accidental pregnancy, the deus ex machina appearance of Dr. Freeman, and the tragic failure of Sandrine Bergeron and Dr. Freeman to marry and arrange for a stepparent adoption of Victoria. But what I mostly spent time on were the Massachusetts common-law precedents that made Dr. Freeman's case hopeless in the absence of Dr. Dagnaud's help. I also described the estranged grandmother's life in small-town Texas, and how she was married to "Preacher Man," as the minister was somehow dubbed for the remainder of the case, and I even got her to smile when I said that a forced upbringing of a little French-speaking child in a tiny town in the Texas desert sounded way too much like a B movie. And, of course, I emphasized that Dr. Freeman made a handsome living, and that he would gladly sign up to fund the entire cost of Victoria's upbringing, including the costs of any visits Dr. Dagnaud and his family might make to Boston over the years. And finally I ended by saying that because it was my understanding that French law would require that Victoria inherit equally with Dr. Dagnaud's other child, Dr. Freeman would voluntarily put precisely the same share-and-share-alike estate planning in place for Dr. Dagnaud's daughter.

Maître Dupont listened throughout my monologue without taking her eyes off mine. When I finished, she stood without saying a word, turned away from me, and walked over to one of the huge French windows that swung open in fine weather to look out over the stunning urban park known as the Place des Vosges. She just stood there, as still as a cat, looking out. A good minute or so later, she asked in a quiet voice, "How good a sense do you have for the quality of the relationship between your client and the child?"

It seemed important not to exaggerate. "What I know is only based on their one visit to my office, and my subsequent visit to their house, so I have limited information. The child jumps into Dr. Freeman's arms to accept his nurturing and love just like my little boy jumped into mine. I don't have the first reason to doubt this man's sincerity; he is desperate to keep Victoria in his life. He'll never have another child—he is irreversibly infertile. So, from the little I've seen, and from the respect I know he has at the Harvard teaching hospital where he works, I'm confident we can count on him to remain a rock-solid parent for Victoria. I really am."

Maître Dupont continued to stare into the slowly softening late-afternoon light, her hands clasped behind her back now, swaying her weight ever so subtly from side to side, thinking it all through. Then, almost abruptly, there was a decision and it came with a strategy. "Can you be here at 21:00 tonight with your client, for dinner?" I froze for a few moments—in wonderment—and then nodded fervently, belatedly adding a "Yes, of course."

"Between now and then," Maître Dupont advised, "give as much thought as you can as to how we keep this easy on Dagnaud and Bernard. It would be one thing for them to support the project. But it would be quite another for them to take the child into their already overly busy lives, what with two careers, a small child, Sophie's time-consuming elderly mother, their modest eighty-five-square-meter apartment . . . and so on. You need to be ready to demonstrate how you can guarantee all this."

It was suddenly clear that I had an unexpected ally: we two attorneys were on the same page that it would be a good thing for everyone concerned if this worked out. Whether she could convince her client of this remained an open question. But at least there was reason for hope.

**

When I emerged on the street, I found that the drizzle had stopped and a partially blue sky had opened above. Enough, anyway, to tempt me to head south to the Seine on foot, cross over the Pont des Arts, and wind my way back to where my little hotel was located.

As I walked along the river Seine—stunned as always by the extraordinary views this provides of the Louvre, Notre-Dame, and a dozen other of the world's most magnificent buildings—my mind wandered to how sad, how tragically sad, it was to have to negotiate the terms and conditions of a custodial arrangement that would determine the happiness of a child. Most children are born into a complex network of relationships that hold and fix their new lives in familial and social space. There is no ambiguity, no uncertainty, no conditionality. But Victoria's circumstances were all about uncertainty. If matters went poorly for us here in Paris—or at trial—a motherless Victoria could soon find herself torn away from the man she knew as her father. She could find herself being raised by two older people whom she didn't know, separated definitively and permanently from all her neighborhood and school friends—and everyone else she had ever known. On top of this, the importance of place in our lives should never be underestimated, and depending on the outcome of the litigation, Victoria would be raised either in the cultural vacuum of small-town Texas—or in the sophisticated urban settings of Boston and Paris. Where we grow up and who we grow up around each play their role in determining who we grow up to be, what values we have, and what life goals we set for ourselves.

Childhood, I mused, is not supposed to be about the ambiguity, uncertainty, and conditionality of everything that is most important to a child. But then childhood is also not supposed to be about war and hunger and chaos—and the other panoply of horrors so many children around the world face on a daily basis. But, I reminded myself, children are remarkably adaptable. They take the world as it is presented to them, as that is all they know. And they are capable of almost unfathomable resilience: they often survive, even thrive, in the midst of terribly trying circumstances. Presumably, Victoria could survive Texas. Others have. But one thing was already clear: little Victoria—all forty pounds of her, if she even weighed that much—would soon need to take charge of much of her own sense of self, whichever of the two lives she would end up leading. She had lost her mother, and even if everything went just right in our custody struggle, her "father" would always be a far more tenuous presence than that of most other fathers. On the other hand—depending on whether Dr. Dagnaud and Sophie Bernard found it in themselves to embrace not just Victoria but also all the change she would bring into their lives—perhaps we adults could cobble together a newfangled blended family for her that would serve her well. Maybe, just maybe.

Still walking as all this went through my head, I came upon a very famous café—Les Deux Magots. It was from this café that the poet laureate of nineteenth-century France, Paul Verlaine, summoned to Paris the teenage poet Arthur Rimbaud. It was in this same café that André Breton created surrealism; it was here that Pablo Picasso and Ernest Hemingway bemoaned the growing threat of European fascism before the war, and it was here that Jean-Paul Sartre, Simone de Beauvoir, Albert Camus, and André Gide argued and wrote about the implications of existentialist philosophy for postwar European politics. If one couldn't think insightfully in this café, in the shadow of such truly great minds, where could one?

And damned if it didn't work. One major problem I knew I would have with the court melted away as quickly as did the sugar cube in my espresso. Suddenly, it was obvious: the way to convince the court that my two-father scheme would work would be to offer to provide the court with ongoing, regular feedback as to how it actually *was* working. How could the court possibly rely on my up-front representation that all would go well in the fluid, complex family setting I was proposing? Such a promise was weak by its nature, and vulnerable: there was no way I or anyone else could possibly know what would come to pass in such a complex arrangement. In contrast, suggesting to the court that it appoint a guardian ad litem—a neutral professional who would serve in an ongoing capacity as the eyes and ears of the court—a professional who would produce a quarterly report for the court detailing exactly how Victoria's best interests actually were (or were not) being served as time went on—this had legs. Yes! I would affirmatively suggest to the court that there was a solution to the weakness in the custody arrangement I was proposing: let's arrange, up front, ongoing systematic feedback to the court—by its own appointed agent. This felt like I'd come upon a missing piece to the puzzle. *Merci bien*, café Les Deux Magots!

***

I returned to my little boutique hotel in the early evening to find two notes at the antique front desk, each neatly folded and carefully placed alongside my room key in the little box for room 204. The first was from my friends, Jeanne and Francis Clement, who had been so helpful to me at our strategy session disguised as dinner. The second was from Dr. Freeman.

Jeanne and Francis wrote, "Terry, we've spoken with our children about the sad plight of the little girl whose life you described to us. The four of us want you to know that if it works out that she ends up spending part of her childhood in Paris, we will gladly serve as a visiting resource for her. If there is any way her legal case could be helped by your informing the Boston judge of our willingness to be a resource for her, please do so. *Bises*, Jeanne *et* Francis."

The message from Dr. Freeman read so differently. "Terry, I am starting to have doubts. Please wake me as soon as you return to the hotel. Jon."

As you might imagine, I went immediately to Dr. Freeman's door and knocked, even perhaps a bit aggressively. A jet-lagged, sleepy-eyed surgeon in his underwear opened the door and asked me in. "Terry, I don't know, this all seems . . ." And on and on he went, full of doubt, uncertainty, and pessimism. When he had talked himself out, I came back at him—somewhat mercilessly, I admit—with a diatribe about how parenting has nothing to do with reservation or hesitation. It's about commitment and it's about certainty and it's about stability. I told him about my progress in the case, but I also told him in no uncertain terms that if he were anything less than 100 percent committed to the project—"emotionally committed, financially committed, and lifestyle committed"—it would fail. I ended with a dramatic—arguably even melodramatic—line. "I'll be in the lobby at eight thirty. We have a nine o'clock dinner at the wife's attorney's apartment with Dr. Dagnaud and Sophie Bernard. If you want to raise Victoria, see you then. But if you show up, you need to tell me that you've put all this doubt and vacillation behind you—*forever*. And I mean for *fucking ever*." With that, I stood up, left the room, and closed the door emphatically.

***

Ninety minutes later, Dr. Freeman was in the lobby, looking refreshed after a shower. He was like a different person: it only took one emphatic nod for him to let me know with no ambiguity that he was now fully back on track for our legal struggles, and—more importantly—for the never-ending trials and tribulations of parenting. So, the rest of Dr. Freeman's life was about to begin with what turned out to be an all-night session—what the French call *une nuit blanche* (a white night).

The evening began at nine p.m. when Maître Dupont greeted us cordially at her door. It was fascinating to watch over hors d'oeuvres and drinks as Henri Dagnaud and Sophie Bernard were introduced to Jonathan Freeman; after all, these people, who had never met, were basically scanning each other to see if they could picture being associated with one another in a blended-family adventure that would stretch out over the rest of their lives. That doesn't happen every day. I'd had a fantasy that the two doctors—two orthopedic surgeons, after all—would share a common story of famous doctor so-and-so, or would both be involved in some international orthopedic society, or that they could at least find *something* in common, anything. But no such luck. Ah well, not all ball games are won with a home run in the first inning.

French culture—like most European cultures—is big on the rituals of the meal. A meal is for eating, for sure, but it is also for talking and for laughing—and for connecting. Any business or serious talk tends to be handled later, over coffee, when relaxing after the meal. And this was the pattern of the evening that would determine the character and quality of Victoria's future life. Dr. Freeman, understandably, didn't fully appreciate this, especially because there was not time or conversational space to translate everything that everybody had to say. I could see the tension rising inside him like the progressively bubbling water in one of those old-fashioned percolator coffeepots.

Maître Dupont finally started off the substantive discussion of what had brought us together with a thoughtful summary of where we were at, ending with the stunning announcement that Dr. Dagnaud in no way denied the responsibilities that he had as the biological father. So long as this adventure in international co-parenting went slowly, step-by-step over time, Dr. Dagnaud and Sophie Bernard were willing to explore where it might lead as time went by. With that, Maître Dupont ceded the floor to me.

Trying to sound both grateful and confident, I tried to speak consistently with Maître Dupont's optimistic opening. "Dr. Freeman," I acknowledged, "finds himself entirely dependent on the goodwill of Dr. Dagnaud and Maître Bernard to help him keep Victoria in his life. I can't be certain, of course, but I think that working together, we have a good chance of making this happen. But I will need to assure the court about the open and cooperative effort the three of you are willing to undertake to design a bilingual, bicultural upbringing for Victoria. Dr. Freeman will cover all the costs—that won't be a problem, given how overpaid American orthopedic surgeons are."

Needless to say, this last line led to a good spate of laughter, and the conversation was off and running on a more informal level. The French love to talk—who wouldn't with such a beautiful language?—and everyone needed to be heard on every possible subtopic. Everyone, that is, except for Sophie Bernard. She remained a quiet presence. I could only interpret this as a sub-rosa announcement that she felt coerced into compliance with Dr. Dagnaud's view of how he wanted to handle his paternal responsibilities, and that she intended to be as uninvolved with Victoria as possible. Without saying so in words, she was telling us that there would be two families, with minimal overlap, and not the one blended family I needed to describe to the court.

And then, by chance, everything suddenly changed. Dupont had an upright piano—and Dr. Freeman turned out to be a wonderfully accomplished jazz pianist. Who knew? I don't know what it is about music that brings people together, but if you could have heard the five of us butchering one song after another—with equal cruelty to the musical heritage of both countries—you might well have guessed that by the time the sky started to lighten with the approach of morning, we five mediocre crooners were ready to engage in just about any joint venture that came our way. Sophie Bernard may have resisted Dr. Dagnaud's arguments, but she melted like a candle in the sunlight of Dr. Freeman's virtuosity with the magic of jazz syncopation.

And just like that, Victoria's family was born.

Of course, working out an agreement between Victoria's two fathers—and her potential stepmother-to-be—was just the beginning. The real work would be to convince the Massachusetts Probate and Family Court of the wisdom of our plan. To my mind, the most worrisome aspect of our newly forged arrangement was the grandmother's advantage if the court were at all hesitant about the wild complexities of our two-father plan. But again, as I had originally said to Dr. Freeman, "One step at a time."

***

Upon my return to Boston the following day, I immediately set out to retain the expert witness services of Dr. Evan Newsom, head of the pediatrics department at Children's Hospital. Later in the week, after he had reviewed the file I sent over, Dr. Newsom called to propose that by far the most effective way to proceed would be for him to visit Victoria at her house at "fall-apart time," as he called it, about five p.m. So that's exactly what we did four or five days later, and sure enough, just like any other child her age, as Victoria became progressively more tired from a long day at school, she got cranky.

Normally, this time of day was handled by Dr. Freeman's nanny, who had worked for the family since just after Victoria was born. But this particular afternoon, at Dr. Newsom's request, Dr. Freeman was on his own. Dr. Newsom quietly observed as Dr. Freeman played on the floor with Victoria, animating a tea party that was quite formal given that there were two queens in attendance. He joked around with her, fed her dinner, bathed her, put her in her pajamas, and finally read her bedtime stories as she fell asleep. Victoria essentially ignored the silent presence of Dr. Newsom throughout the evening. In contrast, she couldn't possibly have been more inclusive of me—always, and I mean *always*—speaking to me in French. Perhaps her use of the language kept something alive inside her, something from her mother. In any case, it reminded me that there actually was light at the end of the tunnel—if we could get over the legal hurdles—because in speaking French with Dr. Dagnaud and his family, Victoria would reuse and thereby keep alive the sounds her mother's voice made as she held and nurtured her little girl. And these would be the sounds she would one day use when it was her turn to hold and soothe a child of her own.

As we left the house that evening, I was not in the least surprised to learn that Dr. Freeman had passed his test with flying colors. Dr. Newsom had zero doubts about the depth and solidity of the parent-child relationship between Dr. Freeman and Victoria, and the following week, he gave me a signed and notarized affidavit to that effect.

We were now ready to file papers with the court, and, of course, I would be required to fill out a form listing all persons of interest who should receive formal notice. I thought about drafting a personalized cover letter to Victoria's grandmother, somehow cleverly assuring her that all would go well if she declined to appear, and that she would always be welcome to visit her granddaughter as the years went on. But I abandoned the idea—it was too manipulative a step, and I feared it could do more to provoke the grandmother than to calm any concerns she might have. So I just mailed copies of the court filings to her home address, return receipt requested, with a simple cover letter stating that she was entirely welcome to call me if she wanted to speak.

Within ten days, an attorney named Michael Torper called and left a phone message that he would be representing the grandmother. As was my practice, before I returned any call from an unknown opposing counsel, I had an associate research his background and performance history. It turned out that Attorney Torper was better known for his plaintiff-side tort practice than for his occasional representation of clients in Probate and Family Court. This gave me the idea—a pipe dream really—that he might be someone who was retained to approach Dr. Freeman about the possibility of a financial resolution of the matter. I returned his call, wondering how I would ever broach the topic of "settlement," but I needn't have spent a moment concerned about this. It was he who wondered aloud if there wasn't some way we could potentially work the matter out without a trial, to which he gratuitously added, "Who would want their child raised in *France*?" I was a really good boy and didn't say a thing about the relative merits of small-town Texas versus Paris, France.

It took me a day and a half to reach Dr. Freeman, who was ecstatic at what seemed like a hint by the grandmother's counsel that she might want to use her leverage in the custody struggle to extract some money from him. I warned him that a plaintiff's tort attorney like Torper might operate by exploring our appetite for a financial resolution before he even broached the idea to his client. Nevertheless, Dr. Freeman authorized me to go as high as $50,000 without even checking back with him if I saw any opportunity of buying off the grandmother's sudden concern for Victoria. He also reported that he was nearly done creating his list of the professionals who could testify about his parenting of Victoria, including her pediatrician, her pediatric dentist, her teachers, her play-group leaders, and her day-care crew—as well as all the families who had children with whom she played. The plan was for my office to interview all these individuals, and then to determine who among them would make the most effective trial witnesses.

Several days later, Attorney Torper came to my office for a meeting, and it turned out he was completely up front about what he had in mind. Don't let me sell the man short: he went on for quite a while, like any good salesman, about what a great sacrifice the grandmother would be making, and about how her only concern was whatever was best for the child. I listened politely, and did quite a bit of disingenuous nodding. In the end, Torper announced he would recommend to his client the sum of $100,000, plus attorney's fees. I thought it best to avoid negotiating price and instead suggested that I agreed with him: we should each get back to our respective client and see what could be done to come to an arrangement, and I would encourage my client to be "open-minded" about the idea.

In the meantime, I had my associate attorney working day and night interviewing our potential witnesses, and every single person the associate contacted willingly dictated an affidavit about Dr. Freeman's solid parenting skills, and signed their notarized document under the pains and penalties of perjury. I also arranged to visit the household again, this time with a professional forensic photographer. She took shots of the house in general, of Victoria's room in particular, and of Victoria at play with her best friend, who lived down the street. At the same time, a parallel process was ordered up in Paris. Dr. Dagnaud's flat near Parc Monceau was an ideal neighborhood in which to raise a child, and the photographs that were taken there amounted to a brief documentary designed to introduce this to the court.

We were also simultaneously investigating near Fort Worth, Texas, to learn just exactly who Grandma and Preacher Man actually were. The initial feedback from the private detective I hired was enormously disappointing from an evidentiary point of view. There was *nothing* he could find that was unusual or abnormal about either of them— even about Preacher Man's tent revival scene. Damn it. On the other hand, I had to admit, this meant Victoria had a viable grandmother, which, of course, was a good thing, in and of itself. She checked out to be a normal middle-aged housewife in her early sixties, with a routine middle-class life, a respectable set of lady friends, and so on. We also struck out with Preacher Man—no police record, no bankruptcy

filings, no involvement in lawsuits, either as a plaintiff or as a defendant. Nothing. Grandma and Preacher Man were not interestingly, let
alone threateningly, abnormal in any way we could make use of at trial.

And then things took a disappointing turn: Attorney Torper called
to say his client had "changed her mind," and no amount of money
would convince her to forsake her granddaughter. My suspicions about
Torper having initiated negotiation of a financial settlement of the
matter without first having discussed this approach with his clients
remained as previously mentioned, but it really didn't matter. We were
headed to trial.

**

As the petitioner, I had the advantage of doing some judge shopping,
and shopping I went. One of the great lessons I'd learned from my long-
since retired senior partner and mentor was that being consistently
polite and considerate to court clerks was about as good an investment
as an attorney could make. And sure enough, I learned sotto voce from
one of the clerks that Judge Sheila McGovern, chief judge of the county's Probate and Family Court—who always sat in Cambridge—had
just agreed to fill in the following month for one of the Dedham judges
who required a break for some surgery. *Bingo.* No judge in the Probate
and Family Court system went more directly to the heart of a matter
than she did, and no piece of evidence escaped her laser-like focus. The
only problem was that this meant we would have to expedite matters—
but then again, so would Attorney Torper. I marked up my motion
and petition, and mailed notice to opposing counsel. My friendly clerk
called three or four days later and announced that we were on trial just
six weeks down the road.

That evening, I called Dr. Freeman and asked him to arrange a
meeting at his home to rally as many as possible of the potential witnesses who had signed affidavits. For those who couldn't come, I asked
that he arrange convenient times for each of them when my associate
attorney could prepare them for their testimony via telephone. As it
turned out, the substantial totality of the listed witnesses were such
committed fans of Victoria and Dr. Freeman that they were willing
to forgo whatever other plans they had, and well over a score of them

came to our meeting at the Freeman household the following Sunday. I arranged to arrive two hours earlier, first to spend a little time with Victoria, and then to begin my preparation of Dr. Freeman for his testimony.

I wanted to meet with Miss Victoria to talk with her about her likely one-on-one meeting with Judge McGovern in the judge's chambers—a particular habit of hers that was utterly unique. I was in the midst of explaining that this would give her a chance to tell the judge whom she felt safe with, when Victoria interrupted. Actually, she explained, the meeting would not be one-on-one: Françoise, her stuffed giraffe, would in all likelihood attend as well. I found that to be an excellent idea. But even as I said this, my plotting little trial lawyer mind was at work: I knew from my past meetings with Victoria that this particular giraffe spoke only in French. We were just weeks away from when she would meet Dr. Dagnaud—who also spoke only French, which Victoria still described as "speaking like my mommy." My dream—my scheme—was that this would play a significant role in hastening the bonding between the father and the child who had never met.

I know this must all sound manipulative and cunning, but that's only because it was. Such is the nature of trial law. While an attorney must strictly comply with the rules of the game set forth in the Rules of Evidence and the Rules of Civil Procedure, and while there are important normative principles—like insisting that one's witnesses actually need to live up to their oath of telling the truth when they testified—otherwise, a trial is a sphere of combat. Controlled and bloodless, to be sure, but combat nonetheless.

The meeting in the living room was a delight, even an honor, to attend. Gathered in front of me were the lion's share of Dr. Freeman's family, friends, neighbors, fellow parents, and work colleagues—as well as the professionals who provided Victoria's pediatric and dental care. They comprised nearly all the adults who formed the most important connections in his and Victoria's life—save for her schoolteachers, who were being separately contacted. As I waited for the assembled multitudes to settle so that I could speak, my mind wandered to what I'd learned in a comparative law class, now so many years in the past. In Continental civil law, the professor had told us, unlike in the common-law tradition we took from the English, as early as the sixth century there was a firmly established principle that a single witness was insufficient to establish *any* given point. Here, in contrast, I had a roomful of unimpeachable witnesses, each ready, willing, and entirely able to testify about Dr. Freeman's attentive parenting. My only problem, of course, was that legal precedent held that the issue of the quality of his parenting could not even be reached unless the court deemed Dr. Dagnaud's minimal involvement as adequate to see the case as having petitioning family on both sides of the matter. But there was hope. Judge McGovern was what lawyers call an "equity judge," as opposed to a "law judge"—she was far more likely than most of her brethren to bend legal formality if that was what was required to achieve justice, particularly if the well-being of a child was at stake. I was growing more optimistic day by day.

The next day, and the day after, I kept waiting for Attorney Torper to send me discovery documents asking for the details of my case— whom I would have testify, what they would say, and what documentary evidence I had to support our case. Nothing came. My equivalent documents had long since gone out and been returned by him with cursory, useless responses: "To be determined," or "This response will be supplemented in a timely fashion." I also kept expecting Attorney Torper to call and arrange for Victoria to spend some time with her grandmother during the week before trial, but that never happened either. I never knew whether that was a function of his lack of experience in creating the type of evidence that impresses a Probate and Family Court judge, or whether the grandmother was somehow not adequately invested in the case to have arrived in Boston early enough to allow such a strategy.

But, overall, while there was a pool of disquiet deep within me— worry that Attorney Torper might be hiding some masterful strategy—the louder voice in my head was one of increasing confidence that we had put together a case that was custom designed to help Judge McGovern get beyond the legal hurdles we faced, and to go straight to the heart of the matter. Prior to going on the bench, after all, the judge had worked in the Child Protective Unit at the Middlesex District Attorney's Office, and had later played an outsize role in the Juvenile Rights Advocacy Project at her alma mater, Boston College Law School. In the myriad of cases I had presented in her courtroom, she had always adhered strictly to a principle of juvenile law that my office had established in a Massachusetts Supreme Judicial Court case: the "best interests of the child" test. Given that we now had family on our side of the case—if, admittedly, to a markedly limited degree—I was becoming increasingly convinced she would consider Dr. Dagnaud's involvement adequate to allow her to proceed to apply the "best interests of the child" test, and thereby compare the two proposed home lives for the child—in which case, we should surely prevail.

**

On November 1, 2002, I received a phone call from the trial clerk of the Norfolk County Probate and Family Court courthouse in Dedham, Massachusetts. Our trial would begin on Wednesday, November 13. I immediately contacted Dr. Dagnaud, who had been waiting to plan the timing of his weeklong "get to know her" visit to the Freeman household before the trial. I assured Dr. Dagnaud that I felt more and more confident that we had put together a remarkably strong case.

Just as planned, exactly a week before trial, Dr. Dagnaud arrived in the afternoon at Boston's Logan Airport. I picked him up, and off we went to Brookline—to the home of Dr. Freeman and the little girl they were hoping to raise together, Miss Victoria. I had told her that her "other daddy" was coming from far away by airplane to meet her, and that he was bringing a special surprise for Françoise. On this last point, I actually had left nothing to chance, and had searched in three or four toy stores before FAO Schwarz had come through for me big-time: I had found a slightly larger, rather similar—if shockingly turquoise—stuffed giraffe that had agreed to being introduced to Victoria as "a daddy giraffe looking to find his little girl giraffe." What an amazing coincidence.

As general counsel to a dozen adoption agencies, over the years I had been asked to facilitate at six or eight reunions of adopted persons whose search for their birth parents had led them to such encounters. But they were all adults, save for one teenager, so the first encounter of Victoria and Dr. Dagnaud was to be a new experience for me. Also, in each of the cases of adult adoptees meeting their birth parents, save one, there had been a striking differential in class and education.

This was typical in Massachusetts, because persons of humble means were statistically more likely to give up their children for adoption, and persons of substantial means were more likely to be involved in the lengthy and expensive process of infant adoption. The effect of this differential was almost universal: the reunited parties found almost nothing in common to talk about, and with only a few exceptions, there was no significant follow-through after the initial (usually, disappointing) reunion.

How different this all turned out to be with Victoria and Dr. Dagnaud! Part of this I attribute to the special role Victoria's "mommy language" had always played in her life: it turned out to afford Dr. Dagnaud an extraordinary entry point for connection with his daughter—even more than I had predicted. For the first hour, the three of us sat at Victoria's tiny plastic table with its even tinier chairs, except when we lounged out on the carpet, playing with the puppy or acting out the joyous reunion of the daddy giraffe and his long-lost daughter—Françoise. It was an amazing experience to watch Victoria give voice to Françoise's delight at meeting her daddy giraffe—and welcoming him into her life. Bit by bit, my role in the interaction became increasingly marginal until, at one point, I was able to slip out almost unnoticed and leave the two of them alone. Needless to say, Dr. Freeman was delighted to hear that everything was going so well.

I clearly remember humming to myself on the ride home that day as I left Dr. Freeman's house: the father and daughter were bonding, the two doctors were getting on swimmingly, the two-daddy plan made great good sense for Victoria, and the trial preparation was complete. What could possibly go wrong?

***

On Wednesday, November 13, 2002, those scheduled for the first day of trial on our side of the case met at eight a.m. on the steps of the Dedham branch of the Norfolk County Probate and Family Court. Sure enough, the elusive Attorney Torper was present with two young associate attorneys, as well as both the grandmother and Preacher Man. Victoria's grandmother looked young for a woman in her early sixties; I had been hoping for quite the opposite. Preacher Man was as Texas as possible, including sporting the single biggest belt buckle I've ever seen, along with an impeccably clean cowboy hat that was potentially the only one in the entire Commonwealth of Massachusetts belonging to someone over the age of five. He was cold and ill at ease, and there was no mistaking that he considered my involvement in the case to be on the side of evil and sin. I shook their hands and assured them that no matter how the court determined which custody arrangement would be best for Victoria, Dr. Freeman hoped they would play an ongoing role in Victoria's life—she was lucky to have grandparents committed to her well-being. The grandmother smiled, but not Preacher Man: I had the distinct impression that if he could have turned into a rattle-snake for a moment, I would have had a major problem.

At nine a.m. sharp, we entered the courtroom and awaited the appearance of the clerks. Normally, the trial clerk should have been arranging her files and preparing for the session, and the court reporter should have been fiddling with wires and microphones and getting prepared to start. I was just beginning to note the anomaly of how unprepared the courtroom was to begin trial when the judge's trial clerk came out and stood behind the judge's chair on the high podium—rather than going to his place on the level below. "Ladies and Gentlemen," he announced, "I have devastating news. Judge McGovern died last night."

***

We were asked to return to the courtroom at two p.m. for a status con-ference—without our trial witnesses. I packed up the trial bags with the folders I'd been arranging on the petitioner's table and sent them back to the office with my associate attorney. The two doctors and I had no choice but to stay near the courthouse, so we drove to a local strip mall of chain restaurants and chose one that advertised the avail-ability of private rooms for events.

Once we were ensconced in our private space and had arranged for a little buffet lunch, I set out what little I could for the two doctors about what was likely to happen—significant delay being one almost certain outcome. But then, unwisely, I got off into an appreciation of Judge McGovern—about how she had been such a great champion of children's rights, and how our case had been "custom designed for her to hear." An uncomfortable silence followed my ill-chosen words, and I could see the increasing doubt and consternation on Dr. Freeman's face. Dr. Dagnaud—for whom I translated—also began wavering. "Maybe it's a sign," he said.

"No, it's not!" I insisted—a bit loudly. And so began two hours of painful, draining, repetitive argument—two arguments, really, one in each language—about how to interpret what had happened, and what our response should be. Dr. Dagnaud began wondering out loud about return flights to France, and Dr. Freeman waxed ever more pessimistic by the minute. I was arguing—sternly—that everyone should just calm the fuck down until two p.m., when we would learn where this was all heading. This torture session went on until 11:45 when, *thankfully*, the waitstaff came in to set a table with a little luncheon buffet. I was never so glad to see a bowl of iceberg lettuce in all my life.

***

At two p.m., the three of us, along with Attorney Torper and his clients, were in the courtroom, as directed. It was empty. It was fifteen minutes later that the judge's trial clerk came out of her chambers to tell us the news: while all other cases and motions scheduled to be heard by Judge McGovern would have to wait some indeterminate amount of time to be rescheduled, because our case involved an essential party who had come from Europe to testify, Judge William O'Connor had agreed to emerge from retirement to hear our case beginning at nine a.m. sharp the following morning. The papers had already been delivered to his house.

Attorney Torper shot me a look that was either a smile or a smirk—I didn't know him well enough to discern which. He and his clients seemed pretty perky and ready to roll with the change in trial judge, whereas my team was visibly down in the dumps: I could see Torper pick up on this.

Custom clothing not picked up at the tailor must be very hard to sell to another customer—especially if there is no time to alter it. Judge O'Connor—an ancient, dried-up, humorless man—was fairly well known to me, and to the entire bar, as being an absolute stickler for procedural process and evidentiary rules. The judge was all about form and formality. Whereas Judge McGovern would take a child into her chambers for a private talk about where and with whom the child felt safe, Judge O'Connor considered a six-year-old a viable witness, so if you wanted a child's testimony, you had to examine the child on the stand. No exceptions. And whereas Judge McGovern was willing to work with the complexity of modern-day blended families, Judge O'Connor—so far as I knew—was convinced it was still the 1950s, and that was just fine. So now the question became: How much of this to share with my disheartened and decidedly disillusioned doctors? I called my office and told the associate to meet us an hour later at Dr. Freeman's house.

First things first: it was Victoria time. The two fathers engaged her—and her now-inseparable puppy—in a host of games and stuffed-animal discussions, which were followed by dinner, a bath, and, finally, bedtime stories. The associate and I spent the three hours all this took at the dining room table, marking up each and every witness examination outline to reflect the formal procedural requirements that Judge O'Connor would surely impose.

Once Victoria was finally asleep, I explained to the doctors how, with the change of judges, they would have to listen super closely to my questions, because, with the new judge, I would not be allowed to ask leading questions—questions that contain a hint to remind witnesses what it was they were going to say. I would be strictly held to very general questions like: "What did you do after that?" Or: "What happened next?" We also discussed how to deal with the fluster factor. Witnesses need to know how to recover when objections are called out and sustained by a trial judge—they can be very unnerving. And, of course, some of these procedural complexities would presumably be exaggerated for Dr. Dagnaud, as he would be testifying through a court-certified translator.

When the four of us finally got up from the table at 1:30 a.m., I tried to give a little pep talk about looking and sounding confident, and about being infinitely polite on cross-examination no matter how repetitive or annoying they found the accusative questioning. I closed by coaching: "Believe in what you can do for Victoria. Give the court every reason to know that you fully believe in what you are proposing.

And no matter what subtopic you are testifying about, always express a quiet, calm confidence about the sense of connection that you each have—or will develop—with Victoria."

***

And so, at nine a.m.—and I mean *exactly* at nine a.m.—the judge exited his chambers, took the bench, and looked down at me. "Mr. Freiberg, your opening argument, please." For the first half of the thirty minutes I was allotted, I gave His Honor the general outline of Sandrine Bergeron's history and the unusual circumstances of Victoria's birth.

The second half of my opening was about how wonderfully everything went for six years. I also began describing how Ms. Bergeron had been totally estranged from her mother, who had never visited Victoria, and who—

"Objection, Your Honor," interrupted Attorney Torper. "That's not—"

"Mr. Torper," the judge cut him off. "You just interrupted an opening argument. I'm shocked; I understood you to be an experienced trial attorney. If this had been a jury trial, I probably would have asked for a motion for a mistrial."

"But, Your Honor," Torper followed right on, "I wanted—"

"Mr. Torper, sit down. Don't say another word until I invite you to." The judge was positively glaring at opposing counsel. I was busy studying my shoes, staying completely out of the line of fire.

"Carry on, Mr. Freiberg, and see that you don't make any similar misstep yourself."

"Yes, Your Honor." I went on to describe the grandmother's total absence of involvement with the child and finished with a brief description of how this hyper-busy couple—Sandrine Bergeron and the petitioner, Dr. Jonathan Freeman—kept putting off their marriage and a stepparent adoption, for which they have no one to blame but themselves. "We are here before Your Honor to correct this terrible error, and as Your Honor can see, we are here with the co-petitioner, Dr. Henri Dagnaud, the biological father of the child, who wants to join Dr. Freeman in raising Victoria." I closed with a very brief description of the proposed parenting plan of the two fathers. My last line was: "It won't be a routine upbringing, Your Honor, but we can't get to routine in this case. And sometimes upbringings that aren't routine work just fine. I'm confident this one will." With that, I sat down.

When I was finished, Attorney Torper sat stone-still instead of standing to make his opening argument. I was just beginning to delight in the trial clerk's puzzled glance at me over the top of her half-glasses when His Honor ended my daydream of a courtroom melt-down. "Sorry, Mr. Torper; I did ask you to wait until being invited to speak. So tell me your version of the story, what you think my judgment should be in this matter, and why you think so."

This would be my first chance to watch opposing counsel at work, and after his initial faux pas—truly an awkward and inexcusably amateurish move—I was hoping for the worst. No such luck. Torper, who was a rugged, weathered-looking man—with a touch of the unkempt, "old salt" look of a wizened sailor stuffed for a day into someone else's suit—undeniably had a certain allure, and he turned out to be a superb storyteller. He was also blessed with a honeyed voice, which he was masterful at modulating, and I began to wonder if his initial stumble had been a ploy embedded in a strategy. Torper crooned the tale of an ungrateful daughter who had often rejected her mother's repeated efforts to mend fences, and he made much of the "embarrassing out-of-wedlock surprise pregnancy." It wasn't the grandmother who prevented a wedding—if to a man other than the child's biological father—it was Sandrine Bergeron and Dr. Freeman, who seemed to have other things in their lives more important than marrying and safeguarding the child with a stepparent adoption procedure. He assured the court that his client would have attended the wedding—if only there had been one to attend.

The best plan for the child, Torper argued, would be to be raised in the Christian and moral community where her grandparents lived—a small town about twenty miles from Fort Worth, Texas. Dr. Freeman could visit, if he indeed maintained and exhibited a legitimate ongoing interest in the child, but the presence of the biological father was a fiction, a legal fiction concocted to introduce a blood relative onto Dr. Freeman's side of the litigation—precisely because without that fiction the law was clear: the grandmother's case would prevail as a matter of law. "This man didn't even know about the pregnancy, let alone about

the child, and, on information and belief, was contacted by Attorney
Freiberg to strengthen the legal case of his real client, Dr. Freeman."
Attorney Torper's opening argument ended with his summary of the
case: "No doubt Dr. Dagnaud is a fine doctor, an honorable gentleman,
and a good family man. But he let himself be talked into joining this
litigation on the condition that the role he and his wife were to play
would be only minimal. That doesn't sound like a father to me," Torper
concluded. "It sounds like a nice guy trying to help out another nice
guy trapped in an otherwise unwinnable legal struggle."

The main problem I had with Attorney Torper's opening argument
was how accurate it was. It was suddenly crystal clear that this trial
was going to be a struggle, and I could only hope the judge was ready
for protracted warfare. I had a truckload more witnesses than did
Attorney Torper, and I'd be damned if I wasn't going to take advantage
of that. From that moment on, I began thinking of protecting and per-
fecting the record to build a case that could possibly prevail on appeal,
should that ever become necessary. I began to think that perhaps this
case had just the right set of facts to convince the appeals court—or
even the state's Supreme Court—to expand the application of the "best
interests of the child" test to cover a circumstance like Victoria's. Why
shouldn't a trial judge be able to think through which setting is best
for a child, even if one of the options does not contain a blood relative?
But, again, one step at a time.

***

For my first witness, I called Victoria's pediatrician, followed by her
pediatric dentist, her past play-school teacher, her past after-school
administrator, her current kindergarten teacher, and the pediatric child
psychiatrist she was seeing to work on grieving the loss of her mother.
The main point of this string of professionals was to document in the
record that every single need of the child was being dutifully attended
to. Additionally, I inquired of each of these witnesses the role, if any,
that they had seen Dr. Freeman play in their particular sphere of contact with Victoria. Each and every witness testified consistently with
what they had told me on that preparation day at Dr. Freeman's house:
he had always been a completely reliable parent. When I inquired of

them what, if anything, had changed after Sandrine Bergeron's death, they each gave identical responses: he was brokenhearted and tragically alone, but always appropriate in the presence of the child. And he hadn't missed a heartbeat in picking up the other half of the parenting work.

There was also an ulterior motive to deciding to lead off with the professionals. My hope had been that Attorney Torper's cross-examination of these professionals would be inappropriate—too harsh, too aggressive, too disbelieving. No such luck. He knew when there was nothing to gain from crossing a perfectly credible professional witness—such efforts almost always serve only to reemphasize their testimony. Torper clearly was in control of his argument. It wasn't that Dr. Freeman didn't do a good job parenting—he clearly did. It was that he was a legal stranger to the child, unlike the grandmother, and that he therefore had no further legal right to parent Victoria, however good he was at it. "No questions, Your Honor," he repeated after each of my witnesses, to the visible approval of the court.

Next came a stream of personal reference witnesses selected from among the friends Dr. Freeman had made through co-parenting Victoria. These witnesses were young pillars of the Brookline community: doctors, attorneys, shop owners, teachers—all sorts of people whose kids associated with Victoria in school, after school, in dance class, and the like. None of them had changed the play patterns of their children with Victoria after Sandrine Bergeron's death. They expressed complete faith in Dr. Freeman's parenting skills and testified that they felt entirely secure that their child was safe when playing with Victoria at her house with Dr. Freeman supervising.

Again, no cross-examination from Attorney Torper. This made for a very happy judge, since it moved along my side of the case at breakneck speed and didn't waste the court's time with needless objections and nit-picking cross-examinations.

I then called Dr. Freeman's father to the stand. Now the logic of examination underwent a major shift. The thrust I wanted from his testimony had nothing to do with the parenting skills and consistency the doctor had unarguably shown: here, I wanted the witnesses to tell the court who Victoria was in his life, and how connected he was to her. Dr. Freeman's parents were working-class Jewish people—the father was a cobbler who still worked daily in his shoe repair shop, and the mother was a skilled seamstress. They were both short, stout of build, humble in nature, and full to the brim of everyday-life wisdom. And such gentleness. They spoke with softened European accents—vestiges from their youth before their respective parents had managed, just barely, in each case, to send them off to America to survive the Holocaust.

The tone and tenor of the parents' testimony were remarkable. It came from the center of their hearts. Asking these people how connected they were to Victoria was like asking them how connected they were to their arms; it was like asking one side of a coin how connected it is to the other side. Removing Victoria—or any of their other three grandchildren—would be an amputation, pure and simple. Deal with that, Mr. Torper.

Given the wise restraint he had exhibited up to this point, I never expected Attorney Torper to cross-examine Victoria's grandfather. Even the judge was surprised—to the point where he shot me a quick look. Moreover, to my complete surprise, Torper began by affirming everything the grandfather had testified to, adding that he had "zero doubt that you adore little Victoria." Torper's remark garnered the full attention of everyone in the courtroom, and he knew it, so he paused for dramatic effect before asking, in an almost casual tone of voice, "But that being said, sir, you agree, don't you, that it's not love and nurturing that bind families together through truly hard times—it's the irreducibility and the certainty of blood relations. You admit that, don't you?"

I got one more quick glance from His Honor, which said exactly what I was thinking. Torper had violated one of the primary rules of trial law: *never ask a witness a question unless you know how he's going to answer.* What came back was: "Are you kidding? Both my wife and I were sent off as little children on a ship to America—separately. Each of us at about age five was completely alone. Not a single relative. The ship only took little children. We were each taken into an American family that raised us through the hard, hard times of World War II. Neither family had any money. My parents were American Catholics, and my wife's parents were Lutherans. And each family not only took us into their homes but also into their hearts. My sisters and my brother, and my wife's sister, were the American children of these couples, and they are to this very day our beloved siblings—some alive, some now gone. It was *exactly* love and nurturing that bonded us all together—some glues just don't come undone. I know you're a very educated man, and I'm just a simple cobbler, but this one thing you have wrong: family is *all about* love and nurturing."

Torper just stood there next to the witness stand, frozen in time: he seemed like a man who, having been punched in the belly, couldn't catch his breath. It took him quite a while to speak the four words that needed saying: "Nothing further, Your Honor." You won't be surprised to learn that he subsequently refrained from cross-examining Dr. Freeman's mother, sister, and niece.

After the family, there were three witnesses left on our side of the case—and possibly a fourth, if it felt like I needed her. These, of course, were our key witnesses, and it is an easy matter to summarize their direct testimony.

Dr. Freeman's testimony flowed seamlessly. When I asked him why he and Sandrine had not married, he just shook his head back and forth. "Because I was an idiot. Between our two careers and raising Victoria and spending time with my family—whom you just met—and taking care of the house we owned, our days ran from six in the morning to midnight, seven days a week. Every week. Of course, I see now that this is no excuse, and that I missed the chance to marry the love of my life, and even more importantly, I failed to do what I needed to do to keep my daughter safe."

I asked Dr. Freeman if he had a will and/or trust, and he testified that indeed he had a pour-over will and a revocable trust that he had had drafted by an estate-planning attorney soon after Victoria was born. I had asked him to bring a certified true copy of the documents, which were then offered in evidence. The will poured over all his assets into his living trust, and the only beneficiaries of the trust were Sandrine Bergeron during her life, and Victoria. There was life insurance as well—all of which was aimed at keeping Victoria safe.

Needless to say, I had Dr. Freeman describe how he regularly takes Victoria to her children's dance program at the Boston Ballet, and how they also make frequent weekend trips to the Boston Museum of Science and the Boston Children's Museum—of which Victoria was particularly fond. But by far the most effective part of Dr. Freeman's testimony was when he told the court who he was as a person—above and beyond being a parent. It came out best in his answer to the question: "What, if any, hobbies do you pursue?" Dr. Freeman responded that he had been a music minor in college and was a lifelong pianist. His specialty was Chopin, but in his heart of hearts, his true love was jazz piano. This had worked out well for him, he told the judge. He had been able to support himself throughout his internship and residency by playing at a variety of clubs and events. The judge's left eyebrow shot up just a touch at hearing this; could this apparently dried-up prune of an elderly man take in a little Oscar Peterson from time to time? A touch of Herbie Hancock? Perhaps a pinch of Thelonious Monk?

The further along the trial went, the clearer it became that the case might well turn on Dr. Dagnaud's testimony, and, more precisely, on whether or not Dr. Dagnaud's presence as co-petitioner was perceived as legitimate, or whether it was seen to be—as Attorney Torper had labeled it—simply a handy fiction trumped up for the litigation. Accordingly, more and more of the strategic trial planning was concerned with thinking through what we could do to bolster both Dr. Dagnaud's credibility as a witness and the believability of his willingness to meaningfully participate in the co-parenting we were proposing. He had, after all, just met the child.

In practical terms, the first thing this meant was that Dr. Dagnaud would have to stay throughout the trial. To me, it was now obvious that if he could only be present for the first part of the trial, we risked that his subsequent absence might be interpreted by the judge—and argued by opposing counsel—as evidence of his lack of commitment. The problem was, of course, that it was a double disaster for Dr. Dagnaud to take practical steps to prolong his stay in Boston. In the first place, he had already bought favors from other surgeons on his team that would deprive him of any vacation days for months and months to come—and this sacrifice on his part, obviously, redounded to his wife and child. Secondly, Dr. Dagnaud cautioned us that his wife would see a postponed return as mission creep—as a sign of her loss of control over his life and, thereby, over her child's life. The best the doctor could do—and I had every reason to believe him when he told me that he was paying dearly for this—was to stay through Wednesday of the second week. So that was what we had to work with—and then the judge left the courtroom an hour early on the Friday for "personal reasons." Great—every minute mattered now, and we'd just lost an hour.

Clearly, I needed to trim down Dr. Newsom's expert testimony in order to get Dr. Dagnaud on the stand as early as possible on Monday. In the first days of trial, Attorney Torper had not been a stickler on forcing me to "qualify" my expert witnesses to the court; this had saved all of us from the tedium of having to ask each such witness a spate of questions about their education, occupational history, specialized training, and the like. But Torper was preceptive and resourceful. It became progressively clear that he had figured out that I was running up against time pressures. So, notwithstanding the fact that Dr. Newsom was by far the single most qualified professional in the trial—he'd practically been born on the Yale campus, educated there as both an undergraduate and a medical student, with an equally sterling professional career—at Attorney Torper's insistence, I had to spend precious time having Dr. Newsom describe his education, his work experience, and the many honors he'd received. After fifteen minutes of questions and answers repetitively establishing his expertise, I finally offered the doctor as an expert witness to the court. Torper, confirming his shift into delay gear, objected loudly—but he made a mistake, because he failed to state a sound basis for his objection, such as: "Could we get some more information, Your Honor, about his experience with children this age who have just lost their primary parent?"

He'd made a strategically clever move—but he'd been careless with his tactics, and the judge let him have it right between the eyes: "Attorney Torper, this court is well aware of what Dr. Newsom has done at Children's Hospital for, what?" the judge asked, looking over at Dr. Newsom. "Over thirty years?" Newsom nodded yes. "And you're not going to waste any more time. I intend to keep this trial moving, and now that I think about it, I intend to speed it up. And that applies to you as well, Attorney Freiberg, do you understand that?"

I have no present memory of ever so entirely welcoming such a sternly voiced reprimand from a judge. "Yes, Your Honor, I hear you loud and clear." With this, I immediately turned back toward Dr. Newsom and asked: "Do the factual findings and expressed opinions in your report on whether Victoria Bergeron should remain in Boston in the joint legal and physical custody of Dr. Freeman and Dr. Dagnaud constitute findings and opinions reached with a reasonable degree of medical certainty?" When he affirmed this, I asked him to summarize his findings, which, as you might imagine, were all about the importance of certainty and continuity, and the importance of not introducing any additional loss of connection into the life of a child who has so recently lost her primary parent.

When Dr. Newsom had answered my final question, it was time for Attorney Torper to decide whether or not to cross-examine him. I could see him struggling with his quandary: cross-examination would help in his new slow-the-trial-down strategy, but on the other hand, it exposed him to giving the witness the opportunity to emphasize and reiterate important points that he'd testified to. And it could outright piss off the judge. Wisely, I thought, Torper declined to cross-examine.

I next called Dr. Dagnaud to the stand, not wasting a moment of time. Dr. Dagnaud—through a court-certified translator—described a life not unlike that of Dr. Freeman. Both men had come from humble families and had worked hard—rather against the odds—to achieve their medical training and professional stature. I had Dr. Dagnaud describe his father, who was a *traiteur*—a chef specializing in making first-course dishes like terrines and pâtés and all sorts of salads that are as appetizing to look at as they are delicious to eat. His description of his mother, who ran the family's charcuterie where these beautiful food products were sold, became a brief trip out of the dusty courtroom when we introduced in evidence—and showed to the judge—half a dozen photographs of the charming small village in the Beaujolais region of France where the parents lived and worked.

Dr. Dagnaud went on to describe how his extended family had been informed about our two-dad plan, and how they were absolutely prepared to welcome Victoria into their lives. Multiple additional photographs—of his wife and child, of his extended family, of his home in Paris—were duly identified, briefly described, and offered in evidence. When I had shown the doctor a photograph of his parents posed in front of their shop, Dagnaud had spontaneously—without a question from me—turned toward the judge on his own, and through the interpreter told the court: "You know, Judge, my parents are sad that my wife—like many people in busy Paris—has only one child. They want more. So, for them, they see this as a chance to add another grandchild. No problem!" Then, to my complete surprise, Dr. Dagnaud reached in his breast pocket, took out an envelope, and continued his direct conversation with the judge. "And I just remembered, Judge, I brought a letter from them also. Can I give it to you?" After which he added one final line, in beautifully accented English to boot: "It is in French, of course; so sorry."

"Objection. Hearsay," called out Attorney Torper, jumping to his feet.

I stood as well. "Unavailable witness, Your Honor; it's an exception to the hearsay rule."

Judge O'Connor went stone silent and sat perfectly still. Torper was correct, the letter was hearsay. But there are exceptions to the hearsay rule, one of which is the unavailability of a witness to be present for cross-examination. It was a close call, and this aged stickler for the rules—and their exceptions—was no doubt running through all the relevant case law on hearsay exceptions. When he'd thought this through, he spoke with considerable judicial wisdom: "I'm going to allow the letter to be read and the translator to translate it, while reserving my ruling as to its admissibility."

Since I hadn't heard a word about the letter, I was in the same position as opposing counsel. We each grabbed our pencils, ready to scribble the notes we would need to support our respective arguments as to why the letter from the grandparents should or should not be allowed in evidence. But as it turned out, the warm and inclusive tone of the letter spoke louder than its content. The note ended with the line: "We'll welcome our new grandchild; we have plenty of love to share with her, and plenty of beautiful food to eat together as a family."

The judge, without saying a word, peered down from the bench at Attorney Torper. There were ten seconds of complete silence before opposing counsel once again exhibited evidence of his appreciable trial skills: "Objection withdrawn, Your Honor."

When I look back over my career, it seems that in almost every trial, there was one witness—or one part of a key witness's story—where the testimony was both critically important and monumentally at risk of going badly. The reasons for such extreme vulnerability varied wildly, of course. Some witnesses were just terrible witnesses:

they couldn't express themselves succinctly, or convincingly, or credibly. Others had no problem delivering their testimony—but what they had to say wasn't backed up by any other evidence, and they simply lacked the weight of character to be convincing in the absence of corroboration. When I think back on Victoria's case, and ask myself why I was so fearful that Dr. Dagnaud's explanation of his relationship with Victoria's mother could go so wrong, the logic for my trepidation was clear. What I had was a tall, movie-star-handsome Frenchman trying to explain through a translator to a white-haired, wizened, little old dried-up, very Catholic retired judge why there was nothing fundamentally unacceptable about his having come to Boston for a two-week medical training seminar, during which time he'd met, seduced, and impregnated a beautiful young nurse. How the hell was that going to work?

But I had no choice but to ask the question—if I didn't, Torper would do so on cross.

"Dr. Dagnaud, can you describe in detail to the court how you met Sandrine Bergeron, and what happened during your two-week visit to Boston seven years ago?"

"Oui, bien sûr." These first three words, delivered in Dr. Dagnaud's deep baritone voice, brought the courtroom to complete silence. He turned toward the judge as he answered—as I had asked him to do—and spoke slowly for two or three sentences, and then sat as calm and still as a cat while the translator put his words in English. The judge seemed spellbound and hung on every word. "Your Honor, I was fortunate to be invited to the surgical training session at Harvard Medical School, which took place at Beth Israel Deaconess Medical Center. It was an amazing professional opportunity for the twelve of us young surgeons fortunate enough to have been chosen from more than a hundred applicants. We worked from six a.m. straight through to six p.m., and then we were off for the evening."

He cleared his throat before retaking up the narrative in his resonant voice. "At the hospital, there was an operating-room nurse—Sandrine—who had been assigned to my team. She had"—here, Dr. Dagnaud paused just long enough for me to realize he was time traveling back those seven years—"such enormous and beautiful eyes. When she looked at me over her surgical mask, I was . . . captivated . . .

captured. As our surgical team was scrubbing down after the first day, I asked her in my terrible English if by any chance she would like to take a coffee with me. When she responded in French, I think I nearly fell over, especially because she said '*oui*' in the way only a single woman does . . . you know what I mean, Judge"—and then Dr. Dagnaud added in his Maurice Chevalier English—"with a little smile." And damn if the judge didn't smile right back at the witness.

"Judge, it was the most beautiful two weeks you can imagine . . . Days full of new, cutting-edge surgical technique, nights full of love . . . We were so young, Judge . . . It was as if sleep really didn't matter . . ." Again, Dr. Dagnaud paused, and the room remained perfectly silent.

"And then, somehow, the two weeks had passed by, and it was time to leave. Sandrine drove me to the airport, and we parted as lovers, with all sorts of plans and ideas about when and where we would see each other next. We called and spoke for, I don't know . . . a number of weeks, and we talked about a visit to Paris for the Christmas holidays. And then . . ." This time when the doctor paused, he wept silently, needing to use his right hand to chase down a few tears. "Then, suddenly, for no reason I could explain, she stopped calling, stopped taking my calls. I was heartbroken. I thought . . . I don't know what I thought . . . You know how young people are, Judge . . . I thought it had ended because I was so far away. So busy in my life as a young surgeon. I never knew until a month ago about the pregnancy . . . about Victoria. If only Sandrine had told me, Judge, if only . . ." And then there were no more words, and the doctor again had to use the back of his hand to wipe away the final tears and give the judge one final, small—and very gentle—smile.

At this point, Dr. Dagnaud turned forward in the witness chair to face me for another question. I waited as long as I dared to lend gravitas to the testimony he had just finished, and then inquired about his reaction to learning about Victoria, and what arrangements he was prepared to make with Dr. Freeman to raise Victoria, if the court were to approve their plan. The doctor's emotional openness in his testimony to this point, not to mention his personal charisma and sonorous tone of voice, lent enormous credibility to his description of how he and his wife were perfectly willing to participate with Dr. Freeman. Then, entirely on his own once again, he turned to the judge. "Your

Honor, I know I need to promise you that I will take my role in parenting Victoria very seriously—and, as she is my daughter, I can make this promise to you in perfectly good faith. I will never let my daughter down, Judge. I will never let you down, Judge, if you find that giving me and Dr. Freeman this opportunity is what you think is best for Victoria, I will never violate your trust." With this, the doctor turned back square in his chair, looking out at me for another question.

Sometimes you just need to stop, even if there are more questions on your notepad. This was such a time. "I have nothing further, Your Honor."

No one had noticed—or cared—that Dr. Dagnaud's testimony had busted right through the planned 2:00 p.m. lunchtime; it was now nearly 2:30. The courtroom clerk, no doubt thinking about the poor stenographer who had taken down all this testimony without any break, announced there would be a forty-five-minute lunch break, after which cross-examination would begin sharply at 3:15.

The two doctors and I had a sandwich at a small shop in the tiny little town center. I told them that, if it was okay with them, I wanted to put Victoria on the stand first thing the next morning to close our case. We all agreed that I would go home with the two of them to prepare Victoria for her testimony. For the remaining ten minutes of the meal, the two doctors struggled to find enough shared language to discuss some newly developed prosthetic hip replacement hardware—and I was left alone to ponder what I would do if I were Attorney Torper cross-examining Dr. Dagnaud. My conclusion was that, unless Torper had something good on Dr. Dagnaud from an investigator, he would probably refrain from calling this captivating and credible man back up on the stand.

Torper saw it differently, thereby confirming that he was indeed in stall mode. He crossed Dr. Dagnaud for the rest of the afternoon. He got Dr. Dagnaud to readily admit there were unknowns about how things would work out in the future, to which the doctor spontaneously added, "But that's the nature of the future, *non*?" a line that made the judge openly smile and nod. He got Dr. Dagnaud to admit that his wife had some concerns and worries about how things would work out, to which the doctor added, "But that's the nature of a wife, *non*?" And he got Dr. Dagnaud to admit that after only one week together, he didn't yet know Victoria very well, to which the doctor countered, "But didn't your client only see the child once, as a tiny baby, and for just one or two days?" After this last stinging retort, and somewhat abruptly, Torper finally sensed the warmth the judge felt for the witness and announced that he had nothing further.

With this, the judge looked over at me, sternly. "Are you calling any further witnesses, Counselor; when will you rest your case?"

"Judge," I answered, "I have only one more witness for tomorrow morning, and she will be exceedingly brief. I want to call the child, Your Honor, if you feel that would be appropriate."

The judge was silent for a moment, considering the offer. "Yes, I think that is entirely a good idea; I want to meet this young lady. But I don't want her put on cross; I want the two of you attorneys to agree that she will be available for gentle direct questioning by both of you, with no cross. And I do mean gentle; she's six years old."

"Yes, Your Honor," we intoned in unison.

***

Back at Dr. Freeman's house, cheese and wine were brought out to celebrate. Our case had gone in well—very well—and there really wasn't much more we could say to convince the judge of the viability of our two-dad plan. Of course, we had all learned to respect Attorney Torper's skills, so perhaps he had magic up his sleeve that we knew nothing about—yet.

At some point, Miss Victoria came skipping into the living room, where she found the two doctors relaxed on the sofa and me sitting across from them in an easy chair, all of us exhausted after the day of trial. Victoria, accompanied by Françoise and the puppy, as always, jumped up between the two of them and launched into a manic tale about how Françoise had been giraffe-napped at school before being belatedly returned.

Victoria's story provided me with just the lead-in I needed with her. Speaking in French, I asked Victoria if she and Françoise could come tomorrow to talk to a man who was very important both to her daddy and to her papa—as she called Dr. Dagnaud. "This man, the judge, will be making the decision as to where you will live now that your mommy is gone."

Just as I began to wonder if I was getting any part of this across, Victoria surprised the hell out of me. "Is this the judge you told me about a long time ago that I might get to speak to in her office about where I want to live?" I began to confirm to Victoria that she was exactly right, but before I could really get started, she interrupted: "But I thought the judge was a lady judge—that's what you said."

The last thing I was going to tell this little girl was that another adult in her life had also passed away. So I lied. "Being a judge is a job, Victoria—like both of your daddies have the job of being doctors. The lady judge left her job as a judge, so another judge is responsible for your case now. And he's a man. Both of your daddies have met him and want you to come in tomorrow to tell him who you and Françoise—and your puppy, of course—feel safe with, and where the three of you want to live. Is that okay?" Victoria said it was okay, indeed, and as soon thereafter as I could manage, I took off for home to get as much sleep as I could.

***

Once we were all seated the following morning and the courtroom was called to order, I called Miss Victoria Bergeron to the stand, and she popped up into the seat, and decided—all on her own—to stand on it rather than sit down. This put her little face directly on a level with the judge's, which I realized was a brilliant decision on her part. Of course, she was holding Françoise, but not clinging to it, as children sometimes do. I asked her to tell the judge her name. Then I asked her about who she lived with, and she pointed to Dr. Freeman, and answered, "With my daddy, of course. My mommy got big sick and died, but my daddy is a doctor and he's not sick at all. I'm not either." I inquired who the other man sitting next to her daddy was, and she responded without hesitation, "That's my other daddy, my new daddy. He talks like my mommy, and he has a baby girl at home who'll be my sister when I meet her . . ." With this, she sort of jumped through a ninety-degree turn and faced the judge. "Isn't that fun? I'm going to have a sister!"

I could tell the judge felt a bit cornered, but damned if he didn't rise above the technical legalities that disallowed Victoria to presume the outcome of the trial in posing a question directly to him, and replied, "That is indeed fun, young lady. Very fun."

And then, having gotten a smile out of the judge, before I even understood what was happening, Victoria went rogue. She asked the judge if her new daddy could come over for a second, since she wanted to show the judge something. His Honor, whose hard surface was visibly melting in the presence of this little Shirley Temple ball of energy, said he supposed so unless Attorney Torper had any objection. He didn't dare. So, Dr. Dagnaud walked up to the side of the bench next to the witness chair. "Lean close, Papa," Victoria instructed him in French. "Put your face next to mine." He did so, and then both of them leaned in over the bench toward the judge, their faces almost touching, ending up not more than four or five feet from His Honor. "What do you see?" asked Victoria.

"Two faces, two very nice faces," Judge O'Connor replied, sounding a bit stumped by the exercise.

"No, no," scolded Victoria. "Look at our eyes."

There followed ten seconds of stunned silence, and then the judge did just what Victoria had plotted and planned—totally on her own. "Oh my goodness, they're identical! And so, so green. I've never seen such green eyes . . . Now . . . uhm . . . uhm . . . now . . . everyone back to their place."

It was time to ask Victoria the three questions she and I had talked about in her room, although by this point, I had no idea how she might answer. "Victoria, how would it make you feel if the judge thought it was better for you to live far away from your daddy?"

"You mean without Françoise and my puppy?"

"No. With Françoise, and with your puppy, but far away from your daddy."

"I can't lose my daddy," she replied. "I already lost my mommy." Then, out of the blue, she created an entirely new way of answering my question. Covering her right eye with her right hand, she faced the judge and explained: "It would be like if you lost one eye, that would make you sad." Then, putting Françoise on the chair, she covered both eyes with both her hands. "But if you lost both eyes, that would make you blind. My heart is sad because my mommy died, but it's not blind. It would be if I had to move far away from my daddy."

Then Victoria pivoted—or sort of jumped, actually—to face me again for the next question. "And how would it make you feel if you had to move far away from all your friends?" I asked.

"You mean Betsy, and Hillary and Louise, and my friends at school, and my friends at dance class, and Kathy next door? Well, not next door, but almost. And Christina?" I nodded yes. Once again, she turned toward the judge and placed her arms on the side of his bench. "That would be so terrible," Victoria moaned. "Those are the people I share with. Who would I share with?"

I had one more question for her. "Victoria, how does it make you feel when you talk to your new daddy?"

Once again hopping around sideways to face the judge, and this time putting her elbows on the edge of his bench and her chin in her two hands, she thought for a good ten seconds before she replied, "It makes me feel safer, because he talks like my mommy and like my storybooks that my mommy used to read me but can't anymore. It feels fuzzy and warm when he talks to me in my mommy language 'cause that's how I would fall asleep or when I hurt my knee."

"Fuzzy?" I asked, taking a gamble.

"Yea, fuzzy, like Françoise when I hug her. Here, Mr. Judge, if you pet Françoise, you'll see what I mean."

With that, she held good old Françoise out, and not only did the judge stroke the smiling giraffe, but he also got a laugh out of everyone in the courtroom when he followed up with: "Let the record reflect that I am taking judicial notice that Françoise is, indeed, quite, quite fuzzy."

Finally, I asked the court if Attorney Torper and I could approach the bench on the side away from the witness chair. The judge looked a bit surprised but allowed my request. When we were huddled there, I asked if he would mind if I posed a few questions to the witness in French, which the interpreter would translate, just so that he could feel comfortable, and the record would reflect, that the child was fully bilingual—given how important that skill would be to the proposed co-parenting plan we were putting before the court.

When the judge assented, I realized it was time to quickly bring my case to an end. I asked Victoria—in French—if she knew who the woman was sitting next to Attorney Torper. *"Non,"* she replied. After the translation, I asked Victoria to tell the judge where she wanted to live, and why she felt that way. "With Françoise and my puppy, of course." I told her we knew that, we all did, and that that was going to happen for sure. But what house would she and Françoise like to live in? She answered, "With my daddy, of course. With both of them." And when I asked why she felt that way, she responded—speaking for the very first time in a shaky, little-girl voice: "Because that's where I feel safe enough to cry when I need to."

Once Victoria's response had been translated, I turned to the court and closed my case. "Nothing further, Your Honor. The petitioner rests."

The clerk called for a fifteen-minute break before the start of the respondent's case, and this gave me a chance to speak with Attorney Torper. I tried to convince him to speak with his clients about resolving this matter between us. They had been present throughout the trial and had heard that the petitioners' case was strong and—more importantly—that there was a healthy and good life for Victoria with her two dads. My last line was: "We can all walk out of here winners today, Counselor, and all these clients of ours can end up one big, super-complicated blended family. Why the hell not?"

Attorney Torper had listened politely but gave no sign of his position on the matter. He did say that he would take my suggestion to his clients and get back to me before we took up in the afternoon. But when we all reentered the courtroom ten minutes later, Torper didn't even look in my direction. Once the judge was seated, the court reporter was ready, and the judge had asked Attorney Torper if he was ready to proceed, Torper asked if he could take a few minutes to supplement the opening argument he had given. The judge looked over at me with a furled brow—perhaps it was an invitation to object—but I thought otherwise, and replied, "That's all right with me, Your Honor, if I can reserve the right to reply."

"All right, gentlemen. Here's how we're going to handle this. You can speak to me now—one or both of you—but any time you use will be subtracted from the one-hour time limit I intend to allow each of you for your closing arguments. So have at it."

As he had in his opening, Torper signaled that this case was all about morality and propriety and Christian life. It seemed as if Preacher Man was setting the strategic plan. There was, of course, a chance that Torper knew more about this judge than I did, but there seemed to me to be a greater likelihood that his clients just saw this case from a small-town-Texas point of view, and had insisted that their attorney argue the case from that perspective. As counsel phrased it in his second go at an opening statement, the petitioner's case was all about asking this court to sanction a "sinful, nontraditional lifestyle, a lifestyle where there is nothing unacceptable about having sex outside of marriage, getting pregnant without even telling the father, quickly seducing an infertile man and using that to get him to agree to help raise the child." Torper argued, "Judge, you heard about how Victoria gets medical and dental care and dance lessons—but you didn't hear a word about church, about her getting religious guidance. How could she—her mother was a lapsed Catholic, and her mother's boyfriend, who petitions to raise her, is a Jew." This line caused the judge to cock his head to the right, and to slightly open his mouth.

"The birth of this child," Torper stormed on, "was not important enough to the deceased mother, or to her boyfriend, to take the time to get married. That, Your Honor, is a perfect image of how secondary this child has been to their work lives. And they think this will be improved by bringing in the biological father, who lives three thousand miles away and is even busier than they are with his own medical practice and his own family?

"As the evidence will show in the respondent's case, the best plan for this bastard child would be for her to be rescued and placed in the bosom of the Christian and moral community where her biological grandmother and her ordained preacher step-grandfather live just outside of Fort Worth, Texas. This is a community, Your Honor, in the old and biblical sense of the term—a town of four hundred and fifty souls where everybody knows everybody, and everybody supports the moral upbringing of all the town's children. The witnesses for the respondent will testify to all of this, Your Honor.

"Finally, Your Honor, I want to warn opposing counsel that I shall be arguing in my closing argument that he has attempted to defraud this court—"

At this point, the judge interrupted. "What are you referring to, Mr. Torper? You're making a very serious allegation in open court, and you expose yourself greatly by what you've just said. I want to know right now what you are referring to when you claim that Attorney Freiberg has attempted to defraud this court."

"I'm referring to the fiction that Dr. Dagnaud would be a second father for the child. This is a narrative cooked up by Attorney Freiberg to defraud this court. Dr. Dagnaud's only relationship to this case is that he immorally seduced and carelessly impregnated the child's mother over half a dozen years ago. He knew nothing further about his despoiled victim, or her sad, lonely pregnancy, or the child, until a month ago when Attorney Freiberg probably flew over to France to find himself the one witness who could challenge the legal right the child's grandmother has to take and raise this orphan child. Your Honor, I don't doubt that Dr. Dagnaud is a fine doctor over in France, and a fine husband, and a fine father to his legitimate baby girl. But he has allowed himself to be manipulated into being used as a pawn in a fraudulent lawsuit. He should go back to France and rejoin his own family, where he belongs. He testified, Your Honor, that he has no time at the present to participate in raising Victoria—he claimed only that he would visit from time to time, and that in later years, who knows, maybe more contact would be possible. That doesn't sound like being a father or a co-father to me. It sounds like a nice guy who was talked into helping out another nice guy in an otherwise unwinnable legal contest for the custody of this lovely child."

Clever. Mr. Torper had maneuvered the court into letting him give his opening a second time. But there had been a little frown on the judge's forehead throughout Torper's argument that led me to believe he was well aware that he had been manipulated. While I couldn't be certain of this, of course, I decided to allow its implications to guide me.

I rose from my chair to speak. "Your Honor, I'm a firm believer that the rules of this court permit one opening and one closing. I'll reserve my closing until after the respondent's case, as the rules foresee. Thank you, Judge." Just the tiniest upturning of the judge's lips told me what I needed to know.

***

After an early lunch break, Attorney Torper launched into his case. The grandmother testified throughout the rest of Tuesday about how she so loved her daughter, and how heartbreaking it had been for her to be rejected and unappreciated. She then testified that she also had been taken advantage of as "just another pretty face" by Sandrine's father—yet another Frenchman on the prowl for naïve American girls. She went on to claim that it was clearly the work of the devil that another Frenchman—a generation later—should despoil her daughter's virginity and propriety, just as had happened to her. The world for the grandmother was all about Sodom and Gomorrah, good and evil, propriety and sin.

I thought I saw the judge fidgeting a bit more as the stale, dry heat of the courtroom was progressively exaggerated by the increasing afternoon sunlight gleaming in through the tall, century-old windows. It was as if the rising temperature intensified the grandmother's hellfire-and-brimstone view of the world, and I could see the judge becoming increasingly impatient with testimony that was both off point and a century out of date—and that was just fine with me.

Then Torper opened up a new line of inquiry about the religious practices to which the grandmother subscribed, how she had been saved, and how the child would be saved . . . and suddenly the judge could take no more. "Sidebar!" he called out to both attorneys, and we scampered over to the side of the bench away from the witness. "Counsel," the judge whispered to Attorney Torper, off the record, "why are you doing this? I don't care about your client's religion or her worldview—I want testimony about her plans for this child. How would she raise the child? At her age, does she have the energy, the health, the stamina? What about all these little-girl friends the child has here; can they be replaced down there in that little town? How so? How soon? What about all the extracurricular activities you heard about—do they have dance classes down there for little girls? What about childcare? What about help with her homework? What are the schools like down there? Your opposing counsel painted me a very clear picture of what life is like for the child up here. Do you hear what I'm saying, Counsel?

Let's take a ten-minute break, and you talk to your client about what I need to hear."

After the break, everything changed. The grandmother metamorphosed from south-of-the-Mason-Dixon-Line ideologue to super-grandma. She articulated well-conceived plans for Victoria, with names of schools, teachers, extracurricular activities, doctors, playmates, and so on—with each category supported by written documentation and photographs, all of which paperwork was offered in evidence. Somehow, she had morphed from an annoying, grating presence into an extremely effective witness. And she did an even better job with questions about why she had felt uncomfortable, even unwanted, in that single visit to see her baby granddaughter, and why—at "great emotional cost" to her—she had written off her daughter and her daughter's baby as a lost cause. I found myself wondering if Attorney Torper had orchestrated the strikingly sharp contrast between the initial testimony and what I was hearing now, because the disparity was definitely serving to enhance the grandmother's position. In any case, she had the court's full attention now—that was clear.

Oh boy, just when I thought the chess game of the trial was over, it was back on again—big-time. No way was I interested in cross-examining the witness. If the judge was going to apply the "best interest of the child" test and compare the two environments, we still came out ahead—way ahead.

Next up was Preacher Man. If only my investigator had found something—*anything*—out of order at the tented, Holy Roller proceedings he staged where, according to my private eye, the same half-dozen zealots were saved—week after week. Couldn't there have been just a *touch* of scandal—any kind of scandal would have done just fine. I didn't need Jim and Tammy Faye Bakker—but just a little comingling of funds, just one little complaint of sexual impropriety, or even one itty-bitty touch of fraud? No such luck. I had nothing to work with. And to my surprise, the man was an effective witness: there was no evidence or reason to believe that he wouldn't live up to his promise to be an engaged and effective step-grandparent. Alas, there was nothing to be gained from cross-examination, so I again declined the opportunity.

Preacher Man's testimony concluded the Tuesday trial session, and once again, I went back with the two doctors to Dr. Freeman's household to debrief the day and plan Wednesday's session. Wednesday, of course, was not just any day—at the end of the day, Dr. Dagnaud would be leaving for France, so we had a major decision to make as to how to announce this to the court.

***

As soon as I saw Attorney Torper the following morning, I asked if I could briefly interrupt his case to put Dr. Dagnaud back on the stand for a quarter hour to explain to the court why he needed to return that evening to Paris. Torper's eyes opened as wide as saucers—he was thrilled, as one would expect, that the principal petitioner was disappearing from the trial.

I began my redirect examination by asking Dr. Dagnaud to explain to the court his normal work schedule back in Paris, and what he had arranged with his colleagues in order to free himself for the nearly two weeks he'd been in Boston—first to meet Victoria and spend a week with her, and then to attend the trial through today. He replied and then added, through the translator, "Basically, Your Honor, I'm going to be living at the Cochin Hospital for the foreseeable future."

Suddenly, I had a major decision to make: I wanted to ask my witness a question for which I hadn't prepared him. I took a gamble and went ahead. "Dr. Dagnaud, how does it make you feel to have to leave this trial proceeding before it's finished?"

The witness's eyebrows shot up on his forehead when my question finally arrived via the translation process. He cocked his head slightly to the right and looked down toward the floor, and then, after taking the time he needed to formulate his answer, he turned to his left and directly faced the judge.

"Having to leave this trial proceeding makes me worry, Judge. It makes me worry that you might misinterpret my absence as a lack of interest in Victoria, or an absence of commitment to the co-parenting plan Dr. Freeman and I have placed before you. Nothing could be further from the truth. If I were free to stay, I would, but I am part of a surgical team in Paris, and it is not fair to my colleagues to place any further burden on them, or increased risk on our patients. Tired surgeons make mistakes, just like tired anybody else.

"Judge," Dr. Dagnaud continued, "I don't know anything about American law, or how you are going to weigh and decide between the very real and wonderful life Dr. Freeman and I can give Victoria and the life her grandmother and step-grandfather could give her in Texas. All I can do is assure you of this: I will be involved in my daughter's life either way. I would far prefer to coordinate with Dr. Freeman to construct a fascinating bilingual childhood in Boston and Paris for Victoria, but if you think it is best for Victoria to live in Texas, then I will buy a big hat and visit her there. Victoria is as much my daughter as my little Yolande in Paris, and I am already committed to Victoria for the rest of my life. Period. You met her, Judge—she is a little jewel of a person, and she will enrich my life, and eventually she will enrich the life of her half sister—and my wife—wherever she lives. So I ask you, please don't let the fact that I have to fly back to Paris tonight— and operate in the morning on a man about your age who needs a new hip—influence which of these two childhoods you determine is best for Victoria." The doctor than paused for a moment before delivering a punch line I could tell he had preconceived. "Just be glad you are not that patient!"

***

Dr. Dagnaud hadn't fully left the witness stand when the judge—now clearly in let's-speed-this-trial-up gear—told Attorney Torper to call his next witness. Torper called three additional witnesses, each of whom testified about the availability of educational, medical, recreational, and social facilities, as well as friendship networks, in the town where Victoria would live. How all this was available in a town of four hundred and fifty souls was a bit of a mystery, and while I had determined to forgo cross-examination, I couldn't resist inquiring of the final witness how so many resources were available in such a small town. The reply was an admission: most, if not all, of the services and facilities were actually located in the town of Aledo, which was "only eight miles up the road." I asked the witness if she could estimate the population of Aledo. "About fifteen hundred," she replied. I looked over at the judge as I restated the number "about fifteen hundred." I had no further questions. The numbers spoke for themselves.

The judge then entered into a prolonged whispering session with his trial clerk, after which the clerk announced that closing arguments would begin immediately after lunch.

***

As respondent, Attorney Torper argued first; the petitioner (like the plaintiff in a civil matter) always gets the final bite at the apple. The heart and soul of his argument, as the following quotes from the trial transcript show, was that even if the court found Dr. Dagnaud's involvement adequate to allow application of the "best interests of the child" test, the court should think long and hard about which blood relative would actually have the time to raise Victoria. "I don't in any way mean to denigrate this fine French gentleman," Torper intoned, sweeping his hand toward Dr. Dagnaud. "But the evidence is undisputed, Your Honor. Dr. Dagnaud's life is in Paris, where he has a busy surgical schedule and a family of his own to take care of. He is clearly an honorable man, an admirable professional, and no doubt a committed parent to his own child, but," Torper emphasized with dramatic flair, "he can be only a very, very, very part-time father to Victoria for the foreseeable future."

The final paragraph of his argument seems worth quoting. It was delivered in a calm and thoughtful tone of voice: "I would even suggest, Your Honor, that for reasons Dr. Dagnaud explained to us so elegantly yesterday, it is not fair to his wife, his child, his surgical colleagues—or to his patients—for Dr. Dagnaud to be absent too often from Paris. And add to that, Your Honor, that while Dr. Freeman remains interested in participating in raising the child he has nurtured since her birth, he also is a busy surgeon. He told you, Judge, that the main reason he and Sandrine Bergeron never formally married was because their careers were so busy that they couldn't even find the time to wed one another. In Boston, Judge, this child will be raised principally by neither doctor: she will be tended to by hired help, by nannies. In contrast, in Cresson, she would be raised, day in and day out, by her nonworking grandmother. I don't disagree with Dr. Dagnaud that you have two viable possibilities here—but only one of them involves significant presence by a blood relative."

All in all, it was a well-argued and quite persuasive closing. After about half a minute of thinking things through, the judge looked down at me to follow on with my closing. But I couldn't, and I knew I shouldn't. So, I swallowed all pride, stood up, and announced: "Your Honor, I am, in fact, not ready to proceed. It is now nearly three thirty in the afternoon, an hour before Your Honor normally ends the trial day. I would ask that Your Honor allow me to argue first thing tomorrow morning, if Attorney Torper does not object. I have no doubt, Your Honor, that every single person present in this courtroom would like to see Your Honor divine whichever of these two alternative home lives is best for this lovely child. Attorney Torper raised and argued important points, Your Honor, and to do justice to them, I need the evening to contemplate what he said, and to think through what a thoughtful response would be. I hope you will grant me that time, and that Attorney Torper will join me in asking you to do so."

Torper looked over at me with an unmistakable "you've trapped me here, you son of a bitch" look. The price I paid for Attorney Torper's reluctant assent was that it gave him one last opportunity to underscore the strongest point in his case—the part-time involvement of Dr. Dagnaud—which he took advantage of in a wordy and barbed assent to my motion. But I had no choice but to pay that price, and opposing counsel's assent gave the court little choice but to grant my request, as the judge laid the ground rules for the final day of trial:

"Very well, since you two seem to be in agreement, I'll allow what you ask for, Mr. Freiberg. Court is adjourned until precisely nine a.m. tomorrow morning, when counsel for the petitioner will have exactly one hour for his closing argument. That will conclude the trial. It is currently my plan to rule from the bench tomorrow, if I possibly can." Something in the judge's tone of voice, and in the seemingly ominous look he shot me, made me concerned that, currently, we were losing the case. His brief but telling look at me had subtitles, and it seemed to me that they read: "Be careful, Counselor. Even if there is enough Dr. Dagnaud to get you over the blood relative issue, that doesn't mean there is enough Dr. Dagnaud to be meaningfully present in this child's life while she is young and in need of family connections." Somehow, I had to find an argument that outweighed the distinct advantage Torper had with his full-time grandmother over my very part-time fathers. I had no idea what that argument might be, but at least I had the night to figure it out.

***

As I packed up my briefcase, I realized that, once again, as happened with every single damn trial in my career, the night before a closing argument would provide little or no sleep—as I worked at the last minute to try to piece together a cogent and moving closing argument. I had long since learned that the trick to an effective closing argument was exactly the opposite of what I had first thought as a beginner. I used to run through a list of all the evidence in my client's favor, and then pronounce to the jury—or the judge in a bench trial—that *therefore* my client should prevail. In total contrast, after a decade of watching experienced trial attorneys steal juries away from me, I finally learned that while it made sense to mention three or four of the strongest items of evidence in my client's favor, it was crucial to use the rest of the allotted time to paint a picture for the jury or the judge with an image or a metaphor. What you want, in other words, is to forge a connection with the fact finder so they don't feel like you are facing them and lecturing them. What you want is to get them to feel as if you're sitting side by side with them in the jury box, with everyone looking out at a film of the evidence. You're just reading the film's subtitles out loud.

The most salient evidence? That was obvious: it was the expert opinion of Dr. Newsom, coupled with the contrast of the two potential life spaces. But what parable to describe? What metaphor to make? What image to paint? I had no idea.

***

For some reason, I thought that spending an hour with Victoria that evening might lead to garnering an idea from the child's innocent, unfiltered perspective on all that was going on—some hint of an image I could use in my closing. Also, it would give me a chance to thank and say goodbye to Dr. Dagnaud, who was taking a cab to Logan Airport from Dr. Freeman's house.

I began by asking Victoria how she felt about what was going on in court. She thought for a few moments and then answered, "Safer. I miss my mommy. I mean, I hope I'll have two daddies to keep me safer. I don't want things to change; I don't want to go somewhere else with that woman and lose my friends." Safety. Continuity. Connection. I was getting an argument from her, but not an image.

Then, when Victoria changed the topic of discussion to the puppy and lost my attention completely, I began glancing around her room— plotting my escape. But in doing so, I spotted a small scientist's scale on one of her toy shelves. It looked like something Dr. Freeman or Sandrine Bergeron had used in some long-past laboratory class in medical school or nursing school—but, for me, it morphed into the scales of justice. *Of course!* That's what Dr. Dagnaud's appearance in the case changed—however little he would be available to Victoria in the early years. Unless the judge found Dr. Dagnaud's participation in raising Victoria so minimal that it didn't count, he should be free to apply the "best interests of the child" standard—and, fairly enough, he would put some weight on the grandmother's side of the balance to account for Dr. Dagnaud's long-distance, very part-time presence. The image I needed to fix in the judge's mind, I decided, was a picture of the scales of justice—because the image of his doing the balancing got him beyond the threshold question of whether Dr. Dagnaud's minimal presence "counted." Boston and Paris in one pan. Cresson, Texas, plus a full-time grandmother in the other pan. That should work. It didn't take me long to excuse myself from Miss Victoria and explain to Dr. Freeman that I was heading home to write my closing.

On my traffic-clogged drive home, I became more and more con- vinced of the usefulness of the scales-of-justice image, and of the wisdom of emphasizing Dr. Newsom's eloquent testimony about the psychological ramifications to Victoria if she were ripped out of her home and neighborhood—out of her network of connections. Dr. Newsom had testified that she could become emotionally adrift, like a boat that had broken the lines to its mooring. But what could I say that would convince Judge O'Connor that Dr. Newsom's warning was the key item of evidence that should decide the case? I had a fishing pole. I had a fishing line. But I had no hook.

I eventually came to a stop sign where traffic was horrifically backed up. Only one car at a time from our little street could squeeze out and turn right into the solid lines of traffic that choked the boulevard ahead. Understandably, the fellow in the car in front of me was becoming more and more agitated at not being able to pull out and make the turn, and then, just when he finally had an opening to do so, he found his car blocked by a very elderly lady who was slowly making her way across the crosswalk with a walker. In frustration, he honked— long and loud. The elderly woman was so startled by his boorishness that she came to a full stop, turning her head to stare disdainfully at him before looking away and continuing her way across the street. One part of my brain thought, *Rude son of a bitch*, but another part exploded with the image: there it was—*my hook!*

What I'd gleaned from the plight of the mobility-challenged elderly lady was that the way to bring this elderly judge *personally* into giving proper weight to the overriding importance of Dr. Newsom's warning was to remind him that people of his age often face the same issue. That is, elderly persons who still live at home can be vulnerable to being pressured by their children—or by the elder service authorities—to leave their house and their possessions and their neighborhood connections in favor of an institutional retirement setting. The challenge, I suddenly saw, would be to sneak in a few lines that would make the judge *feel* what that would feel like to Victoria.

All that remained to be done now was to somehow get through the damn intersection, get home, make a pot of coffee, and get down to work. Below you will find some of the more significant parts of my closing argument that I came up with that night. But what turned out to be the most amazing thing about the following morning was not my argument—it was the fact that Miss Victoria sat perfectly still and listened attentively throughout the entire proceeding. It seemed as if this diminutive six-year-old had come to fully understand that the quality of her life hung in the balance. But then again, it did.

***

"Today, Your Honor, you are faced with the awesome responsibility of deciding which of two very different lives Victoria shall live. And given that there is a blood relative on each side of this case petitioning for her legal and physical custody, you will find no guidance in the statute books, nor any helpful controlling precedent in past jurisprudence. This case, accordingly, cannot be decided on the law: it must be decided upon the evidence and upon the expert opinions that Your Honor has allowed to be placed in evidence. My argument today, Your Honor, shall therefore expressly *not* be concerned with my analysis of the underlying statutory and case law that frees Your Honor's hand to balance these two very different potential lives for Victoria. My legal analysis of the case law, Your Honor, is covered in the memorandum of law and fact that I am submitting to Your Honor this morning.

"When I say, Judge, that you must *balance* against each other the two very different lives Victoria would have in the two very different settings that have been described in testimony, I have a particular image of a balance in mind, Your Honor. I am picturing the scales of justice, where a blindfolded lady—representing the moral force and neutrality of the judicial system—holds in her left hand a balance, where the evidence on one side of a legal dispute is weighed against the evidence on the other side.

"The single goal of my argument today, Your Honor, is to convince you that when *you* hold up the scales of justice to weigh the matter before you, the scales will tip in favor of Doctors Dagnaud and Freeman, because the undisputed evidence is that Victoria currently enjoys a magnificently safe and happy life, save only for the tragic loss of her mother at such a tender age. And let's talk about that loss for a moment, because the evidence, Your Honor, shows that this lovely child has somehow weathered this momentous setback with remarkable composure and tons of charm. The very fact that she has been able to do so, Your Honor, the very fact that she has come through her loss so intact, so vibrant, so full of life, is in and of itself powerful evidence that Victoria feels safe and nurtured and loved in her current life. Dr. Newsom told us all this, Your Honor.

"What I would like to speak about now, Judge, is exactly *why* Victoria feels so safe and so nurtured and so loved in Dr. Freeman's household. Why do any of us feel safe and nurtured and loved in our lives? It's because of the *connections* we have to other people in our lives, and because of the *connections* we have to the spaces and places where we live. It's all about connections, Judge, it's all about connections. We humans are social animals, Your Honor, and isolated individuals who are not securely connected to others in their lives experience one of the most debilitating sensations to which human beings are subject: loneliness.

"In the memorandum of law and fact I am submitting today, Your Honor, I have included references to the most recent psychiatric and psychological research on the effects of chronic loneliness on the morbidity and mortality of children who are torn from their web of connections to their parents, to their friends, and to their life spaces. The statistics are appalling, Judge, and easily summarized in one sentence from Dr. Newsom's testimony: young children seldom thrive when they lose both their parents. Victoria—whom Your Honor met up close, very up close—has clearly thrived, and continues to do so, notwithstanding the sudden death of her mother. Again, I ask Your Honor: How has she been able to do so? The evidence on this single most important fact is uncontradicted, as Your Honor heard from half a dozen fact witnesses, three expert witnesses, and most especially from Dr. Newsom, one of the most prominent pediatricians in the country. He testified that, based on Victoria's record, and also based on his examination of her in the Freeman household, he found her to be, and I quote, 'an entirely intact, psychologically healthy, happy, thriving child.' He strongly recommended to this honorable court that the child, and again, I quote from the trial transcript, 'remain in the Freeman household, where she both feels—and is observably—safe, nurtured, and loved.'

"I also want to review the importance to Your Honor's upcoming deliberations of the testimony of the child's biological father, Dr. Henri Dagnaud. When opposing counsel argued that it was I, as counsel to Dr. Freeman, who proposed reaching out to Dr. Dagnaud, that was entirely correct. The evidence is clear, and the petitioners have never denied, that Dr. Dagnaud not only had no relationship with Victoria prior to this litigation but that he didn't even know of her existence. But what you need to put on the scale, Your Honor, is what Dr. Dagnaud's *future involvement* in his daughter's life will be like. Dr. Dagnaud took off nearly two weeks from his professional and personal life in Paris to come live in the Freeman household with Dr. Freeman and Victoria. I spent a good deal of that time there with them, Judge, and what I saw was remarkable. Your Honor, while most love stories are written about a man and a woman falling in love, there are many other kinds of love in the world, beginning with the love a parent has for a child. I saw this type of love story blossom during those two weeks, as Dr. Dagnaud fell in parental love with the little girl he had sired but never known. Less than two weeks is certainly not a long span of time, Your Honor, but it is far longer than the respondent in this matter has ever spent with the child. And it was, in my observation, a long enough period of time for a very loving bond to be forged—a bond between father and daughter, and also a parenting-partnership bond between Dr. Dagnaud and Dr. Freeman.

"Your Honor, you are tasked with balancing which of two very different lives would be better for Victoria. So let's take a look at what is in evidence about what each of these two lives would be like, above and beyond the benefits of continuity and connection over disruption and disconnection.

"Victoria's grandmother—in good faith and with good intentions that are not in question—asks to raise the child in Cresson, Texas, a tiny little town of four hundred and fifty people eight miles from the local small town of Aledo, which has a population of about fifteen hundred people. While one of Cresson's residents testified that everyone in Cresson would welcome Victoria with everything they have to offer, one has to ask, what exactly is it that they have to offer? Not much, I would submit, at least when compared with Boston and Paris. Boston draws about nineteen million tourists a year, and Paris draws about twenty-three million. Why? Because these cities have a lot to offer. While lovely lives can be lived in small towns, there are undeniable advantages to the great cities of the world. The evidence submitted in this case indicates that Victoria's life in Boston is replete with dance and music lessons, and that she is a young fan of the Boston Ballet. The Freeman family are members of the Boston Children's Museum and the Boston Museum of Science, both of which Victoria often visits, to her delight. Dr. Freeman owns a house in Brookline near his work at Beth Israel Deaconess Medical Center, a Harvard teaching hospital. Brookline's public school system is one of the best in the country: it sends the vast majority of its graduates to America's finest colleges. There was testimony to this effect, while there was no testimony as to the quality of the educational system in Cresson. Victoria's pediatrician and pediatric dentist—both of whom testified in this case— are each on the Harvard Medical School faculty, in contrast to the no doubt competent but presumably less stellar caregivers she would encounter in a small Texas town.

"And then there is Paris, ready and waiting to welcome Victoria when she is a bit older and stronger. This child speaks native French, as Your Honor heard in court. Now, with Your Honor's assent, she will have a French father, a French stepmother, a French half sister, French grandparents, and an extended French family. And when the two doctors determine it to be age appropriate, some of Victoria's education can take place in Paris. Your Honor, for over a thousand years, young people have gone to Paris to study at its world-class universities, located among its urban splendors. All of this will be available to Victoria as she grows and expands her horizons.

"And so, in closing, Your Honor, I want to argue that the evidence in this case indicates that while the child's grandmother offers to raise Victoria, there is a far better offer on the table. The scales of justice Your Honor holds are a balance, and you are charged with determining which side outweighs the other. Dr. Freeman and the child's biological father, Dr. Dagnaud, offer Victoria a safer and far more vibrant life. Her life would be safer, Your Honor, because the entirety of Victoria's current *network of connections* would remain intact. In contrast, every single connection in her life would be torn asunder and ripped apart if you were to send her to live with a grandmother she does not know, in a house she's never seen, to play with other children and people she's never met, in a small town that would seem a desert to her after all the cultural richness she has been accustomed to in Boston.

"Your Honor, a metaphor, if I might. What Victoria would face if involuntarily removed from her home, from her life, is not unique to her stage of life. Many of us have known elderly persons, particularly aged widows and widowers, who have been forced out of their personal homes and placed in retirement homes by circumstances not of their own choosing. All their memories, all their associations, all their neighbors, all their photographs, all their worn but familiar furniture—*all those connections*—are left behind for a sterile room that is identical to the other rooms up and down the hall. The effect this has on advancing dementia, and diminishing will to live, is hardly a surprise.

"I urge you, Judge, to issue an order that joint legal and physical custody of Victoria be granted to her biological father, Dr. Henri Dagnaud, and to the man who has lovingly raised her since the day she was born, Dr. Jonathan Freeman. If Your Honor has the slightest doubts of any kind about whether Dr. Freeman will remain the totally committed father he has been up to this point in Victoria's life, or if Your Honor has the slightest doubts about whether Dr. Dagnaud will make good on the promise he made to this court that he intends to devote the time it takes to become ever more engaged in his daughter's life, then my suggestion is that this court should, in its judgment and order, appoint a guardian ad litem. The order should instruct the guardian ad litem to return to this court for further proceedings if at any time he or she finds the performance by either Dr. Dagnaud or Dr. Freeman to be wanting with respect to any of the material representations they have each made to this court in these proceedings. Thank you, Judge; I have nothing further."

***

Silence flooded the room after I finished my closing and took my seat at the petitioner's table. The judge remained entirely still, and the courtroom was, correspondingly, utterly silent. Two or three minutes passed before the judge's serene inactivity came to a sudden halt, at which time he began to furiously write on a yellow pad of paper. On and on he wrote, never looking up at the courtroom, never saying a word. Complete silence continued to reign. Finally, the judge stopped writing and set about reorganizing the scattered pages he had ripped off the pad one by one and tossed about his bench. When he finally had them gathered up and put in order, he cleared his throat, scanned the courtroom from one side to another with an intense stare, and then referenced his findings and read his judgment:

> My written Findings will come to counsel by mail in
> the following weeks. I am, in contrast, going to issue

from the bench my Judgment and Order, after weighing all of the testimony, documents, and expert opinion allowed in evidence over a full week of trial.

JUDGMENT AND ORDER OF THE COURT:

1. Joint legal and physical custody of the minor child, Victoria Bergeron, is hereby granted to Dr. Henri Dagnaud and Dr. Jonathan Freeman.

2. Dr. Jonathan Freeman shall be solely responsible for all costs of raising and educating the minor, Victoria Bergeron, expressly including reasonable sums to enable cost-free, regular visitation by Dr. Dagnaud and his family from France. Any contribution by Dr. Dagnaud to the costs of raising the child shall be voluntary and made at his sole discretion.

3. Until such time as the minor, Victoria Bergeron, reaches the age of majority, there shall at all times be a guardian ad litem to review the status and adequacy of the co-parenting of Dr. Dagnaud and Dr. Freeman, and said guardian ad litem shall, if at any time he or she finds said parenting wanting in any aspect and is unable to resolve such issue with the joint custodians, bring such further proceedings before this court as are necessary to achieve a resolution. The costs and fees of said guardian ad litem shall be paid for in their entirety by Dr. Jonathan Freeman.

4. The guardian ad litem shall ensure that during the minority of said Victoria Bergeron, that her maternal grandmother, Louise Gully, shall have full and unfettered visitation rights, such visitation not to

unreasonably interfere with the minor's educational and recreational activities.

SO ORDERED AND DECREED THIS DAY

William O'Connor, J.

***

And so, Victoria's story comes to an end—at least the part of the story
that has to do with how tenuous and how at risk were her connections
to her stepfather, his family, and her friends following the death of her
mother. Victoria could have lost everybody and everything she loved
and knew, as well as all of her connections to the places of her life, had
Dr. Dagnaud and Sophie Bernard not come to her rescue with such
open and generous hearts, or if we had run into a judge with less vision
and daring. Or if Dr. Freeman had not been one hell of a good jazz
pianist!

What has not come to an end is my relationship with Victoria,
given that I undertook several routine legal projects for Dr. Freeman
in the years that followed the trial. So, I can report to you that today
Victoria is a vibrant young married woman living near Aix-en-
Provence, France—with a beautiful child of her own. What the petitioners argued to the court came true: Victoria ended up thriving
from the complex blended family that even included, after a two-year
hiatus, establishment of a relatively normal, if long-distance, relationship with her maternal grandmother. After finishing elementary and
middle school in Brookline, Massachusetts, Victoria was admitted to
Lycée Louis-le-Grand in Paris—one of France's top high schools. From
there, she went on to an equally prestigious university, École normale
supérieure, from which she graduated with distinction. Today, Victoria
works as a high school teacher specializing in comparative literature,
and on the side, she translates texts between English and French with
remarkable aplomb, specializing in the quasi-impossible task of translating poetry.

Victoria and I have remained in touch after she married one of her
university classmates and moved definitively to France. And, just a few

years back, she was kind enough to work her magic on the translation of a little story of mine, "The Loneliest Boy," into its French version, "Un Garçon si Seul." When she was partway through this task, and pregnant with her child, by chance, we discovered that we were both to be in Paris at the same time. We took the opportunity to meet in a café across the street from the Gare Saint-Lazare train station to touch base, and especially to discuss how best to translate several terms that I had used in my story. It was a delight to see her—and her still-remarkable jade-green eyes—once again, and to learn how wonderfully well her life was going. Just before she headed into the station to board her train back to Provence, she shook my hand, looked me straight in the eyes, and told me that she and her husband had declined the doctor's offer to learn their child's gender, but that, "If it's a boy, we're going to call him Thierry, after you."

I'll treasure that gesture until the end of my days.

THREE SOULS CAUGHT IN A SPIDER'S WEB

"Terry, how the fuck are you?" Before I could even identify the voice on the phone, it took up again. "Look, man, we need your help. I mean that. I know I said I wouldn't be calling so soon, but we've got the weirdest goddamn Supreme Court disbarment case. We are absolutely at loggerheads in my office about what's going on with this guy, and you're our psych lawyer, baby, so you're getting the call. Please hear me out. This guy's going to get disbarred and then sued up the ying-yang—and we're not at all convinced that's the right outcome. Worse still, there are others involved who have really been hurt. We need your help, man ... *he* needs your help ... *his victims* need your help." A pregnant pause followed, which I waited out, silently. "Oh yeah, and I probably should mention that this guy doesn't have a dime to pay you with."

By this time, I knew it was Mike Jepson on the line. Mike is an attorney and a friend; I'd known him for years, since we were on opposite sides of a trial case. He had long since given up the practice of trial law to become chief counsel to the Board of Bar Overseers. The board regulates attorney activities, promulgates ethical practice rules, and investigates complaints against attorneys that allege unethical conduct. It contains a semiautonomous prosecutorial wing called the Office of the Bar Counsel that prosecutes attorney misconduct cases before the Supreme Judicial Court of Massachusetts—the oldest court in the entire United States.

"How weird are you talking, Mike?" I responded in jest. "Is this a 'nine'? I had an 'eight' come into the office just last month, so that slot's taken, and I have an ongoing 'ten.'"

Jepson sidestepped my flippant response. "Seriously, Terry, hear me out on this." He paused for emphasis. "None of us here on the board can figure out what the hell is going on with this attorney, and his entire career is threatened. The Bar Counsel side of our office is hot to disbar him for life—they're going after him as hard as they can. They absolutely won't listen to our investigative wing—they've gone rogue in my view. We had a really hot argument with them a week ago to give us more time, but I just learned twenty minutes ago that they filed a complaint today with the Supreme Judicial Court praying for an order of permanent disbarment. The complaint claims that he sold out his clients' best interests in order to make more money, but my side of the office doesn't think that fits what we're looking at. I already told you he qualifies for pro bono counsel, so how could it be about money. We feel certain something else is involved—but we have no fucking idea what that could be. Like I said, we've had big arguments with the prosecutorial staff asking for more time to continue our investigation, but they've totally disregarded us and gone ahead and filed. There've been some very heated arguments up here about this case . . . very heated . . . Bill Watson called me a 'dumb motherfucker' last week. You know him?"

"No. But the dumb part can't be true—you were *Harvard Law Review*."

"Okay. That's pretty funny actually. But listen up. It all started when the board received three completely independent, almost identical accusations—*within a month.*"

"Saying what?"

"Saying that his guy, Herbert Britton, cajoled each of these criminal defendant clients into rejecting normal and reasonable plea bargain offers in favor of asserting their right to a full jury trial. Bar Counsel's argument is that Britton's conduct constituted an ethical violation because by single-handedly rejecting the entire plea bargain system of the criminal justice system—without regard to the merits of any particular case—he unreasonably and unprofessionally exposed his clients to conviction on multiple felony counts. And sure enough, each of his clients was slammed on nearly every count they faced—with just one or two exceptions. So, for example, all three of his clients whose cases are cited in the complaint are serving long, hard stretches in maximum security, and they each blame him for the length of their sentence."

"Humph. What's this guy's practice like?"

"He's a simple guy, from a simple law school, with a simple law practice. He does public-defender-type criminal defense work; I think his entire practice is court-appointed representation of defendants who can't afford private counsel. He's one of those attorneys who hang around the district courts waiting for a judge to assign them a case."

I made one more feeble effort at staying uninvolved. "Mike, I'm completely out of date on criminal procedure; I haven't done any criminal work in years."

"I thought about that, of course, but I don't think it's important. I think the psych element in the case far outweighs the criminal procedure element. And you have law partners who do plenty of criminal work—hell, Christina Lorenz is still at your firm, isn't she? She's a superstar criminal defense attorney; bring her into the case if you need to. Terry, we need someone who cares about making justice happen here—for all four of these people, if possible—whatever the fuck that might turn out to mean. You figure it out; you've done it for us before."

"Keep talking, Mike; there's something else. What haven't you told me yet?" This led to a round of his deep-throated chuckles—his laugh wasn't like anybody else's.

"All right, all right. Look, one thing we do know about you is that you snake around better than anybody. Or maybe I should say that private detective of yours does. So, what we were thinking is that if you could bring your investigator into this case, we might *all* learn what's going on, and maybe, just maybe, justice can prevail. Terry, we have three people rotting away in prison who have decades to serve—and that should never have happened. And we have a public defender criminal defense attorney running around loose who might be doing more harm than good to his clients. That's a problem." We were both silent when he finished, but my reluctance was apparently palpable. "Come on, we need you to jump on this case. And here's a sweetener: if you accept this case, I won't call you again for a full year—I promise."

"Two years. And this time you have to mean it."

"Eighteen months."

"Done."

**

Of course, I didn't know it at the time, but Mike was introducing me to a case that would teach me more than I ever wanted to learn about how intensely injurious "one-way" relationships can be. Before this case, the only one-way relationships I'd ever known—personally or profession-ally—had been those that had begun with a shared understanding of what the affiliation was supposed to be all about. So far as I knew, it was only later that, all too often, one person remained deeply commit-ted and involved, while the other had long since jumped ship and emo-tionally disconnected. But, as I was to learn, this quotidian path to a one-way relationship is not the only path—some relationships are one-way from the get-go. Who knew that sometimes the two entrants into a new relationship *never* shared a common conception of what their newfound connection was supposed to accomplish—even though they both joined in good faith? I sure didn't.

**

And so I ended up representing Herbert Britton. And although Mike must have felt a little ill at ease asking me to use an expensive private eye in a pro bono case, I was actually thrilled to have a case that would provide me an opportunity to work once again with Reginald Brooke—the master private detective he had referenced. Brooke was practically a generation older than I was, and there simply weren't going to be that many more opportunities.

But let me take a moment, my reader, to more formally introduce you to Brooke—or "Longfellow," as he was always called, due to his lean, six-foot-four frame—as you will meet up with him again in other cases later in this collection. He was British by birth and had been educated at Eton and Cambridge before the war. His soaring command of the English language, coupled with his very proper accent and his quirky sense of humor, made him a pleasure to listen to. And Longfellow was equally engaging to look at: he had the chiseled features of marble statuary, which were decidedly exaggerated by his wildly generous pure-white eyebrows—they lifted halfway up his forehead when he was about to say something either shrewd or sardonic. To my mind, Longfellow was the finest private eye in Boston—an opinion I found convincingly confirmed by the fact that the entirety of his agency's time was booked out on a yearly retainer basis by just six law practices, as it had been for over thirty years. One of those practices had belonged to my now-retired senior partner and mentor, so I had, in effect, inherited Longfellow.

Longfellow had served with the British intelligence services during World War II, and while he consistently declined to discuss anything about this period of his life, I knew from my mentor—himself a naval aviator—that Longfellow's contributions during the war had been quite significant: at the conclusion of hostilities, he had been awarded the Order of Merit by King George VI. The war also changed Longfellow's personal life: while taking shelter from a V-2 attack in a London tube, he had met—and later married—a young American Red Cross nurse. The couple moved to Boston after the war, where Longfellow soon opened his private detective firm, which he called "Solutions and Outcomes, Ltd."

Longfellow offered far more than typical private eye services. Most private detectives are limited to shadowing a subject, casing out a venue, perusing court records, and subsequently presenting written and photographic reports—and court testimony, if necessary—of what they had learned. Longfellow provided me with much more, just as my mentor had promised. He was, to put it succinctly, a master strategist—a skill that I always assumed he had honed in the British secret services. Besides his strategic genius, he also brought—and infused in others—a remarkable sense of calm in case management, especially in moments when setbacks were experienced. In part because Longfellow had worked for so many years for my senior partner, and in part because of our large age difference, the master spy took on the role of guiding me through the subtleties and complexities of developing effective case-specific strategies. And that was just fine with me: I had enormous respect for the man and was honored recently when his wife asked me to speak at his memorial service. I should mention that were he still living, I wouldn't have breathed a hint of his existence into these pages.

***

Later in the morning that Jepson and I spoke, a messenger from the Office of the Bar Counsel arrived at my door, visibly straining under a full copy of the Britton case file that entirely filled a Xerox box. I stepped out, bought a sandwich, and brought it back to my office, where I dove into the record. It was over three hours before I surfaced.

The disciplinary complaint to be heard by the Massachusetts Supreme Judicial Court indeed sought disbarment for life of Attorney Britton—as Jepson had forewarned. The complaint named three criminal defendants whose cases Britton had allegedly prejudiced: Linda Sikes, Peter Sanders, and William McDermott. Sikes was doing hard time for shooting and seriously wounding someone; Sanders had broken into a house and brutally beaten its elderly residents; and McDermott had been found guilty of the statutory rape of a fifteen-year-old girl. In all three cases, Britton had been appointed as a public defender to represent these hapless individuals, none of whom had had the financial capacity to retain private counsel.

But there was one aspect of the complaint that Jepson had not mentioned and that immediately caught my eye: Bar Counsel expressly *stipulated* that Britton had worked long, hard, and diligently on each of the three cases. I was familiar enough with Massachusetts criminal law practice to know that this work ethic was monumentally atypical for court-appointed counsel. These low-on-the-food-chain attorneys earn a meager hourly rate, which is paid by the Commonwealth. The hourly rate is about one-tenth of what would be charged by a private criminal defense attorney. And then, adding insult to injury, their modest paycheck on a given case notoriously arrives the better part of a *full year* after their legal services were rendered.

When I looked further into the details of Bar Counsel's stipulation, my puzzlement grew exponentially. The complaint expressly granted that Britton met all his case deadlines, thoroughly prepared his witnesses, performed accurate and extensive legal research, wrote cogent and well-argued legal briefs, and litigated well-conceived jury trials. The one and only point at issue in the case was the allegation that Britton had unreasonably pressured his clients to reject any and all plea bargains that had been offered—without any regard or concern for how this might affect any given case. What was curious to me, however, was that absent some element of bad faith, Britton had every right to advise his clients as to the pros and cons of accepting the terms of a particular plea bargain they'd been offered and, with their informed assent, to reject the proposed deal and proceed to the trial of their cases. That is a constitutional right, no less. So, I was totally baffled.

The author of the complaint, which I read over and over again, seemed equally puzzled, because he or she felt constrained to conjure up a hypothesis as to *why* Britton's advice to his clients to exercise their constitutional right to a jury trial should be construed as an ethical violation. The proffered argument was the obvious one: that Britton earned more money this way, since a great many more billable hours are generated by taking a case through trial than by settling it. But what really caught my eye was the conspicuous absence of facts in the complaint to support such a supposition—none whatsoever, as far as I could tell. Where was the expensive sports car or the lavish lifestyle? Or the offshore banking account? And if Britton made so much money, why did he qualify for pro bono counsel? It just didn't add up.

***

I nearly always met with a new client before beginning investigation on his case, but in Herbert Britton's matter, I found myself tempted to speak first to his ex-clients who were named in the complaint. My thought was that this might prevent me from becoming entrapped in whatever rationalization Britton would espouse for his aberrant manner of practicing criminal law. And besides, I had an appointment at a law firm in Framingham—a city on the western outskirts of Boston that happened to be the location of the women's maximum-security

facility where Linda Sikes was imprisoned. Ms. Sikes had been in residence there for just over eighteen months, and she was scheduled to
remain there for more than another decade.

So, without yet having even spoken to my client, I found myself
going through multiple identity checks, an almost embarrassingly
thorough frisking, and the half-dozen locked steel doors that divided
Framingham women's prison from the outside world. This facility is
the oldest women's prison in the United States, opened in 1877. And
when you entered it, you felt very much like you were stepping back in
time.

As I reencountered the ice-cold, hardened steel and cement envi-
ronment, my initial introduction to the facility came rushing back
to me. I had come to the prison with my criminal law class decades
earlier, and the shock of seeing hundreds of women, each as hard as
stone—along with the odor of so many prisoners sharing such a modest amount of space—turned out to have never faded from my somatic
memory. About six hundred and fifty women are held in the prison
at any time—roughly 125 percent of its official capacity. Needless to
say, any prison stands in stark contrast to everyday life in the outside
world—but a women's maximum-security facility somehow seems just
that much colder, just that much harder.

The prisoners I walked past on my way to meet Linda Sikes were
of all ages, all races, all sizes and shapes. However, because the women
could wear their hair as they pleased, they looked almost like any other
collection of women one might see—save for their dull-gray prison
uniforms, which no woman on the planet would have elected to wear
by choice. These prisoners were doing hard time; there are lower-
security facilities elsewhere in Massachusetts for shorter sentences and
lesser crimes. The fact that the complaint had mentioned that Britton
had come here unusually often to meet with his client said much about
something, assuming that my suspicion was correct that it wasn't about
running up his bill. I just had no idea what that something could be.

**

The officer who saw to visiting attorneys led me into the barest room
imaginable: there were four light-green walls, one antique ceiling lamp

that I immediately began to covet, two chairs, and one small, very old, scratched-up wooden writing table. Period. Sikes—in handcuffs—was led in two or three minutes later. She proved to be an extremely attractive thirty-nine-year-old woman with striking blue eyes. Her light-brown hair, drawn back in a long ponytail, reflected softness—even in the room's dullish light. Once the cuffs were removed and the noticeably polite guard had withdrawn from the room, Sikes greeted me coldly in a classic South Boston accent as she took a seat in the chair across from me. Above and beyond being so pretty, Sikes clearly had a perceptive eye because she sized up my discomfort without a moment's hesitation: "You don't practice criminal law, do you?"

I was taken aback—if impressed. "No, I don't," I admitted. "Not my thing—to be honest. Nothing personal. It's that obvious?"

"Oh yeah. It definitely is." No smile followed. Then Sikes immediately shifted gears. "Let's get down to business, Attorney; they've only given us ninety minutes. You're defending Herbert Britton, am I correct?"

"Precisely," I replied. "And I'd like to record our conversation—my leaky memory requires it. Okay by you?"

"I don't care. Record away. Now, you do know that I wrote a letter to the Board of Bar Overseers explaining how Britton mishandled my case. Correct?"

"Yes. I've read it."

"And if I have it right, other letters were written by several other former clients of his, correct?"

"Exactly. Your case, and two others, make up the core of the complaint filed against Attorney Britton."

"All right. And it was these three complaint letters that led the board to send one of its investigators out here to talk to me—and, I would presume, to the other two victims. I assume that the outcome of that investigation process was what led the board to file the complaint against Attorney Britton. Do I have all this correct?"

"Yes. Precisely."

"So, why in the hell would you think I'd say or do *anything* that might help Attorney Britton? He screwed up my life. So, my story, or my testimony, or whatever it is, will *support* the board's effort, not your defense of Britton. By the way, I imagine you won't be surprised to hear that I have a new court-appointed attorney who is filing a motion to vacate my conviction—on the basis of ineffective counsel."

"I'm not at all surprised."

"And he is also looking into a possible malpractice action against Britton."

"Again, no surprise there," I responded.

She crossed her arms over her chest and cocked her head defiantly to the right. "So what's up?"

"Ms. Sikes, I'm not at all asking you to help Attorney Britton. Of course, that would be idiotic on my part—you're correct. But the overall situation in this case is . . . complicated—complicated enough that it just might be true that what is best for your case is to help me figure out what really makes this guy tick. Will you at least give me a chance to try to explain myself?"

"Hey, baby, it's either listen to your bullshit or go rot in my cell. I'm easy."

I laughed and felt myself relax. The reward was one brief, very lovely smile.

"Okay, here goes. And let me start by saying, first, I personally have nothing to gain here: I'm volunteering my time to defend Britton on a pro bono basis. I'm not being paid a dime. Second, I haven't even spoken with Attorney Britton yet—so I have no preset assumption about how I'll find him. Something made me want to start learning about this case by starting with you—I'm not at all sure why, really. Anyway, what I want to know—what *I need to know*—is who you really are, what Britton's handling of your case was really like, and whether you think Britton pressured you to forgo your chance to cop a plea."

For some reason, what I said caused Sikes to stand up, spin her chair around, and sit on it backward, resting her arms on its back. "Well, hot damn. The lawyer man can talk. You're doing good so far; let's see if you can keep it up."

Ignoring her sardonic tone, I did indeed keep going. "Look, before I even meet the man, I assume he's going to say he deserves an award, not discipline, for his heroic battle against the evils of the plea bargain regime of modern-day criminal law. He's going to tell me about how defendants plead to a lesser charge—even when they're wholly innocent. He's going to say defendants are forced to cop a plea because it's just too big a gamble to go to trial, especially if you're black or Latino. I can hear it all coming."

"And you don't buy that?" Sikes interjected.

"Not at this point. I don't know what to believe. But what I want to hear is *your* story—*your* experience with Britton. And the other two ex-clients' stories as well. It's the three of you who can help me understand what the hell is going on in this guy's head."

"Why do I care if you understand what's going on?" Sikes shot back just before something emotional boiled up inside her, cracking through her tough shell. A sheen of tears suddenly covered her eyes. "Look, Attorney, you seem like a nice enough guy, but I'm sorry—I need to do what's best for *my* case, not Britton's. I'm *dying* in here. Every day, I age a week. Can you even hear me on that? I need to get a new trial with a new plea bargain to save as much as possible of what's left of my life. *I can't take this for another decade; I just can't.*" Again, she paused, and this time, a single tear went trickling down the left side of her face and then splashed almost audibly on the ancient table. We both fell silent as she took a minute to collect herself.

There seemed to be an opening here to get through to her—quite possibly the only one I would have. "Ms. Sikes, my goal here is to find a way to help everybody involved; there is no reason why the three of you who wrote those letters should not get relief if Attorney Britton advised his clients to take sure-loser counts through to trial without good reason. But I need to learn the details of precisely what took place to have a chance at pulling this off. Does this make any sense to you?"

She stared at me, sizing me up before replying. "Actually, no. My attorney says that if Britton is disbarred, it would *increase* the odds that my motion for a new trial would be allowed. So if you're defending Britton, I don't have a clue how you can help me—I would think whatever you come up with would work against me."

"Please give me a chance to explain, Ms. Sikes, please," I interjected. "I think I see a way I can help you—without in any way prejudicing my client's case. Please hear me out." Sikes took her arms off the back of the chair and crossed them defiantly over her chest; whatever portals had briefly opened on her emotions had once again slammed shut. "Ms. Sikes, I get called into cases—including this case—because I have double training; I was a social-psychology professor before I even went to law school. Something is up with Britton on a psychological level, Ms. Sikes—but I don't have a clue as to what that might be. Look, if Britton has some psychological issue that overrides his professional judgment, it won't be hard for your new attorney to convince your trial judge to grant your motion for a new trial. Do you hear that? Your ineffective counsel argument will prevail—easily. But I need you to help me *learn* what's going on in the man's head. What was he like? Was he delusional-sounding on his anti-plea-bargain stance? Did he give you a reasoned argument about why he rejects the plea bargaining system of criminal justice? Did it sound like an ongoing crusade with him—you know, above and beyond your individual case? Ms. Sikes, help me here. Help me help you. What makes this man practice criminal law the way he does?"

Sikes remained completely frozen with her arms still crossed in front of her. I could sense that she felt increasingly doubtful that I was in any way interested in helping her. Then she let me have it. "Attorney, cut the bullshit. You need to tell me right now, in unambiguous terms, what you could *possibly* do to help me. Otherwise, this interview ends."

"Okay. Okay. Here's my proposition. Tell me what you know. Help me learn what makes this man tick. And concretely, in exchange, here's how I can help you—or at least how I can try." Her frown turned to a look of cautious curiosity with nothing more than the slightest raising of her left eyebrow. "If what I learn is that the reason Britton discouraged his clients from accepting advantageous plea bargains is a function of some psychological pathology, then I'll do everything I can to convince him to let me settle his case with Bar Counsel without making the 'constitutional right to a jury trial' argument . . . and . . ." I stopped in midsentence, well aware of how obtuse my effort was. "Wow, that's totally not clear. Let me figure out how to say this in different terms." I looked away and took a few moments, trying to find a way to express what was just developing in my mind. "Okay. Let me say it this way. Ms. Sikes, if I can argue to the Supreme Court that Britton's campaign against plea bargaining was a function of some psychological pathology, then I can easily ask the Supreme Court justice who hears the case to get involved and be *actively helpful* in all three of your cases. In other words, if Britton biased your case to fulfill his own psychological needs, then I will formally request that the Supreme Court justice call your three trial judges and recommend that each of you be allowed new trials based on Britton having been an ineffective counsel. And you know what: in this scenario, I can almost promise you that the Office of the Bar Counsel will join with me in asking the Supreme Court justice to make these phone calls. Obviously, if you three defendants get new trials, you will encounter new offers of plea bargains. Then each of you and your new attorneys can do whatever is best for you in your individual case. Am I making any sense here at all?"

Sikes paused to think this through, staring deeply into my eyes in what clearly was an effort to ascertain if I could be trusted—or not. After a set of facial contortions that I misread as her being about to cut off our conversation, she asked just the right question. "What if you *don't* find anything about the man's psychology that would work for that strategy? What if you feel compelled—or what if you *are* compelled by your client—to make the constitutional hero against plea bargaining argument? Could you still talk to the Supreme Court justice about calling my trial judge—I mean, in that scenario?"

I was ever more impressed with Linda Sikes. "Look, Ms. Sikes, I trust you can see the problem I would have if, for some reason, I have no choice but to use the constitutional hero argument. If the only argument I have is that Britton did nothing wrong in representing the three of you, it would seriously undercut my position if I added at the end, 'But even so, Your Honor, even though Ms. Sikes and the other two defendants were advised by Attorney Britton that they had the right to accept or reject the plea bargains they were offered, and then they chose to go forward to trial, and lost their cases. Could you please help them out anyway?' Do you see that: either he did something wrong in handling the three cases—or he didn't. I can't argue it both ways."

"I get that," Sikes replied after a moment, taking her arms from around herself and entering back into full conversation. "But isn't there some way you could still help if the case takes off in that direction?"

"That's a fair question. Look, by all odds, I'll find myself working with Bar Counsel for a solution—like a settlement of Britton's disbarment proceedings. That often happens, just as in any litigation matter. In that setting, I can say anything—including, 'How can we help out the three clients who are referenced in your complaint?' In that scenario, Britton would have nothing to lose by my asking Bar Counsel to join me in being helpful to the three of you—whatever the disposition of Britton's disbarment negotiations. So here's what I can tell you today, Ms. Sikes. I can give you my word of honor that I will include your interests in any dealings I have with Bar Counsel, *with one caveat.* And that one caveat is that I can't do or say anything that would prejudice my client's interests—you know that. Other than that, you'll have a new ally in me—if you'll accept that one caveat. Now, can we get down to work before we run out of time?"

Linda Sikes sat absolutely still and remained perfectly silent for almost a minute. Then she broke. "Fine. I'll accept your word. But I have a condition as well. My story of how Britton kept tempting me not to settle for the simple assault-and-battery plea bargain that was offered is set forth in the new court papers that my attorney is working on. I've seen a draft. I'm not going to say anything to you that contradicts the papers that will be filed."

"Absolutely. I would say *precisely* the same thing in your place. Now, can we give this a go before the guard returns?"

There was one last, long look before Sikes plunged into our newly formed joint venture. "Okay, then. Let's start at the beginning. You need to know me—my background—to understand what I did and why I did it. That's all relevant for why and how a competent attorney would have negotiated a plea bargain for me."

"Let me stop you for one second," I interrupted, coming to my senses on one critically important point. "I need to tell you that, since I'm not your attorney, there is no formal attorney-client privilege safeguarding the confidentiality of what you say to me. That being said, again I will give you my personal word: I will treat what you disclose to me exactly as if there were a privilege. So, if I think anything you say would be useful in Britton's disciplinary hearing, I will check back with you or your counsel for your consent prior to disclosing it. No exceptions. Is that fair?"

"That's a deal. We understand each other." She cleared her throat, gracefully stood and flipped her chair around to face me, then sat back down and launched into her story. "Attorney, as you can see, I'm a pretty woman—I always have been. You'd think that would be a plus in life, like being born smart or rich. But it has led to more trouble than joy, I can assure you. Pretty women are just that much more of a target. So, like a lot of women—maybe most—I'm a survivor of a lifetime of sexual harassment and multiple physical assaults. Southie—where I grew up—is a tough part of town, as I'm sure you know. My high school had more than its fair share of punks, so my teenage years in the crowded hallways were a fog of sexualized remarks, 'accidental' tit brushings, and straight-out ass-grabbings. Then I was raped. The first time was in high school—by a huge kid on the football team. After he finished, he threatened me: he knew I have a much younger sister, and he said that he would leave her alone—*unless* I told someone what he'd done."

Sikes's breathing had become shallow and audible. She paused for a few moments, sighed from somewhere deep, deep within herself, and then continued. "There was another time, the year after I graduated high school. I was a 'barista' at a Warbricks coffee shop. Early one day when the assistant manager and I were the only ones there, we were changing into our uniforms in the employee room prepping to open the store, and he came up from behind and raped me. I needed that job because I was saving up to move out of home . . . I . . ." At this point, Sikes's crying completely overcame her speaking, and she just allowed her tears to stream unimpeded down her cheeks.

"Did you do anything about that assault—did you tell anyone?"

"Oh yes. But it took me about seven months to tell my parents—I just didn't know how to tell my father that I wasn't a virgin. He called a lawyer, and the lawyer called Warbricks. But it turned out that Massachusetts had a six-month statute of limitations on sexual harassment, and Warbricks took an ice-cold hard line because I was just beyond that time limit. They didn't have an ounce of pity for me—even after my attorney learned that the employee had been moved from another branch for similar behavior. The Warbricks attorney told my attorney that since the deadline for a sexual harassment complaint was passed, my claim against Warbricks was worth very little money. It was a just a worker's compensation issue—which only allowed me very minimal compensation. I hate that fucking company. How could they have *not cared at all* about a teenage employee who was taken advantage of by her supervisor? How could they have treated me so heartlessly?"

More tears followed, and as neither of us had any tissues, we shared a smile at Sikes's not-so-successful efforts to use the back of her hands and forearms to wipe her eyes and cheeks. She took four or five deep breaths and exhaled slowly to soothe herself. Then she started right up again. "Then, more recently, there was my asshole ex-boyfriend, who was always pressuring me for sex, completely disinterested in what I was feeling. He even refused to move out of my apartment when I finally asked him to; I had to go to court to get a judge to order him out. I was *so* afraid that he'd seek revenge that I told all this to an older friend at work—I was a waitress by then. You know what she said?" Sikes asked touchingly, even softly.

"What?"

"She said her husband had gotten Alzheimer's, and she'd hidden away a gun he owned. She wanted it out of their house, and said that she'd be glad to give it to me—so long as I promised never to give it back or tell anyone where I got it from. So the next day, she brought it to work, and I took it from her."

"Uh-oh."

"Uh-oh is right. It was just a matter of time, I suppose. I mean, I don't think I would have been crazy about it—women don't have a lot of choice but to learn to dismiss and ignore the small crap: the stares at your breasts in elevators, the 'accidental' brush-ups, the catcalls on the street. But, bit by bit, I was becoming more combative about all this, and then something snapped. I started *doing* something about it. If a man in an elevator or on the street did or said something sexist, I'd call him out. And women around me would usually support me, laughing out loud at the asshole, or whatever. Those moments were beautiful. The best was one day when I was standing on the T at rush hour and a guy making his way down the aisle pretended to stumble, ending up with his hands cupping my breasts. I returned the favor by reaching down, grabbing his junk, and giving the hardest yank I could manage! And I yelled at him, 'How do *you* like being grabbed, asshole?' Four or five women around me who'd seen the whole thing broke out laughing at the prick, and we literally shoved him out the door at the next stop. We all cheered out loud—and there were even men who joined in. God, it was such a beautiful moment!" Sikes looked over at me with a radiant smile.

"So, tell me what happened with that goddamn gun," I asked.

"Yeah. Shit. I should have stuck to the verbal comebacks. What was I thinking . . . ?" Her voice trailed off as she said this, and she spent fifteen or twenty seconds far away before shaking her head to clear her mind and then looking back at me. "Anyway, one evening I came out of Filene's Basement at about eight thirty to go to my car. I was parked on a little side street off Washington Street, and it was dark out. I was reaching in my purse to get my keys, and some big dude came up behind me, put his hands real tightly on my sides, and spun me around. In a split second, the hand I had in my purse went from the keys to the pistol, and just as he began to pull me in toward him, I fired it off right through the purse. 'Bang,' it exploded—it was incredibly loud—the loudest noise I've ever heard. He just stood there, looking puzzled, still holding my sides. You know what I said to him?"

I shook my head.

"I said, 'You going to let go of me, asshole, or do you want me to shoot you again?' When he did let go, he fell straight backward—and that's when he whacked his head on the sidewalk. That turned out to be the serious injury; the .22 shell went right through his thigh and didn't do much damage." No tears came this time; she was scanning my face for any sign of approval.

Something deep inside me told me not to smile, not to approve of a point-blank shooting of anybody by anybody. But that little voice was overruled by everything I'd just been told by Sikes, plus everything I'd been told by dozens of other harassment and assault victims: "Holy fuck. You shot the guy, and then you said *that*?"

"Yep. Sure did. I keep trying to regret it, but I'm still having trouble getting there. That, by the way, is just between us—I keep telling my prison social worker that I'm the most remorseful girl this side of the Rockies. There were all sorts of charges brought against me, as you probably know. Besides the assault and battery with a dangerous weapon and the lesser included charges, there were two counts growing out of my illegal possession of an unregistered weapon. Anyway, the police and an ambulance soon came, and I was arrested. The rest of the story you know."

I was so taken aback that it took me quite a few moments to gather myself and ask Sikes my questions. But there wasn't time to delay. "I'd like you to tell me as precisely as you can the exact words Britton used when he talked to you about rejecting the plea bargain you were offered. And tell me roughly how many of these conversations took place, and how your thinking on the matter evolved over time—if it did. And I want to remind you that I'm looking for any insights you might have into Britton as a person. What do you think was going on inside his head? What do you think motivated him to spend so much time on your case? These guys don't get paid much for all the extra work. What was up with this guy?"

Sikes drew in a deep breath, looking sideways and down, thinking back. When she finally spoke, her voice had softened, and it had an empathetic touch to it, a caring quality. "Okay, let's give this a try. I—" We were interrupted at just this point by a knock at the door, and the officer who had originally ushered in Ms. Sikes entered to tell us our ninety-minute visitation session was up.

We both stood up to comply, crushed by the timing—at least I was. Before I could plead for more time, the officer sensed that we were at an awkward stopping point, and completely of his own initiative asked, "Would it be helpful if I gave you two another hour to finish up? That works for me if you want the time."

We both profusely thanked the officer, who closed the door.

After a pause, Sikes plunged right back in. "You're right, he did work hard. I wasn't expecting a public defender to be as diligent as Attorney Britton was. In fact, I was amazed when he suggested we take our time to think through the plea deal that had been offered. He told me that first we should get control of the evidence to see if we could find a way out of the entire matter—it was an act of self-defense, after all. And he told me the very first time I met him that his way of practicing law involved working super-hard on a case—from 'soup to nuts' was his phrase. And I have to say something else, with respect to what I told you before: one of the positive traits of Britton was that he didn't come on to me—*not at all*. Sometimes men who are dorky looking like Britton just want to be friends with a good-looking woman, and that can be nice, frankly—I mean, for the woman. So, I figured if I could trade friendship for hardworking legal representation—we'd both be better off."

"Why do you say 'friendship'?"

"Why not?" Sikes asked, furling her brow and tapping her fingers on the table. "Look, Britton seemed to be a lonely, fat guy who was interested in a warm, cordial working relationship. I assumed he got a kick out of working with a pretty face. Fine. I certainly couldn't see any reason not to be warm and friendly to a public defender who was working hard on my case, who was taking the time to seek out the witnesses we needed, and who was meeting with me on a regular basis. I mean, it's sort of like soldiers in a battle: why wouldn't we develop a warm team spirit—like teammates or soldiers do? And he never hit on me once—never even gave a hint of it—and that's a big deal to me."

"I hear you," I replied. "I hear you loud and clear. Let me steer you to the discussions you had with Attorney Britton about whether or not to accept the plea bargain you'd been offered. Can you tell me what was discussed between the two of you on that topic? And who actually made the decision not to accept the offer and to proceed to trial?"

Again, Sikes took the time she needed to think before she spoke; this was, after all, the heart of the matter, as she was well aware. "Well, there were discussions of the pros and cons, to be sure. But the decision turned on the *weight* you gave each pro and each con—and that, in effect, had to be his call. It's like in a doctor's office when they always have the patient make the decision, but they know we'll go along with what they signal to be the smartest thing to do, right? How could we not?" I nodded, having done precisely what she was talking about only a week before our meeting. "So, formally, yes, he did ask for—and, I suppose, wait for my decision. But the real question, I think, turns on the degree to which I gave my *informed* consent. And that's tough, like in my doctor's office example."

"I get it. So let's move on. How did you experience Britton, *as a person*, not just as your attorney? And not just what you saw or heard, but what you *felt* about what really makes him tick—deep down inside."

She stared at me, parsing my question. "Well, mainly, I felt lucky. I'd been assigned a lawyer who seemed to care about me, and not just about my case. I'd heard horror stories from other prisoners about how they were treated like trash, whereas Britton made me feel like I was . . . his . . . his . . . friend."

"So, did Britton's friendliness seem in any way inappropriate—I don't mean sexualized. I mean, did you ever find him to be inappropriate, you know, like being overly friendly, even if not in a sexualized way?"

"Well . . . no. He was just friendly. There were no boundary issues—not so far as I ever sensed. He showed concern, friendly concern, with respect to what I was going through personally. Hey, I shot a guy—it's an upsetting thing to do. I'm not a violent person. And I was living in this hellhole. Perhaps his hard work on my case and his concern for how I was dealing with having so totally fucked up my life got me swept up in the excitement of our joint campaign. Maybe that clouded my thinking about whether or not to accept the plea bargain that I was offered—I don't know." Here she paused, and when she took up speaking again, her voice had changed: now she sounded almost dreamy. "I mean, maybe the friendliness played a role in leading me to make the wrong decision, but how can you blame someone for being friendly? Looking back . . . it seems so clear now that I was a fool to get caught up in Britton's fantasy of winning an acquittal. But he was *so* enthusiastic and *so* hardworking—and *so* supportive of me as a person—what I was going through. I don't know, maybe all that together made the self-defense argument seem more powerful to me than it should have." With this, Sikes looked away from me and let out one of the saddest, most touching sighs I'd ever heard. Then she turned back and asked: "You know how long the jury deliberated in my case?" I slowly shook my head no. "Forty-five minutes. What does that tell you?"

I paused at the impact of this information. "It tells me he didn't convince a single juror." Sikes just scrunched up her mouth in an ironic little smile and stared at me. I needed to get her back on topic. "Ms. Sikes, tell me, what were these working sessions with Attorney Britton like? What was discussed about the plea bargain? Can you remember the specifics?"

"Sure. We discussed the advantages and disadvantages of accepting a deal. And Britton was clear: it was my decision to make. There was no ambiguity or doubt about that on either of our parts. But his enthusiasm and friendliness swept me up. And I believed in him; why wouldn't I—he was my hardworking ally, my champion . . . my friend when I didn't have any friends. He was here at the prison a lot, willing and eager to work on my case. It's hard to condemn that, isn't it? And when the trial drew near and we worked on my testimony, he was even more generous with his time. And it isn't like we spent time talking about the Red Sox or my pipe dreams about what I would do when I got out. We talked about the case, not much at all about other stuff. I have no doubts that Britton tried to put together a winning case; it just didn't work out."

"I'm not surprised at what you're telling me," I broke in. "He's clearly a competent attorney. I'm just trying to figure out if he's a competent person."

Sikes was about ready to say something, but then stopped short with a quizzical look on her face, and shot back at me, "What the fuck is a 'competent person'? That sounds a bit condescending to me."

"It does, doesn't it?" I replied, somewhat embarrassed. "I just mean that competent adults don't have character flaws that bring their lives crashing down. That's really my question to you, I suppose. Looking back, do you see any type of character flaw in Britton? Can you think of anything about his character or his behavior that has brought his law career to the brink of disaster?"

She took a while to find her answer. "I see what you're asking, but I'm not sure I have an answer for you. Maybe he just needs to think of himself as . . ." And here she raised her right arm defiantly, modulated her voice to the lowest tone she could muster, and in a wonderfully humorous accent, called out, *"Herbert Britton: the great trial lawyer who dares try cases that lesser attorneys fear to handle."* Sikes stopped speaking when I laughed out loud at what she'd said. Then, with just a hint of a wry smile, she told me, "You know what? Now that I think about it, what he did *was* pretty macho—in a good sort of way. He was the only one in my corner at the time. I was a broke, unmarried woman who had just lost her job and who was facing a truckload of felony counts. I was desperately in need of legal help, and of a little friendship as well, to be honest with you. And I have to tell you, he stood right up to the prosecution. Britton was resourceful—and strong with the judge. At trial, I thought he did a much better job than the prosecution. The only problem was, Perry Mason couldn't have won my goddamn case." She paused to think about what she wanted to say next. "You can't imagine how many times I've thought this through in the past eighteen months, and the only thing I can fault Britton for was not recognizing that my case couldn't possibly be won with a self-defense argument. I mean, what was the guy on the sidewalk going to do—hug me to death? I had no cause to shoot him—and you need that to use for self-defense to work. But as for how diligently he fought that fight, and as for how friendly and supportive he was throughout the almost nine months the process took—I have nothing but praise for the man. Does this make any sense?"

Now it was my turn to pause for a moment to think through what all this meant. "Look, Ms. Sikes, what I don't get is why an experienced trial attorney would ignore the obvious weaknesses in your case and expose you to such long incarceration. Why would he do that—especially since you said he was friendly and supportive?"

"Like I said earlier," Sikes answered, "my take today is that this had more to do with him than with me. Maybe it has to do with how important the act of trying a case is to him—all the grandstanding and posturing in front of the judge and the jury. Pretty heady stuff for an otherwise fat, dorky guy, don't you think?"

"Absolutely; I totally follow that. But, look, could you take one more stab at telling me how he seemed to you as a person—not as an attorney?"

"As a person." Sikes paused again. "Well, he never spoke about his personal life, so I'm just guessing. All I know is that everything he did, he did in a gentlemanly and professional way. And like I said, he was appropriate and friendly and warm with me when I desperately needed it. But it was more than that: he was . . . sensitive . . . in a way that most men aren't—no offense."

"None taken."

"He'd ask how I was *feeling*, how I was *dealing with having shot someone*, he asked whether I was getting enough sleep. So, that's why I guess he's probably a prince to his friends. But I'm just guessing here; he never talked about his own relationships. I could be way off."

I nodded. "By the way, Ms. Sikes, any news as to how the guy you shot is doing?"

"He's a mess, as I understand it. He got a very serious brain bleed from hitting his head, and we heard at trial from his doctor about how they had to drill holes in his skull to relieve the pressure, and how all this has compromised his balance and coordination. I should have had one of those pepper spray things—that would have done the trick with him—and kept me from ruining my life. Twenty-twenty hindsight works great, doesn't it?" These were her last words before the guard reentered, and it was time for us to part. "Ms. Sikes," I said as the guard handcuffed her, "I made you several promises. Please trust me: I will keep them. And I will do everything I can to be helpful, you can count on that."

"Thanks, Terry. I trust that you will." Sikes ended the interview with a smile as she was led from the room. She had saved using my nickname for her final words—I hadn't even known that she was aware of it. I had to figure that Attorney Britton was as subject to her charms as I was—and that he had been out to help, not harm, this captivating person. What had gone wrong? Ten minutes later, the last of the six steel doors slammed shut behind me with a steely thud, and I was back out in the sunlight and fresh air.

***

As I drove back to the office through Boston's ubiquitous traffic, I pondered Sikes's analysis of Britton. I could easily see her point: How could Britton *not* find trial work to have an element of gladiatorial excitement? It is captivating—sometimes exhilarating—and it's a great chess game to play because it isn't *your* ass, or *your* wallet, that's on the line. The moves and countermoves during discovery and trial reward strategic insight, and the presentation of your client's witnesses—and the cross-examination of the other party's—provides a forum for tactical virtuosity. On top of that, outfoxing opposing counsel in navigating the complex Rules of Evidence provides yet another opportunity to test one's comparative mastery of the profession. It seemed to me that Sikes's insight was probably right on the money: Britton's preference for trial might very well be based on his psychological need to access the courtroom—just as actors presumably hunger for time on the stage.

And I couldn't help thinking more about Linda Sikes. Southie—the neighborhood traditionally associated with working-class Boston Irish—is a tough place to leave. They say you can take a person out of Southie but you can't take Southie out of the person. And it's not just the accent that marks you for life. It's the poor schooling, the hard-edged people, and the limited opportunities. This bright, beautiful woman could have done *anything* with her life if she'd been born a few miles west to a middle-class family in the Back Bay or a few miles southwest in Brookline or Newton. Those few miles made all the difference: they played a role in how many times and how relentlessly she had been sexually harassed and assaulted; they played a role in her decision to carry an unlicensed gun; they played a role in her having to rely on a public defender; and they would play an even more out-sized role in what she could possibly make out of the rest of her life. One thing was for certain: I needed to find a strategy to the case that allowed me to help her find a path out of that soul-crushing prison.

***

Three or four days after I met with Linda Sikes, I received a call from Herbert Britton. He was quite pleasant on the phone, and was thrilled to have pro bono representation. It turned out he knew of me and my practice from several sources. "Keep track of your time," he told me. "If I ever get any money, I'll pay you every dollar I owe you." I admired his saying this. People have a right to self-respect, no matter how modest their circumstances. We arranged for a meeting early the following week.

***

In the interim, my associate attorney reviewed the entire record in all three of the cases referenced in the complaint, plus the litigation spindles of five additional cases that he'd located by visiting the local district courts and searching their dockets. He also interviewed two of the assistant district attorneys who had prosecuted two of these eight cases, and he had an upcoming telephone conference with a third. The two prosecutors confirmed that Britton had unquestionably taken the time to master the detailed fact pattern in each of the cases they had had with him. Both of the ADAs—on their own initiative—contrasted this with the mediocre quality of work they all too often saw from other court-appointed counsel. The more I learned about Britton, the less I understood.

In the five additional cases that had been reviewed in detail, Britton had achieved one full acquittal, as well as dismissals and acquittals as to several counts in four of the other cases. Otherwise, Britton had lost every other count of every other case. My associate had been able to confirm that Britton's cases were disproportionately "dog cases"—those that are almost certain losers, so there was little or no stigma attached to his losing them at trial. I began to question if Sikes had analyzed Britton's motives correctly: Why would a skillful attorney take almost certain losers all the way through to predictably disappointing jury verdicts? How could the quasi-certainty of loss not outweigh the thrill of presenting the case at trial? Do actors take mediocre roles just to be on stage?

***

I went back and read through the disciplinary complaint once again. Bar Counsel was careful to state that any individual criminal defendant could elect to reject a plea bargain and exercise their constitutional right to a trial by a jury of their peers. That was not in question. But, as the complaint phrased it—somewhat intriguingly, I thought: "Rejection of a plea bargain is a *retail* matter, a case-by-case decision. What we have here is a *wholesale* rejection of all plea bargains engineered by Attorney Britton for nearly *all* of his clients. This is not permissible, and constitutes a breach of the code of ethics precisely because it is fair to infer that it was Attorney Britton who was making the wholesale rejection decisions, and not the individual clients." This ethical code violation, Bar Counsel went on to argue, "undermines the criminal justice system in an important way, as evidenced by the appended complaint letters filed by Sikes, Sanders, and McDermott. Once these defendants found themselves to be convicts serving far longer sentences than they would have served under their respective rejected plea bargains, they felt cheated not only by Attorney Britton, but by the criminal justice system itself."

The complaint was sensitive to the fact that an ethical violation is quite a different matter than legal malpractice. Malpractice is a question of practicing law below an expected standard of competence, whereas an ethical violation necessarily involves an element of bad faith. In Bar Counsel's analysis of Britton's case, the bad faith motive was straightforward greed: he was out to maximize his legal fees by drawing out his cases. But this theory came with two glaring anomalies. First, it was clear that Britton worked many, many more hours than he actually billed for. Second, there was universal agreement that he worked diligently and consistently produced technically excellent legal work. Greedy people are not at all like this, at least in my experience. They generally take as much as they can get and give back as little as they can get away with. So, it had to be something other than greed—and the more I thought about Linda Sikes's concept of just what made Britton tick, the more sense it made to me. Why wouldn't a guy like Britton get addicted to jury trials? I certainly found them as exhilarating as hell. They are absolutely packed with action and emotion, and they reward those who can think quickly as testimony goes off on a tangent one could never have planned for. Sikes was proposing that the courtroom drama of arguing a case to a jury was to Britton what bullring and a corrida are to a matador. I could see her point.

***

Attorney Britton lumbered into my office just a few days later and plopped down heavily in one of the client chairs facing my desk. He turned out to be a few inches over five feet tall and quite conspicuously rotund. Just shy of his fortieth birthday, he was perfectly bald—save for a one-inch-wide swath of gray-brown hair that encircled his skull from temple to temple. He had a pleasant face, really, and wonderful hazel eyes. But, best of all, he had a sunny smile featuring straight bright-white teeth. Apparently, his significant paunch rendered belts problematic, and I was soon to learn that he owned an impressive collection of flowery bow ties that matched his many sets of suspenders. His persona seemed twofold. On the one hand, it was immediately clear that he was someone who liked to be liked: he was a good conversationalist with well-honed listening skills. On the other hand, he was a study in self-doubt, tension, and anxiety: I never, ever saw him sit still. Of course, by the time I met Attorney Britton, he was under tremendous pressure. Technically, his law practice was still up and running, but it was gravely threatened by the ultimate sanction: publicly announced disbarment for life by the Supreme Judicial Court. On top of that, he had every reason to worry that a disbarment would trigger a number of civil suits for legal malpractice. It made perfect sense that he was a nervous wreck.

I opened the conversation by asking Attorney Britton what he made of Bar Counsel's argument that he was out to drag out his cases so he could bill for more hours. "Can I assume that this was not the case?"

"Are you kidding?" Britton shot back with a smile. "Who's going to sell out clients for thirty-five dollars an hour? And more importantly, I'm actually not a person who cares much about money."

"So why didn't your clients take more of these plea bargain offers like the rest of the world?"

"Because the Constitution guarantees their right to a jury trial. And on top of that, I was sure I could win each of those trials. And I worked my ass off trying to win each case. You've tried a lot of cases; how did you find the quality of my work?"

I hesitated for a moment, trying to read his body language—but all I saw was a small symphony of nervous twitches. "From what I could see, you consistently filed well-researched, well-drafted paperwork in each case we've reviewed, and your trial preparation and courtroom performance were equally admirable. None of that is in question; in fact, Bar Counsel even concedes all this in the complaint. But what I really need to know is whether, in any way, no matter how subtly, you set out to influence your clients to elect to forgo the plea bargain offers they were given."

"I didn't pressure them!" Britton shot back defensively. After a pause, and stammering about somewhat, he continued, more calmly. "I mean, I presented the pros and cons of going either way. I explained what the plea bargain path looks like. Then I explained what the trial path looks like. Each client could do whatever they wanted." I was silent when he finished, and sat still, staring into his eyes. This elicited one last outburst: "I mean, I *did* tell them that I was a very hardworking attorney and that I would investigate every detail, prepare every witness, research all the controlling law, and put on a vigorous trial." He

paused a bit, looked me straight in the eyes, and finished with emphasis: "And I fulfilled each and every one of those promises in every single
case—as you said, Bar Counsel concedes that in the complaint. But the
three cases referenced in the complaint were hard to win."

When he finished, there was a deep silence—partly due to the
room's floor-to-ceiling bookshelves, and partly due to the aftereffect
of Britton's loud outburst. Okay, then—Britton was not going to voluntarily reveal to me the secret to the case—if he was even aware of
what that might be. So that meant it was time to start digging into the
myriad of details I would need to learn in order to try to figure things
out for myself.

"Herbert," I began my refocused inquiry, "what I need to do for
the rest of our meeting today is learn as much as I can about your
background, your education, your private life, and, of course, your law
practice. It's in the richness of all these details that I often find my best
arguments. Remember, in a disbarment hearing, unlike a civil trial, I'm
able—I'm even encouraged—to talk about you as a whole person, and
why the court should be lenient, and why the court should consider
your overall circumstances, and so on. You probably already know
that, right?"

"I understand perfectly, and I do the same thing in my practice. It's
the only way to fly the plane. Where do you want me to start?"

"Start at the beginning. Tell me what your childhood was like, tell
me about what your schooling was like, and then tell me about your
former and current social life. And if you don't mind, I'm going to
record this conversation so I don't lose any details. Okay by you?"

"Sure. But why do you want to hear about my childhood?"

"Humor me, Counselor. I was a PhD social-psychology professor
long before I was an attorney. I want to listen to your story with that set
of ears as well. Who knows what I'll I find that I can use."

"That's fine. You're calling the shots here." Then another heavy
silence fell upon the man. Something was building up inside him and
was taking control of his emotions. With each breath, he grew progressively choked up, and by the time he spoke, his voice was tremulous
with tears. "Counselor, I'll do *anything* you say not to be disbarred. You
need to understand, I *can't* lose my license to practice law. Law is what
I do. Law is *all* I do. If I'm disbarred, I'll die. What would I do if I can't

practice law? I don't have any other skills, no family company to slide into, no hobbies—no nothing. Nothing." Here he stopped, breaking down completely. I handed over my box of tissues, and only after several minutes and a dozen room-rattling nose blows could we take up our conversation again. "Sorry about that. Look, what I'm trying to say is that practicing law isn't just how I earn my living; it's much, much more to me than that. It's what I do when I'm awake; it's what I think about when I get into bed; it's what I dream about when I'm asleep. I'm not a guy who has hobbies or plays sports. I'm just not"—he searched patiently for the words he wanted—"*involved* in anything else. I'll do whatever I need to do to keep my ticket. Help me, for God's sake, *please help me.*"

I had the distinct impression that Herbert Britton was now ready to get down to work on his case. These were the moments when I was most aware of the distinct advantage of law work over clinical psychology: the fear of imminent real-world consequences motivates clients to move beyond their defense mechanisms much more rapidly than does a proffered hope of greater inner calm and improved social relations.

And, indeed, without further prompting, Britton got serious about telling me who he was as a person. "To be frank, I haven't thought much about my childhood in a long time," he began. Bit by bit, his emotions and tenor of voice calmed, and he gradually shifted into an almost dreamy tone of voice. "I was alone a lot as a little kid, to be honest. And my parents couldn't provide me comfort; they never really liked me very much. And I know my brother didn't either—he still doesn't. We haven't spoken about anything meaningful in years—twenty years—more."

"What's his first name, and where does he live?" I interrupted.

"Jeremy. Spokane, Washington. Anyway, physically, I was always pretty much the same guy you see in front of you today: double-chinned, overweight, and underpopular. I've been fat my whole fucking life. But I wasn't bald." I giggled at his line and expected him to look over and share a little smile with me. He didn't. "My brother—two years my senior—was the opposite of me, exactly the opposite. He was thin, cute, and popular. Everything he touched worked out. He was the co-captain of the high school baseball team; I couldn't even get myself selected as the team's equipment manager, goddamn it. And there was only one other applicant—Tommy Clarke's brother who had Down syndrome. Actually, it was that particular fiasco that embarrassed the hell out of my brother and soured our relationship. For life, I guess. But it had been the same before that in junior high school. As far back as I can remember. Every day, I was immersed in humiliation, drowning in a virtual sea of fat jokes and insults—verbalized or not. Fat people live with that, you know. And there wasn't a moment of relief, including at home." He teared up a bit again and began shaking his head back and forth. A good while passed before he could speak again. "But there was one fun thing. One incredible sphere of sunshine and warmth." He looked over at me, and a little smile broke out across his face, the way the sun can briefly shine through a small break in an otherwise thick cloud cover. "The only fun thing I did as a kid was to spend time working with my dad on a really big stamp collection that *his* father had started. That was our one moment of contact, and it was *all mine*, because—*thank God*—my brother was completely disinterested in stamps." Britton then fell silent, looking down at the floor, waiting for a follow-up prompt.

"Tell me about your childhood friendships," I offered.

After a few moments, a second, fleeting smile flashed across Britton's face. "I did once have a friend—a really good friend—the only one ever . . . really. When I was about twelve or thirteen—in junior high school. I learned that one of the . . . popular kids was also interested in stamp collecting. He was the only other kid I ever met who could relate to stamps—he had learned from his father, like I did." Britton paused, clearly immersed in warm reveries of long-ago good times. After fifteen seconds or so, he absolutely floored me by looking straight in my eyes and adding, "I think I loved him, actually. He was so handsome—dark-black hair and sky-blue eyes—and his smile was so beautiful." Another pause ensued, followed by a long, sad sigh. "No one else in my entire life has ever so completely forgiven my fatness and my homeliness and my awkwardness. Jon was amazing. When we peered through a magnifying glass at the tiny details of the stamps, and when we read about the old stamps my grandfather had collected, we lay side by side on the floor. We'd discuss and analyze the most minute details of a stamp. We always did this in the same way. One of us would hold the handle of the magnifying glass; Jon would use his right eye, and I my left, which caused our cheeks to touch. I remember my heart beating so hard when we did this that I thought it would explode." He looked up and over at me, staring directly in my eyes again. "Can you imagine how much that friend meant to me?" Britton looked away, paused for twenty seconds, and then continued. "Then, one day, Jon told me that his family had to move to Seattle because his father got a new job with Boeing, and a couple of months later, the best friend I ever had was gone. Like that, poof, gone from my life . . . forever." Britton somehow slumped even more deeply into his chair. "God, I can feel the emptiness in my chest right this moment, even after all these years." Again, he slipped into silence for a few moments. Then, looking down at the floor, he added, "You're the only person I've ever told that to."

"Thank you, Herbert, thank you for sharing that with me, and especially for trusting me with it." I followed on, acknowledging his opening up to me, just as I'd asked him to do. "You obviously loved having such a wonderful friendship—who wouldn't? How sad that he was torn away from you. Did you try to make other friends?"

"Of course. But it's tough when you're fat; kids didn't give me a chance. And, frankly, at some point, I gave up exposing myself to being hurt, to rejection. I just gave up."

"All right," I said, searching for another prompt. "Tell me about your college years."

"I went to a public school, Fitchburg State University. I was in their criminal justice program because my guidance counselor thought it was my best route to law school, and from the age of fifteen or so, I knew I wanted to be an attorney. I've never been certain why, really. It could have been the law shows on TV—you know, Perry Mason, that kind of thing. Prancing around a courtroom—it looked great to me. It was something a fat guy could do. And I thought I could gain respect if I got good at it. I never had any doubts. I graduated in about the middle of my class, and got into Western New England University School of Law—out in Springfield. Of course, I needed to find a job to support myself—it was going to take me a lot more than three years with the evening program that I enrolled in. The only work I could land was bagging groceries, but that wasn't as bad as it sounds. It gave me access to the produce and meat that were too old to sell. Six years later, I had enough credits to graduate."

"When you have a moment, can you make a list for me of the professors or fellow students who would give us an affidavit about how devoted you were to your studies, or about your general character—whatever?"

"No. I don't think I can. I never got to know anyone there; I was just present for the classes. Otherwise I was working at the market."

"Okay. Well, who *do* you know now who would vouch for you? What about people at the market?"

"No, definitely not. I didn't leave there on the best of terms."

"Okay. How about the client for whom you obtained the full acquittal?"

"No way. That was a private case, not a court-appointed one. And we parted with a fundamental disagreement. He thought because he was acquitted it meant he was innocent of the crime he and I both knew he had in fact committed. I tried to gently disabuse him of his revisionist history, and all I got was not paid."

"Oops. I hear you. All right. Well, let's definitely leave that one alone. How about this: Have you worked on the same side of a case with another attorney—or even if you were on opposite sides, can you think of any member of the Massachusetts bar who would stand up and say good things about how you practice law?"

Britton thought for a moment. "I wish I could help. But no. I'm not really in contact today with anyone I can think of right now. I'll keep thinking about this."

"All right. Keep working on it; see if you can come up with an idea or two. So, let's change tracks here. Tell me about your law office."

"I practice out of a rent-a-room suite of attorneys who share an office in Brockton. But I don't have anything to do with the other lawyers; it's their lease, their office. I just pay my share of the rent and my share of the receptionist's salary."

"Can we approach these guys for an affidavit?"

"Oh, definitely not. That would involve my telling them about my disciplinary hearing, and they'll go bananas because of the malpractice policy. The only thing they know about my law practice is that I exclusively do criminal defense. And that's all they need to know."

I was astonished at what I'd just heard. "Are you saying you haven't notified your malpractice insurer yet about the complaint? That isn't wise, Herbert. You'd better reread your policy. Some require immediate notification as soon as the insured learns of a claim or even of a potential claim. I wouldn't delay. You don't want to end up fighting with your own insurance carrier about whether they have to defend you if a claim is filed. My advice is that you inform your insurer immediately, whatever the reaction of your office mates. Do you hear me?"

Britton nodded his consent.

"Okay," I replied, trying to think where to head. "So, let's take a different route here. Uhm . . . have you done any pro bono work, or are you linked in any way with any charity—anything, Herbert, anything . . . ? Give me some help here; I'm grasping at straws."

"Counselor, I don't think you're hearing me. Let me try again. I live by myself in a room I rent in an old house in Framingham. Each room is rented separately, and we share the kitchen and bath. I know one first name—no, that's not accurate—I know two first names of the other guys, and none of their last names. My office situation, I told you about . . . It's just like my home, isn't it? I never really thought about that before." Britton sighed deeply and sat hunched over now with his elbows on his knees, looking down at the floor, shaking his head back and forth in slow motion.

"Okay, then; I hear you," I responded, with no idea where to head next.

"No, no you *don't* hear me. Not really," Britton cut in. "You have no idea how hard it is to be me. No offense, but you can't possibly hear me."

I started to respond, but he didn't allow it—something had opened an avalanche of emotion in the man, and it came spewing forth: "Counselor, if I tell you this society is as 'looks-ist' as it is racist, you'd probably agree on an intellectual level. But you can't imagine what this *feels like* if this makes up the framework of your everyday life. When you're fat, people essentially don't see you. They choose not to see you— they look away, just as quickly as they can. And even when people do look at you—like when they're selling me something in a store or whatever—they don't *see* you. This is a looks-ist society, and if you're fat, you end up being sort of . . . invisible. And people don't make friends with people they can't see."

I hadn't thought the air in the room could grow any thicker, but it had—quite considerably. Part of me recognized that it would be prudent to move away from questions about Britton's personal life, but another part of me just couldn't believe his claim that I wouldn't be able to locate even a single favorable character witness. And, for sure, his wallowing in self-pity was starting to prejudice the case. So, unwisely, I decided to try one last time. "What I'm looking for here, Herbert, is support from *somebody—anybody*—so that I can litigate your case. We have to gather some evidence in your favor, *you know that*. We're not doing clinical work here. This is not the time or the place to feel sorry for yourself. This is the time and place to defend yourself. There *must* be some attorney whom you worked with—or against—who came to respect how hard you work for your clients. Or some past client, or some district attorney, or some court clerk, or some court reporter, or some neighbor—there must be *someone* who will give me an affidavit supporting you in one way or another. You're a skillful trial attorney, Herbert—a very skillful one. You *must* have impressed people along the way. Think about it."

Britton remained perfectly silent as the atmosphere in the room vibrated off the walls from my insensitive flare-up. Then he looked over at me, tears once again welling up in his eyes, and simply said, "There's no one."

Where I had only heard the man before, this time I finally listened. "Okay, then. Let's forget that approach." I shifted gears, trying to sound encouraging. "Don't worry about that approach. We'll find something else . . . And if we don't, there's nothing wrong with arguing that you should be admired, not admonished, for bucking the plea bargain system of justice with all its inequities. Think about it, Herbert: either you'll prevail or you'll be a culture hero. That might give you a soft landing, even if you're disbarred. And I can argue that you should be respected for putting in all the time and hard work that you did—much of it unpaid, the rest of it underpaid—to protect the constitutional rights of people of modest means. I was just looking for a backup argument—if there was one to be found. You understand that, you're a trial attorney—a damn good one."

The silence grew oppressive at this point. I was groping for something to say, and I ended up asking if he managed to get enough clients to fill his practice.

"That's the beauty of what I do," he responded, his tone quickly turning somewhat more upbeat. "I never need to attract clients by advertising or anything like that: all but a few of my cases have been court-assigned public defender cases."

"Your entire caseload is court appointed—or almost so?"

"Yep. And it works really well—for me, anyway. The only downside has been that you don't make much money in this practice. But I really don't care much about money—you heard how simple my life is. Do you realize how liberating that is? All I need is enough to cover my office and home rents, and to buy gas and groceries—and my life works just fine. Or at least it did before all this shit hit the fan."

"Do you get enough cases from the courts?" I asked.

"Yes and no. I could take on more cases. But I put so much time into each case that my time is always filled up no matter how many cases I have."

"How long does your average case take to resolve—from assignment to its final resolution?"

"As long as possible," Britton quickly responded before realizing how strange that sounded and then jumping back in to modify his answer. "What I mean is that I believe in the saying 'Once a client, always a client.' My goal is to do such good work for each client that even after their case is over, I've become their go-to attorney for life. I want to become their consigliere. You know what I mean? You saw *The Godfather*. My clients become important to me. I stay in touch with them. I send Christmas cards and birthday cards—marketing, you know. I suppose you could call this a type of advertising, but it's the traditional way attorneys advertised—before it became legal to put out regular ads."

I had no idea how to proceed with this consigliere issue—whatever precisely he had in mind—so I backed off and asked what I had thought would be a benign question: How would he compare his style of practicing criminal law in the district courts to the work of other attorneys he worked alongside?

Bingo! This inquiry elicited as emotional an outpouring as had my former line of questioning—if from an entirely different direction. Britton seized the opportunity to criticize how his fellow attorneys had no problem with the plea bargain system of criminal justice, and he went on and on in an almost transported tone of voice. "The difference is night and day," he began. "Most of the other attorneys who get court-appointed work plead out their cases right away. And sometimes they do this using only the preliminary case conference memorandum that comes from the court when you get the appointment. It's not rare for that to be the single piece of paper they ever see—that and the police report, of course. And the assignment memorandum contains only the most minimal summary of the case—we're talking about a paragraph, sometimes two. I've seen plea bargains happen within an hour of an appointed counsel first receiving a case. What the fuck is that? That's not justice. That's not practicing law. It's not that the lawyers aren't bright and capable people—some are, some aren't. It's that our criminal justice system pressures them to talk their client into accepting a plea very, very early in their case—the deals that are offered at that point are far better than they are later on in the case. I suppose this is because the earlier you accept a plea bargain, the less work it takes by an already overburdened prosecutor's office."

Suddenly, the conversation had turned interesting, and far more promising. Britton sat up straight in his chair—and I suppose I did the same. "Herbert, have you ever seen the plea bargain system lead fully innocent defendants to cop a plea to avoid the risk of trial?"

This lit Britton up like a neon sign. "Sure, it happens from time to time, particularly with minority defendants. And that's another problem with plea bargain justice: it's inherently racist. It's a goddamn factory production line, and more and more so all the time. The United States has about five percent of the world's population but about twenty percent of the world's adjudicated prisoners, a third of whom are African Americans. Black men are five times more likely than white men to be imprisoned, and black women are two times more likely. And when I say it's a factory, check out this statistic: in 1980, there were about five hundred thousand prisoners in the US. Between 1980 and today, the population of the country has gone up about fifty percent, so at the same incarceration rate, you would expect about seven hundred and fifty thousand prisoners. But you know how many there are? About two million."

I was stunned at the transformation in the man; this animated, passionate Britton was the one I wanted to introduce to the Supreme

Court, not the lonely sad sack. And it turned out he hadn't even really begun yet. "And I need to add something important," he continued. "Being guilty of an underlying criminal act is not the same thing as being guilty of all the charges the district attorneys pile on. The plea bargain system encourages them to pile on extra charges to create pressure—and then they use the surplus charges as bargaining chips in cutting their plea deals. So, if you were to listen in on a week's worth of negotiations between assistant district attorneys and the court-appointed attorneys who churn out these plea bargains—most of what you'd hear would be wheeling and dealing about the charges to be pleaded to and the charges to be dismissed. You'd seldom hear discussion and debate about the underlying guilt or innocence of the defendant. And remember, it's not just guilt in some abstract sense. There's also the question of whether or not the prosecution has the evidence to prove a defendant's guilt *beyond a reasonable doubt*. Terry, you're a civil trial attorney. You win cases with fifty-one percent of the evidence in your client's favor. Contrast this with the prosecution in a criminal matter: it has to come up with ninety percent certainty. Big fucking difference."

Wow. Britton's distaste for plea bargaining was turning out to be based on a sophisticated-sounding critique of the current criminal justice system. All of a sudden, I began to see his case in an entirely new light. While I hadn't at all thought through at this point what this might imply for the defense of the allegations brought against him, it signaled that I just might be able to make an entirely different set of arguments in his favor. Far sexier arguments.

"Look, here's the problem," Britton continued. "If you allow the plea bargain system of criminal justice to force you to negotiate a plea deal when you know almost nothing about your client's case, you end up encouraging your client to make a decision before you could *possibly* have an accurate assessment of whether the prosecution can meet its tough burden of proof. And that 'beyond a reasonable doubt' burden applies to *each and every required element of each and every count.* You know that."

With that, he fell silent, and so did I for a bit. Then, to give him yet another prompt, I asked to learn more about how he operated his practice.

"I try to practice criminal law in the opposite manner of what I've been describing," Britton replied in the first confident tone of voice I had heard him use. "I don't give a rat's ass about how much time it takes me to properly investigate a case or research the relevant precedent—nor do I particularly care about how much of that time goes unpaid. It takes me weeks, sometimes months, to do discovery before I have an adequate grasp of the fact pattern and the witness availability. This is the information I need to be able to analyze whether or not the prosecution can meet its burden of proof. To me, it's legal malpractice to advise a client on a plea bargain offer during this period. The problem is, most of the assistant district attorneys won't wait that long. They put time limits on plea bargain offers that are designed to force clients to make early decisions. And the weaker an ADA senses his or her case to be, the shorter the time limit they tend to give you. I refuse to be part of today's industrial criminal justice system. It's designed to feed an ever-increasing stream of defendants—regardless of whether they are completely innocent or couldn't be proven guilty—into the ever-expanding *for-profit prison sector* of today's economy. A significant part of the plea bargain criminal justice system is not about dispensing justice—it's about making profit off us taxpayers who pay the bills of these privately owned prisons. I don't want any part of that."

Okay, then. This turn in the case was starting to fire up my imagination. "Herbert, who in your experience actually makes the decision about accepting a plea bargain in your colleagues' cases—not in your cases, but in the cases of the colleagues you were describing?"

He answered without hesitation. "Formally, of course, it's their client. But I've overheard attorneys in the hallways *berating* their clients to accept the plea bargains that they'd negotiated, and I've seen defendants assent with tears streaming down their faces."

"So, I want to get this straight. Are you saying that for those of your colleagues who are at peace with the plea bargain system of justice, behind the formality of obtaining the consent of the defendant, in reality it's the attorney who is actually making the decision?"

Britton looked over at me, now clearly aware of where I was heading. "Let me tell you what I said to every single client I've had for years and years who has faced a plea bargain decision. And you can—*and you should*—go ask them to confirm this. I tell them: 'Let the Commonwealth prove each count *beyond a reasonable doubt*. Let's see if they can scrape together enough evidence to convince the jury. If not, we'll beat this thing—count by count. And remember, counts we lose, we probably would have had to plead guilty to anyway.' So, my clients get their day in court—which is their constitutional right. Could you *please* tell me what's so wrong about that? Especially in the framework of the plea bargain conveyor-belt system of justice that makes a mockery of a major constitutional right? They should give me a fucking medal, not a disciplinary hearing. Am I making any sense here?"

I could barely keep my bearings. "Oh, I hear what you're saying, Herbert, and it could be a powerful argument, especially to the SJC.[9] But for this to work, you understand, you'll need to be able to testify that you fully informed each of these clients of their options and their exposure."

"That's not a problem at all; I did that over and over again. Go ask my clients."

My mind flashed to what Linda Sikes had told me; it was not at all inconsistent with what Britton was claiming. Interesting. "Okay, but let me take a step back and ask you an altogether different question about the three cases named in the complaint: Did these three defendants actually commit the underlying crimes they were charged with?"

Britton looked away and pondered my question for a while, holding up his thumb on his left hand, then ten seconds later, his pointer, and then . . . no third finger. Only after that did he look over at me. "Sanders didn't. His crime was being black. The others committed the underlying acts that precipitated their respective indictments—but in each of their cases, there were additional bogus counts piled on by the prosecution, like I was talking about. Never forget for a moment what an important element that is of the industrial criminal justice system."

"Did you file pretrial motions to have those bogus counts dismissed?"

"Of course I did."

"Were they?"

"In part. But the judges are part of the system, by and large."

---

9.   Nickname for the Massachusetts Supreme Judicial Court.

"So, were any of these defendants convicted at trial on counts that would have been dismissed by the prosecution had successful plea bargain negotiations taken place?"

Britton hesitated when so directly confronted, took in a deep breath, and released it audibly. "With Linda Sikes, the answer is yes. There had been an offer to dismiss all but the least serious of the lesser included felony counts. So, her case didn't work out well. I have to admit that. But you need to understand: I felt so certain that she had a valid self-defense case; I still can't believe the jury nailed her."

"Really? I thought the jury was out for forty-five minutes. And the other two cases?"

Britton sighed before answering. "Well, yes . . . there were counts in each case that came out the wrong way for us. I still don't see how that jury convicted Sanders; the man never littered, let alone committed a violent crime. Racist bastards. But these cases are outliers for me: normally I get the pile-on counts dismissed, and the client is no worse off than if he'd copped a plea. That's why these three cases were chosen by Bar Counsel."

"No, Herbert. They weren't 'chosen.' These were the three clients of yours who filed independent, and highly consistent, complaints against you. But let me ask you this: In the three cases we're talking about, did you continue to examine the plea bargain option with the prosecution and with your clients as the cases progressed?"

"Of course I did. And you can confirm that when you speak with my clients."

We both fell silent. I was stunned, actually, that an argument of constitutional merit had arisen in Britton's case. One of the reasons I'd taken the case—and one of the first pieces of bait Mike Jepson had dangled in front of me—was the opportunity to argue before my state's Supreme Court. But it's one thing to present a lame, uninteresting argument and quite another to argue on a fundamental constitutional right. I began to think that *just maybe* Britton's case had legs, after all.

"Herbert, it sounds more and more like we have something very interesting to work with here." I tried to sound as upbeat as possible in saying this, and waited for a smile, or some sign of camaraderie, but none was forthcoming. Britton just hunched back down in the chair, looking sad and tired; for some reason, the enthusiasm that had accompanied his ringing critique of the industrial criminal justice system had subsided as rapidly as it had appeared. We planned the date of our next meeting and called it a day. But I left the meeting uplifted, to be honest, having fallen quite enamored with the prospect of arguing constitutional law to the court.

***

Later that same day, I did some library research and learned something I certainly had not known: there was a powerful partisan element to the ongoing industrialization of imprisoning American citizens. Of the fifty-one legal jurisdictions in the United States (the fifty states plus the federal system), sixteen now held more than 10 percent of their prisoners in private, for-profit prisons. Eleven of the sixteen state jurisdictions were solidly Republican voting states. Over 8 percent of imprisoned American citizens were currently held in these for-profit, corporate prisons, one chain having the charming name "Corrections Corporation of America." Recent years had seen a mushrooming growth of more than 45 percent in this "business sector." Given that the Massachusetts Supreme Judicial Court was consistently progressive in its jurisprudence, I began to see where, just perhaps, I could use this information to mount an effective argument on Britton's behalf. Perhaps Sikes was wrong about Britton; perhaps he was motivated by something altogether more noble than what she had proposed.

***

One fine July day not long after my meeting with Britton, I went for a swim off a Cape Cod beach. I made my way out to a swimming float, climbed its ladder, and lay in the warmth of the sun for ten minutes or so, catching my breath. This sublimely peaceful moment, however, came to a sudden end when four teenage boys swam up and clambered aboard the other end of the float. They dangled their legs in the water, splashing about, and using the word "fuck" at least twice in every sentence. Their conversation bounded around from one inanity to the next until it landed on the topic of some poor bastard named Richie. Over and again, he was described as "fat," "blubbery," "a tub of lard," "the slowest runner in school," and "Mr. Wilson's pet" who "actually likes algebra." Next, they proceeded to concoct explicit plans to torture this poor fellow with exclusion—just before bellowing out cross-volleys of ludicrous dares and then cannonballing themselves back into the water and heading off toward the shore and, thankfully, out of my life.

But these boys had served a purpose. They had caused me to remember how incredibly cruel children can be, and how conspiratorial they are by nature when they get around to the business of marginalizing the odd kid out. What they had said brought Herbert Britton's story to life for me: they reminded me that, while I was handling a case that was routine from a legal point of view, it was anything but routine from a social-psychological point of view. Britton was, and apparently always had been, profoundly excluded and disconnected. This meant that while it was conceivable that I could formulate an argument for the court that Britton was a skillful, hardworking trial attorney and a constitutional hero, I also had to admit to myself that this analysis and approach failed to account for many facets of my client's character.

In fact, the more I thought about what those boys had brought to mind and the more I contemplated what approach to the court would be the wisest, the more I had to admit to myself that it might well be shrewder to petition the court's sympathy for the man as opposed to trying to elicit sympathy for a constitutional position that the court had never supported in past jurisprudence. Britton's stance, after all, challenged the entire procedural reality of how criminal law is practiced in our era.

The problem with returning to this more sober approach to the case, of course, was that it meant that I was back in the game of needing to figure out the social-psychological puzzle of just what made Britton tick, and that clearly involved trying to understand how his professional behavior was impacted by his profound and chronic loneliness. In *Les Misérables*, Victor Hugo famously taught us how hunger led an honest man to steal a loaf of bread; listening to those boys reminded me that I needed to learn what hunger's sister sensation—loneliness—had led Herbert Britton to do. Something about the piercing brightness of the sunny summer day had clarified my thinking: I was forced to admit to myself that it almost certainly wasn't wise to rely on Britton's self-understanding of what led him to practice criminal law so strikingly at odds with how all his colleagues plied the trade.

***

Clearly, it was time to bring Longfellow into the case, and garner some help from a man who, as I mentioned earlier, was at once an accomplished private eye and a master strategist. We met for lunch, and I described the complaint, the fact pattern of the case as I understood it, and what I had learned from Linda Sikes. I also described Herbert Britton in full detail, and explained my temporary infatuation with Britton's constitutional rights explanation for his aberrant mode of practicing criminal law—and my fear that that approach could blow up in my face if I argued it to the court.

At the end of my somewhat lengthy presentation, I handed Longfellow an expandable folder containing numerous files, including a transfer memorandum summarizing all that my office had learned about Britton and his law practice, and copies of the litigation spindles from all eight of the cases we were reviewing. I proposed that Longfellow's team investigate how Britton was perceived in the criminal clerks' offices of the district courts in which he practices, and also that we gather evidence on Britton's lifestyle to rebut Bar Counsel's argument that Britton's law practice was designed to maximize income. In sum, I needed to learn who Britton the person actually was—both in his personal life and in his professional practice.

Longfellow had been looking down as I spoke, diligently taking notes. When I concluded, he looked up at me, took a sip of his coffee, and then pronounced in his gentlemanly accent, "If I understand you correctly, Counselor, what you want me to do is gather information that would allow you to determine whether the motivating cause of Mr. Britton's manner of practicing criminal law is something other than his proclaimed crusade against plea bargain justice. Do I have that correct?" I nodded. "But how would I go about learning what's inside a man's head? How do you propose that I discern if what actually drives the man is some deep psychological need other than the one Ms. Sikes proposed? Please tell me."

As he had consistently done for years, Longfellow was challeng-
ing me to clarify my strategic approach to a case so that he might, in
turn, refine his investigation tactics. It was one thing to have a vague
theory about Britton derived from those teenagers on the float—a theory about rejection and disconnection as a child affecting how you
approach others throughout your life. But it was quite another thing to
translate an unarticulated hypothesis into a concrete investigative task
for a private detective.

"Well, what I had in mind was that we would do well to learn as
much as feasible about Britton's personal life. Let's take a look at who he
sees, how often, where, and for what purposes. I'll personally interview
the other two prisoners named in the complaint, but I would think
we should broaden our scope. I think it makes sense for your team to
locate some additional ex-clients; I'd like to learn how often he met
with them, and if they ever felt that he violated boundaries by either
prying or inserting himself in any way into their private lives—beyond
what was necessary to create a defense. Obviously, it's key to get as
much detail as we can about his conversations with them concerning
plea bargain offers in their cases. And it would be helpful to know if he
ever expressly described to anyone his crusade against plea bargaining—I'm baffled as to whether that is a rationalization or whether it is
the reality."

Again, Longfellow tranquilly sipped away at his coffee, thinking
through his response. "That all makes sense. But do us both a favor.
Take your plane up to twenty thousand feet and tell me what you see;
tell me about the general topography of the case—at this point—when
you look at it from altitude." When Longfellow asked questions like
this one—even though the years were passing and my hair was gray-
ing—I invariably felt like an undergraduate responding to his professor's inquiry, and that was *just fine*.

So, I gave it a try. "Let's see," I said, closing my eyes and taking a
deep, slow breath. "My take from altitude is that Bar Counsel jumped
way too fast to assert the churn-more-hours/make-more-money theory of the case. My suspicion is that whoever drafted the complaint
for the Office of the Bar Counsel proposed this 'to make more money'
theory of the case because that's what they had in mind before they
ever interviewed the three clients who submitted ethical complaint

letters. I've only spoken with one so far, Linda Sikes, but at least from what she said, the make-more-money hypothesis doesn't fit the facts—it leaves far too much unexplained. Tell me if you think I'm wrong, but in my experience, what Britton did is *not* what greedy people do. What I mean is, greedy lawyers—like other greedy people—put out as little work as possible while billing for as many hours as they can get away with. Sikes's take on Britton is that his quasi-insistence on taking her case to trial wasn't *at all* about the money: it was about the metamorphosis he experienced in the courtroom, where his trial skills transformed him from an overweight nebbish to a skillful gladiator. Why wouldn't he want as many jury trials as possible if this emanates from his underlying psychology?"

"Interesting theory," Longfellow responded, taking a moment to think through the implications. "Might I assume that, even if that were true, it would be a losing argument to use at the SJC hearing?"

"Absolutely. An attorney can't sacrifice his clients' best interests to burnish his ego by prancing around in front of a string of juries. I would never argue that—but I'd love to know if that's what's going on."

"So, what's your take on the psychology of your client at this point; do you think Sikes has thought it through correctly?"

I took in another unhurried lungful of air and exhaled just as slowly as I could, thinking over Longfellow's question. "Is she right . . . ? Is she right . . . ? This is just a hunch, Longfellow, but if I had to give an answer to your question at this point, I'd say that while Sikes's ego-trip theory explains a good deal of what we see, there are elements of Britton's behavior that aren't well explained by her theory of the case."

"Such as?"

"Such as not distinguishing between those cases that were certain losers and those where he had a chance to prevail at trial—at least on some of the counts. I don't know this, Longfellow, but I think it's safe to assume that matadors love their time in the bullring. But even so, I would think they would adapt their tactics depending on the ferocity of the bull they're facing on a particular day."

"Ah, so you've read your Hemingway. Clever lad. So, if it's not ego assuagement, then what would you propose as a more powerful explanation of what's going on here—psychologically?"

"Frankly, Longfellow, I don't have a clue. But my guess is that the key to the case lies somewhere else than where any of us have yet looked. I keep thinking of those teenage boys I told you about; how could anyone emerge from a childhood like the one Herbert had, and *not* have that play a significant role in who they become and how they interact with others?"

Longfellow allowed a small smile to flash across his lips as he transitioned back to his mentor/teacher tone of voice. "You're learning to listen, Counselor. You're learning to look beyond your law books. That's good. That's very good. You're growing into your work." He stopped again to finish his coffee. "Finally. Anything else I can try to learn for you?"

"Yes. Let's locate Britton's brother in Spokane. Britton told me they've had no meaningful interaction for twenty years. Let's see what his brother makes of their relationship—and of Herbert in general. Britton told me he had had only one childhood friend; is the brother's memory consistent with that? And let's learn what you can from the brother about Herbert's involvement with their grandfather's stamp collection; that seems to be playing some role in his psyche."

"Righto. I've got all that. Now answer one final question for me: What is your single biggest concern about this case?" I wasn't at all prepared for this question, and sat silent, flummoxed. Longfellow pushed harder. "Take your time; look deep—take a deep breath. Think about what you *feel*, not about what you know."

"Well, I know I don't want to look like an idiot in front of the Supreme Court."

"I understand that, but that's not at all what I was getting at. Go deeper. Far deeper."

I closed my eyes and tried to quiet my mind, seeking to somehow sense what I *felt*, instead of what I *thought*. I took at least a full minute, perhaps longer, to allow the petty thoughts in my mind to quiet down. And then, when they did, quite suddenly, my *feelings* about this case came rushing at me like a runaway train. I looked over at Longfellow and let the answer spew forth—almost on its own. "Holy shit, Longfellow. What I feel is *fear*! Fear that this guy could implode if he loses his bar card. If Britton's life is as empty as he says it is, he would have no support system to weather the storm—none whatsoever. Who knows what he might be capable of doing? What I fear is that I might read a headline in the *Boston Globe* about a lonely, friendless attorney blowing his brains out in a cheap rooming house. What I fear is that Britton and I could *both* really lose this case—big-time."

Longfellow just smiled without saying another word. There was at least a minute of silence between us as I gave my credit card to the waiter. Only as we were actually leaving the restaurant did Longfellow add, "Well, then, we'll just have to find a way forward. Give me a month, old chap. How long before the SJC hearing?"

"I think it's scheduled for about three months from now, but I could extend that another month or two if we end up needing the time."

"I see. I'll get you an update in about a month, then." We shook hands, and off he went. I walked back to my office wondering whether I was more concerned about my client perishing, or about the stain Britton's suicide would leave on both my reputation and my psyche. I couldn't find the answer.

***

About two weeks later, I met with Britton again. I had, by this point, learned that questions posed to Attorney Britton about what underlay his crusade needed to be posed obliquely, since he was thoroughly convinced of his constitutional heroism. Actually, I was relatively confident that he would have passed a lie detector test on the matter; it's amazing how one can be both terribly certain and utterly mistaken about why one does what one does.

One thing I insisted on and extracted from my client that day: a list of names and details about additional past clients beyond the five cases we had discovered on our own. His recall of past client names and case details was quite remarkable, even startling, and he revealed that he was still in touch with almost all of them. There was pride in his voice when he told me that he visited his incarcerated clients on a regular basis—including those for whom he was not actively processing an appeal. That registered as odd. Finally, and quite usefully, he remembered the names of nearly all the assistant district attorneys involved in the matters he listed out that day. I very much looked forward to hearing their reactions to having worked with him: *somebody* had to have the key that would unlock the mystery of Herbert Britton.

***

Just over a week after my second meeting with Attorney Britton, I was able to meet with the second of the complaining witnesses—Peter Sanders, the assailant of the elderly couple. Sanders was serving hard time at the Commonwealth's medium-security prison in Concord. Entering "MCI-Concord," as it's called, is like entering a Hollywood set of a prison. A tall wall with guard towers at the corners surrounds the facility, with razor wire coiled along the top of the wall. It is everything filmmaker Cecil B. DeMille could have asked for—except, perhaps, for the irony that it sits in the midst of one of Boston's wealthiest and most historic towns.

Inside the high walls, the atmosphere was far harsher than at the Framingham women's facility: the coldness of the steel and the austerity of the concrete were the same, but the harshness of the atmosphere was magnified a hundredfold by the pervasive ambience of raw violence. Relations of force are what men's prisons are all about—that's the medium of exchange. The administration intimidated the guards; the guards bullied the prisoners; the white prisoners intimidated the black inmates, who in turn were at loggerheads with the Hispanics. MCI-Concord, in other words, was defined not only by its high walls, iron bars, and inflexible rules—but also by an entirely separate but equally important network of prisoner-defined rules of where one could be, what one could do, and with whom one could associate. The challenge for each new prisoner was to accurately perceive where he stood in the context of both the official rules and the prisoner-defined hierarchies. Getting any of this wrong could be dangerous business. Even deadly business.

My meeting with Peter Sanders took place over a telephone through a three-inch-thick plastic window. Sanders sat across from me, alongside a dozen or so other prisoners who were each also speaking to their visitor by phone. While you couldn't hear anything from the prisoner side save what came through your phone, there was a cacophony of noise on my side of the plastic wall, and a pattern to the din. The volume in which we visitors spoke into our phones would constantly escalate—until, at a certain point, the prison guard in charge of the visitor side gave off an earsplitting, fingers-in-the-mouth whistle, after which we all restarted at a lower volume. Every ten minutes or so, the cycle would repeat itself.

Sanders took care to look and hold himself as a gentleman, even in the humility of his prison uniform. And even more wondrous, this tall, broad-shouldered man emitted nothing but gentleness. He wore his hair in a short Afro, sported scholarly-looking wire-rimmed glasses, and spoke in a voice that was so pleasant and temperate that it seemed almost mismatched with his massive frame.

I introduced myself and described how my goal was to deal with the Supreme Judicial Court on behalf of my client in such a way that it would end up supporting the efforts of all three of Britton's past clients to be granted a new trial on the basis of ineffective counsel. I explained that I had told Linda Sikes that I was investigating the possibility of an underlying psychological reason explaining Britton's universal opposition to plea bargains, and that she had opted to trust me and had been very forthcoming and helpful. And I ended by saying that I had given my word of honor to Linda Sikes that if there was any possibility of helping her case, I certainly would do so, and I was prepared to make him precisely the same promise, *on my word of honor.*

Sanders stared through the smeared plastic window. Then, for reasons I probably will never understand, he smiled ever so slightly, nodded his head yes, and joined my expanding team. "Okay. I'll accept your word. Let's give this a go."

I then told Sanders that I'd read the police report and his trial transcript but that I'd very much like to hear directly from him more about his background, about the crimes for which he had been convicted, and, especially, his take on Attorney Britton.

"To tell you my story is to tell you about my family," Sanders began. "A lot of black kids in this country grow up without fathers in their lives. Not me; I had a fabulous father—even though he died in a work accident when I was only twelve. He dug trenches for the electric company, and the walls of one gave way, crushing him and three others. But what he taught me in those twelve years has never left me—not for one moment. He was as big and strong as I am, and yet he was as soft spoken, as calm, and as kind a man as God ever made. He set my image of who I was determined to be, and of how I wanted to be seen by others. I still want to be seen like that—even in here.

"As you know from what you've read about my case, I had zero police involvement of any kind before this case—ever. That's not a big deal in some communities—probably like the one you grew up in. But it's harder for black kids from working-class neighborhoods, way harder. That's hardly a secret. Anyway, I finished up high school with a solid B average, and was never in trouble of any kind at school. Never. I'm totally aware—always have been—how extra important this is for a black man in America. If there's any trouble in a black man's life, it leads to more trouble, and if there's any jail time, it always leads to more.

"Anyway, so there I was, a solid, honest citizen of this country, forty-one years of age, with seventeen years of steady work at a first-rate lumberyard, an apartment with the rent paid on the first of every single month—never missed it once—and a fiancée who was the apple of my eye. And just as important to me, my reputation was getting to be more and more like that of my father; I treated everyone with respect and never went anywhere near drugs or alcohol or any other form of trouble. But then trouble found me all on its own.

"As you know from what you've read, some big, strong black maniac broke into a house in Dorchester about half a mile from where I lived. He beat up and terrorized the elderly Irish couple who lived there, and stole everything he could take. A week or so after this happened, the police came to my door one evening, and were quite polite. They didn't arrest me, or even make it sound like I should be worried; they just asked if I would come to the police station to answer some questions the following afternoon. I was an honest man. I had nothing to hide. I had no problem cooperating in every way. The rest is history. It turned out that the purpose of my visit was to participate in a lineup. I found myself in a lineup with seven other tall, strong black men who wore their hair in a tight Afro—like I do. I wasn't even smart enough to be worried. Well, I should have been: the elderly lady victim identified me as the perpetrator, and everything I had worked so hard for melted away like snow in the sunlight. Everything.

"Anyway, I was put on unpaid leave of absence when I told my employer of my arrest, so I qualified for a public defender, and Attorney Britton was assigned to represent me. He believed in my innocence from the moment he met me, and he put in all the time it took to interview everyone, and I do mean *everyone*, whom I identified as a potential witness. His investigation confirmed my innocence, or so we thought. There was no evidence against me whatsoever, other than the lineup identification. The footprints in the mud by the victims' broken window were smaller than mine would have been; I'm left-handed, while the male victim was punched on the left side of his face—presumably by a right-handed blow; and, of course, none of the stolen property was found in my apartment. Just as importantly, Attorney Britton had well over a dozen witnesses: my neighbors, all the local shopkeepers, and my supervisors at the lumberyard. They all swore under oath that I might be big and strong, but that I have always been of a gentle and peaceable nature. But none of it mattered: the prosecutor was out to convict a big, tall black man, and I fit the bill. I don't doubt they would have rather found the right one, but second best was to just go along with the victim's misidentification of me. It counts as a conviction, and the press goes away."

With that, Sanders fell silent, looking through the plastic divider with one of the saddest but most earnest looks I think I've ever seen. And while some vast percentage of incarcerated inmates will profess their innocence on a stack of Bibles to anyone who will listen, everything about Sanders's composure and tranquility convinced me that he was not to be disbelieved.

"I hear you, Mr. Sanders. I really hear what you have to say, and I don't doubt you for a moment. Can you give me more details about how Attorney Britton handled your case, and especially more about the offer of the plea bargain that you wrote about in your letter to the Board of Bar Overseers? How was that handled, and how was it discussed between the two of you?"

"Well, as my letter said, there was an offer to plead guilty to breaking and entering and simple assault and battery. The police prosecutor apparently had some significant doubts about my guilt, at least according to Attorney Britton. He told me that the offer was also based in part on the district attorney's worries about losing the case; after all, there was no evidence whatsoever other than the elderly lady picking me out of the lineup. And, of course, there was my completely clean police record. Attorney Britton told me that the district attorney said— off the record—that such a horrible crime like this didn't sound at all like something a first-time criminal would commit." Sanders took a momentary breather, and shook his head back and forth. "You know, whoever did this, whoever punched out these frail, elderly people . . . how can someone do something like that? I not only didn't do it, I can't even understand how someone else did it."

Sanders fell silent again, somehow looking even sadder in his empathy for the victims than he had earlier when reexperiencing his own sorrows. I prompted him out of his silence: "Mr. Sanders, can you please tell me in detail how you and Attorney Britton thought through what to do about the plea bargain offer? Who made the decision not to accept the offer?"

Sanders contemplated his response for a good ten seconds. "You'd think that would be an easy question to answer, but it's not. Remember, I knew full well that if I agreed to the deal and pled guilty, I would have publicly failed my life's goal of being a fully honorable man, like my father. On the other hand, you don't need to be a college graduate to know that black men in America need to think these things through with a different logic than do white men." He paused. "It was the toughest decision I was ever forced to make. I think what finally made the difference was how enthusiastic Attorney Britton was about my chances at trial; he talked on and on at each visit about how he had located yet another witness who would testify in my favor. He would tell me that he kept reminding the DA about his duty to disclose any evidence he intended to use against me, and how there was still nothing other than the testimony of the victim witness— her husband never claimed to have seen the perpetrator. So, I'd get pumped up at each visit, because one thing was for sure: Attorney Britton worked hard on my case, and with each visit, he became ever more important in my life."

"Why do you say that?" I asked.

"Well, my fiancée called things off after my arrest, and my mother was way too frail to visit. Attorney Britton was like a friend to me by this time. He believed in me—in my innocence. He believed me deep down in his heart of hearts. I never had any doubt about that. And his belief in my integrity and honor was as nurturing to me as the air I breathed. It got to the point where I thought the only hope I had to regain my honor, the one and only hope, was in a full acquittal."

Again, Sanders stopped, patiently waiting for another question. "Mr. Sanders, why do you say Attorney Britton was 'like a friend'? Was he friendly, or had he become a friend, if you see what I mean?"

This time Sanders didn't hesitate in the least. "He was friendly and considerate and compassionate. And he continued to visit me after the jury convicted me, and probably still would if I hadn't asked him to stop."

"Why'd you ask him to stop?"

"Because my new attorney said that I should do that; that it could come back to haunt me with respect to my motion for a new trial."

"I see. But I'd love you to answer my question as to whether you are saying that he was friendly, or that he had become a friend."

Again, Sanders took a moment of repose to consider his answer. "Well, he certainly started off as being a friendly presence. That was just his mode of dealing with others, I suppose. But did he become a friend?" Sanders took more time to think through the rhetorical question he had asked himself. And then, with a warm smile, he had an answer. "No. He didn't step over that line. We spoke only about the case—we never chatted about all the other things friends talk about. He was a hardworking attorney—friendly and supportive. And we were sort of a team in our effort, after all, and that makes teammates close for a while, doesn't it? But friends aren't friends 'for a while,' are they—friendship is all about staying linked up with each other indefinitely, don't you agree?"

"Sure I do. One more question, sir. When you think back, do you find that Attorney Britton pressured you in any way to reject the plea bargain that had been offered? Or were you free to make the choice that you thought was best for you?"

Again, no hesitation. "Pressured? I don't think so, really. But when we were thinking through what to do, I remember one conversation in which he encouraged me to make one last effort to salvage an honorable life. But . . ." Sanders's voice trailed off.

"But what?"

"But he shouldn't have. It was his job to know what a white jury was going to do to a black man in a case like mine, and to warn me about that. On the other hand, that's not entirely fair. It was my job to remember that I needed to think this through with a black man's logic. Attorney Britton was using a white man's logic—how could he not? And I should never have overlooked that, no matter how friendly and hardworking he was."

The guard's whistle this time was followed by a warning: five more minutes and visiting time was up. I looked back one last time at Sanders. His eyes had teared up, and he just sat there, staring out at me. I was enormously impressed with him, and choked up a bit when I told him, "You have my word of honor, sir. I will figure out a way to ask the Supreme Court justice to call your trial court judge. I promise you that." Sanders didn't say a word in response; he just put his left palm flat up against his side of the plastic barrier. I placed my right hand directly over his. We didn't smile. We didn't need to. I felt honored.

**

The next time I even thought about the Britton case was a good three weeks later when Longfellow called. That was one thing about a law practice, or at least my law practice: I was always working a dozen or so cases at a time, so when one folder was shut waiting for a call to come or some procedural step to occur, the case went almost entirely out of mind. I remember as a raw beginner how hard, how monumentally uncomfortable it was to handle multiple cases at the same time. And it wasn't just dealing with the content of one fact pattern at 10:00 and a completely different one at 10:20: it was often a matter of ricocheting from one extreme emotion to a completely opposite one. You might share one client's exhilaration at ten and another's despair just twenty minutes later. No wonder one of the most important functions of the Board of Bar Overseers is the program they provide to attorneys who develop alcohol problems.

**

"Counselor," Longfellow began on the phone, "I have quite a good deal of feedback for you on the Herbert Britton case. Is this a good time?"

"It is. You sound psyched."

Longfellow paused, completely taken aback. "Really?" he asked in his most proper British accent. "Sorry about that. I shall try harder to keep my emotions . . . invisible and out of my work . . . British thing, you know." I laughed. "Anyway, you might want to take this down." I grabbed a pen and pad of paper with such exuberant suddenness that I almost knocked over a full glass of water.

"To start with," Longfellow began, "your client is just as isolated as he described. We've tailed Mr. Britton on a twenty-four-seven basis since about two days after you gave me the assignment. 'No surprises' would be an accurate two-word summary. We haven't seen him get together with a soul—other than at work or chatting with a merchant as he made a purchase. He was at all times in his office, or in court, or in the room he rents in the boardinghouse. Or in transit between them.

"Secondly, when Mr. Britton was home, we sent an agent into the house posing as an exterminator. He went first to the kitchen, then to another of the tenants with a story about having to spray the house against cockroaches, and this subsequently set him up to knock on the door of Mr. Britton's room. No problem: Mr. Britton let him straight in, and went to wait in the shared kitchen. Our man got some excellent photos of the room, as you'll see when I send them over. Executive summary: there was not much to see. Certainly no evidence of any other person being involved in Britton's life. No photographs. No signs of a personal life at all, frankly: no mementos, no trophies, no travel trinkets. Stark, I should say, quite stark. The only object of any interest was the stamp collection you mentioned, as you'll see in the photographs. The stamp books fill up an entire almost-floor-to-ceiling six-shelf bookcase. My agent reported that when Mr. Britton came back into the room from the kitchen where he'd been waiting during the spraying, he had one of the stamp books under his arm. That prompted the agent to make up a story about having a brother-in-law who is a philatelist; he asked if the collection was a serious hobby for Mr. Britton. Mr. Britton replied that it had very much been when he was young, but that he hadn't expanded the collection much since the death of his father—apparently, the truly significant contributions to the collection were made by Mr. Britton's grandfather. He told the agent he was a busy attorney and hadn't had the time to do anything much with the hobby in years, but that perhaps someday he would get re-involved."

"Anything else about his private life?"

"That's about it, actually. The agent reported that when he sprayed the rooms of the remaining two tenants to perfect the con, he tried to chat them up about Mr. Britton. One of the gents didn't engage, while the other one told the agent that the tenants in the building didn't know each other, or socialize together, so far as he knew. He only knew Mr. Britton's name from the mailbox, and had only spoken with him to the extent of exchanging an occasional 'Hello, how are you?'"

"Got it. Any luck locating the brother?"

"Oh, we easily located Jeremy Britton. He lives in the center of Spokane, Washington, as you told me. I retained a fellow practitioner out there who was able to arrange for the services of a Gonzaga University social work graduate student. The agent worked with the student to cook up a staged interview with Jeremy, who was told that he had been randomly selected to earn a cash stipend of five hundred dollars if he would submit to a two-hour interview on the topic of sibling relationships in contemporary society. No problem there; he accepted at once. The interview was presented as being part of the student's master's thesis research, which was tentatively entitled 'The Changing Nature of Sibling Relationships in an Increasingly Atomized Society.' They met, they spoke for nearly two hours, and while some of the interview was padding to mask what was really going on, a lot of it was dead on point. Clever as hell, I'd say."

"Amazing setup. What did he learn?"

"No surprises. The brother confirmed that Herbert had always been a loner, even as a child. He described him, and I quote . . ." Longfellow paused as he flipped through some pages. "Ah, here it is: 'an obese, awkward, unpopular child who had no friendships as a kid.' As he phrased it, 'What you'll see now when you go interview him is what you would have seen then—overweight, out of step, and spurned by everybody.'"

"And the relationship between the two brothers?"

"Nil. Jeremy told our student researcher that the two brothers hadn't had any meaningful contact *at all* since their late father's services. When queried as to why there was so minimal a relationship between the two of them—remember that was purportedly what the study was all about—Jeremy responded that while geographical distance was certainly a factor, the reality was that even as children they had never had a meaningful relationship. Jeremy reported that he knows next to nothing about Herbert's current life, except that he is an attorney. He said he initiates a ten-minute phone call between them about once a year, and that he fills in Herbert on the status of his children, while Herbert never adds anything at all about his own personal life—quite precisely, and again I quote, 'because there's nothing to add. He doesn't have one.' Jeremy said his two children have no relationship whatsoever with their uncle—in fact, they don't even know him, except for meeting him at their grandfather's funeral. Jeremy disparaged Herbert for living in a rooming house, and in general was entirely disdainful about Herbert's lifestyle. He knows nothing about Herbert's nonwork activities, his hobbies, and so on. Jeremy said they had had no disputes about dividing up the father's property. There wasn't really very much, and the only thing Herbert wanted was their father's stamp collection. Apparently, the one and only moment of anything even approaching inter-sibling warmth in the interview came up on this topic. Jeremy said that Herbert's interest in the stamp collection was, without question, linked to some lovely times he had had working with their father on the stamp books."

"Learn anything about Herbert's relationship with his parents—I mean, other than the stamp story?"

"Yes indeed. Jeremy described how their mother was openly and unrelentingly critical of Herbert's weight issues. The obesity issue was obviously front and center in the household, essentially on a daily basis. When Jeremy was asked, 'How did *you* feel about having an obese brother?' he responded: 'I hated it. I was embarrassed as hell in front of my friends; I never once included Herbert in what I was doing. I never even called him Herbert until we were adults; his nickname was Tubster. Even our mother called him that occasionally when she was particularly fed up with him—like when she caught him with a bag of chips or some such. His refusal to stay on a diet was a nonstop battle between the two of them.'"

I was impressed. "Productive interview technique, don't you think?"

"It's more than that, Counselor: apparently there was a stunning collateral outcome to the staged interview. My colleague told me that the graduate student who did this work for us told him that he'd been casting about for a research topic for his master's thesis. Apparently, after this interview, he decided to do his *actual* research work on the status of contemporary sibling relationships. Your law case may have launched the next Sigmund Freud."

"Righto," I replied with a laugh, trying to imitate Longfellow's accent. "What else? How about your investigation around the court-houses; find anything interesting?"

Longfellow described how the fellow attorneys among whom Britton practiced were dismissive of him. One was quoted as saying he "hadn't seen the fat-ass around lately." Another among them, however, was rather more generous. He told the agent that he felt sorry for Mr. Britton and understood how hard it was for him. "I have a quote from this attorney here . . . somewhere . . . um . . . here it is: 'I feel for the guy because I have an obese sister, and her entire life has been so hard for her. Never a boyfriend, never even a really close friend—just evenings and nights by herself, and lots, and lots, and lots of television.' So," Longfellow continued, "no surprise: Britton was seen by three of his colleagues as the odd guy out, the courthouse rebel—the one and only attorney who bucked the plea bargain system."

Longfellow finished his report with some remarkable statistics. Apparently, Britton had visited the prison during the past year more than twice as often as the second-place attorney (on a per client basis) and nearly four times as often as the average listed attorney. Moreover, since there were both check-in and checkout times recorded for each visit in the logbooks—which are public record—Longfellow had gleaned that Britton's average visit was just over twice as long as the average visit of other attorneys. This was hard data. I just needed to figure out if it meant anything more than what we already knew—and what had been stipulated to in the complaint—that Britton was a diligent, hardworking advocate.

***

William McDermott was the third and final client of Attorney Britton whose case was described in the complaint. I had reserved McDermott as the final interview of the three prisoners because there was such an appreciable amount of preparation I needed to do prior to interviewing the young man.

McDermott was slogging through ten long years in prison for statutory rape—in some significant part, thanks to the legal antics of Attorney Britton. His mishandling of this case seemed even more egregious than that of the Sikes and Sanders cases. McDermott was—or had been—an eighteen-year-old freshman at Massachusetts Institute of Technology. So far as I know, you have to be positively brilliant in math and the hard sciences to be admitted.

McDermott's troubles began one warm spring evening late in his first year at MIT when he met a young woman a mile down Massachusetts Avenue in Harvard Square. Smiles led to a conversation, the conversation led to a hamburger at Mr. Bartley's Gourmet Burgers, which, in turn, led to a walk back to his apartment. A little pot, a little sex, a little cab ride to drop her off at her home, and everything seemed fine. What a lovely evening. That is, until there was a knock on his door at about two a.m. It turned out that his ladylove still lived at home and that her parents had not only waited up for her but had coerced her into telling the full story of what had happened that evening—first to them, and then to the Cambridge police.

It seemed that the young lady in question was six weeks shy of turning sixteen—the age of consent in Massachusetts. She apparently was well known to the police as a regular fixture at Harvard Square, where, most summer nights, she was invariably found provocatively dressed, her hair dyed in a rainbow of colors, and her arms ablaze with vibrant tattoos. She was habitually glued to the body of one musician or another, begging passersby for spare change that they would subsequently divide between the two of them.

Because the girl was under sixteen, the fact that she went voluntarily back with McDermott to his apartment was legally irrelevant. So was the fact that she was far more sexually experienced than he was, and that it was *she* who'd asked if he had any pot they could smoke.

She had readily told the police that it was she who'd initiated their lovemaking. But none of these facts mattered in the least: he was guilty of statutory rape, *as a matter of law*. This meant there was essentially no permissible jury involvement whatsoever as to his legal culpability, and hence no way to appeal to a jury's sense of fairness. The statute required the Commonwealth to place in evidence exactly two things: her age, and the fact that there was penetration. Period. Case over. Given that McDermott had admitted to the police that they had had sex, and that there was also rape-kit confirmation of the act, this was the *last case* that should ever have been taken to trial. It was literally impossible to achieve acquittal.

Worse still, McDermott's problems didn't end with his conviction. A violation of this statute is classified as an "unnatural and lascivious act with a child less than sixteen," which, by statute, rendered McDermott a sexual offender. Accordingly, McDermott would be required to register *for twenty years* as a sex offender with the Massachusetts Sex Offender Registry Board. Registration can be a life-changing requirement because landlords and employers have access to the registry for "level two" and "level three" offenders. Thankfully, because the difference in age between McDermott and the girl was only three years, there was no chance of a level-three registration outcome. But what was *critical* in the case was to hold the registration to level one, where there is no dissemination of registration information to the public.

Longfellow reported that both the police prosecutor and the assistant district attorney told his investigator that they had been crystal clear about this distinction with Attorney Britton. Because the girl was nearly of age, and because of the modest difference in their ages, coupled with the fact that it was undisputed that she had consented— even initiated—the entire matter, a very attractive plea bargain deal had been offered. In exchange for a plea of guilty to the statutory rape charge, the prosecution was willing to recommend to the court three important concessions. First, they would ask the court to overlook the fact that McDermott had supplied marijuana to the victim, which by statute can be an "aggravating" factor calling for a harsher sentence. Second, and even more importantly, they would recommend that the court find McDermott to be only a level-one offender. And third, they were prepared to ask the court to minimize prison time in exchange for a prolonged probation term. Britton was gambling with McDermott's entire future by encouraging the young man to turn down this offer in favor of going to trial. In this case, it was crystal clear that Britton's crusade made no sense whatsoever, given the statutory scheme. Longfellow reported that the assistant district attorney who prosecuted the case had told his agent that she had been "shocked" by Britton's intransigence. He had insisted—on behalf of McDermott— that while he would agree to stiff probationary terms being placed on his client, the prosecution needed to agree to "minimal imprisonment." Britton seemed convinced that he could convince the court of this in the sentencing phase of the trial. The ADA who had tried the case told Longfellow's agent, and I quote her, "Attorney Britton kept repeating, 'The girl is a slut. Why do you want to ruin a brilliant MIT student's life?' I never understood why he showed such complete disregard for the controlling statutory limitations on what I could possibly do or recommend to the court. His position was irresponsible."

I was appalled at learning Attorney Britton's performance in the McDermott case. There was never any hope of an outcome in the case better than what was being offered by the ADA—and it was folly to hope the judge would go light on McDermott's sentencing without the ADA's recommendation having been prearranged. Given what was at stake—registration as a level-two sex offender—Britton's strategy was totally imprudent. It wasn't even rational, because level-two offenders suffer additional indignities beyond public access to their sexual offender record, including being required to report in person on an annual basis to their local police station to update all their required information. So, for no defensible reason, Attorney Britton had gambled with McDermott's young life, and lost.

***

I was not looking forward to meeting Mr. McDermott on the early fall day I drove back out to the men's prison at Concord. After all, I was defending the attorney who had so monumentally bungled the handling of his case. I wouldn't have blamed him at all for lambasting me as a stand-in for his nemesis. But that was not at all what happened once I was processed through those six massive steel doors, thoroughly frisked, and eventually led to the nasty plastic wall with its telephone booths.

It was impossible not to like Bill McDermott the moment he came in to sit across from me. He was a tall, blond, good-looking young man, with bright, inquisitive hazel eyes and a smile that wouldn't quit. There wasn't a hint of hardness or meanness or resentment to the young man.

McDermott spoke so slowly and so quietly at the beginning of our interview that I actually asked him if the facility had him on Valium or some equivalent medication. "No, sir, it's just that I'm so depressed I can barely talk—or even breathe. When I wake up each morning—usually from wild dreams—I can barely get my body up off the bed. What's the point? I feel like cement, like I weigh a thousand pounds. I feel like my life is over. All my plans, all my hopes: they're all gone now. It's like I'm a dead man, barely walking." It was crushing to look through the smeared plastic window at this sweet-natured youngster whose legal troubles had been so significantly magnified by Attorney Britton's war against plea bargaining.

I had the same reaction that I had experienced with the other two victims of my client's private crusade: I knew from the moment I met McDermott that I would be telling him at some point in the interview that even though my job was to defend Britton, I fully intended to find a way to plead with the Supreme Court justice who would hear the case to call the trial court judge who would be considering his motion for a new trial. So, once again, I laid out the same promise I had made to Linda Sikes and Peter Sanders. This time, however, my offer was no surprise: McDermott had discussed my upcoming visit with his counsel. "My new attorney thinks you can be really helpful, and I'd be so grateful. It's my only ray of hope. But it's hard to get too excited and optimistic because the best of outcomes involves my pleading guilty and my registration as a level-one offender." A piteous sigh escaped the boy. "But that's way better than what I've got now. But my life will still be a car wreck."

"Yes, that's true, Bill, but car wrecks vary," I shot back. "Sometimes your car is totaled, and sometimes your car is dented—but drivable. Best car I ever had was full of dents, and I do mean *full of dents*." McDermott looked back at me with the tiniest of little smiles. I couldn't resist returning it. "If I can pull this thing off and be helpful to you, I'm going to come back out here to visit you and tell you that story."

"Deal," McDermott replied, sharing another smile with me.

"Bill, I don't mean to make light of what you're going through. To be honest with you, I can't even conceive how you do manage to get up out of that bed you were talking about. But I'm enough older than you to assure you that, at some points in most people's lives, damage control is the only option."

McDermott paused. "All right, let's give it a go. I don't want to sit around a decade from now and regret not having done whatever I could to make things better, even incrementally better."

For the next ten minutes or so, McDermott explained how Britton had impressed him with his enthusiasm, attentiveness, and devotion to his case. He said that Britton had interviewed the girl and that she had been completely open about the sex being entirely voluntary, about her not having been anywhere near a virgin at the time, and even about how McDermott had been gentle and considerate of her. She had told Britton that she would supply an affidavit, or testify, and that the last thing she wanted was for McDermott to be so terribly penalized because she had lied about her age. This last admission was gratuitous on her part, and very helpful, or so Britton had asserted. McDermott quoted Britton as having said to him after learning this, "What's a guy supposed to do, ask for a driver's license?"

McDermott responded to my questions about how he and Britton handled their deliberations on whether or not to accept the plea bargain that was offered. He said that there had indeed been multiple discussions with Britton about the pluses and minuses of the tendered deal. But he also reported that Britton had never made clear to him the important consequences of the differing levels of sex-offender registration. On top of that, McDermott was certain that another important aspect of the case had *never* been explained to him: namely, that Britton would be disallowed by the court *as a matter of law* from arguing to the jury the two principal facts that sounded so strongly in his favor—first, that the girl was only six weeks shy of the age of consent, and second, that she had lied about her age. On the contrary, McDermott's understanding was that these important facts could indeed be argued, and, as he put it, "This was one of the reasons I got swept up in Britton's

enthusiasm to take the case to trial." This last wording was disturb-
ingly similar to phrases used by both Sikes and Sanders.

Toward the end of the interview, I asked McDermott how he
thought Britton construed their working relationship. He answered
with no hesitation. "Attorney Britton was more than my attorney. He
became my ally and my friend at the worst time in my life. My parents had come across the country to see me, of course, but they have
busy lives of their own in San Diego. And after the trial, we were all
so uncomfortable with each other that nobody knew what to say. My
folks are not sophisticated people; my dad's a tailor, and my mom is
a secretary in an accounting office. I was only able to come to MIT
because I won a full scholarship. I don't think my parents could really
distinguish between 'rape' and 'statutory rape,' and my father told me
outright that he thought I'd taken advantage of the young girl, and told
me how thoroughly disappointed he was in me. And neither of them
had had any idea that I smoked pot, so that was another wall that we
suddenly found between us. They left the day after the trial, crushed by
my having wasted the remarkable opportunity I'd been given to make
something interesting of my life. They went back to their own lives—
back to experience shame and embarrassment in front of their siblings
and friends. They've sort of written me off. It's their way of dealing with
all the pain and disappointment I brought them. I can't even blame
them."

Trying my best to not sound choked up, and irrationally hoping to
learn something that might balance what I just heard, I asked if he had
other visiting resources, only to learn, again using McDermott's wording: "My MIT classmates ditched me like a hot potato; not a single one
has come out here to visit me. Not one. And I don't know anyone else
in Boston. I had just moved here to go to school. I cried for the first two
weeks like a five-year-old." He paused, sinking into his despair.

"And then?"

"And then along came Attorney Britton, with his upbeat confidence in what he could do for me. He knew all the facts from the police
report by then, and he had already made an appointment to interview
the girl. And he was so generous with his time. He came to see me tons
of times; can you imagine what that meant to me, locked up in here all
alone? He took pity on me; he was gentle with me. He took the time to

do the law work on my case, but he also was concerned about me as a person. I know my new attorney says it was malpractice for Attorney Britton to tempt me to reject the plea bargain and take my case to trial, and that I should be furious at him, but that's hard for me. We had a real bond with each other throughout those months—we were comrades in arms. That's a powerful bond, you know, when you're fighting alongside someone. To have a friend who . . ." But his voice tailed off, and there were no more words, just one single tear that snuck out of his right eye and crept slowly down his still almost whiskerless cheek.

It was time to say something sage and even paternal, something soothing and reassuring. But when I began, I found that my voice was now so choked with emotion, and my mind so racing with thoughts, that I was forced to clear my throat quite a few times. Bill McDermott sat across from me, patiently waiting for me to collect myself. It was so unthinkably painful to look through the plastic window at this handsome young man . . . And then, in the midst of feeling so emotionally distraught and so minimally professional, I was overtaken by an idea that bubbled up from somewhere deep, deep inside my mind—who knows, perhaps because I *had* been more emotional than rational. "Bill, I just had a sort of . . . a sort of revelation about something you said. I can shut up and leave, if you'd prefer. You've already told me what I came out here to learn about my client."

"No, no. Don't leave. I want to hear what you have to say."

"Can you keep what I say between just the two of us for the time being?"

"I will, I swear."

I thought for a moment, trying to get my arms around my vaguely composed new concept. I knew it wasn't good practice to speak candidly with one of the complaining witnesses about my own client, but I needed McDermott to help me work through my fledgling idea.

"Bill, do you think it could be that Attorney Britton replaces the work of striking out in life to make friends with the notion that his clients *have become his friends*? I mean, I'm beginning to think he allowed himself to ignore the difference between having a friendly professional relationship with his clients, and having his clients be understood by him *to actually be his personal friends*. And what prompts me to even ask this question is that I don't think he has any personal friends."

"Attorneys can't be friendly with their clients?" McDermott shot back at me. "That makes no sense. His friendship saved my sanity; I already told you my family was clearly separating itself from me and moving on."

"No, no, Bill. That's not what I mean. Anybody can be friendly with other people they deal with. That's an important part of life—a wonderful part of life. But's that's different from *being* friends." It was only when I said this out loud that the full implication of what I was saying started becoming clearer to me. "You see, Bill, in a sense, attorneys are not allowed to do the latter—to become actual friends with their clients—by our code of ethics. The code is express and crystal clear—but it's written with only sex in mind. It says that if a lawyer and a client fall for each other and want to have sex, the lawyer *must first successfully refer the law case out* of his or her office to another law firm. Only after that has been fully accomplished can they begin their sexual relationship. That's a perfect analogy, don't you agree? The relevance of that ethical canon for this case . . . I see it now . . . it's perfectly clear. It's not the *sexual* element of that canon of our code of ethics that's key; it's the *personal relationship* part. Does that make sense?" I could tell by his furled brow and doubtful look that he didn't at all follow what I was saying, so I rephrased my point. "Let me put it another way for you, as a question. Do you think Britton could have crossed that line with you? In other words, do you think when he came to see you, to spend time with you, he came to visit you *as a personal friend*?"

McDermott expressed himself carefully. "No. Every single time he came, we worked on my case. We didn't talk about sports or what was in the news or whatever. We always worked on my case. Every single time. I'm sure of that. I agree with you—it would have been weird as hell if he'd come to visit me *as his friend*, and we just chatted or played cards. But that's not what happened. Each and every visit, we worked on my case—only on my case. And, yes, he was friendly to me in the process. But why shouldn't he have been friendly? What's wrong with being friendly, with forming and enjoying a bond between client and counsel? His friendship and emotional investment in my case meant *so much* to me, especially after my parents left me to rot away in here all alone. So, to be perfectly honest with you, no, I don't think you're making any sense."

There was no way I was giving up so soon. "Let me try again, Bill; I know I'm not expressing this new idea in the right words. Think of it this way, Bill. Professional relationships require a certain distance, a certain . . . remove. The classic example I suppose would be the surgeon who shouldn't operate on his own child. I don't really know if this old adage is even true—but I can see why a surgeon who loves his patient might be distracted, or overly cautious, or too nervous—or I don't know what. But it just seems like it would make no sense for the surgeon to perform the operation if another equally competent doctor were available, because it adds a level of . . . complexity . . . to the surgery that isn't there when the patient is a stranger. Maybe this is a dumb metaphor, and not helpful."

"I follow it, though, no problem," McDermott responded. "But I don't see how it relates to my case."

"No, I don't either. Let me try again. Bill, what I fear is—and this is the first time I've ever thought this through, so help me here, if you can. What if Herbert Britton is not actually a dedicated crusader against plea bargaining—what if the crusade is just a rationalization? What if what's really going on here is that Britton—lonely Herbert Britton— doesn't want to let a client disappear out of his life any sooner than he absolutely has to? What if he wants—what if *he emotionally needs*—his clients to stay connected to him for as long as possible—regardless of what this does to their cases?"

I paused for at least ten seconds—and I could see that McDermott was frozen as well. "Bill, that's it," I jumped back in. "That's fucking it! That fits so perfectly with another piece of the puzzle. He said he hadn't thought about how his work and private lives were so identical: he had no connections with anyone in either setting. Bill, that means he's in complete denial of how profoundly lonely he is. And he enables his denial by experiencing his attorney-client relationships as if he were involved in affective friendships—whereas all three of you clients experienced your attorney-client relationship as professional relationships. Do you see the dis-parallel? Am I making myself at all clear? And, Bill, if this still makes sense . . . if I can argue this, it's perfect for your case as well."

There was another period of silence. Fully fifteen or twenty seconds later, McDermott got what I was saying. "I see what you mean, now. At first, it sounded like splitting hairs—but I think I see where you're going with this. I mean, you—you're an attorney too—you must experience the other side of the coin: What does it feel like to you when you finish working with a client after a long case, and they say thanks and you never see them again?"

"Yes! That's the dispositive question, isn't it? Let me answer it: I may *miss* dealing with a client, but it doesn't *diminish* me, like when a friend moves away. It's completely different—I don't dwell on it; I don't think much about it, actually."

Slowly, the first full smile I'd seen from McDermott broke out across his young face, and that smile came bursting right through that dingy, dirty, thick plastic window that no bullet could penetrate. McDermott just sat there seeming to give the idea one final run-through, and then just said in a thoughtful tone of voice: "I think you've nailed it . . . Keep working on it. I'm not going to mention it to my new attorney or anyone else, per our understanding. But keep working on it. I can easily see how you could use it to help my case."

In the silence that followed, a guard took the opportunity to come over to nicely indicate to McDermott that time was up. I just stared through the plastic until the boy was out of sight.

***

Needless to say, I was in an animated and distracted state of mind when I left Concord to drive back to my Boston office. The more I thought about it, the more confident I became that Britton had crossed the line that lies at the heart of the code of ethics proscription. There was—if I had this right—another level at play in Britton's psyche that even he wasn't aware of. But whether Britton was aware of why he did what he did was another matter altogether, and I wasn't particularly convinced that it even mattered.

***

I spent the next several weeks obsessed with trying to think this thing through, without a centimeter of progress. The hearing was now just over six weeks away, and I didn't even have a *hint* of a promising strategy that could make use of what I thought I had finally figured out.

In the middle of the following week, I was scheduled to meet an eighty-five-year-old, particularly charming, long-term Beacon Hill Brahmin client of mine for what would undoubtedly be the tenth minuscule revision of her estate planning. Each summer, she would call my office, schedule a luncheon appointment with me through my administrative assistant, and reserve us an outside patio table at what was then Boston's premier French restaurant, Maison Robert. On the appointed day, I arrived a tad early for our luncheon. This was before the advent of cell phones, so I took a seat at our table, ordered a glass of my favorite white wine—Sancerre—and looked through the menu. Actually, it was that glass of white wine that found the key to the case—not me. It gets credit, first, because it was so enjoyable that my very first sip broke me out of the grind-away-on-the-problem frame of mind that was getting me nowhere. But the Sancerre did much, much more than that.

As I left the office, I had stuck half a dozen letters in my coat pocket. Now I had the chance to glance them over during my wait. One personal letter and five . . . others. I propped the personal one on my wineglass, looked briefly at the others, and pocketed them. Now to the fun one—the letter from my law school classmate who practiced international law in Hong Kong. As I reached out to pick up her letter, the wine in my glass diffracted a ray of sunlight directly onto the letter's exotic stamp, highlighting its bright colors and causing its lively engraving to sparkle in the refracted light—just for a moment. I froze. *Of course!* The family stamp collection! It was the *only thing* other than practicing law in Britton's life, and there had to be some way to leverage it to his advantage. It suddenly dawned on me that perhaps the best outcome to the case had nothing at all to do with convincing the court not to terminate my client's license to practice law. Perhaps an entirely different solution was called for. It was time to think outside the box.

***

I wasn't back at work for a full minute before I called Longfellow's office, and an hour later, I had him on the phone, going on and on about my germ of an idea. He was stone silent for half a minute before he finally brought a full smile to my face. "Good boy. From the wine-glass. You *are* learning."

Longfellow knew no more about stamps and stamp collecting than I did, but he took on the assignment of exploring if we could some-how leverage Britton's stamp collection into a springboard of some sort. And, indeed, just four days after I introduced the idea to him, Longfellow called back. He had quickly learned from a local stamp and coin dealer that a large stamp collection that goes back two genera-tions is very likely to be somewhat of a gold mine. As most of Boston's stamp and coin shops were located on or near Bromfield Street, only a five-minute walk from my office, Longfellow suggested that I stop by to see a certain William Hayes, who owned and ran one of these shops, the Bay State Stamp and Coin Company.

***

William Cunningham Hayes was a sturdy-looking, white-haired gen-tleman whom I took to be in his midseventies. He sported a quite remarkable pair of still-black eyebrows that for some reason refused to follow suit. But it wasn't their color that made these particular eye-brows so noticeable: it was their fullness. These puppies would have kept his cheeks dry had we met outside in the drizzle. When I intro-duced myself, he knew precisely who I was from the conversation he had had with Longfellow.

"Mr. Hayes," I said once we were seated in the back of his shop, "I have a proposition for you with respect to the stamp collection that Mr. Brooke described."

"And what might that be?" he responded, his left eyebrow shooting partway up his wrinkled forehead.

I took just a moment trying to think through how I might plot with this gentleman while preserving my client's privilege and, for that mat-ter, his dignity. "Mr. Hayes, I have a client who is himself an attorney. For health reasons, this gentleman needs to transition away from the trials and tribulations of practicing law." Hayes laughed in a pleasant and alluring way. "Sorry; inadvertent pun," I apologized. "Anyway, sev-eral of us who are involved with my client feel strongly that we would be doing him a great service if we could preplan something construc-tive for him to do after his transition."

At this point, I leaned forward in my chair, engaging Mr. Hayes squarely in the eyes. "This, sir, is where you might come in. We have only quite recently generated the idea that perhaps if my client were to take up work centered around his lifelong hobby of stamp collecting, he could move on from the tensions of practicing trial law to a health-ier, calmer way of life. What we are looking for is a professional phi-latelist like yourself who could . . . guide my client through this career change. But let me begin with a question, and not an assumption: Was Mr. Brooke's impression correct that you personally own this shop, and that your business is linked into a network of collectors, stamp shows, the buying and selling of rare stamps, and so on?"

"Yes, precisely. That is what I told Mr. Brooke; everything you listed is quite accurate. I am seventy-seven years old, and I've been enthralled with stamps since I was five. Five or six; I'm not sure. In fact—and I don't mean to boast, but this seems relevant information for you—I currently hold the office of vice president of the American Stamp Dealers Association. The association organizes three or four stamp shows a month—all over the country."

"Mr. Hayes, may I speak with you candidly, confidentially?"

"You may, indeed," he replied, sitting up straight in his chair.

"What we're looking for is someone in your profession who would work behind the scenes to introduce my client into the world of stamp shows, stamp dealing, and so on . . . Mr. Brooke and I don't want my cli-ent to know that we are . . . how to say this . . . facilitating his transition. You see, Mr. Hayes, our client is a bit of a recluse, and an overweight fellow, and we fear that if he does decide to retire or ease out from the practice of law and is left to his own devices, he'll not get out into the world enough to make new contacts, make new friends—make new connections. Perhaps we're way off base, Mr. Hayes, but Mr. Brooke and I feel that if we help arrange for his introduction into the world of stamps, our client might well thrive. And, frankly, I can't imagine a more clever way for him to make use of his family stamp collection—he has no children to leave them to. Be honest with me, sir—am I mak-ing *any* sense here whatsoever?"

In the most enthusiastic voice Hayes could marshal, he replied with apparent delight, "Indeed, you are, sir. And to be frank with you in return, you can't possibly conceive how interested I am in taking a look at a bookshelf-size, untapped, three-generation-old collection of stamps. So, how can I help—concretely, I mean?"

"My proposition is that I retain your services in this matter so that you can afford to invest some time in linking up with this fellow—*if* I can convince him of the wisdom of such a career change. I haven't even mentioned this idea to him yet." I paused to think up a strategy. "What if I offered to pay you a hundred dollars an hour up to a total of five thousand dollars to meet with the collection owner, invite him to your shop, invite him to work here part-time, or attend one of the shows you help organize to help man your booth—or whatever else you can think of to get him up and running in the field of stamps."

Mr. Hayes's reply was matched by his body language. "This sounds like something I would do with anyone who has an impressive old collection to work with. Why do you want to pay me?"

"Because if this works out, I would want your serious attention to the matter, and until and unless a modest income can flow to my client through sales of some of his stamps, I'd like to see him offered even a little part-time employment here in your shop on an interim basis. He's a man with a very modest lifestyle, so he really wouldn't need to earn very much. You aren't, by any chance, looking to hire an assistant, are you?"

Hays responded with a shrug of his shoulders; I was clearly pressing him too far.

"Tell you what, Mr. Hayes. Let's start with my five-thousand-dollar investment in putting the two of you together. Perhaps there's enough financial value to the collection to pick up after that. If not, we'll cross that bridge when we get to it. Are you interested in joining me in this little project?"

"Yes, let's. I'd like to give it a try," Hayes replied with marked enthusiasm.

"Could we possibly get started soon?" I added. "We think a quick transition might well make my client's upcoming retirement quite a bit more palatable to him."

Hayes took the better part of a minute to think through what was being proposed, and I could see from his changing expressions—those eyebrows told all—that several different thoughts were running through his mind. Finally, he spoke up. "To begin with, when you're seventy-seven, 'soon' is the only time frame that makes sense. And to be honest, I can use the up-front money you mentioned—and I could also use some help running this shop. Currently, I have to close it down when I go to the shows. But there is one assurance I need in return."

"And that would be?"

"If your client's collection turns out to be of little or no interest, or if he and I don't get along with one another, how do I get out of this?"

"You'll call me up, and we'll talk. I'll be available to help work out any issues that might arise, and if what is needed is a peaceful and graceful end to the venture, I'll make that happen as well. Is that assurance enough?" Hayes nodded yes.

"Okay, then. You'll deal from this point forward on financial matters with Mr. Brooke—although you can always call me with a question or a problem. Do you mind if I tell my client that I just wandered into your shop after lunch today, and when you and I spoke, I happened to mention that I had a client who was quite a philatelist? I'd like to add that, in response, you asked me to have him stop by, because you're thinking about the possibility of hiring a bit of part-time help."

"That's just fine, Counselor. I can't exaggerate how fascinated I am to see his collection; an unmined three-generation-old collection has never come my way before, and it could easily contain stamps of some appreciable value. Anyway, I have to tell you, I find this entire idea rather exhilarating; the last time I was involved in anything quite so conspiratorial was . . ." Here, Mr. Hayes paused a good five seconds for dramatic effect, and then, raising that left eyebrow even higher than I had understood it could ascend, he added, "Never." We both laughed.

"There's one other thing," I appended. "All the conversations and details that go on between you and my client will be completely private; I in no way want to invade my client's privacy, if this moves ahead. All that Mr. Brooke and I are trying to do is to increase the odds that my client will make a smooth transition into work based on a hobby he loves."

"Yes, I totally agree about a privacy wall. Consider it to be in place."

"Wonderful, Mr. Hayes," I said, standing to leave. "Mr. Brooke will contact you later today if I can reach him, or tomorrow at the latest. Good luck, sir. You may just save a soul here—and find a future business partner to boot. Who knows? Thank you, sir."

I left the little stamp and coin shop to find that bright sunshine had followed the drizzle I had walked through on the way over. That's the nature of living next to the sea: the weather in Boston can transition in a heartbeat. So, hopefully, could Herbert Britton.

**

I harbored high hopes that my scheme would contribute to producing an alternative and better-connected future for Herbert Britton— as well as producing an opening to help his three ex-clients. But the scheme had its flaws, including the possibility that, if Britton insisted, I would have no option but to argue the crusade-against-plea-bargaining theory of the case. The problem in doing so came into particularly sharp focus two days later when my associate attorney presented me with the two charts he was preparing for the hearing. The first chart unambiguously demonstrated that Britton had billed for *less than half* of the actual hours he had put into the three cases—hardly the mark of a greedy man out to maximize his law fees. The second chart graphically depicted Britton's prison visitation record: it showed that Britton was present at the two prisons far more often—and for far longer visits—than any other attorney (per client), and it also showed that he billed for less than one-third of all those prison visitation hours. This data would blow Bar Counsel's "greed" argument out of the water and deeply undermine their case against my client. What a bizarre piece of litigation this had mutated into: it looked more and more like I had the evidence to deliver a courtroom victory that would end up producing an abysmal outcome for everyone involved.

Worse still, the three clients had each affirmed that they had indeed discussed with Attorney Britton the pros and cons of accepting or rejecting the plea bargains that had been offered, which clearly fulfilled the relevant ethical standard in the Massachusetts Rules of Professional Conduct, Rule 1.4(b). Rule 1.4(b) required only that "a lawyer shall explain a matter to the extent reasonably necessary to

permit the client to make informed decisions regarding the representation." Britton's lobbying for them to accept the risk and grab for the
golden ring of acquittal at trial didn't, at least to my mind, constitute
a violation of the rule—except perhaps in the McDermott case, where
arguably there was no ring to grab. It certainly was a one-off moment:
here I was dismayed, even distressed, at learning that the admissible
evidence was too strongly in my client's favor. How in the world was I
ever going to manage to lose this case?

***

The more I thought about the matter, the more convinced I became
that the best outcome for my client was for him to settle his dispute
with Bar Counsel. My problem—above and beyond the daunting task
of talking the crusader-against-settlement into accepting a settlement
of his own matter—was that any such settlement would necessarily
involve a suspension of his license for some agreed-upon term. How
was Britton going to fund his living expenses in the interim? It seemed
like Mr. Hayes couldn't pay him much more than I was willing to chip
in, and who knew if Britton's grandfather had purchased and saved
truly valuable stamps? I now knew strategically what I wanted to do
with the case, but I had absolutely no idea how to accomplish it on a
practical level.

A few days later, everything came to a head. I had just returned
from a court hearing and was sifting through a pile of pink phone message slips when I saw that the clerk of the Supreme Judicial Court had
called and left a message. Mr. Britton's hearing was scheduled for late
the following week. So, now one thing was eminently clear: whatever
strategy I was going to pursue needed to be finalized at once so that
definitive tactical preparations could be commenced without delay.

The phone notes had been paper-clipped to a memorandum from
our office manager. It announced that there would be a cake-and-coffee
event that Friday for a litigation paralegal who was leaving our office
to get married. The word "paralegal" rang out like a bell in my head.
Years earlier, I had represented an attorney in her effort to appeal a
denial of her application to regain admission to the Massachusetts Bar
Association. In her case, I had been able to negotiate an accommodation

with Bar Counsel whereby the court would deny her appeal, but expressly invite her to reapply five years later—and, in the interim, she would be allowed to work as a paralegal. *Bingo.*

With this in mind, I telephoned Alice Yang, the young, third-year attorney at the Office of the Bar Counsel whom I had been told was my contact person. I asked her if Bar Counsel had any interest in meeting to discuss a possible settlement of the matter that would involve suspension in lieu of disbarment, with the express right for Britton to work as a paralegal during the suspension period. She phoned back twenty minutes later to say that her supervisor, whom she described as the author of the complaint, was "absolutely not interested" but that he would be pleased for all of us to meet to discuss the logistics of reassigning Britton's current cases to other law offices. I jumped at this opportunity to hold the meeting.

Step two in the process was to set up a meeting with the office manager and the then-serving chairman of my law firm—a thankless position I myself had recently escaped from after nearly a decade. I presented the idea that we could potentially replace the departing paralegal with a fully experienced trial attorney who, while on suspension, would expressly be allowed to serve as a paralegal. His work ethic, I was able to assert, was a twelve on a scale of ten. While we all agreed that there would be a host of details to think through, interviews to be scheduled, and so forth, both the office manager and the chairman saw an interesting possibility in the concept—experienced litigation paralegals were very few and far between.

Now, it was time to call Britton. I began by telling him about our rapidly approaching hearing date, about my upcoming settlement discussions with Bar Counsel, and about my needing him to come in to my office the following morning to discuss an important element of case strategy. The last words I left him with—quite on purpose—were, "Herbert, I want you to come in tomorrow with an open mind, *a very open mind.* I have a quirky idea that might resolve everything."

When he arrived the next day, after only the most minimal greeting, I jumped right in. "Herbert, I need you to listen carefully, because I may have found a way to completely remove the gamble of your being disbarred. So, here is my question for you. Could you live with the following, *if I can get it*: a suspension of your license for two years with the right to work as a paralegal in the interim, coupled with a paralegal position here at my firm, where I'm sure your salary would be at least as much as your net take-home from your law practice—possibly more?" Britton winced at the idea, emphatically shook his head no, and started to lift himself out of the chair. I held up both hands with my palms facing him, and said in a tone you would use with a horse, "Whoa there, whoa. Open mind, remember?" He plopped back down, looking exasperated. "What worries me, Herbert, is that your law practice is all about counseling your clients to refuse the criminal law equivalent of a settlement—and here I am trying to talk you into a settlement. Frankly, Herbert, I've put a lot of time into your case, and a lot of money. You owe me the courtesy of listening carefully. Very carefully."

The next forty-five minutes were intense, to put it mildly. Whether I was practicing (unlicensed) clinical psychology or providing legal representation became completely uncertain and ambiguous, but what *was* clear was that Britton went through a significant percentage of the emotional states available to the human psyche. Finally, exhausted and demoralized, he looked over at me with his eyes full of tears and said, for the very first time in the entire case, "What do *you* think is best?"

I didn't answer right away. Instead, I stood up, walked over to the floor-to-ceiling window, and looked out at the majestic view over Boston Harbor, with Logan Airport just beyond the water. As I was standing there, a plane taxied down a runway and took off over the Atlantic. That real-life metaphor—a plane taking off for new horizons—somehow made it perfectly clear what I indeed did think was best for Britton. I turned and walked back toward Britton, handing him the office memorandum about the departing paralegal's going-away party. "Here," I began, "take a look at this memorandum from our office manager that was on my desk this morning." He read it through and looked back up at me, silently, teary-eyed. "I met with her, and with the chairman of the firm yesterday, and, while there are no promises, you would be an extremely viable candidate for that position."

Britton just sat there with his arms dangling off the sides of the chair, the memorandum hanging down to the floor.

The moment of truth had arrived. "Herbert, I'm going to be brutally honest with you here. I've spent months on your case, as has my investigator. I know your life—in detail. Based on everything I've learned,

I don't see a winning scenario for you if we litigate your case. If Bar Counsel prevails, you'll have neither a law license nor the possibility of working as a paralegal. If we prevail—and I think we well might— you'll have the life you had before, minus whatever effect all this will have on your court appointments, which I should think might well be appreciable. And also, if we prevail, you'll continue to have the isolated, solitary work circumstances you've had for years—except you'll probably face at least three malpractice lawsuits, and your office's professional liability policy may or may not cover all that. And, from what you've told me, I would think your office mates might not be too keen on your staying in their firm once the malpractice claims hit."

I could barely hear Britton's totally demoralized voice as he responded. "So, what do you think I should I do?"

"It's your call, Herbert, it's your life. But if I were you, I would take the deal. *If we can get it—and, so far, I've been told to forget it.* If not, we'll tape our ankles, go to the hearing, and try to prevail. I've just learned that Chief Justice Margaret Marshall will be the sitting single justice; I've known her for years, and I couldn't have more respect for a jurist. If we win the hearing, perhaps we could see if there is something we can do to get you involved in a law practice with others so you are not so . . . so alone."

Britton slowly boosted his massive frame out of his chair and lumbered over to the window, now taking his turn to soak in the view out over the water. The day was crystal clear, and the beauty of the afternoon took hold of him for some time. Eventually, and with an uncharacteristic peacefulness, without turning, he simply said, "See if you can get the deal. It's time for me to turn the page, isn't it?"

"Herbert," I replied, "do you have another hour to spare? I want to walk with you over to Bromfield Street. There's someone there I'd like you to meet."

***

The next morning, I walked into the meeting at the Office of the Bar Counsel. I found present not only Alice Yang, with whom I'd spoken, but also Malcom Downing, her middle-aged, dull-eyed superior who had categorically rejected my idea. Somehow, I needed to seize the initiative if I were to even have a chance of accomplishing what I wanted.

So I did. "Excuse me. Please understand that I have *not* come here to deal with case transition issues. I have come here to tell you that if we proceed to a hearing next week, my client will prevail. So, I have an alternative solution to the case to propose to you. *That* is why I am here today." The room went completely silent.

Downing looked a bit shocked and lost, while Yang smiled and held her hands out—palms up—as if to say, "What you got?"

"Mr. Downing, let me show you some charts I brought along which will be presented at the hearing next week . . . if I may." With that start, I walked both attorneys through the hard data documenting that Britton had billed for just a fraction of the time he'd spent on each case, and for an even more modest percentage of the hours he'd spent on his many prison visits. I reminded Downing that, in his complaint, he had already conceded Britton's admirable work ethic and the quality of both his written pleadings and his trial-work professionalism.

Downing started to sputter and become defensive, but Attorney Yang simply cleared her throat to catch his attention, nodded quietly to him, and—quite remarkably, I thought—took over the meeting. "Let's assume for the moment that everything in your presentation is accurate, Counselor. How would it affect the case as profoundly as you claim?"

"Because it shows that the theory of the case your office argued in the complaint doesn't hold water—*at all*."

"And what do you see our theory of the case to be?"

"Your office's theory of the case, Counselor, is that my client manipulated his three clients—Sikes the shooter, Sanders the assailant, and McDermott the statutory rapist—into forgoing plea bargain offers in favor of trial—*precisely in order to increase his billable hours*. Given the data in these charts that I've just shown you, and other evidence I'll introduce, your office's theory completely collapses."

"So, then, Counselor," she came right back at me, "what's your theory of the case that you find so likely to prevail?"

Needless to say, I couldn't disclose my real theory of the case, so I had to sell Britton's. "My client has spent his career watching the abuses of the plea bargain system. My office has collected not just the data you saw on Britton but also data on a significant number of his fellow court-appointed public defenders who practice in the same two district courts that he does. These attorneys literally cajole their clients into copping to pleas within a matter of hours, sometimes within a matter of minutes. Britton is built differently. He happens to be a true believer in the 'right to a trial by a jury of your peers,' a little phrase he picked up from somewhere or other . . . oh yes, from the Constitution of the United States of America."

They were both listening, so I carried right on. "I've interviewed Sanders, Sikes, and McDermott in person, and each of them told me—and I will represent this to the court—that Britton held multiple discussions about the pluses and minuses of accepting the plea bargains that each of them ended up rejecting. Remember, all I need to demonstrate is that there was compliance with Rule 1.4(b), which requires only, and I quote: 'A lawyer shall explain a matter to the extent reasonably necessary to permit the client to make informed decisions regarding the representation.' And there was compliance with this rule so long as Attorney Britton indeed held discussions with his clients in good faith about the pros and cons of accepting a proffered plea deal. Since all three complaining witnesses told me that he had indeed done so, I don't believe your office can demonstrate an ethical violation."

Attorney Yang, not fully three years out of Harvard Law School, turned to her supervisor. "Sir, I'm going to suggest we ask Attorney Freiberg about the suspension idea that he has in mind. If you don't disagree, I would propose that we at least listen to what he wants for his client in return for a voluntary surrender of his license to practice law. Can we move ahead in this way?"

Attorney Downing, seeming a bit lost as to whether or not what I'd argued gave me any real leverage, opted to rely on his remarkably able associate: "Yes, no harm in listening," he replied.

"He'll take a one-year voluntary suspension with automatic reinstatement, so long as he can work during the year as a paralegal."

"Why would you want that if you can prevail at the hearing?" Attorney Yang shot back. "What you are asking for flows from a very different understanding of this case, doesn't it?"

I was clearly up against a young master.

"Counselor," I responded, "I will fully represent to you the following: suspension is the best outcome in this matter for everyone involved; I've thought this through very, very carefully, and I'm entirely certain of this."

"Why do you say 'everyone'?" Attorney Yang responded. "Who else is involved?" Not more than five seconds of silence followed, and by then, she had it figured out. "You must be making reference to the three complaining witnesses. If we did this deal with you, are you going to propose we make a joint appeal to the single justice that she contact the three trial courts about their motions for new trials?"

"That's an *excellent* idea, Attorney Yang," I replied.

Again, she paused. "It is an excellent idea. But it's not my idea, Counselor. It's *your* idea. But it's the right thing to do, isn't it?"

"It very definitely is the right thing to do, Counselor."

"Now let me ask you this," she added. "Do you really want a one-year suspension, with automatic relicensing? I have the feeling you want me to bargain you up to two years with the right to reapply for a license."

"Done. Let's call it a deal."

She looked over at her supervisor, who had clearly not followed the chess moves. He just nodded, rightfully thrilled to have someone so capable on his team. "Counselor," Attorney Yang responded, "why don't you write up an agreement for judgment and send it directly to me; you have more resources." And then, turning once again to her supervisor before looking back at me, she concluded the meeting with, "Attorney Downing will either handle the hearing himself or assign me, as he decides. Whichever one of us appears, we'll approach Chief Justice Marshall together with you at the hearing to try to get some relief for the three prisoners."

***

And so the day of the hearing was upon us. I was delighted to see Attorney Yang when I walked into the beautifully appointed courtroom of the Massachusetts Supreme Judicial Court.

When we had finished presenting our jointly recommended agreement for judgment in the matter, Justice Marshall congratulated us on our having reached a resolution and didn't hesitate to issue our suggested findings and an order of a two-year suspension of Britton's license to practice law, with a right to apply thereafter for readmission. Just as importantly, Her Honor was in complete and enthusiastic agreement with our joint request that she intercede with the three trial courts.

***

While I never knew the final outcomes for Sikes and Sanders, I did learn that, in both cases, their respective motions for a new trial were allowed. The outcome for Bill McDermott, however, is well known to me. He, too, was granted a new trial, which came with a new plea bargain offer that, this time, was readily accepted. While he pleaded guilty to statutory rape as part of his plea bargain, the trial court judge did not accept the rest of the terms of the plea. Instead, the judge took testimony during the sentencing phase of the matter, thereby allowing in evidence all the mitigating factors. He subsequently imposed imprisonment for one year, less time served, in exchange for a lengthy probation period. He had no choice but to impose registration as an offender, but did so at level one. This meant that in a matter of months, young Mr. McDermott made his way out through those six steel doors into the light of day. Within a week, he came to my law firm to look me up to see if I would write a "To Whom It May Concern" letter explaining everything that had taken place. His goal was to apply to colleges in California the following academic year, being entirely up front with them about his circumstances. And it worked: months later, I received a card from him that he had been admitted to San Francisco State, from where his goal was to transfer after two years to UC Berkeley for his bachelor's degree.

***

And so it came to pass that the Britton case was resolved. The position as a paralegal at my firm worked out well for everyone involved; in the following year, I passed Britton in the hallway from time to time, and he seemed to be gracefully making the transition, so far as I could ascertain. You could even see that he was losing weight, rather significantly. Better still, several times when I'd run into him in the coffee room, he'd been so engaged bantering away with his colleagues that he hadn't even needed to acknowledge me. The one and only thing I knew about his personal life was that he was working part-time at the stamp shop. Then one day, roughly a year and a half into his new life, there was a knock on my office door, and in came Herbert Britton. We chatted for a bit about this and that, and then he told me that he had some news to announce. He'd given his notice earlier that day that he would be leaving the firm.

I was a bit surprised, of course, and when I asked why he was leaving, I received a lengthy and animated description of his new career path. It seemed that during the period he had been working as a paralegal, he had once again taken up his childhood hobby of stamp collecting while working very part-time at Mr. Hayes's shop. He proceeded to tell me that he'd already met some interesting people in the world of stamps and that, over the past year, he'd attended a number of stamp shows, helping Mr. Hayes staff a booth. "It's incredible," he ended. "It turns out that I actually had quite a valuable collection—thanks to my grandfather—so I'll be able to live on what I sell and trade, plus what I'll earn at Mr. Hayes's shop in the coming years. Beginning in two weeks, my work there will change to full-time, as Mr. Hayes has some health concerns to deal with. Anyway, I hope you don't think I've let you down by leaving this incredible interim position you arranged for."

"Herbert," I replied, "it's been a pleasure." We shook hands, and that was that. To the best of my recollection, I never saw Herbert Britton again. But I formed the distinct impression that he must have carved out an agreeable life for himself, given that he never reapplied to the bar when the suspension period was over. Several years later, when by chance I was walking along Bromfield Street and passed by the Bay State Stamp and Coin shop, Herbert's name was on the window above another line that read, somewhat poignantly I thought, "Founded by William Cunningham Hayes."

THE WOMAN WHO
WAS NEVER THERE

Once each decade, a case would come into the office that was utterly unique and totally unlike any other matter that I had ever handled. Each time, these one-off cases ended up leading me down pathways I never expected to travel and taught me lessons about connection and misconnection that I never expected to learn.

One such case involved a love affair between a Chinese opera diva and a French diplomat that began in Beijing, China, and ended in Paris, France—with their conviction for high treason. I want to share this tale with you, my reader, because it shines a bright light on the pain and suffering that can be inflicted on a friend or lover whose affection and devotion are obtained by fraud.

***

This curious case of the Chinese opera star who seduced a French attaché reads far more like the libretto of an Italian opera than it does like a description of a legal action—and I am far from the first to have recognized the theatrical quality of my client's life. In 1988, the story you are about to read was crafted into the extraordinarily successful Broadway play *M. Butterfly*, which won that year's Tony Award for best dramatic play on Broadway, and was nominated for the Pulitzer Prize for Drama. Two years later, Jeremy Irons leapt at the opportunity to play my client in a brilliantly made film of the same name.[10]

So, please be my guest for an evening of theater as the lights dim and the curtain rises:

ACT 1: SCENE 1
BEIJING, CHINA
AN EVENING UNDER THE SUMMER STARS

The year is 1964, and the setting is the French embassy in Beijing, China, which had just reopened after twelve long years of cold-war estrangement. The stately building was located in the old Legation Quarter of the city, which in earlier centuries had been entirely walled off, creating a city within a city for visiting Westerners. By the 1960s, however, the walls were long gone, and the approach to the embassy was impressive indeed. One entered through neoclassical gates that were guarded by a pair of massive carved jade lions—as well as a dozen uniformed, very well-armed police officers. Once through the gates and the security formalities, one came upon a long driveway that wound its way through perennial gardens and centuries-old elm trees up to the white marble Italianate building.

These serene gardens and stately trees provided the setting for scene 1 of our drama, a demure soiree to celebrate the reopening of the refurbished embassy. It was a formal, black-tie affair, replete with the finest of French champagne, passed hors d'oeuvres, classical musicians from both traditions performing al fresco, and refined diplomatic chatter. An abundance of high-level Chinese dignitaries were present to greet the new French ambassador and to honor the reestablishment of diplomatic relations, but for our purposes, only the three most humble of the evening's guests are of any interest. By the time the festivities drew to a close in the wee hours of the following morning, their destinies had become inextricably intertwined. Two of these young men,

---

10. Please see "There is a vision of the Orient that I have" on YouTube. This scene from the film is Jeremy Irons's remarkable suicide scene from the film *M. Butterfly*. Several additional clips from the film follow on.

unbeknownst to the third, had commenced a clandestine love affair that would last for nearly thirty years.

The star of our drama is a strikingly good-looking, delicately built rising celebrity of Chinese classical opera named Shi Pei-Pu (Shi, pronounced "she," is the family name). Shi was acclaimed in opera circles for his crystal-clear soprano voice, which, coupled with his boyish build, enabled him to perform female roles with true grace. But it was not his operatic prowess that garnered the young singer an invitation to the night's elegant event: it was the fact that, having grown up near the Vietnamese border, he spoke fluent French at a time when few Chinese did so.

Our costar is a young French diplomat named Bernard Boursicot, who had arrived just days before to serve as the embassy's accountant. Boursicot had classical French good looks: he was tall, with luxuriant dark hair, flawless fair skin, and blue eyes the color of Caribbean waters. The third and final player in the evening's drama is a French college student, Daniel Bertaux, who was touring in China in the very first days of its reopening to Western tourism. Bertaux, who was blessed with both sparkling brown eyes and a radiant sense of humor, had used both of these assets to wrangle an improbable invitation to the event from a charmed embassy secretary.

***

Theater, as we know, is all about deception, and so was that evening. Unnoticed by Bertaux, Shi Pei-Pu whispered a secret to Boursicot as to why he was so adept at acting out women's operatic roles: he was, in fact, a woman, despite his practice of dressing as a man. He explained that his family history had led to this habit: when he was a young child, his true gender had been hidden from his aging grandparents, who were desperate for a male heir. One can imagine the infatuated Boursicot's unbridled delight at hearing this—as the two shared their first secretive kiss behind a stately elm. Ah . . . how Puccini could have written us an aria for that moment.

As the first rays of dawn sent the guests home or to their hotels, Bertaux left the gala evening delighted to have struck up new friendships with the other two young men, along with plans to see them both again. It would be decades before he would learn that Shi Pei-Pu and Boursicot shared an entirely different understanding of what had occurred under the influence of the evening's sparkling champagne and twinkling stars.

But for now, let me turn your attention to the third player onstage that fateful first evening, Daniel Bertaux, for it is he who first revealed to me this remarkable and ultimately tragic story.

ACT 1: SCENE 2
BOSTON, MASSACHUSETTS
MY LAW OFFICE, TWENTY YEARS LATER

I first met Daniel Bertaux in 1969 when I moved to Paris to do research for my doctoral dissertation. Bertaux was also a sociology graduate student, and we spent a great deal of time together during the eighteen months I spent in France working under the tutelage of the great French sociologist Alain Touraine. The friendship Bertaux and I created that year is still very much alive and well today—half a century down the road.

At the time of Bertaux's call to my law office in the late 1980s, at least a year, possibly more, had passed since we had last spoken. He had barely said *"bonjour"* before he asked if I was interested in providing legal representation to a famous Chinese opera star who had immigrated to France only to be arrested, convicted, and imprisoned on charges of international espionage. "A Dreyfus case for our times," he added with the same infectious laugh I remembered from decades earlier. How could I say no?

Bertaux proceeded to describe how he had met Pei-Pu and Bernard, as he called his friends, at the gala event at the embassy. Years had passed, he told me, and then, completely out of the blue, he had received a telephone call from Boursicot. The diplomat, now reassigned to Paris, was calling to solicit Bertaux's help in arranging for the immigration to France of his common-law wife, Shi Pei-Pu, and their teenage son. Bertaux, as you might imagine, was astonished to learn that Shi Pei-Pu, who had unambiguously presented himself as a man in Beijing, was now a woman. Mystified but not deterred, Bertaux used his family's considerable social contacts to put Boursicot in touch with a very well-respected immigration attorney, and subsequently heard nothing more about the matter for several years. And then at some point, he received a call from Boursicot, who thanked him again for the referral to counsel: mother and son had succeeded in their immigration efforts, and were now reunited with Boursicot in Paris.

Several more years passed by, and then one morning, Bertaux, now a full research professor (*directeur de recherche*) at the Centre National de la Recherche Scientifique, glanced at a copy of *Le Monde* and was bowled over by the paper's headlines: both of his friends had been arrested and charged with high treason, and were to be tried for international espionage before the Cour de Cassation—the branch of the tripartite French Supreme Court that handles criminal matters.

According to Bertaux, the indictment of the two alleged spies remained front-page news for weeks leading up to their trial. International treason was itself a headline grabber, but it became all the more so when it was reported that Shi Pei-Pu had been taken to a women's prison after her arrest—and had been summarily *rejected* when the intake shower revealed that "she" was in fact a "he." As you might expect, Boursicot's intriguing failure to correctly note the gender of his longtime paramour itself merited front-page news, and the enigmatic lovers were mocked and satirized on a nightly basis by every television commentator in France.

And then, after all this nonstop press coverage, came the televised two-day espionage trial where both defendants were convicted of high treason and sentenced to six-year prison terms. The press coverage of the colorful case finally wound down—only to flare up again two years later when President François Mitterrand pardoned Shi Pei-Pu under pressure from Beijing. Boursicot, a broken man, was released six months later.

It was only at the end of his breathless description of all this that Bertaux finally got around to my potential role as an attorney. One of the attendees at the espionage trial, Bertaux explained, was a young American playwright named David Henry Hwang. Hwang had had the artistic insight to note that the principal themes of this singular love affair ran enticingly parallel to those of Puccini's magnificent opera *Madam Butterfly*, and he subsequently worked to marry the two stories into the aforementioned Broadway play, *M. Butterfly*. The drama was the hottest ticket of the year in New York City. This highly publicized accomplishment, in turn, generated a full array of proposals and offers for television interviews, biographical books, and film contracts. In response, Shi Pei-Pu—who spoke only Mandarin and French—was searching for a French-speaking American attorney to negotiate contracts for him with the various American media enterprises that sought to interview and film him. He had asked Bertaux if he knew such a person, and Bertaux had recommended his social-psychology professor friend turned attorney—and that would be—*moi*. Sensing a trip to visit Paris, I assured my friend that I was entirely interested in taking on the case. With that, Bertaux gave me Shi Pei-Pu's home phone number, emphasizing that there was no time for delay: *People* magazine had contacted Shi earlier that week about filming a television special and interviewing him for a magazine cover story.

Later that very day, I called Shi Pei-Pu in Paris and told him of my willingness to represent him in these business matters. He retained my services on the spot, and requested that I come to Paris as soon as was practicable to meet with him.

ACT 1: SCENE 3
NEW YORK, NEW YORK
EUGENE O'NEILL THEATRE

Before I called *People* magazine, however, I telephoned the Eugene O'Neill Theatre, where *M. Butterfly* was playing. I used every bit of leverage I could squeeze out of being Shi Pei-Pu's personal attorney (if for only five minutes) to obtain the only two available tickets for the following Saturday night. Before the curtain rose that evening, my wife and I arrived just in time to squeeze our way through seated patrons to what turned out to be the producer's fifth-row center seats.

***

We were, to put it mildly, thunderstruck by the performance. Like everyone else who had seen the masterful drama—critic and patron alike—we were stunned by the brilliance of what Mr. Hwang had created. The Puccini opera, as we all know, involves a tragic love affair between an American sailor, Captain Pinkerton, and a stunningly beautiful young Japanese girl, Cio-Cio San. They are married over the objections of her family, and all goes swimmingly well until one day Pinkerton announces that his ship is leaving port, and that he must leave Cio-Cio San behind. He promises to return as soon as he can, a promise that his teenage lover—shunned by her family and community—holds deep in her heart of hearts. Months later, she gives birth to their son, and mother and child watch out over the Pacific during the next five years waiting for Captain Pinkerton's ship to appear on the horizon. Finally, her confidence proves well placed as the love of her life does return—just as he promised. Alas, Pinkerton announces to her that he has only returned to take the child back to the West with him. Cio-Cio San gives him the boy and just barely finishes one of the most dramatic scenes and most strikingly beautiful arias in all of Italian opera before committing hari-kari. The opera ends with the audience in tears.[11]

What the young playwright had grasped was that the real-world visit of French diplomat Bernard Boursicot to the Far East, and his "fathering" of a son with Shi Pei-Pu—and their return to the West—constituted a tantalizingly parallel story line to the famous opera, spiced up for our times with gender ambiguity and high treason. The marriage of the two plotlines, the subtle handling of the complexities of Shi Pei-Pu's multilayered gender ambiguities, and the artful use of Puccini's celestial music made for an unforgettable evening of theater. How could it *not* have won the Tony?

ACT 1: SCENE 4
NEW YORK, NEW YORK
THE OFFICES OF *PEOPLE* MAGAZINE

Through a series of telephone conferences, I arranged a meeting in New York City with *People* magazine editorial personnel. The wild success of the Broadway play meant that there were competing offers for Shi Pei-Pu's attention, and hence I had ample leverage to negotiate an

---

11. You can see and listen to Puccini's divine aria *Con onor muore* on YouTube with Ying Huang in the soprano role.

arrangement that greatly pleased my client. The outcome was that the weekly publication would remunerate Shi Pei-Pu quite handsomely if he would submit to both being interviewed for a magazine cover story and being filmed for a television special. I insisted that the interview be conducted by one of *People*'s senior staff journalists, in the (not at all realistic) hope that more sophisticated reporting would appreciate the aesthetic importance of capturing the subtleties of Shi Pei-Pu's nebulous gender identity, as opposed to concentrating entirely on the more banal issue of Boursicot's remarkable misperception of his lover's gender. *People* yielded to this demand, assigning one of its foremost journalists, Joyce Wadler, to the task. Wadler, however, did not speak a word of French, and hence it was left to me to act as the translator between Wadler and Shi Pei-Pu.

Above and beyond resolving the conditions for Wadler's interview of my client, the negotiations settled the details for Shi Pei-Pu's performance in full traditional costume at an opera recital that would be filmed in Paris by a *People* magazine camera crew. Shi would sing several arias, which would be edited into a one-hour television special on his life that was to be shown on CBS prime-time television in the United States, and distributed elsewhere throughout the world. Mr. Shi, needless to say, relished the idea of finding himself back in the spotlight—this time speaking about and performing opera, arguably the only thing he ever truly loved.

ACT 1: SCENE 5
CAMBRIDGE, MASSACHUSETTS
WIDENER LIBRARY, HARVARD UNIVERSITY

It was clear to me that if I were going to competently represent Shi Pei-Pu, I needed to quickly bone up on his background in China, introduce myself to what Chinese opera was all about, figure out Bernard Boursicot's role in the French embassy, grasp what espionage actually had or had not taken place, learn how Shi Pei-Pu's and his son's immigration to France had been arranged and accomplished, and come to an understanding of what had taken place in France that had precipitated the trial for high treason.

Earlier in my academic career, I had written a book entitle
French Press, and for it I had interviewed a very considerable nui.
of journalists and editors at major Parisian publications, especiall)
Le Monde, but also at *Le Figaro*, *France-Soir*, and *Libération*. I didn't fi
a moment hesitate to place calls to the reporters and editors whom I'o
met, curious as hell to learn their takes on Shi Pei-Pu. As it turned out,
every single journalist with whom I spoke had an entirely vivid memory of the Shi Pei-Pu story, and a great deal to say about the curious
case of the infamous Chinese opera diva.

Next came three full days of research in Harvard's Widener
Library, where I was able to review back issues of many of the newspapers and magazines that had covered the arrests and the trial. And
what I saw immediately confirmed what Bertaux had told me: not a
single newspaper or weekly magazine available in the library had failed
to report the story as front-page news. It hadn't been just news reporting—it had been a veritable tabloid feeding frenzy.

The deeper I plunged into the matter, the more I could see why
indeed so much press coverage was lavished on the strange affair of Shi
Pei-Pu and Bernard Boursicot. Above and beyond the sensationalist
nature of Shi's gender fluidity and the international espionage, the way
the matter was handled by the French state turned the entire affair into
an *opéra comique*. To begin with, the courtroom in the medieval *pal-
ais de justice* in which the legal proceedings were held (and televised
from) was as ornate as one of Liberace's capes. The high-ceilinged,
Louis XV–style chamber is adorned with rococo carvings covered in
massive amounts of gold leaf. The remaining surfaces feature richly
patinaed wood paneling, on which hang massive eighteenth-century
neoclassical paintings. And all this glittering brightness is exaggerated
tenfold by the quiet of the plush royal-blue upholstering of the seats.

But there's more. To the delight of the entire French nation, the
anachronistic setting, the prosecution's exaggerated fervor, and the
ever-so-serious demeanor of this branch of the Supreme Court of
France were rendered entirely ludicrous by the mediocrity of the espionage. One by one as they were offered in evidence, the documents
that Boursicot had photocopied, spirited out of the Beijing embassy,
and transferred through Shi Pei-Pu to the Chinese police proved to

ential. One, for example, was a set of plans to
bathroom.

thefts of the embassy documents only began
been denounced and discovered, and Boursicot had
ed by the Chinese police. So Boursicot's story was truly
—pure and simple. He had been forced to choose between
ag embassy documents and watching his lover be carted off to
nabilitation" center; imagine loving someone so much that you
would commit espionage to protect them. How beautiful. How operatic. One could empathize with Boursicot—and the press did, in a love-
is-blind narrative. In contrast, we now know that Shi Pei-Pu's interest
in the relationship was never a love story, as he claimed, but a contriv-
ance—at first to ingratiate himself with the Chinese police, and later to
lay the groundwork for his immigration to France. Only one of the two
lovers was in the relationship seeking connection; the other was fraudulently involved from that very first night at the embassy in Beijing.

Not surprisingly, the lion's share of the press coverage was focused
on Shi Pei-Pu's enigmatic sexuality. Boursicot testified under oath
that he had *always* believed and experienced his lover to be a woman.
When he was sternly cross-examined on this testimony, Boursicot
stuck firmly to his position, adding—in a flood of tears—that he had
only learned that his lover's gender *was even in question* on the night
of their arrest when Shi Pei-Pu suddenly appeared in the adjoining cell
after having been rebuffed by the women's prison to which he had initially been taken. By the end of my library research, I had no trouble at
all understanding why scandal-loving *People* magazine was so eager to
get in on the action.

ACT 2: SCENE 1
FONTAINEBLEAU CHÂTEAU, FRANCE
A WALK THROUGH THE WOODS

And so I flew to Paris on Bastille Day, 1987. Bertaux wanted to meet
with me for a strategy session the morning after my arrival, and given
that it was a stunning midsummer day, he proposed that we talk during
a walk through the gardens and surrounding woods of Fontainebleau
Château, just south of the City of Light. He drove us there in his

well-traveled Citroen *deux chevaux* with its suspended canvas seats, and once we had begun our walk, I was treated to an uninterrupted monologue that took Bertaux nearly an hour to complete. Some of his highlights repeated stories I had read in the press, while others were entirely new, since they came from Bertaux's personal conversations with Boursicot.

Bertaux felt certain that when Boursicot had called him searching for the reference to an immigration attorney, he had spoken from his heart in revealing that Shi Pei-Pu was a woman, that they had long since fallen deeply in love with each other, and that Shi Pei-Pu had given birth to a beautiful son. Boursicot described to Bertaux the extreme measures the couple had had to take in their effort to preserve the secrecy of their illegal encounters and the birth of their child. This concealment was a matter of life and death, Boursicot had explained, because personal relationships between a Chinese citizen and a foreign diplomat were strictly illegal at that time under Chinese law, and the French foreign service had its *own* strict rules expressly forbidding personal liaisons of any kind between diplomats and local citizens. But above and beyond the practical goals of the call, Boursicot had bared his soul to his old friend, and in doing so, he left Bertaux thoroughly convinced of the legitimacy of the immigration effort to reunite the lovers, and bring their son to France.

Bertaux described how ever since Boursicot's diplomatic reassignment following his first tour of duty in China, the young diplomat had unsuccessfully applied over and again to obtain a second posting to the Chinese capital. His applications, however, were routinely denied on a yearly basis, given the strict policy of the French foreign service disallowing a diplomat to be reassigned to an earlier posting. Boursicot, Bertaux described, was despondent at not being allowed to return to Beijing, and he might never have seen his ladylove and their child again but for the intervention of historical accident: the outbreak of the violence and chaos of the Cultural Revolution. Suddenly, a diplomatic posting to Beijing had lost its allure in the French foreign service, and there were no applicants whatsoever—save for one. So, Boursicot was indeed able to rejoin his lover, although he never met their son in person during that time period, as the boy was being raised in Central

China by an aunt of Shi Pei-Pu's to safeguard him from the wild uncertainties of the era.

China during the Cultural Revolution, as Bertaux described it, was a very different place from what Boursicot had known half a decade earlier. The Red Guard, the police, and neighborhood informants were everywhere, and the streets of Beijing were filled with hundreds of thousands of marching students—each with their red armband and their personal copy of Mao's Little Red Book. Their youthful fervor could mutate to violence in a heartbeat, and everything that was traditional was under attack. Teachers, intellectuals, and traditional artists, *very much including classical opera singers*, were at great risk of being forcibly torn from their homes and beaten in the street by a mob. But, oh, the power of love: none of this prevented Boursicot from seeking out Shi Pei-Pu and their finding clandestine moments together. Naturally, they greatly augmented their efforts to keep their meetings concealed and brief, but secrecy was far harder to achieve than it had been during Boursicot's first tour of duty.

During these hard times, Bertaux related, Shi Pei-Pu was cunning in other spheres of life—survival depended on it. Traditional opera with its fairy-tale themes, for example, had been labeled "bourgeois" and was disallowed. It was soon replaced by "socialist realism opera" with its dull, dry, ideological productions that typically included rural peasants and urban proletariat workers joining hands to sing homage to the miraculous socialist state and its "great leader." Shi Pei-Pu—ever the sly fox—transitioned seamlessly. Within months, he had converted from singing women's parts in classical gowns to intoning gender-invisible roles in Mao jackets.

That day during our walk through Fontainebleau's vast grounds, Bertaux shared some extraordinary stories he had heard from Boursicot. At times, it had simply not been safe for the lovers to find a moment together, and all that was possible was for them to sit on benches on opposite sides of one of Beijing's massive boulevards and simply stare at each other—not daring to make the slightest signal. Boursicot had described how the lovers had made use of a secret drop-off spot in the knothole of a tree: unsigned love notes were deposited and later retrieved. But by far the most operatic encounter that Bertaux shared was Boursicot's description of one particular rainy

Beijing winter day, when the two lovers, hidden beneath their umbrellas, separately attended the funeral services of a perfect stranger. They sought only to be near each other among the silent mourners: that was all they could arrange, but it was enough.

Bertaux fell silent as we came upon a little outdoor café, and shifted gears into charming a waitress into giving us the last available table. No problem.

ACT 2: SCENE 2
FONTAINEBLEAU CHÂTEAU, FRANCE
A CAFÉ IN THE WOODS

As we sat that day at the forested café in the Fontainebleau woods, I pressed Bertaux into sharing with me his personal views on Boursicot's infamous failure to discover his lover's true gender. Bertaux argued that he found Boursicot's explanation of this oversight entirely credible. Boursicot had told Bertaux that the lovers' trysts were invariably brief and took place in dark rooms. He also had described how Pei-Pu had remained covered, and had "guided him." Bertaux's viewpoint was that this was entirely consistent with the two personalities as he knew them: Shi Pei-Pu was a dominant, manipulative person, and Boursicot was entirely submissive by nature.

But, Bertaux continued, it was more than that. He was particularly fascinated by the depth and certitude of Boursicot's belief that Shi Pei-Pu was truly a woman, and that the boy—named Shi Du-Du—was his biological son. So the key to the enigma, Bertaux proposed, was to analyze the origins of Boursicot's two "certainties." The "son" Boursicot had come to know through photographs was visibly a Eurasian child, so that in itself would have helped convince him of the truth of what Shi Pei-Pu had told him. But, Bertaux theorized, there was a second, even-more-powerful underlying reason for Boursicot's absolute certainty that he had fathered the child with the diva. Bertaux's theory was that there was a type of folie à deux (craziness shared by two people) at play: a mutually reinforcing psychological interdependence of Boursicot and Shi Pei-Pu. In other words, in making the leap of faith that the child was actually their biological child, the two men were simultaneously reinforcing both Shi Pei-Pu's psychological need to believe that he was a woman and Boursicot's endeavor to define himself as a heterosexual male. Shi Pei-Pu, Bertaux emphasized, never at any time varied when he reported to anyone and everyone who asked—including the investigative magistrate judge of the French Supreme Court—that he had always understood himself to be female. As Bertaux summarized his position, "A perfect con job was pulled off by a master con artist on the most willing of marks. We're just not accustomed to seeing con artists fall for their own con."

Was Bertaux right? Was this a con job? And if it was, could that possibly be consistent with the "love story" Shi Pei-Pu was always so eager to tell? What exactly is it that you feel, if you con someone into loving you, and then you discover that you enjoy the relationship? There really wasn't any way I could do anything other than listen to Bertaux that first day in France. To form my own opinions on these issues, I would need to meet the master con artist, and that was scheduled for midmorning the following day.

ACT 3
PARIS, FRANCE
SHI PEI-PU'S APARTMENT

The next day, I took a taxi to a modest neighborhood on the periphery of Paris and climbed four flights of stairs to Shi Pei-Pu's apartment. A handsome and very pleasant young man in his early twenties opened the door. He was, I realized, the famous son, Shi Du-Du. Then suddenly, grandly, Shi Pei-Pu made his entrance into the room with all the flair of an opera soprano coming onstage. I am embarrassed to admit that I was completely and utterly taken aback. The only photographs I had seen of the man were photographs of a trim, delicately handsome young opera star dressed in flowing silk, so I was completely unprepared to meet a puffy-faced, overweight middle-aged man. So far as I could see, there was nothing even remotely feminine—or effeminate—about the man, at least not in this stage of his life.

Shi Pei-Pu, speaking in accented but excellent French, was positively effervescent with excitement about the upcoming fully costumed opera performance he was going to give in two days' time. *People* magazine had rented a ballroom on the second floor of Maxim's bar just off the Champs-Élysées—a highly prestigious venue indeed. Shi Pei-Pu rambled on and on about how he had personally supervised a local tailor with the letting out of his costume, which, he explained to me at considerable length, was an exact copy of a bejeweled gown worn by an imperial princess of some ancient dynasty. He expressed some trepidation about his long unused operatic voice, but overall he was thrilled to have an opportunity to appear once again in front of a live audience—and positively ecstatic about performing in front *People* magazine's television cameras, which would carry his recital to tens of millions of viewers.

During the discussion, Shi Pei-Pu brought out several poster-size pictures of himself in complex and ornate traditional gowns, and the feminine elegance of his once delicate and handsome face made Boursicot's fantasy seem almost plausible. But that was long ago. The day of my visit, viewing the photographs alongside my client in the dim light of the small apartment served only to remind me of how hard the years are on each of us—even on those few among us who begin life with fine-looking faces and graceful bodies. The stark contrast between Shi Pei-Pu's past appearance and the current status of his looks also served to sow in me the seeds of my first doubts about the upcoming recital.

After a few polite inquiries about my flight to Paris, and several questions about how his old friend Daniel Bertaux was doing, we began discussing the interview to be taken by *People* magazine. The inquiry was to be held the following morning. We reviewed how Shi Pei-Pu intended to answer questions about sensitive topics, and, I must say, it was the one and only time I have ever heard a parent speak about the complexities of their gender identity in front of their own child. It was an especially curious moment for me, as a good part of my mind was involved with trying to comprehend the implications of the fraudulent connection that this "mother" had established with "her" child over so many years. There were only two possibilities, it seemed to me. Either Shi Pei-Pu had built an entire parental relationship on the fiction that he was the biological mother of the boy, or the son was well aware of his adoptive status, and hence of Shi Pei-Pu's misuse of him as a chess piece in the con to entrap Boursicot. I found the two alternatives equally aberrant.

ACT 4
PARIS, FRANCE
A HOTEL OFF THE CHAMPS-ÉLYSÉES

As I waited in a hotel conference room for Shi Pei-Pu and Joyce Wadler to appear for the scheduled interview, who should appear but Daniel Bertaux. He explained his unexpected presence by telling me that he had received a last-minute call from Shi Pei-Pu asking him "to back up the lawyer in the translation for the interview." I saw so clearly what my good friend was blind to: he had been manipulated by the master con artist out of a day's work—in all probability not to monitor my translation skills, but to police my efforts to steer the journalist away from the prurient details of the past, and toward the glories of the Chinese operatic tradition.

People magazine's journalistic specialty is to expose as many private details as possible about as public a personality as they can possibly interview. It's that simple. And Joyce Wadler, the senior journalist who had been assigned to the Shi Pei-Pu story, had a reputation as a ruthless and experienced interviewer. In Mr. Shi's case, there could be little doubt that, whatever Wadler's own views were, the mission dictated to her by her superiors was to find what she needed in order to produce an article centered on what most interested the magazine's modestly educated readers: the implausibility of Boursicot's claim to have failed to discover the true gender of his lover.

I felt reasonably optimistic about the likely outcome of the television special; after all, complex sexual matters were essentially taboo on network television at the time. In contrast, we clearly had very little leverage to affect what would make its way into the magazine article, especially because *People* magazine had paid dearly for the right to conduct the interview. I had forewarned my client that however the interview with Wadler went, there was little or nothing we could do to control whatever subsequent spin might be dictated by successive levels of in-house editing at the magazine. But Shi Pei-Pu had been clear with me—and he was the client: the risk involved in submitting himself to the interview was, in his mind, a small price to pay for whatever time in the limelight could be harvested from the wild success of *M. Butterfly*. Mr. Shi, in the final analysis, was an entertainer, and publicity to an entertainer is like water to a potted plant. No one expressed this better than did the playwright who gave us *M. Butterfly*, David Henry Hwang. He wrote: "When I offered a percentage of the play's royalties to its real-life inspirations, Shi instead demanded a recital at Carnegie Hall, a wish as grand as it was unfeasible."

***

Within minutes after Bertaux's surprise appearance, Shi Pei-Pu and Joyce Wadler each arrived, and the interview commenced. The conference room was brightly lit, and from the very start, Wadler's questioning had more the tone of police interrogation than of investigative journalism. On and on she went, grilling Shi Pei-Pu mercilessly with a strategically orchestrated barrage of questions, after having initially attempted to soften him up by posing a number of benign questions about his background as a Chinese opera star. But old foxes are yet more clever than young ones, and he seemed to be anticipating her every move, and weathering the onslaught.

Wadler eventually turned to the topic of how Shi had met Boursicot. What followed, of course, was the story of the 1964 soiree at the French embassy. The difference, however, was that this version was being told by a master entertainer. As I translated, I had no way of knowing if Wadler had any interest at all in the alluring images and careful wordings that Shi Pei-Pu used to paint a picture for us of the champagne-infused evening's events, or if she gave a damn about the fairy-tale-like wording he selected to describe how fate had brought the two young men together that evening, and changed their lives forever. I tried my best to translate beyond the words, to include the sensuality of the starlit evening that Shi Pei-Pu described so vibrantly, even though the eventual futility of his effort seemed a foregone conclusion: *People* magazine, it seemed to me, would almost certainly reduce his lyrical storytelling to a mocking analysis of what exactly Boursicot knew or didn't know about Shi Pei-Pu's genitals.

But whatever the likely outcome was, Shi Pei-Pu was not going down without a fight. That was clear. Wadler attempted every angle of attack she could think of but found herself outmaneuvered at every turn. She wanted data on sex but was only eliciting a portrayal of love;

try as she might, the master was besting her. Simultaneous translation of a running conversation is an engaging endeavor, and yet there
was part of my mind that found the time to be amazed at the old fox's
capacity to carry on the battle of words—especially with his insistence
that Boursicot was "the love of my life." If a con man cons himself into
believing the reality of the fiction he creates, can the fiction of the con
somehow mutate into reality? I kept asking myself: If you fraudulently
induce someone into loving you, but then over time you actually fall in
love with them, does that retroactively eradicate the fraud? Is that what
had happened?

Then, suddenly, Wadler began a series of not-at-all-subtle questions about how and when and in precisely what way the relationship
had turned sexual. Shi Pei-Pu, sensing both Wadler's frustration and
her new angle of attack, retook the initiative by converting one of
his answers into a long, step-by-step description of how the mutual
attraction had blossomed over the months after the young men had
first met. Speaking over the journalist's occasional efforts to break in,
he described in fastidious detail a series of settings where the lovers
desperately sought to be alone together. Shi Pei-Pu's eyes glazed over
as he continued, and I began to doubt my certainty that he had been
out to manipulate Boursicot—not to lovingly connect with him. As
his monologue carried on, Shi Pei-Pu seemed to become progressively
flooded with the sensations he'd felt at the time of the scenes he was
describing—could he possibly be acting this out so convincingly? Why
not? He had been a master entertainer before taking up the art of the
con. It was an amazing performance, whether it was sincere or concocted: his voice had softened, and he seemed unaware—even uncar-
ing—about who else was in the room as he either reexperienced what
the two young lovers had once shared and felt for each other, or play-
acted as if he did. When Shi Pei-Pu finally fell silent, and I had translated his last lines, no one spoke at all for quite a while. It had been a
mesmerizing tale, with strikingly vivid details that, by all odds, didn't
have a chance of seeing the light of day in the *People* magazine article.

Wadler paused to regroup. She took a drink of water, inhaled
deeply, and then counterattacked with a rapid-fire series of even less
subtle questions: "What *exactly* went on sexually between the two of
you?" "How could Bernard *not* have known that you were biologically

male if you were making love with each other?" "Was your penis erect when you made love with Bernard, yes or no?" After I translated the first of these questions, I reminded Shi Pei-Pu—stepping back from my translation duties for a moment to serve as his counsel—that there was nothing compelling him to disclose more than he wanted to. This was not a court inquiry, and he had every right to refuse to respond, or to respond in such a way as he saw appropriate. But with a brief *"Non, non; ça va,"* he sent me back to my translation duties. And, indeed, it soon became apparent that he was well accustomed to protecting his personal integrity from aggressive questioning. I later learned that even the investigative magistrate of the criminal division of the French Supreme Court who had grilled Shi Pei-Pu under oath on these same matters had, in the end, settled for vague verbiage that preserved the privacy of the couple's sexuality. Shi Pei-Pu responded in the same vein to Wadler: his strategy was to swathe his evasive replies in a tone of cooperative compliance whenever an overt question was asked about genitalia or intercourse. At times, he even posed alternative explanations for Wadler, as if he, too, were searching for an adequate understanding of his gender ambiguities: who knows, perhaps he was. When Wadler finally insisted on a direct answer as to whether or not Shi Pei-Pu's penis was erect during the couple's lovemaking, he began to respond with a theory that posed the possibility that he was physiologically hermaphroditic. Wadler, however, was way too experienced not to recognize Shi Pei-Pu's evasive efforts, and repeated and rephrased her question: "Did your penis become erect, yes or no?"

And then, suddenly, Shi Pei-Pu came to the end of his patience with this line of questioning. Without any change in tone of voice, he entirely reversed his strategy of supplying only oblique, ambiguous responses, and said the following:

"Please understand, Ms. Wadler, that Bernard and I dearly loved each other for many, many years. He has been the love of my life, and I the love of his life. During Bernard's first tour of duty in Beijing, we did occasionally find time to be together without others around. We perceived our lovemaking to be between a man and a woman, and I was the woman, a woman who had been dressed as a boy by my family. And this is how I still choose to dress as an adult; it has always been my habit. To the world, I am a man, and to some, I am even an aberrant man who is confused about his gender. But to myself, and to Bernard, I am a woman, always a woman. And as you know, when I sang opera, I was always cast and costumed as a woman, singing some of Chinese opera's most beautiful arias—as a soprano, and when I was quite young, as what you would call a coloratura soprano. You see, Ms. Wadler, this is why I have loved both Bernard and opera with all my being, all my force. Only in their company was I fully the woman that I truly am, and only in their embrace could I be fully myself, could I entirely open up and love—or sing—with all my being. So, yes, I took a man as my lover, but you see, that was only natural because I am a woman. I remained completely devoted to this man until recently when we have gone our own ways because of the extreme pressures put on Bernard by the trial and the press. He has moved from France to escape the cameras and the questions, and I miss him terribly. Ms. Wadler, this is all I am going to say about this topic, not because I am reluctant to speak with you about my private life, nor because I am anxious to seem mysterious, but simply because there is nothing more to add. Nothing more to add at all. Do you understand that? There is nothing more to add."

As I translated these passionate intoned words for the journalist, I could sense that they were having an effect on her, but I was absolutely bowled over when I learned months later that they had essentially torn her in two, separating her heart from her mind. Her heart determined at that very moment to take a year's leave of absence from *People* magazine in order to better comprehend what Shi Pei-Pu had said. From her research, she would produce a wonderful book on his life.[12] But the day of the interview, her well-disciplined mind knew fully well that she was being paid by *People* magazine to not give up. Her job at the moment was to formulate follow-up questions in order to break through Shi Pei-Pu's defenses. At the slightest straightening of her spine, the master fox sensed that she was recovering her sense of purpose. Wadler, at that point, was about ten words into yet another reformulated question about Shi Pei-Pu's penis when it dawned on her that I had stopped translating and was staring at her over my glasses.

---

12. Joyce Wadler, *Liaison: The Gripping Real Story of the Diplomat Spy and the Chinese Opera Star Whose Affair Inspired "M. Butterfly"* (New York: Bantam Books, 1993).

Sensitive to the barrier that had just been raised, quite possibly confused within her own head given her decision to take a year's leave of absence to write an entire book about Shi Pei-Pu, and definitively outfoxed by the master con artist, the experienced journalist gracefully admitted defeat and ended this phase of her inquiry. After a twenty-second pause shuffling through her notes, Wadler ended the interview with a series of benign questions about the nature and themes of the opera arias Shi Pei-Pu would be singing the following evening. The diva, as you might well imagine, became exuberant, even effervescent, in response, and the interview was concluded on an entirely positive note.

***

In silence, in awe really, Bertaux and I walked a visibly exhausted Shi Pei-Pu down the hall to the elevator and, still without a word, went down with him to the front of the hotel, from where we signaled a passing cab. Just before a round of polite goodbyes, Shi Pei-Pu asked me to meet him in his dressing room an hour before the next day's five p.m. performance. The cab edged into traffic and soon disappeared, and only then did Bertaux and I look at each other and nod in agreement, without needing to say a word. We immediately headed to the corner café.

ACT 5
PARIS, FRANCE
LE PONTHIEU CAFÉ, OFF THE CHAMPS-ÉLYSÉES

Bertaux ordered us beer from an attentive waiter who seemed to notice, even sympathize with our desperate need for quick service. For three or four minutes, we said nothing; we just drank the ice-cold beer, letting it do its own magic on everything we'd heard in that dry, stuffy hotel conference room.

Finally I initiated conversation. "So, Daniel. What in the hell do you make of what we just listened to?"

"Could you be a little more specific?" he responded. "We were in that oven of a room for over two hours."

I laughed. "Fair enough. Fair enough. Let's see, what am I really looking for?" I asked myself rhetorically. "Okay, here's what I want to know: looking back now with all we've learned, how do you assess the beginning of the relationship between Pei-Pu and Bernard—I mean the night the three of you first met at the embassy thirty years ago. You were there. Do you buy the version Pei-Pu just told Wadler?"

Bertaux took a long, slow swig of his beer before responding. "Yes, I do, actually. That is, I don't really care who knew what and who fucked whom and how—but on an emotional level, I buy the love story. Let's give them full credit for that. And this wasn't just an everyday love affair. It was a *remarkable* love affair that struggled against obstacles of extraordinary magnitude from its very beginning. And I agree with something else Pei-Pu said today: it probably only ended because of the unrelenting pressures put on it. You've got to at least admit that."

"Actually, I don't, Daniel. You've known Pei-Pu a hell of a lot longer than I have, but from what I've seen, he's one of the most calculating, manipulative, Machiavellian people I've ever met."

"Look, I'll admit he's a manipulative guy—that's obvious—but that doesn't mean they weren't in love."

"I think it does mean that—*at least in one direction.* I know you told me that in the phone calls you had with Boursicot when he was looking for your help with the immigration attorney, you had zero doubt that he sounded head over heels in love with Pei-Pu, and that he fully believed he had impregnated Pei-Pu and was the biological father of their son. I get that. And I totally trust your ability to have judged the sincerity of Boursicot's tone of voice in that call—you knew him personally. But let's agree on one thing: Pei-Pu knew all along that he never gave birth to a child. And, Daniel, don't you think it's fair to say that love relationships aren't really love relationships if only one person is in love? I don't care how fond Pei-Pu became of Bernard over the years—he conned Bernard into loving him for ulterior motives that have nothing to do with forging a connection. I think that's what happened here. In fact, I think there's a lot of evidence that while Bernard truly loved Pei-Pu, Pei-Pu was in the relationship for entirely other reasons."

"Such as?"

"Such as offering the Chinese police the opportunity to turn a diplomatic employee. Who knows, perhaps this was on his mind that very first night when the three of you met as twenty-year-olds. I wouldn't put it past him, not for a moment."

"But why would he do that; what would be in it for him?"

"Are you kidding? That's how he earned a get out of jail free card—a valuable asset in a totalitarian society. Daniel, that very first night he told Bernard that he was a woman—and he knew *that* was a lie. He shakes his dick after he pees, just like you and me. He didn't talk about being 'a woman trapped in a man's body' or that kind of thing. He talks about actually being a woman, penis and all. So one thing we know for certain: he told Bernard a bald-faced and entirely manipulative lie *the very first night he met him.* And what about how Pei-Pu manipulated their sexual couplings? I believe Bernard—and I think you do too—when he told the court magistrate that Pei-Pu used trickery to mask his masculine genitals by insisting that the Chinese way of sex involved a dark room and not undressing completely. That's not true. And I also believe Bernard when he described to the magistrate how Pei-Pu 'guided' his naïve efforts at copulation. Daniel, ask yourself: Why would Pei-Pu do all this lying and manipulation unless he was pursuing his own goals?"

"So, what are you proposing his goals were?" Bertaux asked.

"Initially, survival: to turn a diplomat and offer that up to the Chinese police to earn himself a measure of safety. Later on, my guess is that his goal expanded into the idea of immigrating to France, where he'd be safe from the wild fluidity of life in Maoist China that he'd seen during the Cultural Revolution. Daniel, emigration from China wasn't only a matter of getting France to accept him: *he also needed to find a way to earn permission from the Chinese authorities to leave.* So, in my view, there were two goals—two logics that explain Pei-Pu's manipulation of Bernard by presenting himself to your infatuated countryman as being 'head over heels in love' with him."

"What about the son?"

"Exactly. What about the son? If you're male and you're in love with someone, Daniel, you don't go purchase a Eurasian orphan and lie to your lover that he got you pregnant. Think about it, Daniel: Pei-Pu knew perfectly well that he didn't conceive and bear a child. Talk about manipulation! He went out and bought that Eurasian child to manipulate Bernard—even though I can't tell you why he made that choice.

But there are only a few possibilities. And by the way, it's quite possible that the Chinese police were involved even earlier than we understand; perhaps it was the police who obtained the child to cement the link between the two men that might someday allow them to turn Bernard into a spy—wherever he might be posted. But I don't really care exactly *why* Pei-Pu manipulated their relationship; I just care that he did so. Because, for the purposes of what we're talking about, lying about the origin of the boy constitutes powerful evidence that Pei-Pu was never 'in love' with Bernard. There's no need to lie and manipulate someone you love who loves you back—you just both decide to work together to achieve whatever your joint goals are. If this had been a bidirectional love affair, Daniel, Pei-Pu would have admitted to Bernard that he was a man, and openly discussed how they might engineer a move to France where they could live a gay life together in peace. Am I making any sense?"

"But your theory doesn't explain why Bernard became openly gay after the trial. That's better explained by thinking they were deeply in love—gay love—at a time when neither of them could admit that that was what was really going on. They were both from social backgrounds that abhorred homosexuality. My theory is that Pei-Pu was a gay male who hid that fact from himself by his self-delusion that he was really a woman, and Bernard was a gay male who bought into Pei-Pu's fiction so he could think of himself as a heterosexual man."

"It's a reasonable explanation, Daniel. You might be right. But it doesn't explain what you've always told me: that when Bernard called you for the reference to an immigration attorney, he sounded totally convinced that Pei-Pu was a woman, and that the child was his own biological child. That's what you told me, right?"

"Well, yes."

"And we know that is what Bernard told the immigration authorities. And we know that Pei-Pu immigrated to France as a woman: that's what his *carte d'identité* said. And we know that the allowance of the immigration was based on the argument that the boy was a biological child of a French citizen; that was the legal basis for the immigration application, correct?"

"Yes, that's all true. But that doesn't mean that Pei-Pu wasn't in love, like he said today—how did he put it?—'Bernard was the love of my life, and I was the love of his life.' Something like that."

"Daniel, if there's one thing I've learned from trial law, it's that once you show a jury that a witness lied about *anything*, that witness will have lost all credibility with the jury. We know Pei-Pu lied that first night about being a woman. We know Pei-Pu lied years later about having given birth to a child. So we know that the man is a liar and a manipulator. My guess is that he was *never* in love with Bernard. He may not even conceive of 'love' as we Westerners conceive of it. But even if he both loved and manipulated Bernard, it was still a fraudulent relationship. And like most fraudulently engineered relationships, the person who got conned got hurt—really hurt. You do remember, don't you, that Bernard slit his throat in prison after learning that Pei-Pu was a man, and very nearly killed himself. That's what fraudulent relationships do, Daniel. They hurt people. That's what they always do."

We were both exhausted at this point, and it was time to get the check and leave. I could see my friend looking around to catch the waiter's eye, and I desperately wanted to come up with something light to end on.

"So tell me this, Daniel. After Pei-Pu was released from prison, do you think he ever got the French bureaucracy to change his gender on his identity papers? I have a Parisian friend who, for some Kafkaesque reason, couldn't get his new address officially recognized on his *carte d'identité* for a decade. Can you even imagine anyone succeeding in getting a French bureaucrat to change their *gender* on their *carte d'identité*?" Bertaux laughed out loud at the thought, paid the bill, and we went our separate ways. The plan was for us to meet again at Pei-Pu's dressing room an hour before the next day's scheduled performance.

ACT 6: SCENE 1
PARIS, FRANCE
MAXIM'S BAR

The following day, I walked down the Champs-Élysées to Maxim's bar to attend the much-heralded recital. It was a stunning summer afternoon, and all the glory and beauty of Paris called out to me. Maxim's bar is in the building adjacent to its famous sister restaurant, and it has the same quietly luxurious tone, especially in its art deco wooden bar—a graceful reminder of another era. I was led up a carpeted stairway to the mezzanine, and down the hallway to the door of Shi Pei-Pu's dressing room.

I shall never forget what I saw when I first entered. The room was normally a ladies' powder room, but *People* magazine had hired out the entire floor above Maxim's for the filming, and the room had been converted into a dressing room for Shi Pei-Pu. As I entered, I was coming in from directly behind the diva, who was deeply involved in his *maquillage*, the application of stage makeup. He was staring into a wide, three-panel, well-lit mirror, and he looked up at me without turning, merely by shifting his eyes in the mirror. In front of him on the dressing table were dozens and dozens of bottles and tubes of makeup products, and he was partway through the process of turning his aging face into that of a young woman's. The man who would be a woman was actually becoming one before my very eyes.

On one side of the dressing table, he had propped up a forty-year-old color photograph of himself as a young opera star in full female makeup, costumed and glorious in a bejeweled, silken gown. It was clear that he was trying to reproduce what he saw in the photograph, and also that he was profoundly experienced in the art of applying makeup. He turned his eyes to the photograph every fifteen or twenty seconds, looking for direction, and hoping for progress. But the ravages of forty years, the hardships and deprivations of the Cultural Revolution, the ordeal of immigration, the tribulations of the treason trial, the harshness of imprisonment, and the cruelty of public ridicule—all these had taken their toll. Shi Pei-Pu could make himself into a woman, but he could no longer come anywhere near making himself into the exquisite young princess who gazed back at him from the photograph.

Resigned, the princess rose to put on the layers of her sequin-festooned costume, followed by the final step in the entire dressing process: the donning of a very complex hairpiece and hat that, he told me, connoted regal status. Then *she* stood, drew herself up to her full height, and took my arm to be escorted out of the dressing room to the stage.

Only as we took our first steps toward the door did I take notice of the recent tailoring on Shi Pei-Pu's costume. Long rectangular panels of new material had been inserted at regular intervals to allow the original royal gown to now envelop a quite significantly expanded princess. Notwithstanding the tailor's noble efforts, the coloring of these cloth strips didn't quite match the faded hues of the original silk—and, in fact, they clashed in tone. Worse still, the original silk was almost in tatters, looking as if it had fed a great many moths over quite a considerable number of years. Overall, the gown's hoary condition served only to emphasize the worn-out look of the princess who wore it; one could only hope for dim lighting.

There was a knock at the door, and Joyce Wadler opened it to announce that the film crews were ready, and that the invited audience was seated and becoming restless. She added that she didn't think she needed any additional interview time after all, and asked me to confirm with Shi Pei-Pu that he intended to explain to the audience the operatic setting for the arias he was going to sing, and the general sense of each libretto. She asked me if I would translate these remarks. The princess then closed her eyes for ten seconds or so; took a long, deep breath; exhaled slowly; and retook my arm. Regardless of how she looked, she was clearly 100 percent committed to the international ethic of all performers: no matter what, the show must go on.

ACT 6: SCENE 2
PARIS, FRANCE
ONSTAGE AT MAXIM'S BAR

The room where the stage was erected proved to be much larger than I had expected. It was overflowing with lighting fixtures, cameras, sound booms, electrical cords, recording equipment, and the eight bustling technicians who made up the two film crews. In and around the technicians, there were folding chairs set up for some fifty or sixty invited guests, and there were several score of additional spectators standing behind the television camera equipment. An immediate and full silence fell upon the room as Shi Pei-Pu made her entrance, holding ever-more tightly to my arm. The spectators turned or craned their necks to observe the appearance of the personage whose life story—in lurid detail—was known to each and every one of them. As we approached the front of the room, polite applause brought a small smile to the princess's face just before she ascended the two steps to the stage.

The performance began with a brief synopsis of the story line of the opera from which the arias were drawn. The tale involved the chance meeting of a princess and a peasant boy, each wearing cross-gender disguises. The first aria, my client explained to the hushed room, was about the sadness each lovestruck youth felt at being of the wrong gender to pursue the relationship. The second selection, in contrast, was an aria of pure joy, for not only did the enamored youths discover that each of them had been in cross-dress disguise but also that the peasant boy—unbeknownst to him until just that moment—was actually of noble blood. The third and final aria related the delighted emperor's blessing of the union. A polite giggle arose from the opera-savvy audience, since many of these plot elements had played their role in animating Western opera.

The synopsis finished, a small bow was followed by yet another round of polite applause. Then Shi Pei-Pu turned away from the audience and became entirely still. Remarkably still. The accompanist began to play. Several measures into the music, Shi Pei-Pu turned to face the audience, and there could be no doubt in anyone's mind that he did so as a woman.

**

How to describe the recital itself? It was completely unlike any other performance I had ever attended. Normally, there is a considerable degree of connection, of like-mindedness, between a performer and the patrons who have elected to attend. Here, however, from the very first note that Shi Pei-Pu launched into the air, there was a profound *disconnection*, an unbridgeable chasm that continued to widen, measure by measure. To begin with, there were the costuming issues mentioned earlier, which, as it turned out, were grossly exaggerated by the bright lighting required for the television filming. On top of this was the confusion, bordering on discomfort, that arose from the multiple levels of gender misrepresentation: a female role of a cross-dressing boy was being sung by a male who saw himself to be a female although he always dressed as a male. But these two elements of disconnection between diva and audience paled in the face of the audial onslaught.

It is arguably the case that there is no music on Earth more foreign to the Western ear than Chinese opera. It doesn't matter what level of cultural relativism and goodwill a Westerner brings to listening to these alien sounds, or how open his mind is to experiencing a new and different branch of opera. The chords are dissonant to our audial sensibilities and experience, and are in stark violation of the rules of the chromatic scale that inform our sense of musicality—so there is essentially no way for us to approach the music.

On top of all this, Shi Pei-Pu's voice wasn't in any better condition than was his costume. While no doubt his vocal abilities had once been appropriate for a soprano role, this was no longer the case: his advanced age, his difficult life, his forty extra pounds, and his lack of practice had, understandably, each taken their toll. The delicate soprano tones he so searched to refind were no longer available, and the audience found itself assaulted by an uneven baritone delivery that was farcically incongruous with his portrayal of a young princess.

The more Shi Pei-Pu sang, the greater the estrangement with the spectators became. By the time the third aria was completed, there were tears in his eyes as he looked out at an audience that sat in stunned silence. Three or four seconds passed before a belated and brief round of unconvincingly timid applause broke out. Shi Pei-Pu visibly quivered at being so out of place, so disconnected, so alone, and the recital ended uncomfortably for all involved.

The audience dissipated quickly while the *People* magazine crew—over twenty editors, executives, and their guests—hurried down the richly carpeted stairs to Maxim's bar. I walked with a deflated Shi Pei-Pu as he made his way back to his dressing room. I asked if I could accompany him home or, better yet, take him out to dinner. But he asked to be alone.

Taking my leave, I, too, lost no time in making my way to the first-floor bar, where I gladly joined up with Bertaux and the magazine personnel. We all proceeded to spend a small fortune in *People* magazine funds on drinks that were as overpriced as they were sorely needed. Bertaux, a scotch aficionado, spotted a bottle of scotch that was so "top shelf" the barkeep literally had to go fetch and climb a small ladder to reach it. God knows what those drinks cost the magazine, but as Bertaux had absolutely no sympathy whatsoever for *People* magazine, or its likely treatment of his friend, he couldn't have cared less. An hour later, we gave each other the classical two-cheek air-kisses that are so ingrained in French culture, said goodbye on the sidewalk, and went our separate ways. Although I see my dear friend every couple of years when work or pleasure takes me to Paris, Shi Pei-Pu and his singular life have been conspicuously absent from our conversations. For some reason, we seem to feel that we've exhausted the topic.

ACT 7
BOSTON, MASSACHUSETTS
MY LAW OFFICE, THIRTY YEARS LATER

I never saw Shi Pei-Pu again, although I often spoke with him on the phone as we worked on parlaying his refound moment in the sun into the extraordinary film on his life starring Jeremy Irons[13] and, of course, into Joyce Wadler's well-written book. But during those calls I had the impression that Shi Pei-Pu never again sounded quite the same. Something had been broken the night of the performance; some part of Shi Pei-Pu's spirit had been irredeemably saddened. And I had the distinct intuition that the princess was gone forever.

In due course, I received copies of the television broadcast, one of which I mailed to Shi Pei-Pu. But it was months before he viewed it, he told me, and when I asked him what he thought about it, he changed the topic of conversation. When I asked after his son, he reported that the young man had moved out and was very much on his own. Apparently, he didn't call home much, given the sadness in my client's voice.

***

In June of 2009, Shi Pei-Pu died, and once again, he received a moment of the media coverage he so dearly coveted. But even in the articles

---

13. *M. Butterfly*, 1993. (Directed by David Cronenberg.) I highly recommend your finding this magnificent film, sections of which are readily available on YouTube.

written after his death, he was ridiculed and belittled. Then, in 2014, a scholarly full-length book appeared that documented how Shi Pei-Pu had indeed been manipulated by one of Mao's master spies, Kang Sheng.[14] We now know that from Shi Pei-Pu's side, the entire relationship from the very first night had indeed been a "honeypot" trap—a common espionage recruitment technique involving sexual seduction.

In stark contrast, from Bernard Boursicot's perspective, the entire matter had clearly been all about love. Bertaux had this part right—I feel certain of it. And from this perspective, it becomes totally irrelevant whether Boursicot was, deep within himself, a gay man who needed to participate in a fiction about Shi Pei-Pu's gender to hide his homosexuality from himself, or whether he was a straight man utterly taken in by Shi Pei-Pu's manipulative scheme. All that matters for purposes of our exploration of this remarkable case of a fraudulently induced connection is the fact that the disconnect between Boursicot and Shi Pei-Pu existed from the moment of that first kiss in 1964 behind one of the stately elm trees on the grounds of the French embassy in Beijing. The French diplomat entered the relationship that very first evening looking for love, and he remained in love for thirty years until the weight of all that came to pass made his love no longer tenable. The Chinese opera star, in contrast, entered the relationship to gain favor with the Chinese police. One was in love. The other made a mockery of love.

We can philosophize about the nature of this fraudulent misconnection, we can analyze what it means for a relationship to be so disparate for its two participants, but there is one aspect of this case that words cannot adequately capture or convey: the depth and profundity of the pain and heartbreak that Bernard Boursicot endured. Words just cannot do justice to such coldheartedly inflicted suffering; it seems wiser to leave such a task to the music Puccini composed for the tragic ending of *Madam Butterfly*.

---

14. Roger Faligot and Rémi Kauffer, *Kang Sheng: Le maître espion de Mao* (Paris: Perrin, 2014).

THE BOY WHO WAS OLDER THAN HIS PARENTS

At ten years of age, Billy Denver was easily the youngest person who ever asked me for legal representation. And he was also one of the cutest: his bowl-cut, straight black hair and impish smile set off his eyes, which were precisely the color of a robin's eggs.

I came to know Billy through a phone call from Evan Newsom, MD, chief of pediatrics at Boston Children's Hospital. Dr. Newsom launched one of the nation's first child-abuse counseling and treatment programs, pioneering new techniques in discovering and treating abuse and neglect in young children. I had originally come to know Dr. Newsom when he agreed to serve as an expert witness in a litigation matter involving a sexually abused child, and had subsequently asked him many times to serve in this capacity in other court trials involving related matters.

It was a bright and crisp early spring day when Dr. Newsom telephoned me to discuss a ten-year-old cancer patient in his unit who suffered from stage-three lymphoma. The boy was the only child of educated, high-achieving parents. His father was a hyper-busy hedge fund manager who, in Dr. Newsom's opinion, didn't visit his child often enough—not nearly so. His mother was the twice-elected chief executive of the tony suburban town where the couple lived; from that point on, he referred to her as the "Mayor"—a moniker I hereby adopt. The Mayor visited Billy regularly, but unsatisfyingly to the boy. Something was amiss.

When I asked for more details, Dr. Newsom thought for a moment before he spoke in his deep, airline-pilot-calm voice. "There's a grayness, a sadness, to the boy that I can't explain . . . and I'm convinced that it's not an emotional reaction to his medical condition. I don't think that's what's going on at all." Dr. Newsom assured me that he couldn't discern even a hint of emotional abuse or neglect, which, as a "mandated reporter," he would have been required by law to immediately report to the Massachusetts Department of Social Services (DSS). He believed something far more subtle was taking place. He added that he had used every trick in his bag to get the boy to talk to him about what was worrying him—all to no avail. "All I got out of him," Dr. Newsom continued, "was that there is a 'legal issue' involved—whatever the hell he might mean by that. That's why I called you. Help me figure this one out, would you? This little guy is just a couple of months out from some tough-ass chemotherapy, and he needs these clouds to part so he can help us fight this thing. He's got to really care." He went stone silent after he said this, waiting for my reply.

So, you tell me. What could I possibly say other than "sure"?

***

A week later, I pulled into the Children's Hospital parking lot prepared to meet with Dr. Newsom and his patient. What I was *not* prepared for was the experience of walking into a children's cancer ward. I must have passed by twenty kids lying in their beds, doing nothing. I wildly regretted that I wasn't a sports star or someone else who could have brought a moment of joy just by stopping by. But I was merely another adult in a suit, of no interest to children who, I should think, were seeing far too many grown-ups in suits and white coats and far too few other kids their own age.

I fell under Billy's spell the moment I met him—hell, the moment I first saw him. Perhaps it was those robin's-egg-blue eyes, or perhaps it was the sense of calm and resolve he radiated: rare traits for a boy of ten. When Dr. Newsom initially introduced us, Billy exhibited complete disinterest in me—until the famous pediatrician mentioned that I was a lawyer who did a lot of legal work with children. With that, Billy sat up more against his pillows and announced in as serious a tone of voice as his little body could muster, "Well, that's awesome, because I happen to need to retain counsel. *And right now.*" Dr. Newsom and I burst out laughing, and I think what first really touched me about this child was that he joined right in.

Dr. Newsom soon excused himself. And here, in a few words, is what Billy told me—with an alarming clarity of expression. He first described his financially successful family, where everything material was supplied in abundance. Then, in dramatic contrast, he talked about what was missing—*parents who could soothe him*—as he faced the difficult reality of his illness. According to Billy, his father had neither the time nor the inclination to parent on an emotional level. But, he conceded, many of his friends had super-busy dads, so this wasn't really his principal concern. The real problem lay with his mother, who, again using Billy's words, "doesn't seem to be able to love me very . . . fully." I remember wincing when he said this, and I will never forget his clarification that soon followed: "No, I'm not saying that right. I know she *does* love me"—he took a long pause to find just the words he wanted—"but she does love the way a flashlight shines light when its batteries are just about dead. It's just a glow: it doesn't help you see in the dark."

It took me a while to recover my composure after his remark, and before I succeeded, Billy broke in again: "That's why I need a lawyer." The boy looked over at me and smiled with luminous warmth. It nearly broke my heart to have to tell him that because he was under eighteen, the law didn't allow him to hire counsel. And even if I could be his attorney, I explained, there was no law that I know of that requires parents to be effective in how they love their children. Yes, of course, there are laws, I spelled out, that require parents to keep their children safe, fed, clothed, housed, in school, medically attended to, and so on— *but none compelling effective parental loving.* I explained that there are many, many wrongs in the world for which there are no legal remedies.

I immediately could see the deflating effect my words were having on Billy, and I just couldn't leave it at that. So, probably unadvisedly, and definitely unprofessionally, I asked him to tell me more, to give me all the details he thought were important. I couldn't have known it, but in doing so, I opened the door to a remarkable chain of experiences—and even to an adventure.

**

Billy spoke from his heart for the next quarter hour. He was bound and determined to find out why neither of his parents succeeded in giving him much "emotional juice," as he called it, even when they were together with him—and even when they were clearly trying to do so. Something was missing in their capacity to connect with him, and Billy was out to discover and fix the problem. By the time he had finished speaking, his childish charisma had proven irresistible. But while I admitted that, I couldn't ignore the fact that the law doesn't allow minors to retain counsel. And, mind you, he was not looking for pro bono counsel: he told me that his savings at home were just shy of fifty-nine dollars—and he was willing to invest that entire sum in my law fees. He told me this with complete earnestness, and I didn't dare smile.

I had an idea, I told him. Given that I was general counsel to a children's social service agency called The Home for Little Wanderers, if he met with one of The Home's social workers, and if the social worker called me for a legal consult, then perhaps I could formally represent The Home but still work on his case. I couldn't promise anything: it would be up to The Home—but at least it was a possibility. Now we were back in smiling territory.

Later that afternoon, I reached The Home's clinical director and told her about my meeting with Billy, and especially about Dr. Newsom's concerns. She came through in spades, and arranged for a clinician to visit Billy at the hospital the following day.

Just shy of a week after I met Billy, the clinician gave me a call. Not surprisingly, the little ten-year-old had fully convinced her that there was a significant, if subtle, problem with connection and affection in his home. She, too, was deeply impressed with the boy's determination to get to the bottom of why he felt so emotionally undernourished. She described Billy as "charming" and "insightful," but she also called him "somewhat saddened" and "emotionally hungry." She, as had Dr. Newsom, concluded that Billy's sadness was not a function of his medical issues—serious though those were. The wording she used in her summary really struck me: "According to Billy, his parents 'love' him in some formal sense, but neither of them seems capable of making him *feel* loved." She also reported that her clinical director had told her that I was welcome to intervene in the boy's favor as counsel to The Home, or, if I preferred, that she could call the parents to see if they would come in to talk to her. On a follow-up phone call, we brainstormed about which approach was likely to bear more fruit, and we spoke about how ironic it was that a mother who could entice thousands of people into voting for her couldn't convince her only child that she loved him in just the same way other mothers love their children. We concluded that there might be more to learn if it were I who arranged to meet with the parents, and that I would report back to her if it seemed that family therapy might help the parents get to work on their issues. I couldn't wait to call the boy.

If only I could put into words the excitement in Billy's voice when I reached him on the phone the following day. He seemed in no way surprised to learn that he had convinced the social worker of the justice of his cause, and he didn't sound particularly concerned when I told him that although I couldn't formally serve as *his* attorney, I could keep an eye on his interests as The Home's counsel.

I warned Billy that while I would try to meet with his parents, I would have little or no leverage to use if his parents didn't agree to do so. Billy's response was so notable that I wrote it down in my telephone notes: "Perfect. They'll listen to you, I'm sure of it. I'm a great little kid, except for being so sick. There is no reason why my parents shouldn't be able to learn how to love me better." I remember thinking how remarkable it was that this little guy did not for one second internalize the ineffective love his parents gave back to him—he seemed to have complete confidence that he was entirely lovable, and that the shortcomings of the parental-child connections in the household came from something wrong with *them*, not from something wrong with *him*. It wasn't very long at all before I learned that he was entirely correct.

By the time I finished that phone call with Billy, I was on a mission to get at least one of Billy's parents up and working. This little guy was going into chemotherapy, and if I'd understood Dr. Newsom correctly, his cancer was very threatening and he was going to need radiation therapy as well. More was needed from Billy's parents, a great deal more. In some subtle but important way, the boy couldn't tap into their parental love. He couldn't close his eyes and feel it soothe him as he fell asleep. There was parental connection here, but it was a misconnection.

***

Billy had given me both of his parents' work phone numbers, so it was easy to reach the father's secretary. Reaching the father was quite another matter. Clearly, his administrative staff person was a professional gatekeeper, and entirely skillful at fending off unknown callers. Finally, I had no choice but to pull a rather major bluff: "Tell him if he doesn't call me back about his son, I may file a Chapter 119, Section 51A report of child neglect against him and his wife with the Department of Social Services." The statute numbers did the trick; I had an appointment two days later.

Billy's father ran a private equity company that, I later learned, was a stone-cold player in the game of buying up well-run local companies, immediately loading them up with debt to repay his company's acquisition costs up front, and then cannibalizing them by selling off their intellectual property or know-how to the highest bidder, and what remained of their market share to a competitor. One knowledgeable source told me that these hard-edged tactics had put hundreds of people out of work. Many hundreds. When I walked into Mr. Denver's office, he never even came out from behind his mammoth desk to shake my hand, and his very first words were: "I only have fifteen minutes for this. Big meeting at ten o'clock; and you should know that the only reason I'm even giving you this much time is because my lawyer said I should. He said you could cost me a truckload of wasted time if you hassled us by filing some kind of report about our parenting." I was stunned into silence for the next fifteen seconds or so, hoping that his own words would echo around in his mind. Could the next business deal really be more important to him than the well-being of his only child?

It turned out it was. My effort to explain to William Denver that Billy was emotionally starving at a time when he desperately needed full connection with his parents left the father looking back at me with a blank stare. I knew that blank stare fully well from the time I gave an identical one to a friend of mine who was a mathematics professor: he had just finished trying to explain to me over lunch what his work in "differential equations" was all about. Clearly, Billy's father wasn't going to get anywhere close to understanding what I was saying to him. "Look, Counselor," he replied after thinking quietly for a few moments, "I love my son, of course. The problem isn't me. It's my wife: since she's gotten into politics she's at least as busy as I am. I keep telling her, it's her responsibility to make time for the kid."

I was tempted to just get up and walk out; after all, the quarter hour was almost up. But I had no choice but to take the opportunity to probe about the mother, even if that meant I went—*God forbid*—overtime. "So, let's talk about your wife, then. Billy told our social worker that he knows that she loves him, but that he can't '*feel* her love.' Those were his exact words. What do you think he meant?"

The venture capitalist in his $2,000 suit went silent. He looked down at his right hand, which was skillfully twirling a pencil around his thumb, and then recatching it, over and over again. His voice choked up a bit when he finally responded. "She's like that with me too. Billy's right. I don't know what it is in her that makes her love so lukewarm. It's not just the mayor thing—she was always like that. I used to want to shake her, to try to wake up the last thirty percent of her heart." He paused again, still spinning the pencil around in his fingers, and then he smiled and looked up. "Go see her, Counselor; go figure her out. Get your social workers to work with her. That's how we'll get what we need for Billy." He stood up, ended our meeting, and announced that "we're overtime here, and I need to get into my conference room. But we found the solution for you—I mean, for Billy. And I'll try to spend more time with him too; I know he's about to face some tough procedures. Thanks for coming by, and thanks for trying to do what's best for Billy. *I mean that.*" With that, he picked up his phone and called his administrative assistant, ignoring me as I got up and left. As I waited for the elevator, I kept thinking that it might be easier for me to learn advanced math than to figure out how to reach inside this guy's heart and flip the "on" switch.

Okay, so that left the mother. She must be more accessible than this moneymaking machine; after all, she had twice been elected to office. Her constituents must have seen something special in her.

***

Lo and behold, I was mesmerized by Dianne Denver the moment she sat down across from me at my desk. At first I couldn't tell if it was her attractive face or her long, straight black hair, but within ten minutes, I realized it wasn't her beauty that I found so alluring: it was her ardor, her fire. One hears about "charisma" often enough, but it's rare to meet a truly charismatic person; I suppose, by definition, they are few and far between. You could sense her self-confidence even in the way she held herself; it seemed immediately apparent how this sparkling, five-foot-four ball of energy had twice been elected to high office. But what was not at all clear was how she could possibly be failing to fully and successfully connect with her adorable child. The answer to this riddle was to teach me how otherwise psychologically healthy people can have their capacity to connect compromised by something deep in their background, and how difficult it can be for them to address what lies behind their inability to fully connect with others in their life.

Dianne Denver knew exactly why I had invited her to come into my office. "So, you're the attorney for The Home for Little Wanderers. We send them a check for the children every Christmastime. William told me that Billy had spoken with one of your social workers. Obviously, we appreciate the opportunity to speak with you *directly*." The import of her emphasis on the word "directly" was clear: the last thing any elected official wants is to deal with the DSS authorities.

"So, what questions can I answer for you?" she asked. As general counsel to The Home, and to four of its sister institutions, I'd met with and spoken to scores of parents about problems in their households. But Billy's case was singular because the lackluster love he described and anguished over in no way constituted "neglect" under the statute. It didn't even come close. But what I lacked in leverage, I made up for in determination, and given the father, I clearly had to make an all-out effort with the mother—whatever it took. What was not clear until much later in the case, however, was that I underestimated by several orders of magnitude the work it would take to help Denver come to grips with what rendered her connective capacities so significantly compromised.

"Should I sugarcoat this or just tell you straight up what I think?" I began.

"I can handle it," she replied with the confidence you'd expect.

"Okay. Billy is trying to understand why he doesn't *feel* more loved by you and Mr. Denver."

The Mayor was clearly taken aback, but quickly rallied. "You met his father; my guess is you know the answer to your question."

"I know half the answer, yes. But where do you figure into all this?"

"I love my son."

"Are you sure?"

"Of course, I'm sure!"

"Then why isn't *he* sure?"

She froze. I immediately realized I needed to back down my assertion to something manageable—I meant to be helpful, after all, not insulting. "Ms. Denver, I didn't say that well. What I meant to say is that Billy said that he *knows* that you love him, but that he can't *feel* your love. Those were his words. Why would he say that?"

Denver remained motionless, suddenly looking drained and sallow.

Then the case took its first bizarre turn. The Mayor was slowly getting ready to speak after having what seemed like an intense inner conversation. What she said, however, came out in the softest, most non-Mayor-like voice you can imagine—and it was just five little words that seemed to sneak out the side of her mouth on their own. I could barely hear them, but I did hear them: "That's because I can't either."

Denver looked down, crossing her arms over her chest, and put her right hand over her eyes. She massaged her temples for at least fifteen seconds, contemplating how she wanted to proceed. Then she just stood up and walked right out of my office.

"Ms. Denver," I called to her back, "either you have this conversation with me or I will think seriously about advising my client . . ." But she was out the office door and gone.

The woman had called my bluff, and now I had no idea where to head. Fortunately, I didn't need to: two or three days later, Billy called.

In his deepest, most serious tone of voice, Billy asked me whether I'd met with each of his parents. I confirmed that I had. He had seen them both, he told me, but neither had mentioned their meeting with me. He surmised that their plan was to redouble their efforts to connect better with him—which, of course, was precisely what we were aiming for. Apparently, the father had discussed weekend camping plans, saying that he was really looking forward to some time together when Billy finished up with his treatments. "This," Billy editorialized, "is something he hasn't suggested since I was quite young." Needless to say, this made me laugh out loud again—and once more, sweet little Billy joined right in. "You see, *we've* got some improvement already," he announced, his intonation confirming that *we* were now a team, in this together, wherever it might lead.

***

On my next visit a week later, I asked myself whether Billy's cancer was subtly reducing his vigor, but his strength of character and charm drowned out these early signs of slippage. We spoke openly about the quality of the connection he had with his parents: we must have sounded like two electricians discussing an ineffectual flow of electricity through a line. Billy saw his father's incapacity to emote as intrinsic, or as he phrased it with a sweet smile, "Asking him to get better at loving is like asking me to get taller—it's going to take a while." He saw more promise in working on his mother's inabilities. The exact phrase he used describing her affective incapacities was unforgettable: "There's just no heat in her warmth." I was so taken aback by this wording that I missed the next few things he said, but he got my attention back big-time when he asked if he could ask me a personal question. I reluctantly consented, and he immediately shot back, "Do you have any kids?"

I could see no way out. "I do, Billy. I have a son who's not far from your age."

"Do you think your son has ever felt what I feel?"

Whoops. Now I had no way to avoid indirectly expressing a judgment on Billy's parents, something I had hoped to avoid. But Billy wasn't someone you could tell half-truths to—that was clear. "No, I don't Billy. We—"

Before I could stammer uncomfortably on, Billy picked up on my discomfort and cut me off, telling me: "That's all right; you don't need to say any more. I don't mean to pry into your personal life. I just wanted to confirm that what I get from my parents is not what other kids get." Then he added, with an infectious enthusiasm, *"So, what's our plan?"*

Throwing caution to the wind, I followed up on my own personal motto: when in doubt, dive in. "Okay, Billy, let's get strategic. Here's my take on your parents. As for your dad, it seems to me that you're the emotional adult in the relationship. So, what if we think about it this way: if things were the other way around—if he were complaining to some family therapist that he couldn't get *your* emotional attention—the counselor might tell him to get involved in a couple of your interests. He might suggest to your dad that he should listen to some of the music you like and try to get into it. Or play whichever board game or sport with you that you like best—stuff like that. So, let's flip that around: Why not draw your dad out in the same way? If he's only interested in corporate raiding and business deals, then what about if you go learn something about that kind of thing—and talk about it with him? Draw him out about it in conversation. If he can't do this for you, then you do it for him. What do you think?"

Billy hesitated while he thought through what I was suggesting. "Why not?" he finally replied. "I'll give it a try. Dr. Newsom said I'm going to have a lot of reading time recovering from the treatment. Can you bring me a copy of the *Tall Street Journal*?"

"I think it's *Wall Street Journal*."

"Yeah. That one. Dad reads it first thing every day." He looked away from me, and made a little "humph" sound. Then after a few seconds, he looked back at me. "What about my mom? She's the one who really puzzles me."

"Me too," I said with a sigh. "I'd like to work with her, but she got up and stormed out of my office. Billy, I have no way to force your parents to meet with the right kind of counselor to work on their issues, and I'm sure your parents' lawyer explained that to them. So, how do we get your mom to come in and work with me?"

"I'll make that happen," he replied without a moment's hesitation.

"What will you say to her?"

"Never mind. I've got leverage."

Leverage? I didn't even know ten-year-olds knew the word, let alone had any.

***

It was several weeks before I heard another word from an adult Denver. Billy, in contrast, called regularly—but always only briefly, and always about some discrete issue that was running through his mind. In one call, he reported that his father was now making more of an effort to show up and demonstrate affection, but, as Billy put it, he seemed to have reached "some kind of roof." (I wouldn't have mentioned the word "ceiling" for all the tea in China.) As for his mother, there was apparently no progress in convincing her to come back to see me—I heard this over and over until the eighth or ninth time he called. And that time, he was so excited about what he had to say that he'd told my administrative assistant that his call was "urgent." Apparently—but not at all surprisingly—he had created his own relationship with her, given that she came bursting into my office ignoring that I was in a meeting with an associate attorney. I excused the young attorney from the meeting and worriedly picked up the line, fearing that perhaps something had gone wrong medically. "We did it" were the first words I heard. "She promised me she'd go back to see you at least one more time; the rest is up to you."

"How'd you pull this off?"

"She asked me what I wanted for my birthday; it's coming up soon, you know. I'm not going to always be ten!" When I stopped giggling, Billy transitioned from his silly voice to his serious voice to tell me that his chemotherapy had been delayed for about an extra month while some "numbers" improved, whatever exactly that meant. When he asked me why, I had to tell him: "Wrong guy, Billy. Ask Dr. Newsom—or your oncology doctor. I don't know any more about this stuff than you do."

"That's cool," he replied nonchalantly. "You handle the legal stuff; I'll take care of the medical stuff. Gotta go, bye." Dial tone. Gone.

**

Roughly a month after the Mayor walked out of my office, Billy's persistence paid off. I was uneasy, given our last encounter, but the Mayor immediately dissipated my anxieties by the way she greeted me. "Good morning, Counselor," she said, shaking my hand. "I'm ready to get to work now."

Once we were in my office, the Mayor spoke without prompting—I began to suspect that this might really go somewhere this time.

"So, you've been getting to know Billy."

"I have indeed. He calls once or twice a week. Short calls. I hope that's okay with you; I think it breaks the monotony of the hospital, and after one or two thoughts, he just pops off the line. He's really quite engaging."

She smiled at this, and her charm showed for just a moment through her businesslike exterior. "You have no idea. He insisted that I come talk to you."

"I'm sure he did. But I'm also pretty sure that's not why you came," I replied, determined to take the initiative in the conversation. "I hope you're here because you want to tell me more about what you told me last time."

"What exactly did I tell you?"

"I had just told you that Billy said that he knew you loved him but that he couldn't *feel* your love. That was a quote. It still is. When I mentioned that to you, you told me that you 'couldn't feel it either.' That's also a quote. I've been wondering ever since what in the world you meant by that."

The Mayor fell silent and still. Nothing moved except her facial expressions: I had the impression that there were voices arguing with one another inside her head, so I decided to just sit still and wait until her inner demons settled their affairs. Finally, she spoke.

"I do want to work on what's going on inside me. But it's so complicated; there are so many levels to it all."

"Good, that'll keep it from being boring," I said.

She couldn't resist a quick smile. "If I end up telling you my story, and you end up finding it boring, I'll . . . I'll . . ."

"You'll buy me a bottle of my favorite Burgundy wine," I chipped in.

"You're on. Okay. But a question for you. How confidential can this be? What I need to tell you has got to be completely and totally private between us."

Now it was my turn to go silent while I thought this through. "Dianne, my client is The Home for Little Wanderers, not you, so you would have no legal privilege, as such. You would have to be my client for you to have the kind of assurance of confidentiality you may want. But I—"

"Well, can I hire you to be my attorney?" she interrupted.

I hadn't meant my remark in that sense. But it was an idea. "The problem with that idea, Dianne, is twofold. First, I would need The Home's assent. And second, you would need to understand that if there ever were a conflict of interest between you and The Home, I could no longer represent either of you in the matter."

"Would The Home agree?"

"They probably would if I recommend it. But why are you so certain I'm the right attorney for you? There's a city full of qualified lawyers—some of whom may be specialized in whatever your issues are."

"Oh, I think you're the right attorney. First off, you care about Billy. He speaks very highly of you, you know. When I asked him what he wanted for his birthday—it's just about a month from today—he was insistent that the *only* thing he wanted from me was for me to come talk to you. And frankly, I like your double training; I researched what you taught at Boston University. I know dozens of business lawyers through my husband, and scores more through my own work. But I couldn't share anything personal with any of them, not even close. They're not built for the issues I need to raise."

"And why, exactly, do you think I am?"

"Because Billy thinks so. He thinks you listen. I'm willing to give it a go, if you are—and if you can resolve the possible conflict-of-interest issue with The Home. Can you call them now and see if they mind if you become my counsel for these purposes?"

This whole thing was advancing and morphing at warp speed, and, of course, I had no idea whatsoever what her legal issues were. On the other hand, there was Billy to consider, and if she went to another law firm, I'd lose all ability to try to help him get what he needed and wanted so badly. I asked the Mayor to wait in the reception area while I made my call. As expected, The Home's clinical director had no problem assenting: in fact, she was pleased to learn that Billy's mother was going to work on her issues, and positively ecstatic about my law work on the case being off The Home's tab.

I invited the Mayor back into my office and extracted from her one final, and very singular, condition: she would need to sign a representation agreement establishing that while I served as her counsel, she, as Billy's parent, would authorize me to simultaneously represent Billy. And I was entirely up front with her: my primary interest in the case was his welfare, and if I thought sharing something I learned helped in that way, I needed to be free to communicate about it with Billy without being threatened about having breached her attorney-client privilege. The Mayor stared at me for a good twenty seconds before reluctantly agreeing—after extracting from me the reasonable promise that I would consult her prior to revealing to Billy anything of substance that I learned in representing her. With that mutual understanding, we got down to work.

***

"Please try to understand," the Mayor began her story, "that the single most important thing for you to learn is that I live in constant fear. And fear changes your life—or it has changed my life, in any case. It has split my life in two. One life is on the outside—my family, my public life—all seems well, totally normal, save for Billy's health. The other life is on the inside—I mean, inside my head, inside my heart. And it's a living hell. And it's tearing me apart."

After she said this, some gear switched inside the Mayor. I'd seen this same thing happen a hundred times when a witness took the stand, or testified in deposition, especially if they were recalling a traumatic event. One moment, they are the person who walked into the room, and the next moment, they are the person who they were years or even decades before at the time of the event. The single most memorable example of this phenomenon that I ever personally observed was when a sixty-five-year-old sexual assault victim testified as a plaintiff in a civil case. She had a raspy, cigarette-debased voice when she began her testimony—followed by a much-younger-sounding, almost clear voice when she let the girl inside her tell the jury about how her piano teacher had abused her when she was a teenager. I've never forgotten that.

Anyway, under the influence of whatever it was from her past that I was about to hear, the Mayor's composure and self-confidence began to melt. Little sniffles snuck in between her words with slowly increasing frequency, and bit by bit, her eyes teared up. She began by saying, "I don't know how to tell you what it's been like for me to face this all alone, year after year, decade after decade." The tears increased incrementally, and she had a progressively harder time finding her words. "When you're afraid, and you've never told anyone about it . . . and you're alone with it . . . you can't open up; it's so hard to open up—even with those you love the most. It just . . ." But there were no more words for the moment: just a flood of tears. I got up, handed over the Kleenex box from my desk, and then sat in the other client chair, turning it to face the Mayor. It took a minute or two for her to calm, and then—slowly at first—she began to let out what had been blocked up inside her, apparently for many years. "What Billy is sensing and trying to tell you about comes from . . . something inside me that was . . . deadened . . . by living in fear for so, so long. It's like . . . like it keeps me from *feeling*. It's as if I'm emotionally numb, or partially so. It's like when your arm falls asleep when you sleep on it weirdly, and you touch it with the other hand and it can't feel your touch. But it's not my arm . . . It's my—I don't know what." But she did know, and she fought hard to say it out loud. "It's my . . . my heart." And then there were no more words—just tears again. I asked if she wanted to take a break, but she vehemently shook her head no, and I could see that she was completely determined to let it out—to get it out—because she no longer paid any attention to the flood of tears and deep sobs that mixed with her words. "It's like I'm so fixated on my fear that I can't . . . And my husband . . . and especially

Billy . . . they deserve so much more . . . and this is what Billy senses. I don't know how he sees through my charade; I try so hard to . . . I *do* love him . . . Of course, I love him. I hope you . . ."

"Dianne, take all the time you need. Listen, there is a fitness center a few floors up; I'm going to go get you a proper towel; these tissues aren't up to the job." I was back five minutes later with a clean towel, part of which I had wet down with cold water. She covered her entire face with the cool, damp part—and stayed that way for fully a minute. Bit by bit, I could hear her breathing calm down, and she regained her poise. Then she stood up just enough to pivot her chair so we were facing each other straight on, and with absolutely no apparent embarrassment at what was left of her prominent status—or eye makeup—she finally found the words needed to express what had welled up inside her so powerfully.

"I'm not fully present, not really. Even around those I'm closest to. Even in worrying about and trying to help my lovely Billy. It's like I'm somehow . . . not really here. It's like I'm looking down, and I can see myself going through my mother act from twenty feet up in the air. I see Billy in the hospital. I see my husband talking away about the minute details of some goddamn business deal I could care less about. I see my fellow town employees racing around town hall, doing a hundred tasks. But it's always like I'm in the audience, watching a play from the balcony. Even though one of the players is me. Does this make any sense? It's like I watch myself interact with Billy, or my husband, or my colleagues, as if I were a player onstage, and I'm in the audience—always in the balcony. And I can't feel what's in my character's heart—it's just a script I'm speaking. My character—the one I play—is all motion and no emotion. Even if I watch myself laugh, I don't feel myself laugh. I know this sounds stupid, but I don't know how to say it any better. This is the first time I've ever even tried. I'm sorry I can't . . ." And then the tears again burst forth in another bout of crying.

The Mayor excused herself to go to the ladies' room, while I went to make us some tea in the firm's coffee room. Five minutes later, the Mayor reentered. She was amazingly composed, and I feared that perhaps she'd put the genie back in the bottle. I also feared that that was not what would be best for her or for Billy.

So, I immediately reinitiated the conversation. "Tell me about your fears, or what it is that you're referring to, Dianne. Don't stop. You're doing great. I'm listening, and I am *hearing* you. Tell me more about what you're talking about. Let it out. Tell me about the patterns over time of these feelings."

This prompt worked. After a pause, and after letting out a long sigh, she began to open up. "Patterns. You're right. There was a period when things were calmer for me. At the time, I was so grateful, so hopeful that the memories were resolving, fading. But then once I was elected and stepped into the public limelight—my fears just exploded inside me again. I should *never* have run for office—I know that now. I knew it two years ago and hinted at not running for reelection, but there was no reason I could tell others about *why* I wouldn't run. Especially because it was clear I would win; I ran unopposed. And there were so many people pressuring me and encouraging me—it benefited each of them in one way or another. Terry, since I've held office, I've had terrible nightmares—the kind where you wake up in a cold sweat, gasping for air, overjoyed when you realize that it was just a dream. And even my daydreaming has become more and more focused on . . . on what I did, what I'm exposed to. And I can't keep the images from flashing up in my mind anymore, like I used to be able to do." She went silent with this, looking inward, far away, almost in a trance.

"Paint a picture for me, Dianne. Tell me what you're afraid of. What colors do you see?"

Again, she was receptive to a prompt, and spoke in an almost dreamlike voice, with her eyes closed. "In some of them, it was gray. And there is a recurring image. There's a room. Everything is in different grays. No color at all. A desk, and on it, a desk lamp—the old-fashioned, gooseneck kind. Next to the lamp there is a typewriter—the old, tall black mechanical kind. There's a man at the desk—doing nothing, just staring. Just drumming his fingers on the desk, over and over and over again. Wanting to type." Then she went silent.

"Is this man someone you know or once knew? Is he at work?"

"No, I don't know him." She said nothing for half a minute, and then mumbled: "He's a detective."

"I'm sorry. Did you say 'detective'? I'm completely lost. You mean like a police detective? Is he trying to figure something out?" The

Mayor shivered once, somewhat violently—a sign that she was accessing somatic memory. "Dianne, you're in a safe space here. You can let it out. You can let it all out. It's time to tell someone about it. You're safe. Let it out. I've been here many times, with many clients, Dianne. And it has felt so very good to them when they finally let their fears come out, when they finally sought help in dealing with them. I promise you, Dianne, *I promise you*—you'll feel better. Take the leap. Stop thinking. Take the leap and tell me what you've been so afraid of."

I could see the Mayor struggling to get her mouth to form the words. Twice, her lips moved as she tried—and twice, they stopped. And then . . . and then, something inside her just let go, just gave up, just snapped. She looked up, stared right at me, and told me what I least expected to hear.

"I robbed a bank."

I just sat there, my mouth agape, silenced, dumbfounded, speechless. It must have been twenty seconds before I finally rallied, and even then, I only managed to get out one solitary word, and that in a high-pitched, incredulous voice: "What?"

"I robbed a bank."

Again, I paused, taken aback, trying to find what to say. It took a while. "Do you mean you *embezzled* funds from a bank? Or you found that your bank had erroneously deposited funds into your account and you withdrew them?"

Now that the dam had broken, the story tumbled out; she had someone to tell her tale to, and there would be no stopping her.

"Trust me. I wouldn't be here if I hadn't actually robbed a bank. Of course, I wasn't the middle-aged lady you're staring at today. This happened over thirty years ago when I was a college student. I was young and I was crazy. And foolish as hell. I mean, there were no guns or anything like that involved. It was more what you would call 'breaking and entering'—or something. And amazingly, ridiculously, I got away with it. An amazing case of beginner's luck." With that, she shivered very deeply once again and then went silent, waiting to see how I would reply.

It took me quite a while, I have to admit. "Okay. Okay. So, you robbed a bank. Amazing. I've never met a real live bank robber before. Has it come back to life in some way—have you heard something from the police, or anyone else? Have you received any paperwork of any kind?"

"No, no. Actually, that's not the problem at all," she immediately shot back. "I haven't heard anything from anybody. But that isn't the issue."

"But what can I do for you, Dianne? It doesn't sound like there is any legal action to take if you haven't heard anything from the police. Frankly, it sounds like you might benefit more from talking with the right kind of clinician; perhaps you're going to have to learn how to go on living with this—but with some clinical support. And a good clinician might really help—a lot. And, now that we're on the topic, I've had one in mind for you for weeks."

This was a suggestion the Mayor was fully prepared to reject out of hand. "Not happening," she shot back at me. "That's not *at all* how I want to handle this. I need to get at the root cause of my fear before it drowns me from the inside out. And we're going to do that *now*. I can't live with the fear anymore—I can't. I can't sleep, I can't concentrate, and I can't clear my head enough to . . . to make Billy *feel* the way I love him. And you, Counselor, need to understand one thing very clearly: I am not seeking your legal advice about whether or not I should address this matter. I've already made that decision. What I need is an attorney who will probe the records of the robbery and somehow contact the right criminal authorities to see if this matter can be resolved and cleared up—off the record. I'd gladly give back the money I stole—with interest, fines—whatever. But I need action, and I need it now. And that, in case you're wondering, is why I let Billy talk me into coming back here."

I tried not to pause this time, but I still wasn't in full control of myself. "Okay. Okay. I hear you. I really do. But you need to know that I don't practice criminal law. I have a partner down the hall who does nothing but criminal work—I'd use her in a heartbeat if I had a criminal problem. Wouldn't you rather work with her on your case?"

Denver paused for a moment, sizing me up. Then, in what I imagined was her mayoral tone of voice, she did away with all ambiguity. "No, I want *you* on my case. You're welcome to bring in your partner for her criminal law expertise—that'll be entirely up to you. But I need *you* involved, because Billy needs you involved. And I hope you'll continue to talk with him and comfort him throughout this process, because I really don't know where my head's going to be at, what with worrying about his health at the same time as launching this project. The overlap is coincidental, by the way—I need you to know that. I know it's like a perfect storm. I'd gladly put my . . . my issues on hold—if I could. I really would. *I wish I could.* But I can't." The Mayor fell silent and seemed pensive for a moment before she sighed and then added in a soft, almost plaintive tone of voice, "I need an ally, Terry. And so does Billy. I just can't do this alone anymore."

Silence followed again as the glow of the late-afternoon sun flowed through the window and bathed the room in soft light. At some point, the harsh fluorescents would need to be switched on—but not yet; they would change the mood entirely, and first I wanted to hear her story.

"Dianne, don't worry. I'm not going anywhere. So, let's start with your telling me how you robbed a goddamn bank."

The Mayor just sat there, as still as could be—seemingly in disbelief that, at long, long last, she was free to tell her tale. She gave one last little shiver and then dove in. "Okay, then, the year was 1968, and I was a sophomore at Columbia University. There were protests on campus, as there were all over the country that year—both anti–Vietnam War protests and civil rights protests. One demonstration at school was staged inside the administration building, and it led to six of the anti-war student activists being placed on academic probation. They became known as the 'IDA Six.' One of them was my first lover. Then, a few weeks later, things got far hotter on campus when someone disclosed that a Columbia University think tank had consulted with the military about some of the most unsavory tactics used in the war. This led to much larger protests that culminated in a student occupation of the administration building—more than seven hundred students were arrested. Robbing the bank was my contribution to all this: the purpose was to raise funds for the legal defense fund for the arrested students. What I *hope* you'll be able to argue is that I was so caught up in the student movement that I lost all sense of right and wrong. It was like being part of a cult. The movement swept up its participants and carried us along like an ocean wave sweeps up a line of bodysurfers and carries them all in toward the beach. I've lain in bed awake at night a hundred times thinking this through—and this is the best argument

I can come up with. Hopefully you or your criminal law partner will come up with something better—God, I hope so. Is there any chance this argument will work?" The Mayor had been speaking faster and faster, and was nearly breathless when she finished.

"Dianne, as I've told you, I don't do criminal defense; so let's wait for a knowledgeable answer to your question. But what I do know is that banks are federally insured, so that means there would be two sets of prosecutorial authorities to deal with: state and federal. So, we'd have to win two victories; one without the other might not do you any good."

"Well, maybe it won't work, then. But don't you think, even if it doesn't, we're likely to learn a lot about the status of the case? Maybe some detective will tell you that they never go after thirty-year-old property crime cases. Maybe we'll learn that pre-computer property crime cases didn't even get entered into today's computer data banks. Maybe the paper folder on my case is stuffed in some dusty box in a police department basement, unlooked at for decades. Who knows what we'll learn?"

"Who knows, Dianne? I sure don't. Not my field. But what you're saying makes perfect sense to me. I would think we'd at least find some way to learn where the matter stands—even if in a generic sense, like, 'the police do not put resources into vintage nonviolent crimes.'"

"And you know what I already have?" she said, with a sound of relief in her voice. "I won't be dealing with this *alone* anymore. I've already crossed that bridge—Counselor!" She smiled enthusiastically after saying this. What a massive emotional distance she had traveled in one afternoon.

I smiled back. "I hear you, Dianne, and I'm here for you. But I want you to think about something. And this is important. Let's not leave our plan B to chance. Since your case has been silent for thirty-something years, my guess is that we'll probably learn that there is nothing we can do—nothing we *ought* to do. If that comes to pass, it would mean that you will indeed have to keep on living with this matter remaining unresolved. I want you to let me help you find just the right clinical professional to consult with—beginning now. Working with a good clinician would mean that no matter what legal outcome we arrive at, it will work for you on a psychological level. It takes time and it takes help to find resolution and tranquility. Can you trust me on this?"

"Let me think about it," the Mayor replied. "It's a big step."

"Sure, fair enough. Take some time. But I'm not going to drop the issue. Just warning you." I waited until she nodded yes. "Now, tell me how you robbed that damn bank. And don't skip any details; this has got to be rich."

**

But I wasn't destined to hear the Mayor's story for well over a month—which drove me nuts with anticipation. Halfway through my saying, "And don't skip . . . ," an associate attorney had knocked, entered, and whispered news in my ear of a quite urgent matter. Besides that, the Mayor needed to get to a meeting. So we agreed to meet the following week—but that ended up not working out for some long-forgotten reason; in the end, it was fully six weeks before I heard another word about the bank robbery.

**

The delay served its purpose, however. It left me time to step back and think about the Mayor's case—often while simultaneously dealing with the Boston traffic of the era: the "Big Dig" was then in full bloom. What really caught my eye was how wonderfully well the Mayor's case explored the role and impact of *secrets* in each of our lives.

I'd run into many clients with secrets. In fact, for attorneys, the legal fallout from revealed secrets helps pay the rent—year in, year out. One of my personal favorites was a happily married male client who came in for an appointment one day and told me of some rather significant ramifications he was experiencing from having failed to mention to his wife that an earlier relationship of his with another woman had in fact been a marriage. And not only that: it was a marriage that was never legally resolved with a divorce. When I inquired about what thought process had led him to marry again under these circumstances, his explanation was simply that when he and his second wife had taken out their marriage license, he had ticked the "first marriage" box because, as he rationalized his little secret: "My first marriage was so brief, and in another state halfway across the country, who would ever know?" Actually, it was the answer to his rhetorical question that had precipitated his making an appointment to come in for legal consultation. After more than eighteen years of silence, he had only recently received a phone call from his first wife. Apparently, for all those years she had worked hard to raise the daughter he never knew existed, and now she was seeking financial help from him for college expenses. He was seeking advice on the likelihood that a court would require him to pay his share (I thought so); in addition, he was wondering if I would agree to being present when he broke the news of his bigamy to his second wife (I thought not).

***

In honor of the Mayor's trusting me with the disclosure of her long-hidden secret, I'll do the same with you, my reader. I'm going to share a secret with you that up until this point in my life, I left unspoken for over half a century. Who knows: perhaps you will also pick both a secret and a trusted confidant and unburden yourself. Here goes . . .

***

I had a wonderful friend in college called Barry K. During our final year, one of the many pipe dreams that crossed our chemically enhanced minds was to take a bus to Mexico after graduation from Berkeley, buy a couple of horses in Mazatlán, and ride them about 630 miles to Mexico City. And damned if we didn't do just that.

The day after we arrived by bus in Mazatlán, we set about provisioning ourselves for our adventure. We located the local horse market and picked out two fine specimens, each for about $150. As you might imagine, even in 1966 Mexico, $150 bought you only the most modest of steeds. We bought saddles and bridles and saddlebags, and we had brought our sleeping bags to tie on behind each saddle. All we needed to do was to provision ourselves for the expedition, and we'd be off.

Now, when two 1960s Berkeley boys referenced provisions, one staple they had in mind was some pot. The question was, how to safely score pot in Mexico? Step one, we thought, was to find some guys about our age, chat them up with my high school Spanish, and then hint at what we were looking for. And it worked! Smiles broke out all around, and we agreed to meet at the same spot early that evening. And sure enough, as the sun slowly set in an ocher-toned sky, we found ourselves walking out of the city on ever-more-modestly paved surfaces that eventually became pebble-covered roads, which, in turn, gave way to dirt paths. The boys led us to a simple sheet-metal Quonset hut, and there we met with several middle-aged men, apparently in the trade. I announced that we were looking for *"una bolsita"*—translating "baggie" as best I could—and mentioning that we had ten dollars for the transaction. This led to an animated discussion between the men—in a dialect that I couldn't get a word of. Eventually, their decision was announced as if it were a courtroom proclamation: someone would meet us the following day in the city to deliver our purchase.

Everybody lived up to their end of the bargain, and by late afternoon the next day, we took possession of our *bolsita* of pot. The only problem was one of translation: instead of a sandwich baggie with an inch of grass, our ten dollars had purchased a brown supermarket bag—about one-third full. Between us, there were four saddlebags, which were stuffed to overflowing with our cooking and camping utensils, clothing, and toiletries. It was clear that some of this gear would need to be jettisoned. We ended up devoting one entire saddlebag to our proud new possession.

And so, off we went on our escapade. Over the next three and a half months, we rode across hill and dale in the general direction of Mexico City. There were dozens of adventures and wondrous meetings with rural folks, many of whom had never seen a gringo before. Often we rode into tiny villages that could be accessed only by a dirt path. There were evenings around woodstoves where village women fashioned tortillas by rhythmically clapping their hands together to flatten the cornmeal dough, and there were meals shared with warmhearted peasants who invited us into their homes and hearths. But, if truth be told, there were also days riding along in the rain under heavy gray skies. My swaybacked steed either refused to trot or couldn't remember how—I never determined which—and he only galloped once, and only because we found ourselves in the following predicament.

The two horses would graze when we would stop in the mid-afternoon to set camp for the night, but horses—even horses that only walk—need more energy than grazing on grass can provide. This problem was easily resolved, however: we would simply veer off the path and walk our mounts through people's cornfields. "Rocinante," as we called both horses after Don Quixote's famous steed, would yank one ear of corn after another off the tall stalks as they sauntered through the fields, chewing a couple of times, and then swallowing the whole thing down. One evening, a farmer must have seen us entering his field—where the corn grew well above our heads, even mounted. At first, we heard yelling—far enough away that we barely paid attention. But then it grew louder, and the yells were soon followed by several shotgun blasts. The Rocinantes broke into surprisingly powerful gallops, running wildly at an angle across the furrows. The cornstalks thwacked into us from all sides as we each lay as flat as possible along our horse's necks, laughing wildly at the absurdity of it all.

Anyway, we finally arrived at the capital city, selling off the horses and their tack on the outskirts for the same price we had paid for them. While we were despondent at saying goodbye to the Rocinantes after more than three months of partnership, they in turn gave us the distinct impression that they were looking forward to a considerably tamer lifestyle in the autumn of their days.

Now we had to figure out how to deal with the 99 percent of all that grass we hadn't smoked. We certainly weren't interested in taking it anywhere near the border. For the time being, we took it along to the little hotel room we rented. Our plan was to spend a few days visiting the great metropolis and then take a bus back to California. Ah, but that was not how things played out—not at all. Instead, we went out for a walk around the city, taking a Marlboro box of joints with us, failing to take heed of two age-old adages: "familiarity breeds contempt" and "never carry when you can stash."

It seemed like a good idea at the time to have a couple of puffs just after we had left the city's remarkable anthropological museum. It wasn't. We passed some gentlemen who turned out to be plainclothes police officers, and within half an hour, we were in a jail cell from hell where we waited in semidarkness for four or five hours. The one thing we knew for sure was that we had to avoid being taken by the police back to our hotel room. Somehow, we needed to divert their attention.

An idea came to us. Barry would pretend to gradually show signs of appendicitis. We had heard—probably from television—two things about the malady. First, the pain is felt in the lower right abdomen, and second, if you lie on your back and bring your right knee up, the pain is somewhat alleviated. If we could convince our jailers of this, perhaps we could get Barry taken to a hospital emergency room. Our hope was that once he was there, he would be able to call his parents.

In my entire life, I've seen only two better acting performances than the one Barry gave that day; one was by Alec Guinness, and the other by Dame Maggie Smith. Barry's began with just a few sighs. An hour later, a few moans. Nothing extreme. After about three hours of Barry's distress, a guard came by to bring us some water, and saw what was going on; I said nothing about Barry. Not a word. I did, however, drink down the water immediately, and ask ever so politely if I could possibly have another one—*cuando usted tenga tiempo*—whenever you have time. He came back around the corner with the water within ten minutes, but this time, he had someone with him—a low-level supervisor, it seemed. Barry ignored them, totally engaged in channeling his slowly developing appendicitis. I drank the water, pretending to pay no attention to Barry. The supervisor asked what the problem was with my friend. "Oh, he's had a pain in his right side for the past few days. I guess it's getting a little worse—*un poco mas malo. Pero, no es importante.*" Then came the magic words: he asked me if I knew what pain in the lower right side of the abdomen indicated. Needless to say, I replied that I didn't and asked what he thought we should do. Bless that man: he said he was going to talk to *el jefe*—the chief. About an hour later, we both were taken by ambulance to the emergency room—me for translation purposes—from where we were indeed able to call both sets of parents. Barry was admitted to the hospital for observation, and, lo and behold, his pain slowly subsided. The police left the hospital with our passports, but instructed us to call them and make an appointment to come in with our fathers—who were to arrive the following day. The four of us were to pay a "visit" to the chief.

Barry remained in the hospital overnight for observation, while I returned to the hotel and spent quite a considerable part of the evening

flushing pot down the toilet—being ever so careful not to cause a block-
age. The following day, it was time to pay the piper—and the chief.
Before that, of course, we each had to deal with highly disappointed
but loving fathers. Next, the four of us went to visit the chief. We were
told that the matter could be handled off the record, subject to payment of certain "administrative fees." These were paid by our fathers,
and mine was adamant: I would work and pay him back every cent;
that's how I would learn my lesson.

There, I've done it. I've just written out my own personal deepest, darkest, hidden secret. The stupidity of what I did still haunts
me; things could so easily have ended up much, much worse. I'm still
embarrassed at having been such an idiot, even after over half a century has passed me by. I have, over the years, told friends about some of
the adventures with the Rocinantes—but always without the ending—
and each time my pals have urged me to write something about our
adventures. But, how could I? The story would have revealed my most
carefully kept secret. Well, maybe now I can. Who knows? All thanks
to what I learned from the Mayor.

Could it be that secrets in general tend to create relational blockages that threaten the fullness of our connections with others? Do our
secrets—some of them anyway—create little emotional no-go zones
that interfere with our capacity to emote? Do they function as imped-
iments to fully sharing who we really are with those we care most
about—the way a tiny pebble in your shoe interferes with your stride
as you walk?

***

As the Mayor and I worked on finding a time to meet again, Billy lan-
guished in Children's Hospital, waiting for his tests to finally demonstrate to his treating oncologist that it was appropriate to begin his
chemotherapy. He had turned eleven, which had been duly feted by the
family. As for me, I had pulled out a cookbook and baked him a dozen
chocolate éclairs, which led to more laughter than gustatory delight:
the rock-hard pastry shells, Billy quite accurately noted, could have
been used for hand grenades simply by substituting explosive powder
for the *crème patissiere*. I was standing by his bed—each of our chins

covered in chocolate—when he made this observation, and it was so good to see him crack up and laugh, laugh, laugh.

About once a week, my secretary would buzz me to announce, "Billy's on the line," and I would pick up to hear his tender and amiable voice. Our conversations at this point invariably began with a question Billy had custom designed, as he pronounced it: "Vat zup?" I could be in the bluest of funks about bad news in some law case, or about having just learned that an important client was moving out of state—whatever—and then would come a "Vat zup?" from Billy. I don't think I ever once said goodbye without feeling lightened by having spoken with him.

***

Finally, six long weeks after my first meeting with the Mayor, I once again welcomed her back into my office. We had barely greeted each other when the Mayor took an envelope out of her briefcase and removed an eight-by-eleven photograph of herself as a college girl. She was thin and trim in that era, and wore her straight black hair long and pulled back into a ponytail. She shot a radiant smile back at whoever took the photo, and she seemed entirely at ease in old jeans, sandals, and a washed-out, soft-looking blue work shirt. The photo carried me back to the 1960s—a moment in history when the internationalism of the student movement seemed to portend a brighter future than the wars of the 1940s or the fears of the 1950s.

The Mayor exhaled deeply. "God, how do I do this?" she asked out loud. I didn't say a word; she needed to volunteer the story, not to have it dragged out of her. "To start with, my name was different in college; it was Annie Sher. So, as you can see, I not only took my husband's last name but I also legally changed my first name. I did this . . . to build walls between me and my past."

Then, bit by bit, as the Mayor began to relay more and more of her tale, the younger sounding she became. I progressively had the impression that it was actually not the Mayor who was narrating her story—it was the girl in the photograph. The two voices, by the way, were quite distinguishable. The girl described how her life had changed in college. Brought up on Pat Boone and Eddie Fisher, she found herself at Columbia listening to the Beatles, the Rolling Stones, Simon & Garfunkel, Joan Baez, and Bob Dylan. She was converted into an activist; as she phrased it: "The student movement took hold of my brain, and its music took hold of my body." She told me about the increasing politicization of her worldview, and how she became increasingly receptive to the civil rights activism of the late 1960s and to the anti–Vietnam War movement. "It changed the way I thought, the way I dressed, and the way I groomed, ate, drank, loved— everything. Absolutely everything."

Then, as she had mentioned in our previous meeting, she described how she had met a leader of the Columbia University student move-ment—one of the "IDA Six"; Bob Somerville was his name, and he was responsible for thinking out how each campus demonstration should be organized.

The Mayor paused, took a deep breath, and slowly, audibly exhaled. Then she closed her eyes, allowing herself to drift back, deep inside herself. She began to describe times when she was with Bob at rallies, meetings, and demonstrations during the day—and with him in his waterbed at night, with the Beatles blasting away. Then, she explained, one night after they made wavy, crazy waterbed love, Bob turned toward her and told her he and others had had a meeting to organize a huge sit-in. The strategy was that the administration would take the bait, call in the police, and have hundreds of students arrested. This would give national visibility to the real issue at hand: the Columbia think tank that was so deeply involved in advising the military about how to prosecute some particularly nasty tactics of the war. There were downsides to this sit-in strategy, Bob had explained, one of which was how to raise funds for the legal expenses that would be incurred by students who decided to let themselves be arrested. Bob figured a lot of pissed-off parents wouldn't necessarily come to their children's rescue—or couldn't afford to. The general sense of the meeting, Bob told her, was that it was unfair to tempt kids into being arrested with-out thinking ahead about the realities of raising bail money and legal defense funds.

She paused. "And then?" I interjected after a good twenty seconds.

The Mayor looked over at me, popping back for a moment, before again receding into the past and letting the girl describe how she had told Bob about her idea for raising funds. Apparently, her grandfather had left her a small gold coin collection, and when she was readying herself to go back East to college, her father had suggested she might want to rent a safe-deposit box to keep her coins safe. That very afternoon, she had visited a small savings bank near her parents' house to rent a box. What she saw, however, dismayed her to the point that she ended up renting her box elsewhere: the racking that held the metal safety-deposit boxes formed a square with an opening to enter—a "square horseshoe shape" as she put it. But since the savings bank's vault room was a rectangle, when she walked beyond the square of metal down to the end of the room, she could see that the back of the end wall of the safety-deposit boxes was well away from the room wall—about five or six feet away. She explained to Bob her idea about how to exploit that security breach—assuming it hadn't been discovered and remedied. She told me that she went on to explain to Bob that her father was a heating and air-conditioning contractor, and that she had worked with him during the summers of her high school years. So, she was familiar with sheet metal, and when she had peered that day into the little corridor between the back of the boxes and the wall, she had noted that the back of the safety-deposit box rack was not armored like the front was. It was just a big panel of sheet metal intended to be butted up against a concrete wall. She also noticed that the cleaning crew kept its mops, brooms, and buckets in the little corridor between the back of the boxes and the wall, and she found that "really bush."

Without batting an eye, she reported, Bob had simply asked her what she would need to pull off the operation, and the girl-that-would-become-the-Mayor had responded that all she would need would be three other girls who didn't know her and who didn't know one another. They had to be movement activists whom she could totally trust, and who could trust one another. And, she told Bob, she would need a fake driver's license.

None of this, apparently, was a problem for her resourceful boyfriend. The plan was for Denver to get back between the boxes and the wall and cut through the sheet metal. All she needed now were the tools—so she called her father and made up a story about wanting to cut metal for an art project at school, and asked if he could lend her an electric saw, sheet-metal cutters, and bending tools. The Mayor popped back up into the discussion just long enough to comment, "God, I can't believe I told such a bald-faced lie to my own father."

When spring vacation came, Denver said, she flew out to California to visit her parents—and, borrowing her mother's car, drove over to the little savings bank. She donned a brunette wig, used foundation on her face to darken her complexion, and put nonprescription brown contacts in her eyes—and, voilà, she looked like the girl depicted on the fake license.

Denver said entering the bank was "like stepping back into the 1940s—a time machine." The safety-deposit room was down a hallway, set off from the rest of the bank, and it had its own little reception area where the elderly department manager she had remembered was still on the job. Behind him was a floor-to-ceiling wall of impregnable steel. In the middle of the armored wall, behind the attendant's desk, was the massive walk-through safe door.

The girl described how she chose a large-size box to rent—precisely because it was *not* on the wall of boxes she was interested in, and also because she would need that size to hold the tools she had borrowed from her father. Using the name on the license Bob had obtained, Denver gave the attendant a bogus address, telling him she had recently moved, and paid cash for a year's rental. When I asked how she got to check out the corridor off to the right of the horseshoe, Denver replied that it hadn't been a problem at all. Inside the vault room, she explained, there were two tiny little rooms, each with a little counter and a chair. They were for privacy when a customer was putting items into or taking items out of their box. Once she had finished the paperwork that day, and been offered one of the empty rooms, the guard went back outside the vault to his desk, telling her to call him when she was ready to insert her box into its hole in the armored wall. That had given her plenty of time to walk over, look down the corridor, and learn that absolutely nothing had changed. The brooms and mops were still stored there, about six feet into the corridor, with a plastic trash can behind them. Beyond that, all was lost in dark shadow, except she could see an electrical outlet on the wall. That was critical. Everything she needed was falling into place.

So, the girl's voice continued, she stowed the roll-up of her father's tools and the electric saw in her new safety-deposit box. She also put in an envelope with half a dozen antique silver dollars and three not particularly valuable collector coin books—big enough to create an excuse for the large-size safety-deposit box. The coins and the envelope had all been carefully wiped clean of fingerprints. She explained that she had thought that leaving an empty box at the end of the venture might signal to the police which one of the bank customers had had no real cause to rent a box—even if their investigation would have only led to the girl on the lost or stolen driver's license.

At this point in Denver's story, I had to break into her monologue. "Dianne, our time's almost up for today. Same time next week?" She checked her schedule, and it didn't work, so we settled for two weeks out. Once again, I was going to have to wait for further details on the wackiest story any client had ever recounted.

I had saved the final few minutes of our meeting to talk about Billy. "Dianne, when I talk to Billy, he always asks about how *you're* doing, how *you're* progressing. Perhaps Billy needs something quicker, far quicker than what we're working on here together. And I've got an idea."

"And that would be?"

"Bring him in on the bank robbery. Let's share your story and our efforts with him. He's a kid, Dianne—he'd be fascinated that you did this, and he'd be all involved in the project *with* you. You'd be doing something *together* with him—something fascinating and forward looking and important—and basically organized for his benefit. As for the confidentiality we need, my—"

I was interrupted at this point by her sternest of Mayor voices—so different from the girlish tone in which she had been narrating the details of the robbery. "That is a *ridiculous* proposition, and it's not going to happen. Do you hear me? If you do that, our relationship will be over. I want confirmation *right now* that you hear me and that you will absolutely respect my decision to reject your bizarre idea."

I backed down, of course, but I knew I was right, and my plotting and planning to make this happen kept right on going, if in guerilla mode. In part to mask my scheming mind, I immediately changed gears as the session ended. "Okay, okay. I'll say nothing; you have my word. So, another question for you: What about my idea of your beginning some clinical counseling? I've exactly the right type of therapy—and just the right therapist to suggest."

To my surprise, she didn't shut down the idea this time. "And that would be what?"

"That would be what clinicians call 'relational-cultural therapy'— RCT for short. I could get you in to see the famous psychiatrist who launched this fascinating new field of psychiatry—Jean Baker Miller. Completely by chance, I know her personally. RCT is all about developing a model of clinical intervention that emphasizes the importance of successful human connection and strong interpersonal relationships for psychological health. RCT takes the position that some aspects of mental health are directly linked to having healthy relationships."

She didn't respond right away, so I carried on. "Dianne, I want you to entertain the possibility that you and I may be approaching your goal in a way that just might not work. I think it would be clever for you to work with Dr. Baker Miller *in parallel*—then you'd have two completely different strategies at work, and who knows which one might come through for us in the end?" But then, insensitively, I pressed things too far, too fast, yet once again. "And you could consult with her about the idea I proposed about your bringing Billy into our efforts in order to—"

Again, the Mayor erupted in anger. "I told you, Counselor, the idea of exposing my stupid, criminal behavior to my child is one hundred percent off the table. Why did you even dare to bring that up again after what I told you? Don't you see, Billy's the person I *most* want to keep this away from. Listen to me, and listen carefully. If you *ever* raise the topic again, I'll immediately terminate your representation—and also your representation of Billy. And I'll get my next attorney to serve you with papers ordering you never to speak with Billy again. Is *that* clear enough for you to grasp?"

Stupid me: I'd ignored the fact that pushing her so hard and so directly to explore why she had such defective connections with others was like pushing an alcoholic to get their drinking issue under control. We all know that the initiation of substantive action to deal with alcoholism has got to come from the alcoholic himself—and from no one else. Suddenly, it dawned on me that this was true for the Mayor as well. But it was the Mayor who spoke next, and with great sensitivity.

"Look, Terry, try to understand. It's a huge change for me to begin working with you. This has not been easy for me; can't you see that?" With that, she stood up and left the office.

What I had been hoping to tell the Mayor before I screwed up the conversation was that I had had a long talk with Dr. Baker Miller about the Mayor's case—absent her name, of course. While Dr. Baker Miller couldn't say anything more definite unless and until she came to know Denver firsthand, in our phone call she had brought to light a factor that I had never even considered. To paraphrase her: the nature of social interaction malfunction often has a great deal to do with a lack of self-confidence or a negative self-image, so a positive outcome for the Mayor might not even require that I figure out how to gain her the legal immunity she sought. It might be enough if we simply learned that there was only a minuscule statistical possibility that the robbery investigation would ever be reanimated. The most important factor by far, Dr. Baker Miller had explained, was that my client needed to be truly ready to initiate a clinical investigation of what underlay her emotive limitations.

***

The next day, I paid Billy a visit. Straightaway, my young client gave me his medical news. His "numbers" weren't all that much better, but the oncologist was suggesting that the chemotherapy needed to be scheduled nonetheless. This was to take place in about a month, and Billy was thrilled to get the process underway.

Billy next told me he had read an article from the *Wall Street Journal* on recent merger activity and had more or less memorized it. He said that reading it had been "like eating toast with no butter." But it was worth it, he reported, because our little scheme was working quite well: his father's visits were both longer and more animated as Billy engaged him on their newly "shared" interest in the business of wheeling and dealing.

We had spoken for just about half an hour before Billy visibly began to tire and nod off. Standing there, looking down at my little pal, I became convinced that the advice I had given his mother was precisely correct: she had an enormous opportunity to connect with him just by letting him join our team and involving him in the camaraderie of our joint venture. How to convince her of this, however, was another matter altogether, especially given the very bright line she had drawn in the sand.

***

At our next meeting, the Mayor took up her story once again—or the girl inside her did. The plan was, she and her comrades would drive straight through all the way from New York to Los Angeles the following weekend, taking turns at the wheel. They also took a solemn oath that, without exception, none of them would *ever* tell *anyone* about going to LA. Everyone swore to this security measure, and, so far as Denver ever knew, everyone had lived up to it.

I was amazed. "Were the others as sanguine as you were about the venture?" I broke in. "I don't get why any of you were willing to take on such an enormous risk."

"Mark Rudd" was Denver's two-word answer—this time in her Mayor voice. "He was the spokesman for the Columbia student movement, and he had that level of charisma. Think about it, Terry," she said, "only three weeks later, seven hundred students would let themselves be *arrested* because Mark Rudd thought that was a clever strategy. We were malleable kids, and he was an able sculptor. And as for why we were not more afraid of getting caught—who knows? Frankly, I don't think we thought a lot about the consequences of what would happen if something went wrong. I certainly don't remember thinking much about it, or ever talking about it. We were kids. Naïve, idealistic kids."

"Amazing," I added, gratuitously.

The Mayor, looking a touch annoyed at how my voice from the present broke her absorption into the past, closed her eyes to resume. After a time-travel pause, she described how they had parked the car and walked separately to the bank. Denver, in her disguise, entered to obtain access to her safety-deposit box at precisely 2:30 p.m., making sure to chat for a while with the elderly, somewhat flirtatious attendant. He helped her and one of the girls, whom she introduced as her friend, to get her box, after which he showed the two of them into one of the little rooms, again telling Denver to call for him when she was ready to put the box back—it took a simultaneous insertion of both his master key and her individual key to replace and relock the box in the rack. Once they were alone, Denver and her "friend" exchanged clothes and wigs. Denver took the roll-up of tools out of the box and added them to the huge purse she had brought in. She also had a commercial extension cord, a roll of two dozen large black trash bags, and two rolls of duct tape.

At exactly 2:50 p.m., precisely on schedule, the third girl walked up to the attendant to announce that she was thinking of renting a box and asked for information about the options and the prices. Then, at three p.m., the fourth girl came to the safety-deposit department to wait her turn to rent a box. As planned, the first "new customer" engaged the attendant in a lengthy, indecisive conversation about box sizes and rental rates, while the girl who was waiting fidgeted with impatience awaiting her turn. It was during this double diversionary tactic that the girl who was with Denver—now in Denver's disguise—went to ask the attendant if he could come with his key to replace and lock up Denver's box. Just as foreseen, the sudden rush of business flustered the elderly attendant, and after he and Denver's look-alike inserted her box into its slot, and she left, he returned his attention to his new customers, having not noticed that, whereas two girls had entered, only one had left.

The ongoing diversion with the two new potential customers gave Denver plenty of cover to walk around behind the end of the row of safety-deposit boxes and up into the space between them and the wall. She lay down at the far end of the space in its dark shadows, completely hidden in a sleeping bag she fashioned from doubling up four of the black trash bags, figuring that it would be the longest hours of her life waiting out the end of the banking day and the appearance and departure of the cleaning crew—if this was a cleaning day—and the closing of the vault door. But this turned out to be far less of a problem than she had imagined: the drive across country had taken its toll, and she was soon fast asleep. Eventually she was awakened by the cleaning crew taking out their equipment for the evening. She said she didn't take a natural breath during the next hour; every inhalation, every exhalation, was, as she put it, "managed and silenced."

Then, just as she had hoped, the crew replaced their equipment, left the room, and turned off all the lights. Denver could hear the big vault door slam shut. She waited another ten minutes to be sure—and to get up her nerve—and then exited, full of adrenaline and ready for action. She set up a magnetic flashlight and put her father's headlamp around her forehead. She slipped on surgical gloves that she would wear for the rest of the operation and pulled on work gloves over them to get down to work. As advertised, her father's electric saw cut cleanly through the one-eighth-inch-gauge sheet metal that formed the back wall of the boxes, and within an hour, Denver had cut out three sides of a rectangle that was about five feet high and ten feet long. Then came the one error that could have changed the outcome: when she made the final cut along the bottom, the duct tape "hinges" she had put over the cut along the top failed to hold the weight of the sheet metal she had cut out, and it crashed down about two feet to the floor. It was pure luck that it didn't land on her toes—that would have changed everything. It made a huge clang when it hit the floor, of course—but there was no one in the vault to hear it. It was a struggle to scoot the metal panel over to the back wall, where she taped it up until the end of the operation.

Now she could see the backs of about sixty small-size safety-deposit boxes. The back of each box was made of a somewhat thinner-gauge sheet metal, and with the electric saw, she made two vertical cuts down the corners of each box—that was about 120 cuts, so it took the better part of another two hours. Her arms were killing her, but by three in the morning, she had bent down the backs of all sixty boxes and emptied what she wanted out of each of them into a trash bag. Continuing her extreme attention to reducing the risk of being caught, she expressly took no papers and no objects—only cash. Oh yes, and about a dozen baggies of pot from two different boxes—the young narrator gave out a sweet giggle at the thought that two different bank customers were using the bank to stash their grass. And she mentioned the pathos she felt at finding a very old and threadbare pair of little girl's ballet slippers in one box.

Finally, the student inside the Mayor described how she untaped the heavy sheet-metal rectangle from the back wall and struggled it back over against the boxes. Since she could come nowhere near lifting if off the floor, all she could do was to duct-tape it flat to the back of the boxes and cover the two-foot hole at the top of the entire length of the cutout with taped-on black trash bags. She was very careful with this taping, as she thought it was critical that the cleaning crew see nothing amiss—that could have been a next-day alarm or next-week alarm, as opposed to what she hoped would be a much greater lapse of time before one of the safety-deposit box renters next went in to access their looted box.

I remained in stunned silence throughout Denver's tale, and remained so until its conclusion. She explained how she next packed up the tools, the electric cord, and lights in another trash bag and crept back into her hiding bags. Completely exhausted, she dozed off again, and was awakened only by the opening of the enormous vault door in the morning. When 9:30 rolled around, the girl who had accompanied Denver, with Denver's wig on, was "apologetically" back to access her box to put something additional in it. At ten, a second diversion was orchestrated: one of the two other girls returned for a final round of rental information. This diversion allowed Denver to join her colleague in the little private room, where they again changed clothes and wigs. The girl put the tools in the oversized handbag she had brought, removing from it a second large carpetbag for Denver to use. Denver put the trash bag of cash and the extension cord in the second bag, and left the little room to ask the attendant to please come in so that she could replace her box. As they both stood in front of her box to put their keys in the two locks, Denver "accidentally" dropped her key, and, as she had anticipated, the attendant bent over to pick it up for her. That was all the time her colleague needed to slip behind him and out the vault door. It took only the slightest flirtatious look from Denver to ascertain that all the older gentleman saw was her young and pretty smile. The girl inside the Mayor laughed out loud. And then there was only silence as the Mayor turned back into her adult self once again. It was like watching someone come back from hypnosis.

"So, the scheme worked," I commented, utterly amazed at the audacity of it all. "Do you know when it was discovered?" The Mayor replied that it was about two full months before she saw anything about the robbery in the *Los Angeles Times*, and it was only reported that about $42,000 was stolen—out of the $182,000 the scheme had actually netted. I asked the Mayor what took place when she got back to Columbia, and she reported that, even though she would occasionally pass one of the other girls on campus, she never again spoke to any of them—just as their plan had called for.

"And Bob's reaction when you returned with all that loot?"

"Ahhhhh." The Mayor sighed with a breathy, sensuous sound. "I haven't thought about that in decades. It was, without a doubt, the single sexiest night of my life." Then she became perfectly still, her eyes glazed over—her mind traveling back in time. I kept my silence, letting her savor what must have been an absolutely amazing somatic memory. Then, bit by bit, the girl receded into the distant past, and the woman in front of me seemed to age before my very eyes. The sprite who had told the story was gone with its telling.

Now that the story was told, I assumed the Mayor would want to launch into a serious discussion of case strategy. But that's not at all what happened: instead, she again burst into tears and cried as hard and as deeply as any adult I've ever been with. I assumed that all the emotions she had reexperienced in her visit to the past had overwhelmed her, presumably including reexperiencing the beginnings of the fear that was to plague her for the next thirty years.

"It must be hard to reexperience such emotionally packed moments from the past," I said.

She shook her head, almost violently, from side to side. "No, no, no," she insisted. "That's not it at all . . . It's . . ." But then she went silent.

Finally, I asked: "What is it, Dianne? How can I help?"

There was more silence—at least another half minute. She stood up and walked over to the office windows that looked out over Boston Harbor. Staring out over the water, in a voice I could barely hear, she revealed what actually had grabbed her. "You warned me that in retelling what happened, I might reexperience the emotions that ran through me all those years ago. But I hadn't understood you; I had no idea it could be so powerful."

"Details, Dianne; tell me the details about what you're saying."

"Intellectually, I knew I was here, of course, but *emotionally*, I was back there, not here. And on the level of emotions, it also was then, not now. And I could feel, goddamn it, *I . . . could . . . feel*. I had forgotten what it feels like . . . *to feel*." She exclaimed all this in a delicate feminine voice that was far different from either the college-girl tonality in which her tale had been narrated or the mayoral tones of her current life. "I could *feel*—I could *feel* the love I had for Bob—that full, childish, first-lover love; that unabashed, total, rushing, wild, pulsating, sexy-beyond-belief feeling of love. And I could *feel* the solidarity I had with those girls. Why can't I *feel* anymore? Why can't I *love* like that anymore? Why do I feel so removed and so distant all the time—even from those whom I love the most? Why do my relationships feel so . . . so at a distance? It's not my husband's fault, and it's certainly, certainly, certainly not Billy's fault." She summed it all up, with a noticeable absence of tears: "Something's wrong with me, and it's keeping me apart from my own life."

"Dianne," I followed right on, "now you're asking the very most important questions you can possibly ask yourself. And you wouldn't have asked these questions out loud if you weren't good and ready to go find out the answers. But this office is *not* the place to pose those questions, and I am *not* the right professional to help you find those answers. You and I are working on a law case. Period. But, *please, Dianne, please* let me put you in contact with Dr. Baker Miller—she is exactly the right clinician for you to work with to find the answers to precisely the questions you just asked. The mode of therapy she has developed has *everything* to do with your questions; I promise you, you'll be able to work on exactly the questions you just asked. Please, Dianne. Please trust me on this."

The Mayor had retaken her seat in one of the client chairs, and just sat there across from my desk, as still and calm as she had so recently been agitated and full of angst, her arms hanging down over the sides of the chair as if they each weighed fifty pounds. And then, after a good half minute, she turned her head toward me and simply said, "Okay."

She was so calm, so spent, so centered, that nothing was going to stop me from taking the final step; it was now or never. "And, Dianne, please, I want you to check with Dr. Baker Miller about what I'm going to say, and I hope you'll also grant me permission to speak with her about this. I'm pleading with you: let's work together with Billy on the legal project. I was standing by him a few days ago as he dozed off. We had spoken for about half an hour before that, and I realized that while there are many reasons for you to work *with* Billy on this—I could name a dozen—there is only one legitimate reason not to: fear that he would disclose your secret to someone else. Please trust me on this, Dianne; I'm completely certain we can convince Billy of the need for total confidentiality—I have *zero* doubt about that. And the two of you working together as a team on the legal part—the trust, the inclusiveness it would show to Billy—it would change your relationship with him *on the spot*. And the three of you—Dr. Baker Miller and Billy and you, working together as a team on the psychological part—she'll get you *feeling* again, Dianne, she will. I really do think so."

Complete stillness followed, and then ten seconds later, the college-age voice spoke one last time in the quietest voice imaginable, and just said, without any drama, "We're going to make this work, aren't we?"

I just smiled and nodded yes. Then, in complete silence, she stood up, shared a peaceful smile, and walked out of my office.

***

During the following week, Dr. Newsom called to discuss Billy. The father was now showing up about twice a week on average, typically for the better part of an hour, and the visits were apparently much more animated now that Billy's subscription to the *Tall Street Journal* found its way to his room. Dr. Newsom described how he had recently entered the boy's room at the end of one of these visits just as a very tired Billy had replied to his father, "That's great, Dad," using, to quote the city's best-known pediatrician, "exactly the tone of voice one usually hears a parent use when humoring a child." So, apparently, we were making progress on both parental fronts, and much more quickly than I would have predicted.

***

Now that I had the Mayor's assent, there was no way I was letting Billy go into his chemotherapy without fully involving him in our joint effort to increase his mother's connective capacities by reducing the intensity of her fears. I wasn't about to tell him her story—that was something she needed to do. But I was damned well going to make sure it happened—and without delay, because there just wasn't time to wait for his mother to be healed by Dr. Baker Miller—shrinkage takes its own sweet time. What was needed, at least in my view, was to find a way to *immediately* invigorate the connection between the two of them, and I couldn't think of a better way to accomplish this than for the two of them to be on the same team—a team involved in an active, difficult, high-stakes campaign.

I went in to see Billy about three days after Dr. Newsom gave me the heads-up call, which would have been just about four or five days shy of his first procedure. There he was, propped up against his pillows, being fawned over by three oncology nurses. The little guy shot me a wink between them that I would have framed and hung on the wall, if winks were subject to being photographed. They finished up tending to him, and left the two of us alone. "I'm so glad to see you, Billy," I began.

"I'm just as pleased," he responded, "because I need to consult with my lawyer."

We shared a sweet laugh at his reference back to the first time he'd used those words. And then Billy grew suddenly serious—and he took charge. "Terry—can I call you that? It would mean a lot to me."

"It's my name."

Then, in his deepest voice, he told me, "Terry . . . I don't want you to get discouraged on your end of our strategy. Both of my parents are already trying harder . . . it's *way* better between us now. And I don't want you worrying about me on the health side of our struggle. I've got that under control."

"I know you do, Billy," I replied. "But actually, I've got some good news for you. Some super-good news. Your mom and I have made a breakthrough. We met recently and decided to form a team of three soldiers to fight the secret battle to solve the legal issue you first hired me to resolve. We want to do this because we just figured out that we can't do it without your becoming a full partner in our effort. Are you game to join our team? But you would need to keep everything—*every single word she tells you*—completely secret. Can you do that?"

So far as I know, there is no eleven-year-old on the planet who would not agree to keep something secret. Billy was no exception. "She's going to share with me what worries her so much? *Really?*"

"Yes, she said she would. But first, you're going to have to convince her that you can keep it all a secret, even if a guy points a gun at you. She's really, really concerned about that, because any leak could be disastrous—and I agree with her about that."

"Not to worry; I have that covered," Billy replied, with a gradually tiring voice.

"Really, how so?" I asked, as always being led by Billy.

"You know that money that I'm going to use to pay your lawman bill? Well, she doesn't know I've got that saved up. It's been a secret all along, and it's hidden in my room. Perfect proof that I can keep a secret. True?"

Again, he made me smile and shake my head back and forth. "You got it, pal. How about this? As soon as Dr. Newsom says you're clear to put some energy into our team effort, the three of us will meet to plot a collective strategy. You up for doing this?" Billy didn't answer with words: he just gave me a smile that didn't leave his face until at least half a minute after he'd fallen asleep.

***

The Mayor's office called to change the date of our next appointment—this time to move it *forward* as much as my schedule would allow. She was in my office just three days after the call, and she was anxious to jump back into recounting the remainder of her story.

"So, what happened next with all that cash?"

Now it was the Mayor's story, not the girl's. "Well, Bob's information proved entirely accurate: ten or twelve days after we had the cash, over seven hundred students were arrested in the administration building sit-in. Their bail amounts varied, depending on the charges, but we had our war chest ready to meet the challenge. For the folks with simple trespass charges, we made it possible for them to put down the full bail. For those also charged with resisting arrest, we helped the students with cash for the bail bondsmen, even though their ten percent fee was nonrefundable. We didn't want any suspicion to arise, so we were very circumspect about how the entire matter was handled."

"What about their legal defense; how'd that work out?"

"A half-dozen local, progressive law firms filed appearances as counsel for the students, and cash retainers were supplied to ensure effective representation." She paused one last time to think if there was anything else, but then looked over at me and simply said, "I think that's the whole story."

I confirmed that neither she nor the other women ever heard anything whatsoever from the police.

"No, zero. Nothing, ever," Denver responded with a sly smile. "I don't know what direction they went in, but I never heard a word about any investigation. I was around campus for another two years, so I'm pretty sure I would have heard if something had come up."

"And what ever happened to Bob?"

"Bob and I lived together through the rest of that academic year. We didn't see each other over the summer, but we then took up again the next year—right where we left off. It was his senior year. We had a fabulous time together. Off campus, we were surrounded by mind-boggling events—the developing anti–Vietnam War movement and the civil rights movement—and on campus, we did way more than our professors assigned. Bob and I participated in reading groups where we read on our own Dostoyevsky, Camus, Márquez, Ferlinghetti, Goodman, and so on—and all this in a city that itself had hundreds of non-classroom lessons to teach. It was everything that an undergraduate education is supposed to be."

She paused for a moment to contemplate. "You know, I don't think I've ever again felt that close to so many people. It was an incredible sensation to be part of the counterculture movement and to read about it cropping up in city after city across the US and in a hundred non-US cities as well. It changed my perception of what it meant to be a woman; it changed my sex life; it changed my political life; it changed my musical, film, and dance preferences; it changed how I dressed and how I wore my hair and how I used makeup. It changed *everything*."

I allowed some silence to pass to pay respect to what my client had just said; her words were an homage to connection, after all. "So, tell me what you did after you graduated," I asked.

Calm and collected now, the Mayor described her post-Columbia life. She and her husband were married soon after she finished her master's degree in political science at Princeton. Not long after their

marriage, the couple moved to Boston, where Mr. Denver had landed
a job with a young venture capital firm. The Mayor, for her part, began
her professional life as a certified high school teacher, and taught US
history at her town's high school for a decade. She loved it.

"So, if my math is right," I said, "there was about a decade gap
between when you started teaching and when Billy was born. Was that
on purpose?"

The Mayor froze in reaction to my asking such a personal question. But then she seemed to remember there was no point in keeping anything from me given what I'd already learned, so she described
how her husband's work had been everything to him. She described
how he had insisted that they needed to wait to have children until he
closed some long-forgotten deal . . . and then there were other deals,
and other delays. "That's what he lives for." Denver sighed. "There are
never enough deals, never enough money." Again, she paused completely, sitting heavily, almost limply, in the chair. "I used to cry so
hard about this . . . He gave in . . . finally . . . and we had Billy. Then he
had a vasectomy. We used to argue about whether or not I knew that
he was getting it . . . I didn't. That's just who he is . . . And then me with
my issues . . . It makes me so sad for Billy."

It was time to turn the conversation. I proceeded to tell the Mayor
how my law partner, Christina Lorenz—a specialist in criminal law—
had recently answered several questions I had posed to her. First, no
matter how careful we were in investigating the status of the Mayor's
case, we ran an unavoidable slight risk that our poking around about
the bank robbery could awaken the California authorities. In response,
Denver was crystal clear: she was not only willing to accept the risk but
took the position that, on an emotional level, she had no choice. As she
put it, "I understand that my fears might seem irrational after all these
years—but we're not talking about rationality here . . ." She paused to
find the rest of the wording she wanted. "We're talking about what
goes on so deep inside me that it jolts me awake in a cold sweat. We're
talking about what disables my heart."

"I hear you, Dianne," I responded. "But now you're working with
Dr. Baker Miller, and with her help, you may well regain your capacity
to emote. I just want to say something for you to consider one more
time: you could decide to put off the legal effort until you see what

develops with Baker Miller. You know, we could reconvene here in six months, for example, and see where you stand."

It was only in the Mayor's response that I finally, after all these months, actually heard what she had been telling me. "Terry, for thirty years, every single time there's been a knock on the door, I've flinched. Every time I've seen a film with a related theme, my stomach has churned. Every time I've read in the papers about yet another politician caught up in a scandal from their past, I die a thousand deaths. I can't live like this for the rest of my life. I can't do it. You have to understand that."

I waited a bit before responding to give some weight to my words. "I got it, Dianne, I finally got it. All right. Let's get going on the case then. You ready?"

"Oh yes!"

We were off and running. I informed the Mayor that Lorenz's research, while not yet final with respect to the jurisprudence inter-preting the two statutes of limitations, looked very unpromising. She had learned that when a perpetrator flees the jurisdiction to evade prosecution, each statute of limitations, California and federal, is "tolled"—lawyer-speak for frozen. I explained that this was not a fight we wanted to fight. I also recounted that Attorney Lorenz's research found that the case law in both jurisdictions was entirely settled in that a defendant cannot successfully defend himself in a criminal proceed-ing by claiming that he was swept along by a charismatic leader, or a cult, or—presumably—a social movement.

Understandably disappointed by this bleak review of the con-trolling case law, the Mayor looked down and took a moment to respond. "So, what do I do next?"

"Do you mean what do *we* do next?" I knew my remark risked being taken as a bit controlling or out of place. But damned if for once I didn't say just the right thing to the Mayor.

"Good point. Dr. Baker Miller would want me to say 'we.' And so would Billy."

Wow. This was progress. Now it was time to get to work. "So, Dianne, what we do first is hire a really top-flight private eye to snoop around for us in order to learn whether or not thirty-year-old, non-gun-related bank robberies are actively pursued in California. And I have two pieces of really good news for you on this front. First, I have the perfect private eye to undertake the project, and second, Lorenz says we have reason to be cautiously optimistic about our chances of learning some good news on this front. But it's a seriously expensive undertaking. If I had to estimate—"

The Mayor cut me off. "I don't give a sweet damn about the cost. My sister and I are each beneficiaries of sub-trusts under our grandparents' trust, and I've never touched a penny of that money. This is a perfect use for it. Go get yourself *exactly* the team you need to figure all this out—please. I'd love to have you develop this strategy in detail; will you do that for me?"

"Oh yes, Dianne. Oh yes. That's actually the fun part of what I do. How about two weeks, same time, same place."

"Perfect."

***

So, it was time to bring "Longfellow" into the case, which means it's time for me to remind you of Reginald Brooke, the remarkable British gentleman whose private detective firm, Solutions and Outcomes, Ltd., was, at least in my view, the very best private detective agency in Boston. It took Longfellow three days to return my call, but only three minutes to express a keen interest in getting involved in the Dianne Denver case. He confirmed that there were investigation strategies that essentially eliminated any possible perception that someone was looking into any *particular* past criminal act, but that such black shadow requirements could slow down an investigation quite appreciably. We agreed to pursue that strategy of approach, and noted that he would get back to me just as soon as he had something in mind.

I also told Longfellow that the only two arguments we had thought about to date in defense of our client—if criminal prosecution of the Mayor were ever to ensue—looked like certain losers. Accordingly, I stressed, at the conclusion of our work, the client might well need to be satisfied with confirmation that the likelihood was nil that the dusty old bank robbery case would ever spring back to life. "Got it. Cheerio," replied the master private eye in his Cambridge accent, and he was off the line and on the case.

My next step was to call a law school classmate who practiced in a large Los Angeles firm. He referred me to a partner of his who specialized in white-collar criminal defense. In a return call from this attorney the following day, I explained my need to retain California counsel who knew the inner workings of the case investigation practices of both the Los Angeles Police Department and the Los Angeles County District Attorney's Office. This request led to a second referral, this time to an attorney named Janice McHugh, who had served for over a decade as an assistant district attorney before more recently switching over to the defense side of the bar. When I reached her by phone, she quickly grasped what I was looking for and affirmed that she fully appreciated that the key operational principle for her investigation was to *do nothing that could wake the sleeping dog.* Her first task was to think through and suggest to Longfellow what she proposed as an effective—and adequately stealthy—strategy that would allow her to investigate just how "alive" this unsolved crime was or wasn't under then-current LAPD and district attorney prosecution practices. As a separate task, I asked her to draft a memorandum on the California and federal statute of limitations issues, and to also think through the potential viability in both jurisdictions of arguing a Patty Hearst–type defense based upon Denver's cult-like involvement in the student movement of her college years. No reason not to get a second opinion.

***

While I didn't doubt that California counsel would confirm Attorney Lorenz's total lack of confidence in a Patty Hearst–type defense, I thought it worthwhile to consult on my own a forensic psychiatrist about whether the Mayor's total absorption into the Columbia student movement could be credibly compared to that of a person under hypnotism. His response was immediate: "Nope." As he explained it, "Certain cortical, higher brain wave functions are literally shut down by hypnotism, but not by submission to a cult or cult leader. Fanatical adherence to a social movement is not going to come out any different."

I then sought yet another opinion from a psychiatrist with whom I had recently consulted on another case, but her response was just as pessimistic: "I don't doubt for a minute that an activist's deep involvement in a social movement could trump their normative principles against stealing. But leapfrogging the norm and being unaware of the illegality of the act are two very different things. It takes a conscious decision to proceed with theft, and there typically is admissible evidence demonstrating an array of tactics employed to avoid getting caught—probably the case in your matter. In contrast, a hypnotized person sent to rob a bank would be completely unaware of the risk of getting caught, and hence would take no precautions whatsoever. From a psychiatric point of view, there would be nothing comparable between the two actors. I'm afraid I can't be of help with this case."

So, our one and only theory of how to defend the case against the Mayor, if we ever had to do so, sunk entirely below the waves. It began to seem as if all we could do for her was to confirm the unlikelihood of her case being reactivated by the police. If the probabilities of a criminal investigation of such an old, nonviolent case were slim—which seemed likely to me—the Mayor, now with the help of Dr. Baker Miller, would just have to learn to live with the status quo. That's where I thought the case was at. But then Longfellow called.

***

He started right in. "Terry, the general picture of what we've learned is entirely consistent with what your client told you. Of the one hundred and eighty-two thousand dollars in cash that your client told you about, only about forty-two thousand was claimed as stolen by bank customers. Presumably the rest of the cash in those boxes must not have been reportable—probably for the usual reasons."

"So, the insurer only laid out forty-two thousand dollars?" I responded. "Maybe that's why the investigative effort was so lackluster—but who knows? Learn anything else?"

"Yes, indeed. One little thing. I learned that if your client's identity comes out, she may have a far more serious problem to deal with than her exposure to criminal prosecution."

This statement—the impact of which was exaggerated by the calm of the British accent in which it was delivered—knocked me into silence for a good while. "What in the hell could that be?" I was finally able to say.

"Buckle your seat belt, young man. One of those safety-deposit boxes was rented to a Mr. Pasqualino DiMello, a punk gangster at the time, who subsequently became a 'made man.' He currently resides in Providence, and from what my sources tell me, he is currently one of the two or three major players in Rhode Island's 'organization.' He's a don."

"Does that explain the unreported cash?"

"No, no. It's way worse than that, Counselor, far worse. DiMello, surprisingly, was among those who actually filed a claim—but not for any cash. It seems that he lost his deceased grandmother's wedding and engagement rings. His *family rings*, Counselor. He was all over the police urging them to find out who robbed the bank, and he wanted them back—and seriously so. Can you imagine a mobster who was so upset that he was calling the police on a weekly basis to see if they were diligently working on his case? And he described the rings quite honestly. He said they were costume jewelry with no financial value but that they had great sentimental value to him. My sources learned that this story circulated in mob circles at the time, and that DiMello had everyone on the street aware that he wanted back his family rings in a big way: there was a fifty-thousand-dollar no-questions-asked reward. This was years ago, of course, but apparently 'Pasqualino's rings' is now a generic term on the street. It refers to goods that are accidentally stolen from the mob, or something like that. The implication is that the thief has bought himself a special sort of trouble. Reportedly, this entire matter remains very much a sore point with Don DiMello—presumably to this very day. Anyway, what's clear to me is that if the press learns your client's name and publishes it, she may very well be hearing directly from Mr. DiMello."

"But my client expressly told me that she took nothing other than cash."

"Perhaps she's forgotten," Longfellow shot back. "There is no way DiMello unnecessarily wanted to get involved with the police and the insurance company for valueless costume jewelry, yet he chose to do so. As I already mentioned, the story is widely known, and I checked it out independently with three different sources. Everyone on the street knows that someone ripped off DiMello's grandmother's wedding rings that he was saving for when he got married, and one contact told me that if DiMello finds who did the bank job, he intends to take the rings back, preferably with a finger still in them. I say, your American mobsters certainly use colorful of expressions."

That Martin Scorsese image ended the phone call. Before I could reach the Mayor with my findings, however, I learned that the DiMello problem was not the week's only piece of bad news about the case. The day following Longfellow's call, I received the memorandum I had requested from California counsel, and Attorney McHugh confirmed that California jurisprudence undercut our arguments on both the statute of limitations issue and the Patty Hearst–type defense.

As for the former, McHugh reported, even though we were years beyond the eight-year limit under either statute, there was a fatal problem. Under both lines of jurisprudence, each of the statutes would be tolled if the defendant "avoided the jurisdiction to escape prosecution." And, of course, there was ample discoverable evidence that the Mayor had done just that. As for the Patty Hearst–type defense, the federal Court of Appeals for the Ninth Circuit that had jurisdiction over California took the hardest line on this matter of any of the federal circuit courts: the court's jurisprudence held that the decision to join and remain in a cult, gang, or movement was voluntary and knowing, and that this conscious, purposive decision would be *imputed* to any later criminal act committed under the influence of the cult, gang, or movement.

So I had nothing but bad news to report to the Mayor at our next meeting.

***

The Mayor and I had arranged a meeting in my office to review the status of her case. But just an hour before our scheduled rendezvous, Dr. Newsom called to say that Billy's first chemotherapy treatment had been moved up to two days hence. He thought a quick pep talk was called for, and he mentioned that he had already left the same message for the Mayor, but that she was out of her office. "Not to worry," I cut in. "She's on her way here for an appointment; we'll jump in a cab and be there in less than half an hour."

Forty minutes later, we were each on a side of Billy's bed, with the Mayor holding his hand. The door to his private room was closed, and as far as I was concerned, the time was upon us. The Mayor was babbling away and avoiding the plunge, so I interrupted.

"Billy, remember when I asked you if you could keep the most important secret you'll ever hear? What was your answer?"

"Of course, I can; I'm a specialist at secrets."

"How so?" the Mayor asked, furling her brow as to where this was heading.

"Mom! I can keep a secret! I've saved up fifty-nine dollars that I never told you about, so I can keep a secret. Except now I've spent it."

"Really? Where did you keep all that money? And how did you spend that much?"

"It's under the bottom bookshelf in my room—the one with the stuffed animals. I took the nails out, and that shelf lifts up—tilts up. So . . . my safe is under there. It's in there, mostly quarters, but dimes too. But I owe it all to him," Billy said, pointing to me, "for his lawman fees. We agreed on that."

The Mayor paused, deciding which way to head with what she sensed was happening. "That's excellent, Billy; I'm glad you've taken care of his fees so I won't have to." The two of them beamed smiles at each other that were truly priceless.

Anyway, whether it was the product of Billy's sweet smile or Dr. Baker Miller's good work, the Mayor launched herself into a whole new phase of her life, speaking uninterruptedly for the next fifteen minutes. She told Billy everything about her foolish involvement in the bank robbery, with all the astonishing details of how she and her school pals had pulled it off. Billy's mouth was so wide open throughout the entire account that you could have popped in a cherry tomato. When she was done with the robbery, she broke right into how the three of us were going to work together—*as a team of three*—to resolve her legal issue so she could stop worrying and be a better mom. It was without question one of the most amazing quarter hours of my life.

When the Mayor finished, the room went completely still. Billy was nonplussed for a good twenty seconds, and then—glancing at me ever so briefly before turning his beaming smile back toward his mother—he announced, unambiguously, "Mom, you are definitely the coolest mom in the whole world. That is *so* amazing what you did." But then, allowing a serious look to displace his smile, he turned his head toward me for legal consultation. "Is it okay to be proud of my mom for robbing a bank? It's so illegal. I probably shouldn't be, *right?*"

The Mayor glanced over at me, obviously relieved to let me deal with the moral quandary of it all. What to say . . . ? "Billy, your mom is the first person to say how stupid she was to have done something so illegal. The fact that she did it, and the fact that she might still get caught for it, has worried her every day of her life ever since. Worried her *a lot.* That being said, the three of us are all on the same team now, and we're going to figure out how to help your mom work through this problem. But like you and I talked about, everything your mom told you just now, and everything we do, has to always stay a secret just between the three of us. Zero exceptions to this, ever, Billy. *Zero exceptions.* Do you understand and agree to keep everything about this between the three of us, and nobody else—even your dad?" Billy nodded vigorously that he understood.

Perfect timing. Just after we agreed to the idea of a future meeting of our team, Dr. Newsom knocked and came into the room. Polite though he was, he was basically shooing us out so Billy could get some rest. The Mayor and I jumped in a taxi and were back at my office in twenty minutes.

***

I opened our meeting with the discouraging legal research from California that confirmed how adverse the law was for both our statute of limitations defense and our Patty Hearst–type argument. Denver listened attentively.

Only then did I turn to Longfellow's curious discovery. "Dianne, you told me that you only took cash, except for some little baggies of pot. But I've a question for you, and trust me, it's important. It's *very* important. Could you *possibly* have taken an engagement ring and a wedding band from one of the safety-deposit boxes? I understand they were costume jewelry, but that's not the point. I want you to think back carefully about this; it is *very* important, trust me."

The Mayor pondered my question for only a few seconds before a smile spread across her face. "Damn, you're absolutely right. I did take those rings. I'm sorry, I didn't mean to make things harder for you by not telling you about that. I had completely forgotten about them. It was crazy costume jewelry; the engagement diamond was ridiculous. It was practically the size of a gumdrop. In fact, Bob and I actually called it 'the Gumdrop.' I took it as a joke, because it was so bizarrely enormous. And then I ended up never wearing it—even as a joke. Crazy of me. But how in the world could junky costume jewelry be important after thirty years?"

I responded emphatically: "It *is* important, Dianne—very important. Our private eye learned that the rings belonged to a mobster who in the interim has become a very major-league mob boss. Those rings were his family heirlooms—costume jewelry though they be. Apparently, they were his grandmother's rings, and his intention was to give them to his wife when he married. This guy was so hot and bothered about the rings that he kept calling and pestering the police to solve the crime and get his rings back for him." I paused and allowed her to digest what I had just said. Then I couldn't resist making use of this new fact: "Yet another reason to let that sleeping dog lie, I should think." Then, for no particular reason, I added, "Dianne, you wouldn't be able to find the rings, by any chance, would you?"

The Mayor closed her eyes and rubbed her forehead, searching. "What happened to those rings?" she mumbled, and took more time to think. Then she looked up. "No, I have no memory whatsoever of what happened to them. Zero. Sorry."

"Are you sure? Think again. Think hard. Take your time. This is important. Isn't there any place they could possibly be?"

After another thirty-second pause, the Mayor came up with one low-odds idea. "I have one crazy thought. Years ago, when Billy was about five or so—we gave him a pirate's costume for Halloween or something. The costume came with a little wooden pirates' treasure chest—but it was painfully empty. So I put some of my costume jewelry in the box for him. Perhaps it's still on his toy shelves, I'm not at all sure. He probably hasn't touched it in years—he was way younger then. I could take a look. But that's my one and only idea."

"Oh, do take a look, Dianne. If they're there, my private eye can figure out how to return them to the mobster. That might be a very good idea. We don't need the Godfather out to have a conversation with you."

***

Dianne, sounding a bit anxious, called me first thing the following morning. She had indeed found the pirates' treasure chest—it had survived through the years on the very back of the toy shelf. But it was bereft of the wedding rings. We left it at that, and in some ways, I wasn't all that displeased: after all, this would give me yet another argument to use with the Mayor about the wisdom of our not doing anything that might connect her name to the bank robbery.

Then chance played a role in the game. The traffic on the way home was so abhorrent that I took a different route than usual and found myself within a few blocks of Children's Hospital. I figured, what the hell; I'd slip in to see if Billy knew anything about the rings. I felt a little guilty doing this so soon before his procedure, but something in me wanted to make one last effort to locate the rings.

"How you doing, Billy?"

"I'm ready to kick butt, Terr. I'm tougher than this disease. You know that." I nodded and smiled. Then he added, "Given that you were here yesterday with Mom, I take it you've come back for some particular reason. Am I right?"

I had to laugh at how perceptive the little guy was. "I do have a specific question, Billy. I'll give you details another day because I'm not supposed to be here tiring you out—Dr. Newsom would have my head if he walked in. So, here's my question: You have a pirates' treasure chest on your toy shelf, and two of the jewels that may have once been in it are missing—they're two lady's wedding rings. You wouldn't have any idea where they might be, would you?"

A huge smile broke out across his ever-thinner face. "Of course, I do. They're in my safe with the frog skeleton and a pen that writes in four different colors—or five, I can never remember. You know, with your lawman money. I need them for when I get married someday."

It turned out that on some levels, Billy was a kid after all—because when he figured out that he was about to lose the rings, his face puckered up. Only the truth, I figured, would snap him back into an adult perspective on the matter. "Billy, remember your mom's story about the safety-deposit boxes?" He nodded. "Well, she only took money— and those two rings. To get things solved, I may need—"

He interrupted. "To give them back to their owner?" I nodded yes. "I understand. I see. No problem, then."

"How about we replace them with others?" I offered. "These are fake jewels, but they were the wedding rings of the owner's grandmother—so they are very important to him—a link to his family. He has always wanted to give them to his wife. But for your purposes, we can buy some other ones, don't you think?"

He just smiled back at me in assent, and as I stood there watching, each blink of his eyes was longer than the one before until, in another minute or two, he was fast asleep. I gathered the sheet and blanket up around his neck as the room had a bit of a chill; autumn was upon us once again. Something about Billy brought a sense of peace to everyone he dealt with. Some people exude tension and anxiety; Billy was exactly the opposite.

***

Sure enough, DiMello's rings were safe and sound—and in my hands the following day. The engagement "diamond" was indeed ludicrously large: it was just a little less than twice the volume of a pencil eraser. I was amazed that the band had managed to hold it firmly in place, especially given the tough life it must have led in the world of pirates for the past three decades. The band flared out on both sides of the fake stone, and it was these two triangles that abutted the massive chunk of glass. Each of the two triangles was covered with as many tiny little green stones as could possibly fit in the space. The wedding band, in contrast, was a more subtle effort: it was just a circle of tiny fake diamonds. For costume jewelry, the rings had a certain beauty, I had to admit, and they certainly picked up and refracted the afternoon sunlight coming in through the office window.

I called the Mayor. First, I wanted authority to figure out how to return the rings to their rightful owner without ever speaking to her again about my effort. I wanted neither of them to ever have any knowledge of the other. Second, I wanted authority to spend some money on getting this accomplished in a safe manner. She readily assented.

The first practical step along these lines, accordingly, was to get the rings copied. If Longfellow could figure out how some type of negotiations could be effectuated with Mr. DiMello, it might be useful to approach him first with the copies. So I paid a visit to Martin Warren, a jeweler who was well known in Boston law circles for his forensic work testifying in court proceedings about the value of jewelry pieces. The first thing I explained to Mr. Warren was that the case required complete and total confidentiality. He looked almost insulted that I mentioned this, but reassured me at once. I mentioned that the case involved costume jewelry, which I wanted him to copy, and handed him the envelope. As he removed the rings, I made some kind of remark like, "Ridiculously large, isn't it?" but he didn't respond. Not at all. He had already put his jeweler's loupe in his eye and was surveying the engagement ring. Then, without saying a single word—which was not at all like him—he got up and went back into his shop, returning with a larger, more-sophisticated-looking loupe. Again, he patiently peered at the stone through the magnifying device, and still didn't utter a single word. Finally, after what had to have been the better part of another four or five minutes, he again went back into his shop and came back with a specialized little lamp, and then examined the ring all over again in the lamp's highly focused light—ignoring me completely. This third examination was followed by yet another trip to the back to retrieve jeweler's calipers. As he measured the stone, he took notes on a pad, and when he was finally done, he took off his glasses, placed his elbows on the table, and rubbed his eyes for a good twenty seconds. I was beginning to wonder just how expensive this reproduction venture would be when he finally cleared his throat and spoke.

"Counselor, this stone isn't a fake."

"Well, that's imposs—"

"On the contrary," he interrupted, putting up his right index finger to hush me. "It's a very, very fine diamond." He paused to allow me to digest what he had just said. "How much do you know about diamonds?"

"Me? Nothing, but—"

Again, Warren held up his finger to silence my protestations. "Listen carefully; this is complicated. Diamonds are graded by the 'four C's': cut, color, clarity, and carats. This stone has what appears to be a 'triple excellent cut'—that's a term of art: it means that the proportions, the polish, and the symmetry are all superb. As for color, while I would need more time to be certain, I think this is a blue-white stone; they don't come any finer than that. As for clarity, this stone is loupe clear. As far as I can tell, it is internally and externally flawless. And you can see the size of the thing. That's why you assume it's a fake. As one would expect, the setting is wonderfully done, obviously by a world-class jeweler—I couldn't produce such work. Not even close. The emeralds in the two emerald fields are precisely cut and precisely positioned so as to throw green hues into the luminescence of the diamond. This is a magnificent piece of jewelry."

"Mr. Warren, excuse me for saying this, but you can't be correct," I insisted. "I can't tell you all the details of the case, but I can tell you that the owner of this ring *himself* considers it to be costume jewelry. Why would he believe this if the stone were real?"

"I have no idea—that sounds like a question for a lawyer to figure out. In contrast, whether or not the stone is real is a question for a jeweler to figure out. This is a remarkable jewel stone. And it has been magnificently set."

"Mr. Warren, are you absolutely certain this stone is a real diamond? That will . . . ah . . . change the complexion of the law case dramatically, so if there is any doubt in your mind . . . uhm . . . Would you like some more time to do some double-checking?" I stammered, still stunned and at a complete loss as to where to head with the news.

Warren stared me squarely in the eyes for twenty seconds or so. I realized only then that I had called into question his expertise. Then, slowly and deliberately, he asked me if, when I see a law brief, I can tell if it had been written by an experienced attorney or by a beginner.

"In a heartbeat," I replied.

"I couldn't," he responded.

Okay. Point taken. "Let me think, let me think . . ." I kept saying out loud, stalling for time to recalculate case strategy. Then I knew what I wanted to do. "Okay, Mr. Warren, here is what I need. I need the copies I spoke of. I need them more than ever."

"Very well," the master jeweler replied. "You shall have them in two weeks."

***

Of course, the first thing I did when I got back to my office was call Longfellow with the news. He laughed out loud, and absolutely blew me away with his response: "What wonderful news!"

I had no inkling where Longfellow was heading, or what he had seen so quickly. He sensed that, of course, and switched into strategic mentor mode. "It gives us bargaining leverage, Terry. Can you find it?"

"Whoa . . . Let me think . . . uhm . . ."

"Take it step-by-step, like we've talked about."

"Okay. Let's see. DiMello must know the rings are real, that seems safe to assume. So we know they're hot—*they must be*—he certainly never inherited them from his *nonna*. So, what DiMello lost to the Mayor wasn't his—it was rings he had stolen. So, that still doesn't explain why DiMello as a young gang member would go anywhere near the police—especially if the ring was related to a crime he or his compatriots may have somehow been involved in. That's the key, I think. But I can't trace it beyond there."

"Don't stop. You're doing fine. Keep pushing. Keep pushing," Longfellow insisted.

"Ah, um. Let me see . . . Well, one reason for DiMello to take on the risk of brushing up against the police would be if the person or gang he stole the rings from was even more terrifying than being nabbed by the police. And that would be . . . well, that would be the mob itself—whatever that exactly means. What else could it be? So, here's my guess: he was a low-level mob soldier at the time, and was involved in a heist that included the rings. They're tiny, easy to spirit away from colleagues if the chance arrived. Then what to do with them? To sell them is to announce what he did to just the wrong people. So, he puts them in the safety-deposit box as his rainy-day fund."

"Ooh, this is good work, my boy. But spell out precisely why he would be so aggressive with the police."

"I don't know why," I admitted. "Perhaps he had a pipe dream that the cops would just hand over his *nonna*'s costume jewelry if the loot were located—you know, ending his problem. Perhaps he made the decision to contact the cops without thinking it through . . . I'd have stayed away from them, myself."

I paused, a tad exhausted, to be honest. But not for long: "No, no. Carry on. Push harder, push more," I was instructed.

"Well," I continued, "we know he's a majordomo these days, but he still may need to be wary of a discussion about the provenance of the rings. And even if he doesn't, it could still be in his interest to not have the Mayor precipitate a trial where his name would come up—which it would because he was listed as one of the victims of the robbery. And even if I'm wrong about everything I've said so far, I'm sure he'd still like his rings back—God knows what they're worth."

"Hah!" Longfellow bellowed. "Now listen. Your theory could be right, or it could be wrong—we can't know. But, as you saw, what's important is that we don't need to know. He wants those rings back— one way or the other—and he is a *very* connected man who could perhaps be useful in your effort to deal with the criminal authorities. That's called leverage."

"Why do I think you already have something more specific in mind?" I quipped.

"Because I do. Give me a few days to see if I can find a way for you to meet with Mr. DiMello. This could get interesting." With that he was gone from the line.

***

"Ah, Counselor. How opportune," Billy greeted me the next time I visited my little pal. I burst out laughing, assuming he was kidding around as we'd done so many times. But this time, Billy didn't join in my merriment. He turned out to be entirely serious, and there was no small talk between the two of us that day—none whatsoever. He wanted to speak about how his father's visits were fewer and briefer lately. Apparently, quite a few of the conversations had been paternal monologues about how highly leveraged the family assets were, and how threatened they were, given a recent downturn in the economy, and given that he had made a massive investment in a risky deal that wasn't going well. Billy had me explain to him what "leveraged" meant; it seemed he hadn't dared to ask his father, given all the angst he'd been subjected to.

Billy's report on his mother, however, was decidedly more reassuring. It was clear that the more she worked with Dr. Baker Miller, and the more she openly discussed with Billy how fearful and alone she had felt, the clearer the connection between the two of them was becoming. As only Billy could phrase such matters: "It's like when spring is turning to summer, and you notice how there's more heat in the light." As I stood there shaking my head gently back and forth, I noticed—more than ever—how hard on Billy his chemotherapy seemed to be. But I was never privy to whatever conversations the parents were having with his medical team, or to any other details of his ailments or treatment. There were many boundary proscriptions ignored in my handling of Billy's case, but the sanctity and privacy of his medical chart had somehow escaped that fate.

***

It was fully three weeks later when Longfellow finally had gathered the information he needed to call me back and discuss a strategy for my approaching Don DiMello. Apparently, even the master strategist had needed to take his own sweet time in thinking this one through. Before he presented his proposed approach, however, Longfellow—always the tutor—asked me what *I'd* thought through about how to approach DiMello. I answered that I'd been thinking about telling him the truth: that is, that the bank job was a complete one-off affair—an amateur night—and that the "Midwest-based" amateur had had no idea what "he" was doing, or what the consequences could be. In other words, I'd been planning to stress that the robbery was not pulled off by any organized group of any sort, but was just a one-time adventure. In addition, of course, I was planning to give him back his rings as part of an understanding that he would take no action to investigate who had robbed the bank.

"That's all?"

"Uhm, yes," I stammered. "To be perfectly frank, Longfellow, I'm in way over my head in dealing with Don DiMello. The only thing I know about the mob is what Al Pacino taught me."

"Fair enough," Longfellow replied. "Well, let's see if we can't rethink your strategy. Here's my line of thought. We know that DiMello has a significant interest that the Mayor's case is never brought to trial—or made public in any way. That's what you deduced when we last spoke. If his involvement as a victim of the bank robbery ever came to light, it would be newsworthy—probably front-page newsworthy. Whatever else DiMello is looking for at his stage of life, in all likelihood it's not publicity. And, mind you, if the Mayor's case ever led to a criminal proceeding, DiMello could very well be called to testify at trial about what he lost in the robbery. I think a prosecutor would love to tell a jury the grandmother's rings story—it's a tearjerker. So, we can safely assume that he shares the Mayor's interest that this matter needs to be handled with the utmost of discretion. Do you agree?"

"I do. But no one else knows the rings are real or, for that matter, that they've been found."

"True. But there's still a good chance he doesn't want to have to repeat on the witness stand that implausible story he cooked up about his grandmother and the family wedding rings. It just might expose something to someone we can't be aware of, and minimally, he would look foolish. So, if we can find a way for you to approach him quietly, I should think you might be able to bargain for something far more substantial than just his promise not to try to schedule a meeting with your client. And here's what I have in mind: if anyone can find you a bargaining chip to use with the criminal authorities, it's your new potential partner, Pasqualino DiMello. You just need to figure out the language to convince him that he should get involved as your ally."

"It wouldn't be a language issue, Longfellow; it would be a courage issue. How do I phrase a negotiation like that with a Mafia don that doesn't sound like what I'm really saying is: 'Help my client or you'll never again see the jewels that you obviously stole.' Longfellow, if I get it wrong, he'll eat me with fava beans and a good Chianti."

Longfellow emitted a splendidly British giggle at my quandary. "You'll find a way to word it, old chap. That's what good lawyers do."

"So, you're recommending this step, all things in?" I pleaded, only half in jest, given the involuntary quaver in my voice.

Longfellow took a full twenty seconds to contemplate his answer. "Yes, I am. I can't see how you'll be unsafe, especially if what you take with you are the copies of the rings you've ordered up. Think about this: you have an enormous negotiating advantage in that your client doesn't care about the rings, while he does. That means you can always fold your hand, deliver the rings, and be done with the matter. But on the upside, this development gives you a chance of recruiting a partner to your venture—an ally who is a very well-connected, very powerful man. Who knows where that might lead? I really don't see how we can go wrong here: you'll have a moment of Mafia tourism that should give one of us a good story—either you'll have a tale to share with your pals, or if you disappear with your feet in cement, I'll have one to share with mine. This will definitely work well—for one of us in any case."

Longfellow was entirely pleased with his quip; I could tell by the chuckle that followed. I felt like a boy again, being dared to do something risky. And borderline sketchy as well. But, I had to admit, what Longfellow suggested did make sense: taking along only the copies pretty well guaranteed I'd be safe and sound—at least initially. And when I dared to imagine that this just might open up the possibility of conscripting a powerful ally who could help in the underlying matter—for the price of giving back rings that didn't belong to my client in the first place—that was pretty heady stuff to contemplate. Screw it: when in doubt, dive in. "All right," I found myself saying, "see if you can find a way to set up a meeting, but make it at least a few weeks out from now so we have time to think this through."

"I do have one piece of advice," Longfellow added. "Since you are completely naïve about the mob, use your naïveté to your advantage. I am convinced that's your best approach. Just talk to him like you would anyone else. You're just a civil attorney doing a deal where everybody gets what they want. *Keep it simple.*"

***

And so it came to pass that, just shy of a month after my call with Longfellow, I sat down for dinner with Pasqualino DiMello at Al

Forno, one of Providence's most consistently excellent restaurants. Mr. DiMello proved to be a suave gentleman, and not at all the central casting image of a mob boss that Hollywood had me imagining. He was in his late sixties, I would estimate, and his abundant salt-and-pepper hair was combed straight back, framing his tanned, well-balanced features. The silk of his necktie and the cut of his suit spoke volumes about the subtleties of high-end Italian tailoring. We ate alone at a corner table that occupied a conspicuous amount of open space in the otherwise packed restaurant. Alone, that is, unless you counted the table about twenty feet away that separated us from the other patrons—where two formidably sized gentlemen were clearly enjoying their evening assignment. After our first course, I started to broach the topic of why I had asked for the meeting, but DiMello held the palm of his hand up in front of his face, waving it from side to side, indicating that first we should enjoy our meal—and only later turn to business. We principally spoke about art history—marble polishing to be precise, discovering that we shared a fascination with the statuary of the Italian Renaissance that graces the world's museums.

An hour later, after two unordered espressos arrived at our table, and after Mr. DiMello had taken his first sip—with an approving "hmm"—it was he who opened the topic. "Now," he began, clearing his throat, "I understand that this meeting was set up based upon a representation that a client of yours is in possession of my family's wedding rings, is that correct?"

"Yes, indeed," I replied, slipping across the table a black-velvet-lined ring box that held the two copies for him to examine. "These are copies that I had made. The point of this meeting is to arrange for the return of the original costume jewelry pieces to you." His left eyebrow went up just a quarter inch, but it was enough to signal to me that he had perfectly well absorbed my meaning.

"I assume you're also going to tell me that your client may have the rings, or know where they are, but that he has no idea who pulled off the bank robbery thirty years ago. Am I also correct in that?"

"No, not actually. I'm here to tell you that indeed it *was* my client who was the culprit."

DiMello was visibly startled by my response; his left eyebrow shot up, and he paused for a moment to think of his reaction. "Why are you telling me this? Don't you think I might be just a tad . . . *upset*, shall we say . . . with the person responsible for depriving my wife of my family rings for three decades?"

"Mr. DiMello, I'm here to tell you the full story precisely because what I *don't* want is for you to use what I understand to be your very considerable resources to independently investigate what occurred. I'm hoping you'll see that the identity of my client is far less important than the fact that he fully appreciates the sentimental importance to you of your grandmother's jewelry." I had no choice but to pause after saying this and to stare Mr. DiMello squarely in the eyes. It was one thing for me to wheel and deal about returning valueless costume jewelry to Mr. DiMello; it would be quite another matter for me to knowingly use the delivery of valuable stolen jewelry as leverage to advance my client's interests. The former was somewhat shady, while the latter bordered on being an accessory after the fact. I was willing to stretch the envelope for Billy, but only so far.

"Really?" DiMello responded, obviously picking up on the delicacy of my situation. "And the return of my grandmother's costume jewelry would remain entirely confidential between the two of us?"

"Yes. Entirely so. My client would understand that the costume jewelry rings he stole have been returned to the person he stole them from. Period. He has no knowledge of anything to the contrary, and certainly no knowledge of your name or involvement. And I have zero need to tell him, nor any intention of doing so."

"Reserving for the moment the argument that my agreement to not search out his identity may already be adequate compensation for his returning my family rings, just what is it that your client is looking for in exchange?"

"My client is seeking complete and anonymous John Doe immunity for the bank robbery, and my best guess is that you could be an extremely valuable partner in this effort."

DiMello fell silent, staring at me with an outward calm; his eyes, however, had the intensity of a bird of prey. Finally, he spoke. "Tell me the short form of your proposition—all terms in."

"Your grandmother's rings are yours, Mr. DiMello. They are in my personal possession, and you have my personal word that they will be returned to you whatever the outcome of my client's project. All I am asking you in exchange is that you make a good faith effort to try to help my client clear up the underlying bank robbery matter."

"Are you saying that I have your personal word that for my coopera-tion—whether or not our effort is a success—my rings will be returned to me?"

"Yes. Absolutely so."

"And I can hold you personally responsible for that covenant?"

"That's exactly what I'm saying. But before you think through my proposition any further, I think it would be useful for you to hear the story of the robbery. You'll see why, I can assure you. And it's one hell of a good tale."

The look on DiMello's face confirmed that he was rather bemused. "By the way," he added, "there was also twenty thousand dollars of cash in the box, which, as you might imagine, I did not report to the police at the time, for obvious reasons."

A brilliant chess move. I was glad to assent, actually, because it effectively closed the deal. *Sorry, Mayor.* "Then that will need to be reimbursed to you along with your grandmother's rings."

My host paused while the waiter set down on the table two small glasses of some celestial after-dinner liqueur, and then added, "So, tell me about this job; I've waited thirty years to hear this story."

And so I told Don DiMello the remarkable tale the Mayor had related to me over three or four different afternoon sessions in my office. I spoke slowly and carefully, since Dianne had morphed into a Midwestern male, and I needed to police every word to prevent a "she" or a "her" from slipping out around the edges of my mind. Of course, the story itself underscored what an amateurish effort it was, which seemed to progressively convince the don that there was no rival organization involved. From his body language, and even from a few verbalizations, I could tell he loved the fact that the impregnable strength of the vault door served only to provide the requisite sound isolation, allowing the thief to saw away for hours and hours, mak-ing as much racket as the work required. When the tale ended, Don DiMello picked up.

"You're kidding me," DiMello exclaimed with a huge smile. "It was that simple? Oh, God, that's rich! What kind of kid was so damn smart? Is he looking for work?"

I had to laugh at his line. "Actually, no. He's completely ensconced in a dull middle-class life in a gloomy Midwestern city. I'm thoroughly convinced the bank job was this guy's one and only transgression of the law—ever. In his entire life. I mean that. He even told me he'd never gotten a parking ticket—and I had my investigator check that out. Yep, no tickets."

"What's a parking ticket?" DiMello added with a giggle.

"The problem, Mr. DiMello, is that he's *so* straitlaced that he can't sleep out of fear that this thirty-year-old case will spring back to life one day and bring him down. He absolutely insists on giving restitution a go, including returning your family rings, so long as it can all happen with finality, and be entirely off the record. But here's the strange part that I haven't so far been able to talk him out of: if the restitution for immunity plan doesn't work out, he prefers standing trial to continuing to live in fear that the police will one day knock on his door."

"So how did this get linked to me, again?"

"Well, like I said, I was retained to take my best shot at working out an arrangement with the prosecutorial authorities. My private eye located your name on the list of robbery victims, along with your description of the family rings you lost."

DiMello raised his index finger one inch to order more coffee. I could have stood on the table and not gotten the service he roused. Two new cups of espresso arrived within moments. It wasn't clear when I would next be able to get some sleep, but whatever worked.

"So, it was only a kid, huh?" DiMello chuckled again. "Damn. Who would have thought that? Yeah, in my childish zeal to recover my . . . *grandmother's* . . . wedding rings, I ended up having three or four conversations with the police detective in charge of the investigation. Not too bright, huh? Thank God they didn't catch your client. Anyway, the detective was crystal clear with me: they didn't pick up a single clue, no fingerprints, no word on the street, no names of interest, no reappearance of what was taken—nothing. Your guy was brilliant to leave behind all the traceable stuff. If one of the bonds had been taken and negotiated, they'd have been all over that."

DiMello fell silent for a spell, turning the copy of the engagement ring over in his fingers, contemplating what he wanted to do. Then he added: "I can't believe I'm seeing this thing again after all these years.

This is amazing." Again, he went stone silent, no doubt still calculating what was best for him in this unusual matter. When he finally spoke, he confirmed just how insightful Longfellow had been. "Counselor, it may make sense for me to see if I can find a bargaining chip for you to use. I don't want to be involved with anything public that could come of this, and that's what would happen if your guy ever stood trial. So tell me about what strategy you have in mind."

"My strategy," I replied, thrilled to get down to details, "is to arrange a meeting with three parties: the United States attorney in charge of the Los Angeles office of the United States Department of Justice, the district attorney for the county of Los Angeles, and the successor in interest to the insurer of the bank. My plan is to tell them that I represent someone who wants to make full restitution to the bank and its insurer of all claims that were paid, or any additional losses. This would be in exchange for both federal and state John Doe immunity agreements. I have two arguments that would never carry the day on their own in court—not nearly so—but they should be adequate to provide the prosecutors cover if you can provide a viable bargaining chip."

"And if we try all this, and it doesn't work, then what happens?"

"If we make a solid effort, and we can't make this work, I give you my word of honor: I will do everything in my power to convince my client to walk away and learn to live with his nightmares. So far, he hasn't listened to me on this—quite the contrary. But my leverage to get him to listen to my advice on this has recently increased—even quite significantly so, I'd say. I'm pretty certain I'll eventually be able to prevail on him if I can report that I made a serious effort to deal with the criminal authorities."

"And if the negotiations succeed, what happens to the rings?"

"I was thinking about that. Unless they bring it up, I intend to be silent about the rings. My guess is that the prosecutors would be concentrating on only one thing: whether or not and how they could ensure total confidentiality about the entire transaction without the press getting wind of it. The restitution of the cash part would be to the successor in interest of the insurer that paid out the losses. That part's easy: they'd be party to the negotiations."

"And if they're sticklers for every last detail—including the rings?"

"Then we'll give them the copies you're holding. In this scenario, they would presumably contact you about their return—we know they have your name from the claim you filed all those years ago. Would you care?"

I could see DiMello contemplating this eventuality by the way he looked down and took his time responding. "I need silence in the press, but I could live with the authorities contacting me to give these copies back. Perhaps it could happen through the channels I use to set up what you need. No one need know. There is only one thing: perhaps the copy shouldn't look so exactly like my *nonna*'s actual costume jewelry ... I don't want to lose ... my family's privacy. You follow?"

"I do, Don DiMello."

Then DiMello took a pad out of the breast pocket of his jacket, along with the most stunningly beautiful fountain pen I've ever seen, and in a completely different tone of voice that sent shivers down my spine, he completed our arrangement. "Write down your home address. And sign underneath. This secures your guarantee to me as to the confidentiality of everything we are talking about and doing, and as to your having personal possession of my rings, and as to the return of my *nonna*'s rings after I make what you call a 'good faith' effort to be helpful. But before you sign this, take a moment to think, young man. This is a mortgage. On your body, not on your house. You're okay with that?"

Only for Billy. I signed the mortgage deed, as I was told. DiMello carefully tore out the page, folded it meticulously, and placed it in a stunning alligator-leather breast wallet that he then replaced in his suit jacket. "It will take me a month or two to research what I can come up with for both the California and federal authorities. A tasty morsel, it would take—a tasty morsel. I actually have an idea along those lines, but like you, I need some things to go unmentioned."

"I understand."

"Excellent. And do we also understand one another that no one outside of the two of us and your jeweler is *ever* going to know anything about our transaction, and that includes your client?"

"Yes, except that my private eye knows everything I know—he's the one who performed the investigation, and he's the one who learned how to contact you. My office has worked with him for three decades: there is zero concern about a confidentiality breach on his part."

"That's not a problem; I knew he was involved. Not an issue." With that, we shook hands, under the watchful eyes of the gentlemen at the next table, and I drove all the way back to Boston with a grin on my face. Could Longfellow possibly have come up with a way the Mayor's impossible dream could actually come true?

***

Billy had asked a number of times about my private investigator, and whether what he does "is like I see on TV." So, I asked Longfellow whether, if he had the time one day, he would like to meet a strong candidate for the presidency of the Longfellow fan club. The day had arrived for the much-discussed visit, and Longfellow and I went over to the hospital together after a meeting on another case. By this time, Billy sported a Red Sox cap signed by their great pitcher, Luis Tiant, which I'd scored at a charity auction. He wore it as much to keep warm as to hide his baldness, but tossed it aside in a nanosecond when Longfellow produced two caps he'd had made for the day without having mentioned a word to me. They each bore the name of his detective agency: "Solutions and Outcomes, Ltd."

Longfellow started right in. "I'm looking for an assistant detective, and it needs to be a kid. I already have signed up some older people, people of different races and sizes—because, as you can imagine, you have to assign the appropriate person to the appropriate case if they're going to be inconspicuous. Do you follow what I am saying?"

Billy: "Yes, sir."

Longfellow: "I have a girl who is eight. But I need a boy, about an eleven-year-old. Could be twelve. Do you know of anyone who might be interested?"

Billy: "I'm eleven!"

Longfellow: "Really. Well, that's wonderful news. Do you mind wearing a disguise from time to time; some jobs require it—especially wigs. Some guys have a problem with that."

Billy: "That's opportune; I could use a wig."

Longfellow: "'Opportune'? Kids don't use words like that. You could blow an operation out of the water."

Billy: "Good point. But I can talk like a kid when I need to. I just like learning grown-up words."

Longfellow: "Not a problem. As you can imagine, we would prepare you for the particular circumstances of a given case."

Billy: "Of course. What's the job pay?"

Longfellow: "What?"

Billy: "Yeah. I have legal fees."

Longfellow: "For what?"

Billy: "For him."

Billy pointed in my direction.

Longfellow: "Billy, do you think you and I could speak privately?"

Billy: "Definitely."

I left the room, trying like crazy to not smile until I was outside.

***

I spent the next fifteen minutes chatting with Billy's fans at the nursing station. It was entirely clear that everyone working on the floor had grown just as fond of the little tike as I had. The boy possessed a rare capacity to connect with other people. Connecting with Billy reminded me of when you're driving and you turn the radio dial: static—static—static—and then, finally, you come upon a clear channel. That's what Billy was: a clear channel. No blockages. That, I realized, was why he was so sensitive to the static in the love that was broadcast to him by each of his parents; another kid might never have noticed.

When I returned to the room, Longfellow was preparing to leave. Billy was quite serious in his demeanor and tone, and when I asked if everything was all right, with just a word or two, he made it perfectly clear that he needed to be alone: he was concentrating and thinking something through, because he was, as he phrased it, "on a case."

***

About five weeks later, I returned home one night to find a letter with no return address. It simply contained two names I was to contact. The first was the senior Los Angeles County assistant district attorney, Janet Helms, while the second was the United States attorney for

Southern California, Hendrick Adams. For each, there was a phone number labeled "direct line," and in both cases, I was simply to introduce myself by an arranged phrase: "Terry, from Boston." My calls were anticipated. That was it.

I immediately called Longfellow with these two names. Within a day, he called back to confirm that Helms was the principal assistant district attorney in Los Angeles County in charge of the organized crime unit, and Adams had the same focus for the Offices of the United States Attorney. Longfellow suggested that I should insist on meeting with the two authorities together to avoid any turf wars developing between them as to primacy of contact, and second, he offered to research the name of the current insurance company that was successor in interest to the now- defunct insurer that had paid out the cash losses to robbery victims all those years ago.

***

That afternoon, I met the Mayor in Billy's hospital room, and even though the little guy had a minimum of strength to share, the generosity of his character was evident in how supportive he was of his mother's efforts as we discussed the pros and cons of moving ahead with our project. I reported to my collaborators that, thanks to Longfellow's efforts, we now had something very significant to offer the prosecutors. I had no idea what it was, however: all that I knew was that it had been arranged for, and that it was in place for us to use. Billy asked two insightful questions during our team huddle. First, he probed: "If this doesn't work out, could they find my mom by asking you who your client is, or by looking through your phone records to see who you've been calling a lot?" I explained how the attorney-client privilege works, and how, in theory, it would be illegal for the police authorities to look through my telephone records or in any other way work to trace the Mayor as being the client I would be representing at the Los Angeles meeting.

Billy's second question, which the Mayor seconded, was what I would decide to do in her shoes. Clients often ask this as a way around making decisions themselves. But we were a team of three—and, week by week, it was becoming ever more clear that Dr. Baker Miller was a fourth team member—and it was time for the team to speak as one. "I'd go for it, all things considered," I concluded after taking a good half minute to reflect on the multiple pros and cons.

"How about you, Billy boy?" the Mayor added with palpable warmth. "What's your vote?"

"I like the fact that Mr. Longfellow set it up and thinks it's a good idea."

"Then it's a go," the Mayor said. This brought a smile to Billy's sweet face, and sealed the deal. The Mayor smiled just as broadly and put out her hand with her thumb up. Billy immediately did the same, his hand touching her hand. And a split second later, there were three thumbs up, all touching, all teaming up. Talk about a moment of connection.

***

Three weeks later, just shy of a year after I had first met the Mayor, I flew out to Los Angeles and jumped in a cab, and an hour later found myself in the long-imagined meeting with the California criminal authorities—both state and federal. Longfellow had never come up with any particular approach to the negotiations, and on top of that, neither Assistant District Attorney Helms nor United States Attorney Adams had returned the calls I had made to each of their offices, other than to have assistants confirm the time and place. So, I was going into battle totally blind, with only three meager weapons: an offer of restitution of an embarrassingly small sum of money, a statute-of-limitations argument that was directly opposed to well-settled legal precedent, and a Patty Hearst–type defense that California jurisprudence expressly rejected. Clearly, my only hope was that whatever had been arranged through DiMello would prove adequate. And all I knew about that was that when DiMello's assistant had called me to confirm that I had indeed received the letter with the two names I was to call, he had added: "Set up the meeting; you won't be disappointed." I had tried to pry more information from him, but halfway through my question, I could hear the dial tone.

Sometimes, as an attorney, you know what you're doing, and sometimes you've just got to try to *look like* you know what you're doing—and keep your eyes and ears open as wide as you can stretch them. As soon as I walked into the windowless conference room in the office of the United States Justice Department in downtown Los Angeles, I realized just how little I was going to control what was about to happen. United States Attorney Hendrick Adams was clearly going to be in charge, and that was just fine with me. He was a great bear of a man with a huge barrel chest, hair somewhat reminiscent of Einstein's, a commanding baritone voice, and a twinkle in his eye that you could light a candle with. He had on a flowered bow tie that nearly disappeared between two of his numerous chins—and he wore suspenders that looked to be under significant tension. You immediately wanted to have a beer with the man. Janet Helms was precisely the polar opposite. She was Ms. Plain Jane: a slight, serious-looking, thin-lipped, and seemingly unsmiling woman in her late forties, who, for some unfathomable reason, wore her glasses on the very tip of her nose, causing her to cock her head back when doing anything other than reading. She had dead-straight, dirty-blond, pageboy-cut hair that looked like it hadn't been washed in a week, but—worse still—it undoubtedly had been.

There was only one thing the two prosecutors had in common, and that was that they gave off a myriad of signals that it was an extremely rare thing for them to be personally present in such a meeting, as opposed to being represented by an assistant or an assistant's assistant. It was also abundantly clear that the presence of these two top functionaries—each the number-two person in their respective office—indicated that Mr. DiMello had indeed been hard at work behind the scenes. Counsel to the insurance company that was successor in interest to the insurer that had paid out the claims was also present. Business, very serious business, was meant to be done at the meeting. That was clear.

After we introduced ourselves, and agreed that this meeting was completely off the record, I was asked by the United States attorney to explain why I'd called the meeting. I began by stating that I represented a client who lived in the Midwest who wished to make amends for a crime he had committed more than thirty years in the past. I explained that, as a college student, he had become caught up in the student movement at a major Midwest college campus, and that, to raise money for the movement, he had single-handedly committed the robbery of the Sixth Third Savings Bank in Los Angeles in 1968. All of the $42,000 he had taken had been used to pay movement-related legal fees. I represented that he had been a 100 percent law-abiding citizen ever since, and that he wanted to make full restitution, but only on three conditions. First, there had to be complete anonymity: his identity would never be known. Second, he would have total immunity from both state and federal prosecution under the name "John Doe." And third, the entire transaction would be under seal and not mentioned to anyone outside of this room, ever, including to the press.

I could see as I was finishing that there were two very different reactions brewing as to what I was proposing. Adams listened politely, nodding several times, while Helms looked as if she were watching a particularly violent horror movie. And, sure enough, as soon as I finished, Assistant District Attorney Helms literally exploded. The glare of the overly bright fluorescent lights lit up the droplets of spittle that came flying from her mouth as she spluttered, "This is preposterous. Why in the world would you think that we would agree to such a proposal? I have never, ever heard of anything so outrageous. You go get your guy to fess up, make restitution, and maybe we can talk about a plea bargain, fine. I could probably live with minimal time and a modest probation period. But you're asking for a complete under-the-table whitewash in exchange for nothing? For restitution to the insurer of *peanuts*? Are you joking? There is not a chance in the world I could sell this to my boss, and frankly, I wouldn't even try."

I was about to respond, although I had nothing of significance to argue against her sound logic, when a giant but gentle hand reached out and squeezed my forearm. "Counselor, let me respond to this, if I might," said the United States attorney in a deep and reassuring voice that had just a touch of Southwest accent to it. Turning to the attorney representing the insurance company, he asked, "Sir, I wonder if you would excuse us. The assistant district attorney and I need a few minutes alone with Attorney Freiberg." Counsel graciously excused himself from the room.

"Janet, my office has been in discussions that I am not free to relay to you but which amount to an extremely interesting proposition from a federal law enforcement point of view. *Extremely interesting.*" The experienced trial attorney paused for effect, and then asked that he be allowed "to go over it once, so please listen *very* closely to what I can say, and use your professional imagination to think about what I *cannot* say. Are you listening?" His voice was slow and serious, and he waited patiently to force her to nod yes. "We have been offered information on a completely different matter that is *a thousand times more important* than the one Attorney Freiberg proposes to resolve. Janet, I need you to trust my representation to you that the other matter outweighs this one—literally—*a thousandfold*. When it comes to pass, you will read about it on the front page of every single newspaper in this country." He stared straight into her eyes, and when she did not respond, he simply repeated, "*a thousandfold bigger fish.*" It took her another good ten or fifteen seconds to swallow her pride and do what she had to do; she nodded that she was in accord.

Adams continued addressing Helms, now in a summarizing tone of voice. "I want to say that I agree with every word of what you said earlier, and I can assure you that without the exceptional significance of the collateral matter I've referenced, I would have had *exactly* the same reaction you just expressed." He paused, then stopped. He'd made his best case, and he knew it. While I'm sure the silence that followed was, in reality, ten or fifteen seconds long, for me it felt like it took a week: my whole case was pretty clearly going to turn on the next thing I heard. Finally, ADA Helms broke the quiet. "So, what do I tell the district attorney, Hendrick? I don't make decisions over there, you know that. What do I tell him?"

Adams turned toward me. "So, what does she tell her boss, Counselor? What's her cover story? She's going to go with whatever you've got, so please don't have nothing. What *do* you have for us?"

It was now or never. If there was one thing I'd learned in decades of position staking in negotiations and trial argument, it's that you need to sound unwaveringly confident when you're supporting a weak position. I cleared my throat and plunged in. "Janet, there are at least two skirmishes here, each well worth avoiding," I began, adopting both her first name and a "well, now that we're on the same team" tone of voice. She cocked her head ever so slightly to the right; she was listening.

"The first would be the statute of limitations issue. As a matter of well-settled law, it would turn on the detailed facts as to whether or not my client's absence from California after the robbery meets the 'fleeing the jurisdiction standard' needed to toll the statute. I don't think

California can meet that standard in this case: my client is entrenched in his Midwest life, and from what he can easily demonstrate, he has seldom traveled out of state.

"But far more interesting," I continued, "is the substantive defense my client would make. It would be a novel twist on the defense Patty Hearst used unsuccessfully in 1976 claiming she'd been brainwashed by her kidnappers, the Symbionese Liberation Army. As you well know, that defense failed, and Hearst was found guilty. Arguably, that was because social science knew so little at the time about brainwashing. But a lot has changed in the intervening years. These days, the phenomenon is known as 'coercive persuasion,' and a great deal more is known about how, in a cult setting, an individual can lose control of their capacity to adhere to the norms and respect the laws of the wider collectivity—which is precisely what happened to my client.

"Above and beyond that, an even more powerful explanatory model of brainwashing has been recently developed, and will soon find its way into Patty Hearst–type criminal defense litigation in the States. It's called the 'Stockholm Syndrome Defense.' Defendants citing this syndrome have successfully put expert witnesses on the stand to explain how kidnapping and cult victims progressively display compassion with, and even loyalty toward, their captors—sometimes to the point where they readily cooperate with their captors' orders." I then continued on for a good five minutes with the names and innovative contributions that a number of forensic psychiatrists had recently made in this field, and mentioned that if my client's case needed to be tried, these doctors would be called as expert witnesses. My argument was that settling my client's case would have the added benefit of nipping in the bud what would otherwise be a master class in how to make aggressive use of this revised defense strategy.

Clearly, I had held their attention. Both experienced prosecutors had listened intently—and even Attorney Helms had nodded approvingly several times while I was speaking. It felt like I just needed one more argument to reach the tipping point. And I had one ready.

"Finally, I will represent to you that the investigating police found no evidence whatsoever at the crime scene. There were no security films, no fingerprints, no recovery of the stolen cash, no witnesses—no evidence whatsoever. It was a one-time stupid act by a college kid who today is the most straitlaced, law-abiding Midwestern man you can imagine. If we don't come to an agreement here, I can't imagine how your investigators could ever locate this gentleman, and even if you ever did, I'm quite confident you'd lack the evidence to indict, let alone convict, him."

There was a heavy silence when I finished. Then the resonant voice of the United States attorney boomed out: "Janet, this is perfect for you to use with the DA. Tell him this case is a one-off, nonviolent, thirty-something-year-old case that neither of our offices may be able to prosecute given the statute of limitations, and even if we could, we'd have to be crazy lucky to identify this guy. And even if we did somehow locate him, how are we going to convince a grand jury to indict him? There is no known evidence to convict him whatsoever. On the other hand, if we take the deal, the bank robbery will be resolved, the insurer will receive full restitution, and far more important than any of this, my office will receive what it needs to resolve a matter of a thousand times greater importance. Janet, feel free to have Jim call me directly for more details, but unless I'm missing something, this is a no-brainer." And then, looking over at me in such a way so that he could give me a private wink, Adams concluded his plea to the assistant district attorney with a staged question to me.

"You did say, Counselor, did you not, that the restitution would include compound interest?"

I was as trapped as I had been when DiMello had nabbed the $20,000. "Yes, indeed, sir. And hopefully my client will have enough cash to accomplish this without having to go out and rob another bank."

There was laughter around the table, which clearly signaled that resolution was at hand. At this point, we invited the insurer's attorney back into the room and brought him up to speed on the single issue that concerned his client: the restitution—with compound interest. He had no argument with our proposed resolution.

Adams was ready to conclude the meeting. Everything about his body language and tone of voice made that clear. "Janet, I think this gives you what you need, doesn't it?"

"I suppose so. I'll get this done, Hendrick. But you owe me one."

"I do, indeed," Adams replied with a smile.

Helms took her card out of her briefcase and asked me to call her office in a week for the outcome. And she wanted a written memorandum covering the arguments I'd just put forth. If the district attorney agreed, I was to call an associate in her office named Angela Brady to work out the logistics of the restitution payment that would need to be made to the insurer. She asked me to draft the John Doe immunity papers that I had in mind, and the United States attorney saw no reason for me not to do so for both prosecutorial staffs. There was not a word about the rings.

I have no memory of attending another meeting where the participants dispersed so quickly. Within a minute, everyone had departed and I was left alone for a moment in the conference room, packing up my briefcase. But what I was really doing was trying to get my mind around what had just happened. What in the world had DiMello arranged to exchange that produced such a determined effort by the United States attorney? I had to meet with the don at least one more time to carry out my client's end of the bargain, and I certainly intended to learn what had come to pass—or at least try to learn.

***

On my way home from Logan Airport that evening, I stopped by Children's Hospital to tell the good news to Billy: we were making progress—hopefully definitive progress—on his mother's case, and Dr. Baker Miller would soon be working with a patient freed of fear. How excited Billy would be.

But then the waves of reality washed up on shore and tore apart the sandcastle of the sweet victory story I had drafted in my mind during the return flight from California. Billy's room was occupied by some other child, and Billy, my cherished little guy, was languishing in intensive care. I was only able to peer at him through the ICU glass window, and he just lay there, motionless, with a dozen tubes entering and exiting from the tiny body that inexplicably managed to house such a massive spirit. Dr. Newsom was out for the day, and I couldn't find anyone else who would talk to me about Billy, given that I wasn't family. So, all I could do was stare extra hard and try to beam my affection through the thick piece of glass that divided us. And somehow, just at the last moment before I turned and left, I saw a tiny little smile flash across Billy's lips and then disappear—the way a whip-poor-will darts across your field of vision in the deep twilight of a summer evening. It had happened, I was sure of it, and I've thought of it a thousand times since.

**

Within ten days of my return to Boston, the paperwork in the "John Doe immunity matter" was signed, sealed, and delivered. Something inside me wanted to resolve the matter with DiMello before I called the Mayor with the good news—probably because of my premonition that what she would have to tell me might make our victory seem entirely Pyrrhic. So, I called "Tony" at the number DiMello had given me, and sure enough, five days later, a letter arrived at my home with the name of a Providence hotel I'd never heard of, with an evening appointment time. There was a delivery to effectuate.

It turned out that a room had been reserved for me for the night at the nameless and completely charming boutique hotel located at the address I'd been given, and that was just fine with me—the ride back to Boston from Providence was nothing I needed to tackle late at night. I had time to shower and dress, and then was picked up by DiMello's limousine. The chauffeur mentioned that we had a twenty-minute drive, and that I should feel free to open the bar and make myself a drink. I could find no fault in his idea—none whatsoever.

The car delivered me to an amazing property. As I stepped out of the car, I was politely asked if I would mind being frisked, and once that formality was taken care of, I was led to the room where I was to meet with Don DiMello, as his lieutenants always referred to him. The room was decorated as a sixteenth-century Italianate drawing room, with extraordinary reproductions of Renaissance paintings on the walls, and splendid marble statues in the corners. I was just realizing that it was only my *assumption* that these art treasures were reproductions when a second perfectly matched pair of bodyguards knocked and entered. They politely requested permission to confirm the earlier frisking of my person, this time more for a wire than for a weapon.

Don DiMello appeared soon thereafter, looking elegant in a beautifully tailored suit.

"Did you enjoy yourself in California?" he opened with a wry smile.

"I did indeed," I replied. "I must be Clarence Darrow reborn: I was able to convince the criminal authorities to give my client everything he dreamed of receiving."

"Good going, my boy," DiMello added with a smile. "I'm glad it worked out for you."

There was a pause as he waited for what I might say next. "Seriously, Mr. DiMello, I want to thank you for living up to your end of our arrangement. The senior United States attorney was entirely determined to convince his California state counterpart to join in the resolution of the matter, and they ended up signing off on forms I drafted myself. It was a fascinating transaction. Can I assume that whatever transaction took place between your offices and the federal authorities was subsequently consummated?"

"Indeed, you can. Everything's closed on your side; papers signed and done?"

"Completely closed," I replied with a smile and a nod. "The California attorney general signed off three days ago." Silence followed, and I balked at asking the question I desperately wanted to put to the don—balked for fear of seeming amateurish. But that was ridiculous: I *was* an amateur—a total amateur in dealing with what I was dealing with here, and Don DiMello knew it. Like Longfellow said, I told myself, keep it simple. "Mr. DiMello, can I learn now what was . . . um . . . exchanged?"

DiMello stared at me. "Your client made restitution—that must have been it, don't you think?"

"Oh yes. Or it might have been the argument I made to the two prosecutors. But I have this funny feeling, just a slight suspicion, call it a hunch, that it took a little something special from your end to bend the steel bars of federal prison. You can't possibly condemn me to a lifetime of wondering what that was; you wouldn't do that to me . . . would you?"

Whether it was my friendly tone of voice or the colloquialisms I used, something made the don laugh out loud. I definitely had the impression he wasn't accustomed to being talked to in such a familiar way, or having someone keep insisting that he divulge information he didn't particularly want to disclose.

One more try: "Come on. What in the world was traded to them?"

Again, there was silence while the don looked me over and contemplated what he wanted to do. Then he told me the conditions: "I'm thinking about telling you what you want to know, but if I do, and if you talk to anyone about my involvement in this while I'm still alive, there'll be a problem between us. Do we agree on that?"

"Yes. Of course. You already made that crystal clear to me the first time we met."

"After I'm dead and gone, go right ahead and tell the whole fucking story—tell it out loud—write a book about it if you like. Make a film—be a star!" We shared a laugh over his flippancy, and I definitely had the impression that the don was enjoying himself. "To be frank with you," he said, taking up the point again, "I *love* what that son-of-a-bitch client of yours pulled off, so go right ahead and tell him that it's been my delight and pleasure to help him get away with it. Definitely tell him I said that—*after my days, that is*; that's the only condition." And with that, the don laughed out loud. Something in his demeanor made it clear that he didn't get to be so lighthearted all that often. And then he took right up again: "Give me my ring, and I just might sing." He followed his rhyme with another round of laughter—in which I gladly joined.

First, I reached into my suit coat breast pocket and pulled out an envelope of cash. "Here's the cash part. It's the exact amount that was stolen from your box, all those years ago—twenty thousand dollars. I can't pay you any interest without that having tax reporting consequences, which neither of us needs. You okay with that?"

"Uh-huh. Sure."

Then I produced the two rings. The don's mouth fell wide open as he gazed upon the rings for the first time in more than thirty years. After a long, long silence, during which he turned the engagement ring over and over in his hands, he looked back up to me. "I can assume these are my *nonna's* rings, and not another fucking copy, right?"

"Are you kidding?" I replied with my palms up to the ceiling. "The note setting up this meeting didn't go to a post office box; it went to my home."

DiMello just smiled and giggled lightly to himself. "Good point. Okay, then, let's go spend as much as we can of that cash you brought along. Have you ever *really* been out for a night on the town to celebrate? Do you know how to celebrate, like I'm talking about?"

"I'm open to learning."

"Ha! All right. Let's go see if that's really true."

＊＊

Now that the don has passed away, I can share with you his answer to the question that I wouldn't let go of. About the fifth or sixth time I bothered him about it, he gave a little shrug of his shoulders that signaled he'd finally come down on the side of sharing who the "thousand-fold bigger fish" was that the United States attorney was so interested in—so long as I agreed not to disclose the don's name or involvement in the matter with *anyone* until the legal outcome of the matter had become final, and until he was no longer living.

So, my reader—now that both conditions have long since been met—you get to know as well. The tasty morsel who was offered up was Randy "Duke" Cunningham, a Republican congressman from California. He was subsequently convicted of tax evasion, mail fraud, wire fraud, and conspiracy to pocket nearly $2.5 million in bribes, including accepting a Rolls-Royce and a yacht. Needless to say, he was forced to resign from Congress. "It was the Rolls that did him in," DiMello had declared. "That's the sphere where I learned what I learned. Wish I could share more details with you: they're colorful, you'd enjoy them. You'd definitely enjoy them. But I can't."

＊＊

The following morning, I called the Mayor's office, looking forward to reporting that the transaction was complete in all aspects, and hoping against hope to hear good news about Billy. But she was not in her office, and I was told by her assistant that she was out for two weeks on family matters and would not be given notice of my call until she returned. I tried to learn more, but given that the last thing I could say was that I was her counsel, I had zero leverage to get the administrative staff to open up. So, I had no confirmation of what the issue was, but considering how weak Billy had looked in the ICU, I had a heart full of worry.

***

The greatest moments in an attorney's career are without question when you sit with your client for the final meeting in those cases that have a good outcome. Your hero status may last for just a matter of minutes before your client disappears from your life forever, but those can be sweet, sweet moments. The very most dramatic ones, of course, are when you win a jury trial: there you are, standing next to your client—waiting, hoping, fearing—and then the foreperson of the jury stands up and calls out the good news. It's all hugs and smiles, and, for a moment, there's a bond, a magnificent, electrifying connection between attorney and client. And then, as it must be, everyone goes home, just like at the end of an evening of theater.

In Billy's case, our victory never had even one fleeting moment of the joy of winning. It was all too terribly sad. Irony of ironies, thanks to Dr. Baker Miller—and perhaps, in some smaller part, to Longfellow's and my humble efforts—the Mayor was clear and now able and ready to connect and to emote and to fully love. But sweet Billy was gone. It was one of those perverse ironies that the silent universe we inhabit seems to enjoy inflicting on us mere mortals.

If there was ever a memorial service, I never heard about it. I did, however, receive a sweet gesture from the Mayor that meant quite a lot to me. Her final payment for legal services arrived in a cardboard box. She included a heartfelt thank-you note, which I still retain as a keepsake. Better yet, her check for my legal fees was $59.45 short of the amount billed—because the delivery box also contained a cigar box with precisely $59.45 in coins inside: "mostly quarters, but dimes too." There was also a foil-wrapped object, which turned out to be a frog skeleton, and a pen that allowed you to write in five different colors. Not four. I have no memory whatsoever about the final demise of the frog skeleton, but the pen remained in my desk drawer for the remainder of my legal career.

BREAD SHOULD
NOT TASTE LIKE
KLEENEX

I wasn't a particularly well-behaved child—*except in Margaret's kitchen*. There, total compliance with my great-grandmother's German cook was an absolute and nonnegotiable requirement. Three-quarters of a century down life's road, I can still recall being enormously proud, even prideful, that I was the *only* child in the family allowed in the kitchen on baking day. The basic rule was crystal clear: I was at all times to remain a perfectly still and quiet presence, invariably seated at one corner of the long, heavy wooden table that paralleled the massive black stove. All this took place just after World War II, when large households still baked their own bread—enough for the week to come. Throughout the morning, the multiple small ovens of the massive gas-fired stove spewed forth a dozen different breads, rolls, cakes, and pastries, samples of which were given over for a taste. I found myself amazed—even mystified—at how Margaret could turn flour, yeast, eggs, butter, milk, sugar, and salt into such a panoply of different baked wonders. While I well understand that the luster of childhood recollections can be burnished over time, I have no reason whatsoever to doubt the accuracy of my memory of the extraordinary breads and pastries of my early years.

A second chapter in my love affair with bread began after the summer of my sophomore year of college, when I hitchhiked around a dozen European countries for three months—with all of $550 in my blue jean pockets. That meant nights in youth hostels for a quarter, and bread and cheese for most meals. But what bread it was! Country by country, I was bowled over by their local bread and amazed by the varieties of cheese. And then, at the very end of my summer, I arrived in France and met my first true baguette. Life has never been the same since. It is impossible to exaggerate the importance of bread in France, where it has been the principal staple for hundreds of years—as dominant in a day's diet as rice in the Middle East or pasta in southern Italy. To this very day, the cost of the basic baguette is still price controlled to ensure it remains within every consumer's budget.

**

Fast-forward to Boston, roughly around 1990. There were some neighborhoods of the city that had bakers to admire and fresh bread to revere—Italian focaccia in the North End, Irish soda bread in South Boston, Jewish dark rye in Brookline, and Southern corn bread in Dorchester, for example. But where my wife and I lived, no such luck. It was pretty much a bread desert.

Then, one sunny fall afternoon when I was wandering home from the subway stop, ambling through a neighborhood adjacent to ours and kicking dried leaves on the sidewalk like a child, I turned a corner and came upon a small bakery that must have only recently opened. Customers were patiently, even cheerfully, waiting in a line that wound its way out the door and swooped halfway down the block. The depth of the aromas coming from the shop was something I hadn't experienced since my childhood moments in Margaret's kitchen. Each time the door would open to allow one customer to exit and another to enter, the odors from the ovens would waft down the sidewalk and temporarily quiet the queue. When finally I gained entry into the one-room establishment, it was immediately apparent why such patience was shown by everyone in line: the bread was being baked right before your very eyes. Tall, stainless-steel electric ovens formed a square horse-shoe around the perimeter of the back two-thirds of the room, and the center between them provided space for wooden worktables. Eight or nine apprentice bakers were rolling dough and forming pastries at their workstations, all under the watchful eye of the master baker—a five-foot-two ball of energy with short-cropped auburn curls that surrounded her perky, pretty little face. She moved with grace between the half-dozen stations where her assistants were absorbed in differing tasks, quietly teaching—almost without speaking—as she stopped by each station to demonstrate how to knead the dough effectively, or how to evenly flour a tabletop, or how to roll out and then fold over the dough to create flaky crusts.

The street where the bakery was located soon became more like a village than like urban Boston. As the weeks went on, it became essentially impossible not to smile and warmly greet both neighborhood acquaintances and complete strangers. With the addition of the bakery, there was now a shared connection between all whose lives it graced: there was something communal and welcoming about the shop. Within months, a lackluster café on one side of the bakery was sold or relet, and within a week, it reopened as a coffee shop that openly invited bakery customers to enjoy a cup of joe with one of the bakery's pastries. And only two or three months later, a vibrant children's toy store replaced a moribund beauty parlor on the other side of the shop. Many a crumb fell to its floor as bakery customers and their small children snuck bites from white paper bags as they perused the brightly colored toys. I can't possibly exaggerate how much pleasure and delight this new bakery and these revivified shops added to our little community. But such is the power of well-baked bread. The French bakery seemed almost too good to be true.

**

It was. One icy cold January day when I showed up at the bakery, there was no line outside the shop, and upon entering, I came upon a dark and uncomfortable mood that stood in complete contrast to what I had learned to expect. I chose an *"épi"* form of baguette—where the dough is laid out in the form of a shaft of wheat. But as soon as I lifted it to carry to the cashier, I could feel how limp and crustless it was. I could see the master baker, still wearing her outside sunglasses for some reason, sitting motionless in a far back corner of the bakery, looking listless. The apprentice bakers went about their business, but whatever was weighing upon the queen affected the worker bees as well. Ah well, I thought, a bad day; who doesn't suffer a bad day from time to time?

But it wasn't a bad day—it was a bad month. Something had been lost, something had been broken. I remember thinking that it was probably financial: the little bakery wasn't working out, and soon we would lose this neighborhood gem. A week or two later, on my fourth or fifth visit to the bakery after the downturn in its fortunes, the owner was somewhat livelier and once again moved among her apprentices to exhibit technique, even if there was less lightness to her presence, less assuredness, and far less optimism than there had been in the past. As I paid for yet another soft, flavorless baguette, I began to wonder whether I would continue to patronize the little bakery I had come to love.

And, in fact, it was many weeks before I returned to try the bakery one last time—and I was thrilled that I did. I immediately sensed a change for the better when I was still half a block away. Once again there was a substantial waiting line and a vibrant buzz of chatter from the queued patrons bracing themselves against a late-winter chill. And my impression was immediately confirmed upon entering: all was well once again in the little French bakery, and when I chose an *épi*-shaped baguette as a final test, I could actually hear the crunch of the crust as my fingers pinched down on the small slip of wax paper with which I held it. I could see the baker in the back of the shop, fully animated and clearly returned to peak form. Once again, she was absorbed in patiently demonstrating her know-how to her apprentices, and I found myself utterly delighted that all was well. The croissants I bought that morning had the ethereal lightness that had somehow disappeared during the preceding month—and by this point in time, I needed to buy three of them: our toddler now had enough teeth to attack the buttery bread that greets some vast percentage of Parisians each morning. I have a detailed memory of whistling as I exited the shop and began my walk home—and I never whistle much, given my constitutional incapacity to carry a tune. But whistle I did, so good was the day.

***

For the better part of half a year, all was well again with the little bakery, and then, suddenly—one day to the next—the crust lost its crunch, the bread lost its flavor, and the baker lost her élan. Once again, she sat sullenly and listlessly in the extreme rear of the shop, sporting her oversized sunglasses, unable to mingle with her apprentices. She seemed monumentally grief-stricken—probably, I surmised, because she was a clinically depressed person behind the veneer of productive exuberance. Or perhaps she was bipolar, poor woman. What a shame. That evening, I took home spongy dinner rolls, which proved to be significantly over-salted. It was as if the baker's tears had run down her cheeks and spoiled her batter.

***

Just a matter of days after the second downturn at the bakery, I parked at Boston Children's Hospital on my way to visit a client. It was a rainy, chilly day, so I parked near and made use of the emergency room entrance. I was just about to enter when I noticed, and stepped out of the way of, a very concerned-looking mother rushing toward the door while tending to her young son, whose forearm, given the angle at which it was bent, appeared to be badly broken. Throughout the morning, my mind kept wandering back to the unfortunate child, and I kept asking myself where I had seen the mother before. Had she been a client? I didn't think so. Was she a neighbor? No. Perhaps a Boston University student from my distant professorial past? No, she was too young, given how many years had passed. Ah well, I couldn't place her, and before long, my mind stopped trying.

***

On my next trip to the bakery the better part of a month later, I was both delighted and perplexed at what I found. The line was back, the excited chatter had returned, and once again, the magnificent aroma that wafted down the street put my spirit back in France. Once inside, I could see that everything was again as it should be: beautiful baking, exuberant apprentices, thrilled patrons—and a master baker who seemed to be delighted at making so many people so entirely happy.

Only twice in my life have I experienced what I would call a "revelation"—where in a sudden flash, I came to understand something that had previously eluded me. The first one came when I was about four or five years old. I woke up one morning possessed—*finally*—of the ability to tie my shoelaces. This second time, the mystery of the baker's ebbs and flows—*finally*—became clear to me: the baker was not safe at home. She clearly was a victim of spousal abuse. The visible, palpable state of depression the baker displayed when she'd been beaten, the sympathetic silence and slow-motion movements of her apprentices, and the eerie silence that loomed over the front of the store during these periods—and those oversized sunglasses—all were evidence of what was taking place in my favorite baker's life. But what to do about it? I didn't have a client, or a law case through which I could try to be helpful.

To this day, I can't honestly say why I didn't just walk away from the bakery after all this became clear. Perhaps it had something to do with the five-year-old still inside me, the little boy who sat on the edge of that long wooden table across from the massive wrought-iron stove, watching his beloved Margaret produce a virtual stream of breads and pastries—over half a century earlier. The more I thought about what, if anything, was the right thing for me to do, the clearer matters became. The shop owner—and, by now, I'd learned that her name was Audrey Goodwin—was, like my Margaret, a master baker, and *goddamn it*, the world needs its master bakers kept safe. It was that simple. I couldn't do nothing.

The problem, of course, was how to get involved when I had no client, no law case, no standing, no nothing. Lawyers are expressly not permitted to "foment" legal cases by spontaneously encouraging potential litigants to file suits, for example. To do so is to commit the tort of "maintenance," and above and beyond it being legally actionable, an attorney can lose his or her license for such an ethical violation. This meant I couldn't just approach Goodwin directly as an attorney, proffering the protections the law could provide her. Nor could I effectively start preaching advice to her as a customer—who the hell was I? Just a ten-dollar-a-week customer—one among hundreds.

It was at this point that my frustration led to a tactical error that later in the case almost led to my disbarment. It didn't take long for me to admit to myself that this faux pas was a direct function of my failing to plan strategically before undertaking a tactical move. I should have known better, and it was raw luck that my mistake didn't cascade into big trouble for me—and tragedy at home for Goodwin.

My ill-planned frontal assault involved trying to identify an ally on the baker's staff who could confirm or disconfirm my suspicions. But instead of devising an adequate strategy to pull this off, I impulsively committed the following misstep.

While I had made dozens of visits to the shop by that time, I had barely spoken to any given apprentice enough to matter. It had always been just a few words at the cash register with whoever had that revolving duty on a particular day. The closest I came to a strategic thought about my approach was to select the one apprentice with whom I had shared a few cash-register smiles over the past year. She was noticeably older than the others, who were only in their twenties, and I thought that perhaps her maturity would increase the likelihood she'd be sensitive to the baker's plight—if I had things right. I fiddled around in the shop long enough to wait for an unpressured moment, and only then did I approach the cash register to pay. As this apprentice handed me my change, I mentioned how much I loved the shop's baking and what a fabulous contribution the bakery made to the neighborhood. Predictably, this elicited a big smile, and that was precisely the moment I chose to whisper, *"Am I off base to be worried about the baker? When she wears those dark glasses and the shop is so gray and sad, I feel concerned that she might not be safe at home. Is everything okay?"* The apprentice looked shaken and perturbed by my intrusive question, and didn't utter a word. That being said, the suddenness with which she looked down from the smiling eye contact we had just established spoke volumes to me. But it was time for a strategic retreat: *"Never mind, it's none of my business,"* I whispered quickly. *"Please, just forget that I said anything."* With that, I scampered out of the shop and purposefully didn't return for well over a week.

To my mind, the apprentice's body language had confirmed my suspicion. But then what? To begin with, there was no law case for me here, and on top of that, I had to admit to myself that I knew next to nothing about domestic abuse. The only thing that was clear was that I had nothing to lose by educating myself on the matter, and it was quick work to find the names of half a dozen key books in the field. A month's reading filled me in on the tragic realities of spousal abuse: who knew that well over ten million Americans—over 85 percent of them being women—are victims of intimate partner physical abuse annually?[15] Not I. The effect on me of what I read and learned was that I became yet more determined to find a strategy to somehow intervene on behalf of the tortured baker. What wasn't a case became a cause.

But I was also cautioned by what I read. The literature was crystal clear that to have any hope of developing an effective intervention strategy in a particular case, one absolutely needed to have accurate information about the details of what was happening in a given victim's home. Clearly, before I could even think of developing a strategy, I needed to know where and in what circumstances the baker lived, and I needed to learn as much as possible about her abuser. The literature also made it clear that I had to discover if the baker was trapped in the secluded lifestyle that is so often imposed on battered wives and, with an eye on the future, if she had family or other natural allies who might provide her a safe space if she were ever to gather the strength to escape. Three of the books I'd read were seminal works that presented and analyzed real case stories; one excellent collection had the title *Getting Out: Life Stories of Women Who Left Abusive Men*.[16] And there was one particularly important lesson I garnered from the dozens of fact patterns discussed in the book: extracting a battered wife from an abusive home has its parallels to extracting a prisoner of war from a barbed-wire-surrounded holding facility deep in enemy territory. The more I read, the more clear it became: the idealistic cause I was contemplating bore very real risk—for the baker.

***

---

15. *The National Intimate Partner and Sexual Violence Survey: 2010 Summary Report*, National Center for Injury and Prevention and Control, CDC, 2011, https://www.cdc.gov/violenceprevention/pdf/nisvs_report2010-a.pdf.

16. Ann Goetting, *Getting Out: Life Stories of Women Who Left Abusive Men* (New York: Columbia University Press, 1999).

It became ever more clear that any responsible involvement on my part would require the help of my office's private detective, the inestimable Reginald Brooke, or "Longfellow." The problem, however, was that with no client to pay for his services, I would have to absorb the quite considerable costs that would be generated. Since my commitment to the cause was not yet at that level, I dove back into still more research on the topic. What I learned from my additional reading, however, served only to heighten my fears for my favorite baker. I read studies that documented that the physical violence battered wives endure is almost always accompanied by a relentless pattern of psychological domination that leaves the victims unable to reach out for—or even to accept—the help and support they would need to escape. In addition, most of these women find themselves completely cut off from their collateral support systems because their abusers purposefully and systematically force them to sever relations with their parents, their siblings, and their friends. And it didn't end there: I learned that many escape efforts attempted by entrapped battered wives are horror stories in their own right. Many such courageous women, for example, find themselves permanently on the run, living far from home under assumed names, in abject fear that their torturer-spouse will appear at the door. The articles and books contained appalling statistics, including the fact that this violence can be deadly: in recent years, just under two thousand women were killed each year by their intimate partners.[17]

The more I learned, the more I had to admit to myself that there was a powerful argument against my intervening in the baker's sad story: my amateurish efforts could threaten the status quo in her household and cause matters to go terribly wrong for her. But, at the same time, there was this little voice in my head that kept whispering to me—in Margaret's gentle German accent—"Terry, don't forsake the baker, don't forsake her . . ."

***

17. *When Men Murder Women: An Analysis of 2016 Homicide Data*, Violence Policy Center, 2018, http://vpc.org/studies/wmmw2018.pdf.

Seeking guidance, I telephoned an ex-colleague of mine from when I had been a sociology professor. She had worked and written for many years on women's issues, including spousal abuse. She expanded my reading list with additional important works, including peer-reviewed journal articles that set forth dismaying statistics on just how many women faced psychological terror and physical violence at home. Most importantly, she also gave me a stern warning: do *not* approach the victim again until and unless you know for certain that she has made a decision to leave and you have arranged for a fully articulated escape strategy for her. To do this, she explained, I would need to somehow contact allies in the woman's life who would be available to support her through the entire process, and I would need to confirm that there was a prearranged safe space available to her that was unknown to her abusive husband. Then she added the part that really got my attention: "Her life could be at stake, Terry. I cannot exaggerate how explosive these abusive men can be. You need to approach a battered-spouse rescue with the same degree of caution a bomb-disposal technician uses when approaching unexploded ordnance: he moves slowly, he moves thoughtfully, he moves carefully. If you don't, if you rush this, if you cut the wrong wire, the bomb will explode in *her* face—not yours." Those were her final words. Her final warning. They reverberated in my mind for weeks.

***

The more I began to think as an attorney about the baker's situation, the more I had to admit to myself that I knew nothing whatsoever about the baker beyond what I had surmised from purely circumstantial evidence. Without question, I couldn't take another step in my campaign without seeking help from—and paying out of pocket for—Longfellow's invaluable services. The British-born detective invariably was helpful in designing case strategy—and that would be sorely needed in this campaign if I were to become involved. Still unsure as to whether to proceed or not, I determined to go by the bakery on the way home. My thought was, if the baker's been beaten yet again, it's a yes—hang the expense. But she was fine. The bakery that day was in tip-top form.

Sometimes I wonder if all that was to follow would never have taken place if I had not—on a whim—purchased a pecan roll that day along with my baguette. You see, of all Margaret's beautiful breads and pastries that I had tasted as a boy in the 1940s, none spoke to me like her pecan rolls—although she used the German name for them, *schnecken*. As I walked home from the bakery, each brown-sugary, pecan-laced, buttery-dough bite that I took called out to me more loudly than the one before—and always in Margaret's accent. Fuck the expense: I was in.

***

It didn't take the master detective long to find out where Audrey Goodwin lived, and that she was indeed married. In a meeting with Longfellow about ten days after he first staked out the couple's house, I learned that Goodwin's husband was a man named Steven McCabe, a heavily tattooed United States Marine veteran who had served three tours of duty in an active war zone. He had been honorably discharged, currently received Medicaid benefits as a fully disabled person, and remained at home during the day—all day, every day. Occasionally he would briefly leave the house after Goodwin returned from work, typically riding his Harley-Davidson to an unsavory biker bar called Saigon Sally. One of Longfellow's agents had entered the bar after McCabe one evening, and reported that McCabe drank two beers off in a corner of the room with three other Hells Angels types who had arrived on three additional big bikes.

Longfellow's agent had taken numerous long-distance telephotographs. What was most striking about McCabe was his eyes. It wasn't their color or their shape; it was the hardness inside him that came beaming out. His eyes reminded me of the eyes of a huge tiger I had once confronted face-to-face at the San Diego Zoo. When the tiger and I stared at each other through the plastic window of his enclosure, we were not more than five or six feet apart, and I could see that it looked at me as prey, as dispensable. There was no emotion in the tiger's stare. I was *just* prey, nothing more. And that was what McCabe's eyes exhibited: distance and dominance. Given his Medicaid status, it seemed fair to assume that these were the eyes of a post-traumatic stress disorder

(PTSD) victim—eyes that had seen more horror than the mind behind them could process.

The house the couple rented was an old farmhouse located on part of what had been a two-hundred-acre eighteenth-century farm; it was about an hour by commuter train to the west of Boston. Longfellow also reported that the considerable distance between the road and the farmhouse made his team's clandestine observations hard to accomplish. And since there was no cover of any type available for his team to take advantage of during the day, daylight sightings and filming could only be done by a drive-by. The team spotted Goodwin arriving home from the local train station on a nightly basis, and when this was compared with the timing of her departure from the bakery, it was clear that she had gone directly home, running no errands en route. The grocery shopping, Longfellow added, seemed to be exclusively done by McCabe on his Harley—the only vehicle the couple owned.

Longfellow's report contained a list of mind-numbing observations, especially the discovery that the window shades were down all day, every day. On top of that, there was no telephone line going to the property—and this was well before the era of cell phones. Not a single third party visited the household during the two-week observation period, and Goodwin never left the house in the evening after returning from the bakery. Taken together, these discoveries clearly indicated an extreme isolation of Goodwin: a pattern that had been described over and over again in the reading I'd done of case histories of battered wives. The only observation that remained utterly mysterious, but that seemed of minor importance to us, was that Longfellow's infrared sensors picked up a third, smaller, living being in the house, which he surmised was a good-sized dog. What neither of us thought about at the time, embarrassingly, was why the pet was never taken outside for a walk.

Goodwin was easy for Longfellow to successfully investigate. He reported that she was a graduate of the baking and pastry program of Johnson & Wales University in Providence, Rhode Island—among the region's top culinary programs. One of Longfellow's agents had been dispatched to the school posing as a journalist doing an article on Goodwin's heralded bakery. He had been granted an interview by one of her professors, and this gentleman couldn't possibly have been more complimentary about his former student. The professor explained that after graduating from Johnson & Wales, Goodwin had gone to France for about eighteen months—on only the most modest of budgets. Initially, the agent learned, she had served as an apprentice in Paris for a four-month *stage*, or traineeship, at a traditional family bakery. What was truly clever of her, the professor added, was that she had pressed the Parisian baker to help her find a subsequent apprenticeship in another region of France. This strategy landed her a position in Nantes, where she learned the secrets of *petit beurre* biscuit baking. And partway through this second apprenticeship, she reportedly pressured the Nantes master baker to arrange yet another *stage*; this time, she took the train to Colmar, where she was trained in Alsatian bread and pastry baking. She subsequently learned how to bake *kouglof* in the Hautes-Alpes, rustic sourdough *pain de campagne* in the Auvergne, and *fougasse* in Provence—all because she was so insistent on apprenticing under a string of master bakers.

When the "interview" turned to personal qualities and traits, Goodwin's professor was effusive in his praise for the petite young student who, according to him, had charmed everyone at the school. When I finished hearing this part of Longfellow's report, I remember asking the master spy why in the world this pretty and talented young woman—with all she had to offer—ended up with a PTSD-ridden, agoraphobic, Hells Angel biker. To which he responded, "Well, once you figure that one out, could you try to fathom what my king saw in Wallis Simpson?"

Just a week later, Longfellow came to my office for a meeting on another matter. Once we had finished that discussion, I turned the conversation to the case of the battered baker. I described to Longfellow what I had learned from picking the minds of several mental health professionals who had called me for legal consultations on other matters. Each of the three of them had dealt extensively with spousal abuse, and the fact pattern in my non-case, they all assured me, was a textbook example of cases they had each seen: a PTSD-plagued ex-soldier would isolate his wife, allow her no contact whatsoever with her family or friends, disallow her from making phone calls, and then periodically beat the hell out of her when he would lose control. Worse still, in most of the cases they described, the pattern of domestic violence escalated over time. The typical pattern, I learned, was that each violent attack would be followed by tearful repentance, and often by a considerable interlude of calm. And to complicate matters psychologically, during these interim periods, abusive husbands tended to be particularly solicitous and attentive, thereby interrupting thoughts or plans their victim might have had about escaping. The victims, understandably, lived in constant fear that anything they said or did might trigger the next, still-more-violent event. For them, everyday life was like walking through a minefield, often because abusive husbands typically dictated a playbook of rules, and the slightest breach of any rule could be grounds for an explosive outburst. Battered wives, I was told, spent massive amounts of psychic energy trying to placate their abusive mates by excessive expressions of forgiveness and unmitigated sexual submissiveness. But such strategies guaranteed nothing. Eventually, another beating would occur, which, in turn, would be followed by yet another round of maudlin repentance. And on and on it went until, in the most extreme cases, the wife was permanently maimed or even killed. Every so often, I read, a battered wife would strike back and kill the abusive man in her life—typically with his own gun. But this route of escape led to prosecution and imprisonment: recent case law in many jurisdictions disallowed battered wives from successfully pleading self-defense unless their counterattack actually occurred *during* an active, life-threatening onslaught.

Longfellow remained silent when I finished my monologue. He walked over to the windows that looked out over the harbor, and stood there for a good minute—as still as marble. When he finally turned and spoke, he spun out a strategic plan that was positively ingenious.

***

It took Longfellow about three weeks to locate the key element we needed for his scheme to work. She was a woman named Maria Becker who had herself escaped and overcome horrific spousal abuse. She had subsequently gone on to study such matters in social work school, after which she launched a clinical career dealing precisely with this issue.

Longfellow and I held two long meetings to prepare Becker for the role Longfellow had designed for her. The first phase of the plan was for her to become a three-times-per-week customer of the bakery for a month. After that period, Becker was to board the same car of the 6:20 evening commuter train that Goodwin took home from work. Becker was to do everything she could to sit directly next to the baker, and once that opportunity arose—even if it took more than one evening to accomplish—she was to say the following, which I had drafted:

"Please don't turn toward me, Ms. Goodwin. Just listen. I am a devoted bakery customer of yours, and in the past, I was a victim of spousal abuse. I then became a social worker whose practice is focused exactly on this issue. I'm pretty sure I know what you're going through. And here is what I'm here to say: if there is any way you're looking for someone to secretly talk with who has been through what I think you're experiencing, here is my business card. There would be no cost involved; I do this to help other women because I know how they suffer."

Becker reported that Goodwin emphatically shook her head no, so the card was withdrawn, as we had decided beforehand. Goodwin sat up straight and didn't move a centimeter for the rest of the train ride. She had never looked over toward Becker, and Becker also looked only straight ahead—all as planned. This state of silence and utter stillness between the two women lasted until just before Goodwin's station was coming up. Then, at the very last moment, Becker delivered my catch line. "Do you want me to sit in this exact same seat precisely a week from this evening so you can have time to think about what I've said?" Becker said Goodwin began to stand up, seemingly ready to make no signal, but then, at the very last second, nodded her head yes—twice, in quick succession. And with that, she was gone.

During the intervening week before the next planned meeting of the two women, we met again with Becker. We confirmed that Longfellow and I would be involved only in helping create initial contact; after that, any guidance or counseling relationship whereby Becker would serve to actually help Goodwin escape McCabe was up to Becker and her colleagues—it would no longer be our affair. We knew from Longfellow's due diligence that Becker's office was highly qualified to undertake the arduous task of rescuing a battered wife: she was a member of a good-sized group practice of licensed independent clinical social workers who collectively administered a spousal abuse victims' treatment program. And just as importantly, the program had numerous clandestine safe houses—and a good deal of experience.

So, the following week, we were ready for whatever might develop. And indeed, there were developments—if incremental ones—as I learned in a brief telephone call from Becker the night of her first breakthrough. She had boarded the train and taken the precise seat she had occupied the week before, saving the one next to her. And sure enough, Goodwin entered the car and sat down alongside her, once again facing straight forward. Without a single glance to the side, they spoke throughout the one-hour commute. The details of what the baker told Becker were not disclosed to me, given that the content of the discussion between the two women was a privileged communication under the statute controlling Massachusetts social work practice. Accordingly, I was not made privy to Goodwin's description of the marital abuse, nor was I told whether the conversation advanced to a discussion of an escape plan. When I asked Becker if she thought there was hope, she responded: "Only time will tell; I'm to meet her again, same time, same place, next Friday." And after the next Friday came and went, Becker and I had an essentially identical conversation. After that, however, the pace picked up, as the two women rode together twice the following week, and three times the week after that. From the accelerating pace of their contact, I assumed Goodwin was progressively opening up to Becker, but I learned nothing more specific than that.

**

It was during this period that the proverbial bomb that I'd been warned about exploded. Actually, it was a series of explosions. I first learned of the new developments the day after what proved to be the final social work session on the train. Becker had gone to the bakery to continue her patronage role—only to find the baker hidden behind her oversized sunglasses. Becker planned to simply buy some bread and leave, but Goodwin saw her and approached, initiating a conversation. She asked if Becker had a moment to have coffee in the shop next door.

Goodwin had been very badly beaten and brutally raped. The two women had gone into the coffee shop's restroom, and Goodwin had disrobed to show Becker the marks on her body: welts, bruises, contusions, large black-and-blues, swellings—you name it. Most shocking, apparently, was her entire crotch area, which was bright purplish from the brutality of the sexual assault. McCabe, Becker ascertained, had intended the rape to cause fear and submission: it wasn't sexual pleasure that he had been after.

Becker later told me that as Goodwin described the setting and details of her mauling, her body had broken out into a profound shivering—a textbook somatic confirmation of the depth of the emotional suffering she had endured at the hands of McCabe. Goodwin could take no more: she begged Becker to help her—she was frightened for her life to return to the McCabe household.

Becker proved to be a crackerjack clinician. In their train sessions, she had, clearly, been able to win Goodwin's trust, and she had convinced her that there was light at the end of the tunnel. Now Goodwin sought that light, and Becker reassured her that the safe house she had often mentioned had a bed ready to receive her that very night, and that it would be available throughout whatever transition period proved necessary. As we had arranged, Becker also mentioned that she knew of a trauma therapy center that could work with McCabe, if he was ready to confront his demons—but Goodwin, reportedly, showed no interest in this whatsoever: she sought only to save herself.

Up to this point, all was going according to our plan, but then Becker—spontaneously and on her own—added something that we had absolutely *not* planned: she told Goodwin that she knew an attorney who was both a bakery customer and a resource. Goodwin immediately took her up on this spontaneous offer, at which point Goodwin called me from the coffee shop where the two of them were working all this out. So just at the point where my involvement in the case was supposed to end, an entirely new chapter was about to open up.

***

Ninety minutes later, Goodwin, Becker, and I were seated in my office. Becker introduced us and asked Goodwin for her consent to disclose the details that she had been told in the train-car social work sessions. Goodwin assented, and Becker spoke for nearly half an hour, drawing back the curtains on a domestic horror scene as frightening as any of the reports I had read about. When she'd finished, she turned to Goodwin and asked her: "Please add whatever I've missed or gotten wrong." Goodwin cleared her throat to speak, and tried bravely to work up a small smile to greet me with. She then confirmed the accuracy of Becker's account before adding an entirely unexpected new twist to the case that she had never mentioned to Becker in the train sessions.

"I'm going to be okay, thanks to her," Goodwin said, reaching over to squeeze Becker's forearm. "With the support I'm getting and with the availability of the safe house, I know I can do this. And I'm going to. I have to. That bastard is never going to touch me ever again. Ever. Thank you. Thank you. Thank you both. But I'm worried about the boy."

Becker and I looked at each other in complete astonishment. "What boy?" I finally asked.

"His son," Goodwin replied. "He's not been safe in the house, and it will get worse now that I'm out of there."

"You two have a son?" I asked, completely puzzled as to why Longfellow's stakeout had not discovered this critical fact—a fact that would have prompted an entirely different strategy on our part.

"No. The boy is his, not mine. Or sort of his. He is from a previous relationship of Steve's. The mother was some loose woman he met in a bar not long before he met me. He never even knew her last name. She'd gotten pregnant—whether by him or by someone else, who knows—and had never told him. But about two years later when the toddler proved too much for her—or whatever, I don't really know— she came by our house one evening when I was home and Steve was out at his biker bar. She asked me if she could leave the boy and his bag for a moment to go purchase . . . something . . . cigarettes, I think. I forget what. She said she'd be back in twenty minutes, and meet with Steve that evening about what they were going to do about raising the child. Before I could catch my breath, she was out the door to run her errand. But she never returned—ever. That was about six years ago, because he's about eight now."

"So there's an *eight-year-old child* in that house?" I asked, abso-lutely dumbfounded.

"Yes, it's just the three of us—or rather, it's the two of them, and me. I have no meaningful relationship with the boy—Steve raises him by himself, even homeschools him every day of the week. I was only allowed to be marginally involved when an extra hand was occasionally needed. But somebody will need to keep the child safe now. Can you help him—please?"

I paused for a moment, trying to collect my scrambled thoughts. "What are McCabe's PTSD episodes like with regard to the child?" I asked.

"When he goes PTSD, he goes nuts. Completely crazy. He loses all control. *All* control. That's what happened when he broke the boy's arm about three months ago—I'm not exaggerating when I say he goes completely bonkers."

Finally, I put two and two together and realized who I was looking at. "Aha! Did you take the boy to Children's Hospital emergency room when this happened? In fact, when you took him there, was it raining? I may have been there when you brought him in—if it was the two of you who passed by me at the emergency room entrance. I remember what his arm looked like; it looked seriously broken—strangely bent. It was his right arm."

"Yes, that was us!" Goodwin sat forward in my client chair and put her right hand out on the front of my desk. "The bastard did that to his own kid—he broke *both* of Mickey's forearm bones, for God's sake." She paused when she said this, and her entire body went into a brief but violent shiver. "Can you help him? It could get much worse in that household now that I'm gone—for Mickey, I mean. Can you help him?"

Now what? My baker was safe, and that's when I had always thought my non-case would end. But now I knew there was a child who wasn't safe, and given that a very decent percentage of my client base consisted of children's protective service agencies, I was as trapped in this new chapter of the case as a lobster that struggles its way into one of the lobster pots whose colorful floats I could see out my office window.

"Actually, Audrey, there's plenty I can do to help the boy," I replied. "And we can begin right now if you're willing to sign an affidavit under oath about what you've just told us. With that document, I can call the Department of Social Services, and they'll almost certainly go to court. They'll remove the child today if they think that's what's called for, and he'll be placed where he'll be entirely safe. But all of this depends on whether you're willing to set down on paper what you've just disclosed. Are you?"

Goodwin paused, a look of abject fear on her face. "Worried about McCabe?" I asked.

She just nodded, and looked down. Becker jumped in. "Audrey, if you are definitively out of the house today and leaving him, our team can keep you safe. We have our ways, I guarantee you. And having the court involved is actually a good thing; I'd be advising you to do that even if there were no child. It gets both of you a powerful ally—immediately." She reached over and took Goodwin's hand. "Trust me." Goodwin, looking like a deer caught in the headlights, nodded her fearful assent.

"Okay, then," I inserted. "Who else does the boy know and trust? Are there any relatives?"

"Just a sister of Steve's who lives in Ohio somewhere—but they don't have anything to do with each other, and the boy has never met her," Goodwin replied. "Steve does everything for the boy. Mickey trusts me, of course, but please don't ask me to be involved. I promise you, he won't miss me much: Steve always kept us at a distance from one another. I don't really know why that was so important to him."

At this point, I did two things. First, I explained to Goodwin that I wanted to refer her to an attorney I knew who would be just the right counsel to handle her probate court matters, including obtaining a restraining order to keep McCabe away from her and initiating a divorce proceeding when she was ready. Second, I called in an associate attorney and asked him to take the two women into a conference room to work up the affidavit as to the situation in the McCabe household and the danger that McCabe presented to the boy.

When I was alone in the office, I called the office of the area director for Boston's Department of Social Services, Paul Phillips. Phillips called back within twenty minutes, and I described what I'd been told, and what I expected to see momentarily in a notarized affidavit. When I described the boy as being locked indoors twenty-four seven by a PTSD-ridden, agoraphobic, homeschooling, spouse-abusing batterer—who may or may not actually have been the boy's father, and who had broken both of the boy's forearm bones a few months ago—Phillips's reaction was immediate: "Holy shit. That kid's out of there today. I need your help on this. Meet me in Cambridge at the courthouse in an hour. Bring her affidavit, obviously. I'm going to call the chief judge when we hang up. I intend to get an order from her this afternoon, and then I'll go out to McCabe's house and collect the boy. Are you still counsel to the Italian Home for Children? That would be a great respite care agency for the boy until we figure this all out; he's just the right age for them, and their programs are solid."

"Yep, still one of my favorite clients."

"Great. Could you call them and see if they have a bed for the boy tonight? And if they do, can you get one of their childcare workers to meet us at the courthouse? I'm going to try to find a DSS attorney to go with me to the court and out to the house, and a state police officer as well." Phillips paused, and then added, "Can you come to court? I'm not sure I can rally counsel with zero notice. And would you mind going along with us on the rescue mission? I might need you if I can't get hold of the troops this fast."

Despite sensing that this was my opportunity—possibly my last one—to extricate myself from the entire case, it was just too tempting to see what the McCabe household looked like up close and personal, and I was curious as hell to meet McCabe firsthand. I'd been hearing about him for months, after all, as well as reading all those books and articles about abusive husbands. Still, I was more than a little surprised to hear the enthusiasm in my voice when I answered Phillips: "Oh yeah, definitely. I'm not missing that."

***

I called Bill Winters, the executive director of the Italian Home for Children—a wonderfully administered children's social service agency with a residential program that dated back a century to when such charitable institutions were linked to particular ethnic communities. He indeed had an available bed, and readily agreed to admit the child that day. He also said he would try to get one of the Italian Home's childcare workers to meet us at the courthouse in Cambridge, but that he was short-staffed that day, and it might or might not be possible.

We were at the probate and family court an hour and a half later, where, at the suggestion of Area Director Phillips, I filed a petition for the care and protection of a minor on behalf of the Italian Home, supported by Audrey Goodwin's sworn affidavit. DSS was not represented at the hearing by one of its own legal counsel—none had been available on such short notice—but that was not critical: the department could subsequently file papers to intervene as a co-petitioner. The department had also not been able to produce a social caseworker, and, for that matter, no childcare worker from the Italian Home had arrived by the time the judge's clerk told us that the chief judge, Sheila McGovern, was coming out on the bench to hear our matter. But with the area director urging the court to approve the Italian Home's petition based upon Audrey Goodwin's affidavit, the judge granted all that we asked for, including an emergency order for the removal of the child, with temporary legal and physical custody to be granted to the Department of Social Services.

The next thing I knew, the DSS area director and I were in a state police car traveling by siren to the McCabe household. I was curious as hell to see what was going on in the house—could it really be as grim as Audrey Goodwin had described? And what was this kid going to be like? I had images of meeting a youngster who would be severely limited by never having experienced the outside world—or any other children. And how would McCabe respond to having his demented little world blown asunder? There is no way to exaggerate how comforting it was to have a fully armed state police officer approaching this adventure alongside us.

***

Most of us have probably known someone in our lives who preferred to minimize their interaction with others, but that's not at all what we're talking about here. Assuming the accuracy of the information Audrey Goodwin had given us about McCabe—which was entirely consistent with what had been observed in Longfellow's stakeout—McCabe suffered from severe trauma sequelae, including agoraphobia—the psychiatric illness that drives its victims to cut off contact as much as possible with the outside world.

We arrived at the house, and the door McCabe never wanted any-body to approach was being firmly rapped on by a very large, well-armed uniformed state police officer. McCabe just stood there peeking out at us from behind the edge of a pulled window shade, looking far more like a trapped animal than like a person. And just like a cornered animal, McCabe had no time for either fight or flight—it was over. McCabe left the window, and ten seconds later, he opened the door. With that, the direction of his life changed forever.

The officer was the first to enter. He took one look at the imposing, rather massive biker in his black leather and immediately directed him to sit in a rickety-looking chair that had seen better days. When the officer asked where the child was, McCabe nodded toward the rear left corner of the one-story, cabin-like house. The officer nodded to the DSS area director and me—clearing us to proceed.

Standing in for both the missing DSS social worker and the absent Italian Home childcare worker, I found myself walking back through the room that was lit only by two light bulbs: they each hung down from the ceiling inside nasty-looking, stained shades. So far as I could tell in the dim light, the space looked reasonably tidy and clean, if sparsely furnished. There was a small, old-fashioned kitchen off the main room, and from what I could see, the entire place looked like a film set for a Depression-era drama taken from a John Steinbeck novel. My mind was still wondering whom I would meet behind the closed door: one part of me expected to meet a wild boy who barely spoke, or who, at the very least, would be unable to connect with strangers, given his isolated existence and homeschooling by a Hells Angel.

I could not have been more wrong. Michael—or "Mickey," as he was called—was a cute, small-framed boy with straight, longish auburn hair. Since he had no bangs, from time to time he would toss his head to the right to throw his hair back out of his eyes and behind his ear. By far the most notable trait about Mickey's looks was his incredible light-light-light-blue eyes—they were like the eyes you see on husky sled dogs. Actually, I've never seen eyes that color on another person.

Insofar as the light in his room permitted me to see—the room had yet another single electric wire hanging down from the ceiling with a bulb inside an aged shade—Mickey had been allowed to deco-rate his own room. His walls were as full of life as the main room had been austerely bare. A wondrous cacophony of colorful photographs of nature scenes—especially coastal scenes—had been cut out of magazines and taped up on the walls.

"Hello, young man. My name is Terry. I am the attorney for the Italian Home for Children; that's a place where children can stay and be safe if they're not safe at home. Do you understand what I'm saying?"

"Hello, I'm Mickey."

"Hello, Mickey. What's your last name?"

He shrugged his shoulders. "I don't have one. This is my room."

I was stunned by his answer, and glad to have another direction to head. "I can see that. It's a wonderful room. I love the way you have all these colorful pictures on the walls." Mickey smiled, pleased at the compliment. Now it was time to get down to business. "Mickey, I don't know how much of this you can understand at your age, but the reason I have come here today with some other grown-ups who are out in the big room is because we talked to a judge today who is afraid that you're not safe in this house. Do you know what a judge is?"

"Well, only sort of. We don't have a TV. But Steve tells me about judges. He doesn't like them much. Do you?"

"Yes, actually, I do, Mickey. Judges have the job of keeping us all safe. And some judges specialize in making sure kids are safe. That's the kind of judge we talked to today. Do you want to know what this judge said?"

"I don't know. Do I?"

"Yes, I would think so. This judge thought you might be safer at the Italian Home for Children—at least for a while. There are lots of other kids to play with there, and there is a real school with real teachers. The judge wants to talk to Steve to make sure you're safe here. If the judge thinks you are safe here, then you can come back. But one thing here is going to change for you no matter what. You see, Mickey, Audrey talked to me today, and she is not going to be coming home tonight, or ever living here again. She doesn't want to live with Steve anymore because he hurts her sometimes. Do you understand what I just said?"

"I don't know."

"Well, that's fair. I don't see how you could. But I have a question for you, and this is a really important question. Are you ready?"

"I don't know."

"I want you to think hard before you answer my question. Take your time. And when you look inside yourself for the answer, I want you to think about how you really, really, *really* feel, deep, deep down inside yourself. Okay?" He nodded yes. "Okay, then. Here's my question: Do you always feel safe in this house with Steve?"

Mickey closed his eyes as he thought about how to answer my question. It was quite a while before he spoke, and when he did so, he was almost whispering. "Sometimes I feel safe, like when Steve and I are talking about a book we both read, or how the world works. But sometimes Steve gets wild and scary and hurts us—mostly Audrey, but me too sometimes. But then a few days later, he says how sorry he is, and sometimes he cries when he says that. I cry too, like when I crash into something. But boys are 'spossed to learn not to cry, Steve said. He says he cries sometimes because has ABCD—which is what you get if you kill lots of people in the war and watch your friends get killed. He doesn't mean to hurt us, he says. But he does. But then he's nice later, after he cries."

"Okay, Mickey. I hear you. Here's another question for you. Now that you know that Audrey isn't going to live here anymore, do you think that would that make you feel more safe or less safe—or the about the same?"

Again, the boy looked away from me and took his time to think through how he wanted to answer. When he looked back, he looked anguished. "Less safe. Maybe way less safe. I would be more afraid."

"I hear you, Mickey. And I have just one more question for you. And this is important because we have to talk about this to the judge I told you about who is concerned for your safety. About three months ago, I was going into Children's Hospital on a rainy day to meet with someone, and I passed a boy about your age who had a very scary-looking broken right arm. The boy was walking with Audrey. I think that boy was you. Am I right?"

Tears now glistened in those ethereal blue eyes, and a heart-wrenching moan worked its way out of his throat—seemingly all on its own. Mickey struggled over how to answer: he seemed to sense that his response to this question would determine the direction his life would take going forward. But I knew—or thought I did—how he would answer in the end. I'd seen children faced with this moment in numerous cases over the years, and when they were confronted with the dilemma of admitting to the authorities that that they were living in unsafe circumstances, they would almost always opt for safety and disclose the domestic abuse or neglect they were suffering. In my experience, children tolerated poverty and a hard life—just about anything, including for example living in a car—so long as their connection with their family was the wellspring of their feeling nurtured and safe. In contrast, children whose parent or caretaker was the source of serial physical or emotional abuse were far more likely, once they had the opportunity, to disclose their circumstances and elect to make the leap and move on from their unsafe lives. And sure enough, after a full minute of absolutely silent, internal crying, Mickey nodded yes—three times, unequivocally, even emphatically.

These were the toughest moments for me in dealing with children in the custody of the Commonwealth: there is a strict rule disallowing hugging. Oh, how I wanted to embrace the little guy the way I did my own boy when he was hurting, when he needed comforting and connection. But I couldn't; I needed to make it happen with my words, with my tone of voice. That was all the system allowed me to work with.

"Mickey, how about you gather up some clothes, and toys, and some of these beautiful pictures for sure, and other things you want to take with you and put them all on your bed. We'll wrap them all up in the sheet later and take them along. I'm going to go out now, close the door, and talk to the other adults about what we're going to do. Then, if it's okay with you, I'd like to take you to the children's home that I was talking about—at least for a night or two until the judge can talk to Steve and figure out the best way to keep you safe. Is all that okay with you?"

He thought over my words before responding. "Will you go away too? I mean, after you take me to the place you were talking about? Please don't. I need some grown-up to stick with me if Audrey is gone and Steve is not safe. Will you stay with me through these changes?"

Wow. Normally, when I would come in contact with legally involved children for one of the children's social service agencies I represented, I would steer sharply away from any such commitment. Moreover, I constantly advised the professional clinicians and childcare workers who dealt with these children to do the same. If there was one thing institu-tionalized kids all had in common, it was that they had already endured a lifetime's worth of broken promises, parental letdowns, and loss of connection. Exactly what they did *not* need was some well-intentioned social worker or childcare worker—or agency counsel—making a promise they couldn't keep. But Mickey's case seemed different, I rationalized. After all, I had played a very major role in precipitating what he was going through. And the reality was, I knew, that I probably could manipulate the system to let me stay involved, given how many players I knew after so many years in the field. My indecision to make this commitment came screeching to a halt when I realized what I could extract from Mickey in exchange.

"Mickey," I said in an entirely serious tone of voice, "I'll make a deal with you—if you want. Here's my deal: From my side, I'll promise to do everything I can to stick by you. I'll never be the person who makes decisions about your life; that will be up to the judge I was talking about. But my guess is that if the judge thinks you can't be safe around Steve, you may be headed for adoption by a family—and I think I can help you with that."

Then, in super slow motion, a tiny little smile—the first one I'd seen—broke out on Mickey's face. It was definitely the slowest-developing smile I'd ever witnessed.

I put my right forefinger up in the air. "*But* you have to promise me something too, or I won't make this deal. From your side, you have to promise me to be very brave about all the big changes that may be coming into your life—starting about ten minutes from now. Mickey, when tough moments come into people's lives, some people decide they're going to do whatever it takes to survive. Maybe they're in a life raft off a sunken boat for weeks and weeks and weeks. But they fish over the side, they eat raw fish, they catch rainwater, and they row, row, row—and most important, they remain absolutely determined to survive until they find dry land. Other people just give up, and stop paddling and stop trying when times get tough. If you'll promise me that you'll keep paddling your life raft no matter how tough it all gets, then I'll promise to do everything I can to stay involved in your case as best I can until we find you a safe place to live and grow up—assuming the judge thinks that is the right direction for you to head. So what do you think—deal or no deal?"

"Deal," he said in a tiny little voice, still looking a bit puzzled. And after five or ten seconds of silence, came another, *"Deal,"* this one pronounced much more emphatically. "But tell me how our deal works if I keep my promise."

"Okay, then. Here's the deal. If the judge thinks you need a new place to grow up, and if the plan is to find a family to adopt you, I promise you that I'll do everything I can to help you find a great adoptive family where you'll be safe. I'm the lawyer for a whole bunch of adoption agencies, and I'll—"

"A real family!" Mickey interrupted. "You'll really help me find a real family? You really will?"

"Like I said, if you're willing to live up to your end of the bargain and paddle your life raft through stormy seas and eat raw fish and catch rainwater—then you can count on me."

Mickey held out his little hand, and heartily shook mine. And during that handshake, I was rewarded with a second smile—this one was bright enough to light up the little room far more effectively than did the dangling light bulb in its dingy shade.

***

While Mickey went to work gathering up what he wanted to bring along, I went back out to the main room and spoke with DSS Area Director Phillips. I relayed the good news that Mickey was an intact and alert child, and that he'd unambiguously confirmed that he was not safe in the household and that he would feel still less safe with Audrey Goodwin not returning. I conveyed that Mickey was ready and willing to leave to go to the Italian Home for Children, and also that if the permanency plan the DSS eventually came up with was to search for an adoptive home, he was ecstatic about the prospect of finding a "real family."

Phillips's response was immediate: "Good. We'll work together on this, Terry. Let's find this kid a decent life."

Now came the hard part. I had a duty to serve the court's order on McCabe so that he would have notice about the return-date hearing scheduled for the following day. The point of the expedited hearing, I needed to explain to him, was to allow him to appear and put his side of the case in front of the judge. McCabe hadn't budged an inch from where the officer had sat him down, and at the time I walked over to serve the court papers on him and explain what his options were, he had his elbows on his knees and his face buried in his enormous hands. "Mr. McCabe," I began, standing directly in front of the chair where he was sitting, "here is my card. I'm present today in my capacity as general counsel to the Italian Home for Children, which is the children's social service agency that the Department of Social Services has identified to provide emergency placement tonight for Mickey. I have represented this agency for decades, and I can assure you they do a wonderful job of providing for any child entrusted to them. Mickey will be safe and sound tonight, rest assured of that. Also, here is a copy of the order the court issued today removing Mickey from your custody and granting temporary legal and physical custody to the Department of Social Services. Perhaps the most important thing it says is that you—and all of us—are to appear tomorrow before the judge at two p.m. You'll have the opportunity to tell the judge your side of the story, and even ask the court to return Mickey to your custody. Do you follow what I'm saying?"

Perhaps halfway through what I said, McCabe had slowly looked up at me. But he didn't say a word; he just crossed his arms over his enormous chest, and quietly looked at me like that tiger. "Mr. McCabe, let me be frank with you. I'm going to tell the court tomorrow that, on information and belief, you are not Mickey's biological father. And I'm also going to tell the court that you broke his arm about three months ago. And I know a lot about the violence you've visited on Audrey Goodwin, and I'm going to tell the court about that as well. You should know that Ms. Goodwin is willing to testify against you, and that an affidavit signed by her saying all these same things was filed in court today. And from what I understand, she intends to never again come back to this household. She has left you."

Finally, he spoke. "Why are you laying all this on me?"

"Good question, Mr. McCabe. The reason is that there are two possible directions this case can head. Direction number one: The DSS area director here, and his team, can determine to bring a proceeding before the court to permanently terminate your parental rights—if you even have any. This would be a bench trial, with full discovery. It would be a whole lot of strain on Mickey, as he would have to take the stand and testify about the broken arm, and about a host of other matters. Mr. McCabe, you should consult a criminal defense attorney because, from what I understand, you have significant exposure.

"But then, Mr. McCabe, there is direction number two: You could tell the court tomorrow that you have never believed yourself to be Mickey's biological father, that you've done your best to raise him but that it's too much for you, given your mental health issues, and that you are willing to sign a surrender form to voluntarily relinquish any parental rights you may have. In my opinion, there are several advantages to direction number two that you might want to consider. First, it would probably be better for Mickey to move on to an adoptive family before he gets too old for this to happen. And second, direction number two could significantly reduce your exposure to criminal prosecution. Do you at all follow what I am saying?"

Once again, this human tiger just sat there, defiant as hell, with his massive arms still crossed over his chest, declining to answer.

"That's it, Mr. McCabe," I concluded. "We'll all be in court tomorrow, with or without you. Again, I would strongly advise you to retain legal counsel." With that, I turned away and went back into Mickey's room, only to find that the pile of objects to go along with us had become quite appreciable. I suggested a few edits of some of the larger items, which Mickey very nicely assented to, and then I tied up the rest in the sheet—like a huge Santa's bundle. I swung it over my right shoulder and walked out of the house holding Mickey's hand. The boy never looked over at McCabe as we walked by. Not once.

Mickey and I drove into Boston—against traffic, thankfully—and finally arrived at the Italian Home. As far as I could tell, he exhibited little or no separation anxiety and a palpable excitement at spending time with other children. When we arrived, Executive Director Bill Winters joined us and welcomed Mickey with the warmth of a man who had devoted his entire adult life to bettering the lives of children in need. I told Bill that a childcare worker would need to bring Mickey to court for the two p.m. hearing the next day, as we would be required to "identify the child to the court" as part of our petition for care and protection. With that, the Italian Home's chief executive officer and its newest resident headed down the hall hand in hand to find where Mickey would be spending the night, and beginning the rest of his life.

***

The following day, I arrived early at my office to place calls to several adoption-agency clients of mine in order to start the process I'd promised Mickey that I would attend to. I did this principally so that I could report to the judge that the process was already underway—I wanted her mindset to be forward looking, as opposed to thinking this was a case that should be controlled by the Commonwealth's general policy of "family reunification." It just wasn't a family—not to my mind and, far more importantly, not in Mickey's mind.

My first call was to Evelyn Elson, who ran a small but sophisticated adoption agency that specialized in placing older children. Most potential adoptive parents have the dream of finding a healthy newborn to take into their home. But, statistically speaking, that is not at all how adoption operates in our era. In the time frame of Mickey's adoption, only about 15 percent of the roughly 135,000 legalized adoptions in the United States each year were relinquished US babies. (Older children from child welfare or foster care settings made up 59 percent, and about 15 percent were international adoptions.) But the statistic that really concerned me came from a then-recent study showing that, for children over six, only about 41 percent developed warm and close relationships with their adoptive families, as opposed to 84 percent of children younger than six. A 41 percent success rate was completely unacceptable to me. I'd made a promise to the boy that I fully intended to keep, and if I needed to spend some time to up his odds, so be it.

When Elson answered, I described the circumstances of Mickey's upbringing, how intact and alluring Mickey was, and what a wonderful addition he would be to a well-functioning household. Elson was more than willing to look through her agency's files, but warned me that the relatively small number of qualified families currently listed with her agency meant that the odds were not great. In any case, she promised to give me an update within a week or two.

My second call was to Marilyn Morningstar, who had—for more than twenty years—directed the very large adoption program at another longtime children's social welfare agency client of mine, The Home for Little Wanderers. The Home is the oldest child welfare agency in the country, having been launched in the eighteenth century. It was also the largest such agency in the Boston area, with dozens of different programs specializing not only in adoption but also in treatment and residential programs tailored to the widely divergent needs of children and families with their broad range of issues. Morningstar and I had worked together for well over a decade on a significant number of cases, including foster care and adoption placements, as well as the resolution of problems that arose in foster and adoptive homes postplacement. She was the perfect ally to recruit for what I hoped to provide for Mickey.

Because Mickey's case took place in an era when there were far more pre-adoptive couples hoping to adopt (nationally, roughly 2,000,000) than there were children freed for adoption and waiting in child welfare and foster settings (about 420,000), and because a vast majority of couples hoping to adopt in Massachusetts listed themselves with the large and sophisticated adoption program of The Home, Morningstar had long since developed a policy on how to queue up the prospective adoptive couples. She was a proponent of what she called a "hybrid approach," by which she meant that couples were seen as being simultaneously in line—and in a pool. What she meant by this was that while it was fair to have some part of the process be first come, first served, it was equally arguable from a best-interests-of-the-child point of view that the best-suited family should be chosen for a particular child or sibling group, even if they weren't first in line.

I told Morningstar about eight-year-old Mickey, describing him as "healthy, articulate, and forward looking." I told her about the highly unusual circumstances in which he had been raised and the domestic violence Mickey had both witnessed and suffered. I also mentioned the fact that his stepmother was now gone forever from his life. "Marilyn," I added, fessing up to my compromised position in the case, "I made a promise to the boy, and I desperately need your help in order to keep my word."

Morningstar giggled at the transparency of my manipulative efforts, and then responded in her inimitably gentle and warm tone of voice. "Counselor, don't worry so much. I have a number of families looking to adopt an older, healthy child. But for now, don't you think you should concentrate on getting this child legally freed for adoption? You know perfectly well that that typically doesn't happen very quickly. I don't want to contact a family only for them to suffer ongoing disappointment if the child's legal status is in limbo for a year or two."

"Marilyn," I responded, "Judge McGovern is not going to put up with this guy: he broke both bones in the boy's forearm three months ago, and he serially battered the wife who just today walked out of his life for good. I have an affidavit from her, and I could fill the courtroom with witnesses as to her sufferings at the hand of this sicko. We'll all be back in front of the judge this afternoon, and hopefully McCabe either won't show up at all, or he'll be there only to arrange to trade a custody surrender in exchange for immunity from criminal prosecution. One way or the other, I'll bring you a surrender before the adoption process can get halfway done. The facts are that bad for the father—if he even is the father. That's why I'd love to move simultaneously on finding an adoptive family, even though I know it's unusual." In the end, we agreed that I'd report back as to what transpired in the court hearing, and that I'd keep Morningstar up to date on what the likely timing would be for Mickey to become legally freed for adoption. I had to smile when I hung up the phone: I had found precisely the ally I needed to keep my promise to Mickey.

***

Sometimes I'm wrong about things, and sometimes I'm just dead-ass wrong. I could see McCabe down at the end of the courtroom hall, and he was not only present at court but also dressed in a suit and tie. I noted as well that he was accompanied by legal counsel—Mike Miller, a skillful and experienced practitioner whom I'd known for years.

So, I did an unseen about-face and headed back down the courthouse hallway to make some calls. Experience had taught me—and Attorney Miller as well, no doubt—that in these types of custody battles, it is critically important to have the court award your client physical custody of the child during the pendency of the litigation. The litigating party that enjoys this advantage can be counted on to later argue, with good reason, "Judge, you really don't want to move the child now: the child has been stable and well cared for during all these months, and it would not be in the best interests of the child for you to order a change in custody at this time." Now that McCabe had experienced counsel in his corner, it immediately became obvious that the complexion of the case had changed dramatically.

My first call was to Children's Hospital to leave a message for Dr. Evan Newsom. Newsom was a pediatrician by training, and years earlier he had initiated the hospital's cutting-edge program on how to identify and treat very young children who had been victims of sexual and physical abuse in their homes. Earlier in the day, I had spoken with Dr. Newsom about serving as an expert witness in Mickey's case, going over everything I had learned about the boy and the mistreatment he had experienced in the McCabe household. He had agreed to serve, but we had both been operating on the assumption that the evidentiary court hearing at which he would testify would come weeks or even months later—that is, that it would occur in the context of the termination-of-parental-rights aspect of the case. Now, that timing assumption was almost certainly erroneous, and I needed Newsom to be at court today.

My next call was to my law associate. I asked him to get his car out of the garage and head over to Children's Hospital: his assignment was to locate Newsom and get him to the courthouse by about three p.m., even if he had to physically kidnap Newsom from the hospital. I also asked the associate to call Maria Becker; we desperately needed her to come to court today as well. I wasn't heading into battle against a skillful attorney like Mike Miller without my troops.

Returning to the courthouse hallway, I found Attorney Miller and Mr. McCabe, and—disingenuously, to be sure—acted as if I had just become aware of Miller's presence. He excused himself from his client, and the two of us left the crowded hallway and sat in the jury box of the empty courtroom we would soon be using.

"Good to see you again, Mike. How've you been?"

"Great. Wife and kids healthy and thriving, law practice running at a good volume, so can't complain. You?"

"Yeah, same."

"So, what's up in this McCabe case? I hear you went in and kidnapped his son yesterday afternoon."

"Yep, kidnapped. Spelled 'R-E-S-C-U-E-D.'"

"Terry, what the fuck is this case all about? This guy knows my receptionist—I think her boyfriend is a motorcycle aficionado like McCabe, or something like that. Anyway, he reached me at home yesterday evening—in a complete panic. And, by the way, what the hell did you do with his wife? He hasn't heard a word from her either. You kidnap her too?"

I had to laugh; Mike was a good guy, and a highly competent attorney. Where to start? "Mike, do you know what this guy normally looks like? I'm actually amazed that he even owns a suit and tie."

"He didn't. He bought them this morning—on my instructions." We both had to giggle at this revelation. "No, really," Miller continued, "tell me what the hell's up here. I really don't get it yet." And so, for a solid ten minutes, I disclosed everything I knew about McCabe's background, his PTSD, his agoraphobia, and his occasional violent outbreaks. Finally, I described the boy as I had found him yesterday, including my amazement at how he had presented as remarkably intact, despite his upbringing in complete isolation. When I finally finished, Miller looked decidedly stunned. "Wow. I have a bit of an uphill march here, don't I?"

It was always good to have an opposing counsel whom you could work *with* instead of *against*. "Mike, I have to tell you, from what I've learned about this case to date, you're not marching uphill. You're climbing a mountain."

"I hear you, I hear you," he replied with a little giggle. "Sometimes you get the bear, and sometimes the bear gets you. No big fucking deal. You work with what you get. But I'm fascinated: What the hell did his place look like?"

"Dark, sparse, and grim—except for the kid's room. His walls were papered with magazine photographs of seascapes—it was all about light."

"Huh. Interesting . . . Look, Terry, you know perfectly well that my job is to try to get my guy's son back *now*, with a big request for help for the household from DSS—obviously that's needed. We could be headed to a trial that won't start for months, and this entire case could be determined by where this kid stays during that period—and hence where he stays tonight. So, I need to disclose something to you: I've got a shrink here today, a developmental psychology professor from Boston University named"—Miller opened his folder to find the doctor's name—"Dr. Harold Cummings. I don't know him; do you? You were a prof at BU, weren't you—years ago?"

"Yeah. Decades ago. But I didn't know Cummings. Thanks for telling me. And, Mike, by the way, I want you to know that I've also retained an expert: Dr. Evan Newsom from Children's Hospital. I'm trying to get him to come in today to talk to the judge, but I have no idea if he would have any free time this afternoon."

"Damn it, man! You bring the fucking A-team, don't you. *Is he coming today, or not?*"

"I don't know, like I said. I told my Patriots-frontline-size associate to go over to the hospital and kidnap him if necessary."

Miller put his hands together in prayer position, and in a flawless Boston Irish accent, he looked up at the courtroom ceiling and spoke to his deity: "God, it's me, Michael Miller. The one from 218 Franklin Street. I know me body has not been present at Mass too terribly much lately, but me spirit's been there without fail. Really. Now, God, I've a small favor to ask. Please make Dr. Evan Newsom busy this afternoon. It's really not a lot to ask, as I see it. Amen. PS: It's N-E-W-S-O-M." Then he looked up and over at me, and we shared a good belly laugh. "Listen, Terry, about Newsom. Normally I'd agree in a heartbeat to continue a hearing to accommodate an absent witness. You know that. But the nature of today's hearing doesn't allow that: the whole issue today is who the kid goes home with tonight. So, it's got to be hardball; I don't have any choice. So, if Newsom can't be here today, I hope you see why I can't assent to a continuance."

"I totally understand, Mike. Let's see what Judge McGovern does with this."

I returned to the hallway just in time to see Mickey skipping down the hall toward me—smiling from ear to ear. He was trailed by a child-care worker from the Italian Home who was falling farther and farther behind. Mickey was positively ecstatic in telling me all about what fun he'd had at the Italian Home, playing with a whole circle of kids his age. He went on and on about details of which kids he'd played with, but it wasn't the content of what he said that mattered, not to my ear. It was his tone of voice, because it so clearly conveyed how powerfully he'd been moved by playing with other children *for the very first time in his life*. It was hard to get my head around that; I don't think I'd ever run into that before.

For the moment, however, I needed Mickey to concentrate on the court hearing we faced. "Mickey," I said slowly, looking him right in the eyes, "I need to say something important to you, okay?" He nodded. "Today, right now, you need to figure out which way you want to row that life raft of yours—the one we talked about. If you think you want to live with Steve as long as he never hurts you again, tell me that—and you'll probably have a chance to tell the judge that as well. And that may be possible, if that's what you want. The grown-ups here today could all try to figure out how to keep you safe in his household—even without Audrey. But if you want to row your life raft in a different direction, if you think you no longer want to live with Steve, that may be possible also—or at least we can ask the judge for that. It's up to you, Mickey, to choose the path that you think is best for you—all things considered. It's your life."

Mickey floored me with his response: "Is your promise from yesterday still your promise today?"

"Absolutely."

"Then let's row my life raft to happier places than Steve's. He told me a hundred times he's not really my dad. I get it. I'm going to tell the judge that I want to find a real family with other kids. Please, *please* help me do that; you said you would."

***

No sooner had we all entered the courtroom than the uniformed bailiff belted out in his window-rattling bass voice: *"Court! All rise. This court is in session, the Honorable Chief Judge Sheila McGovern presiding. You may be seated."* Judge McGovern sat motionless for a good five minutes reviewing the petition for care and protection, reading and rereading Goodwin's affidavit, and browsing through her order from the previous day.

"Good afternoon, everyone. Is the child here to be identified to the court?"

"Good afternoon, Your Honor. I am Attorney Harry Jenkins, from the Office of General Counsel of the Department of Social Services. The child, who spent last night at the Italian Home for Children after his emergency removal from father's residence pursuant to Your Honor's order, is here to be identified to the court. For the record, Your Honor, I'll be filing papers tomorrow morning whereby the Department of Social Services will join the Italian Home for Children as a co-petitioner in this matter."

Mickey was brought forward into the court's well, just in front of the judge's bench.

"Good afternoon, young man," the judge greeted Mickey.

"Good afternoon, Mrs. Judge."

Judge McGovern couldn't resist a smile. This happenstantial early smile led to his smiling back—and I think that changed everything. "You can just call me 'Judge.' Now, young man, please state your name and date of birth for the record."

"Michael, but you can call me 'Mickey.'" Another warm judicial smile. "We don't know when my birthday is; I'm sorry."

"One thing at a time, Mickey. What is your last name? The space on the petition is blank."

"I don't have one, Judge," Mickey replied, looking down, ashamed and embarrassed.

"*What?*" called out the judge, loudly enough to visibly startle Mickey. "Counsel to sidebar." With that, we three attorneys gathered at the edge of the judge's bench. In a whispered tone, the judge asked, "Which one of you knows the most about the background of this boy?"

I seized the initiative: "That would be me, Your Honor."

"Good morning, Mr. Freiberg. Good to see you as always. I assume you're representing the petitioner, the Italian Home for Children. Tell me what you know."

"As I understand it, Judge, Mickey is the child of a woman the respondent dated a couple of times. According to Ms. Goodwin's affidavit, the woman dropped the boy off at about age two at the McCabe household under the pretense that she'd be back to discuss who would raise the child. She never returned. When Mr. McCabe was dating the mother, on information and belief, other men had access to her as well. In the six years since that event, Mr. McCabe, and he alone—according to Ms. Goodwin—has raised this child. According to the child, Mr. McCabe often told the boy that he was not actually his father . . ."

"Objection, Your Honor," Attorney Miller whispered emphatically.

"Sidebar is not appropriate for objections, Counselor; we're not on the record. Please introduce yourself."

"I am Attorney Michael Miller, in for the father."

"Nice to meet you, Counselor. You need to know that Attorney Freiberg has had scores of cases in front of me, given his representation of so many of Boston's children's social welfare agencies. I have never, ever heard him make a representation to this court that wasn't backed up by the evidence in the case. He quoted the child as saying your client has told him on a number of occasions that he was not the boy's biological father. Obviously, I will need to hear testimony on this issue during this proceeding. But, Mr. Miller, please do not challenge an off-the-record representation made to this court by a brother attorney unless you have extremely good reason to do so. Am I clear?"

"Yes, Your Honor," Miller replied. "I just meant—"

The judge interrupted him: "I'll take that as a yes. Now, Mr. Miller, is it true that your client does not know this child's last name, or his date of birth?"

"Yes, I believe so, Judge. I just spoke to him last night for the first time, and, of course, I asked him to bring the child's birth certificate to court today. But he told me he never had one, because he has absolutely no idea where the child was born, and so he had no way to order a copy."

"Do you know what steps he took, if any, to try to locate the mother, or the place of Mickey's birth?"

"No, Your Honor, this is all so new to me; I first heard about this case just last night."

The judge was looking progressively bewildered. "Mr. Miller, please feel free to walk over and ask your client for an answer if I ask you something that you don't know but your client might know. Attorney Freiberg mentioned that he had been told by your client's estranged wife that the child was homeschooled. Is this correct?"

Miller replied that he had not had a chance to discuss this level of detail with his client, and that he would like a moment to consult with his client. Two uncomfortable minutes later, Attorney Miller was back at the judge's sidebar to report that, yes, the child had been home-schooled from the day the mother had dropped him off, and also that it was true that Mr. McCabe had no idea where or when the child was born, or what his last name might be.

"Fine," the judge replied. "So what name did your client put down for the child on the form for the submission of the annual notice of homeschooling to the local school district? Let's use that name for the time being." Once again, Miller traipsed back to his client for a whispering session, and then returned to the sidebar. "He didn't know he was supposed to submit any form to the local school. He said he kept thinking the mother would reappear to claim her child, and the months and years just flew by."

The judge was not happy. That much was obvious. "Mr. Miller, how much do you know about whether your client took the child to a pediatrician on a regular basis?"

"I would need to ask him, Your Honor."

"And a pediatric dentist?" the judge added.

"I would have to ask about that as well."

"Then go do so."

Sixty seconds later came the response: "Mr. McCabe used the emergency room of Children's Hospital when something came up. He said he did so even though it was far from where he lives because it is such a renowned hospital."

"Mr. Miller, I read in the petition that was submitted that your client allegedly broke this boy's arm about three or four months ago. How much do you know about that?"

"He says it was an accident, Your Honor." I could hear Judge McGovern tapping her fingertips on the bench as she contemplated where this was heading.

"Did you speak to him about the serious allegations of repetitive violent spousal abuse? What do you know about that?"

"Again, Your Honor, I haven't had this case for even twenty-four hours."

Now the judge looked down, furiously writing notes in her trial book for the better part of three or four minutes. Then she looked up at Attorney Miller and gave him full warning of the problems he faced: "Mr. Miller, if we proceed with the hearing today, I don't see how your client can possibly prevail. The Department of Social Services is taking the position that the best interests of the child would be served by removing Mickey from your client's home and placing him in a residential program—namely, the Italian Home for Children. I occasionally rule against administrative agencies, but I'm sure you understand that I owe them a considerable degree of judicial deference—it's their job to be experts, each in their own sphere of competence. I'm just a judge."

"I understand that, Your Honor," Miller replied.

"Step back, gentlemen," she directed. The case went back on the record, and the judge now spoke to the entire courtroom. "Let the record reflect that I have spoken at sidebar with all three counsel in order to develop a basic sense of what the differing positions are of the petitioner, the Department of Social Services, and the respondent. At this time, as a final preliminary matter, I would like to ask Michael to come with me into my chambers so that the two of us can have an informal talk. Is that all right with you, Mickey?"

"Yes, Mrs. Judge. I mean, yes, Judge." And so the two of them trundled off into Judge McGovern's chambers and weren't seen for almost three-quarters of an hour. When the boy and the judge finally did emerge, they each had an ever-so-tiny smile on their face, and Mickey found just the right moment to flash me a clandestine wink. I think that was the exact moment when I first realized how thoroughly pleased I was to have a chance to help this little guy get his life straightened out.

"Counsel to sidebar," the judge called out once she had regained the bench. "Mr. Miller, what witnesses do you have today other than your client?"

"I have Dr. Harold Cummings, PhD, a Boston University professor. He will testify as an expert in these matters."

"Anybody else? Any family or neighbors of Mr. McCabe who can testify as to his parenting of the child?"

"No, Your Honor. I would need time to develop a proper witness list and to gather the evidence I would need to support the respondent's objection to the petition."

"Well, then, Mr. Miller, do you have any objection to my setting a hearing date down the road so you can put together a decent case for your client? Talk to your two brother counsel in this matter, and see what the three of you can work out—either as a real-world solution to the entire case, or at least to select a hearing date that you can all live with. Tell the clerk when you're ready for me to come back out on the bench."

"But, Your—"

That was all Attorney Miller got out before the stentorian voice of the courtroom bailiff rang out once again through the centuries-old oak-paneled courtroom: *"All rise. This honorable court is in recess."*

Ten minutes later, a very bedraggled-looking Mike Miller found me in the hallway. I put my finger up, asking him to hold on until I could locate DSS Attorney Harry Jenkins and ask him to join us. Two minutes later, the three of us stood together. "I thought you said I had a mountain to climb?" Attorney Miller began.

"You don't?" I asked.

"No. Not at all. 'Climb' is not the right verb. It's more like one of those technical ascents where they hammer little hooks into the rock face and pull themselves up with ropes. Look, I can't talk my guy into continuing the matter—he wants it done today, whatever the outcome." I just shook my head. "I know, I know," Miller responded. "I did too good a job on him with that where-the-kid-sleeps-tonight thing. And he's wedded to the advantage that we've got in having our expert here, while you don't necessarily have yours. But I think the big issue is life change—who knows, maybe with the wife gone, there's part of this guy that wouldn't at all mind being free and clear of raising the kid. But I don't know him well enough to know that—just a hunch."

I excused myself from the conversation, noticing that the Italian Home childcare worker and Mickey had come into the hallway. "How's it going?" Mickey asked when I walked over to them.

"I don't know for sure, Mickey, but pretty well, I'd say. How did your talk with the judge go?"

"You told me to be ready to talk to her, and when I was lying in bed last night, I thought over and over again about what I wanted to say—about how I want my life to be. And you know what I kept coming back to?"

"What's that?"

"I want to move on from Steve's dark house. I want a real family. With brothers and sisters. I want light in the house. Especially that. Especially light. And I want friends. And when I grow up, I want to be a lawyer and help kids like you do."

***

I had no sooner high-fived Mickey when the bailiff's voice careened down the hallway announcing that the judge was coming back out on the bench. I walked in with Attorney Miller, who had been speaking with Mr. McCabe.

"Did you have a chance to speak with your client?" I asked. "Any change?"

"Nope. There's no deal. He thinks our best shot is today, despite what the judge said. He seems to have some other agenda going."

"All right, let's go with what we've got. This isn't a trial; it's just a return date on yesterday's order of emergency removal. She may only want counsel's arguments, plus offers of proof. No big deal. But, Mike, I won't object if you want to put your expert on. Saves me doing discovery if we're heading toward trial."

***

Into the courtroom we went, only to find a somewhat annoyed-looking bailiff who was clearly ready to bring out the judge and call the session to order. *"Court! All rise. This court is in session, the Honorable Chief Judge Sheila McGovern presiding. You may be seated."*

Out shuffled the somewhat portly judge, visibly ready to make progress. "All right, gentlemen. Did you reach an agreement on rescheduling today's return-date hearing?"

Both DSS Attorney Jenkins and I looked over at Attorney Miller: it was his client who had refused to listen to the judge's advice, so the judicial heat should be his to take. "Your Honor, my client, Mr. McCabe, prefers that we hold the hearing today, as originally scheduled."

The judge was motionless, save for a little cock of her head to the right. "Bring your client up into the well with you, Mr. Miller." A minute later, speaking directly to Mr. McCabe, the judge was quite clear: "Mr. McCabe, did you hear me in court earlier today when I explained to your attorney that I thought the odds of your prevailing today over the recommendation of the Department of Social Services would be significantly increased if we put this hearing off for a month or so? During that period, your attorney could gather and prepare witnesses who could testify on your behalf. Did you hear me tell him that?"

"Yes, Your Honor," Mr. McCabe replied.

"I have just one more thing to say to you on this topic: you might want to rethink your position if your decision is based on the idea that wherever the child spends tonight and the following few weeks will, in and of itself, essentially determine where I will ultimately decide he should reside. Because that would be a misunderstanding. When I make a final decision as to the best interests of the child, I will move hell and high water to implement that decision—very definitely including moving Mickey from any temporary residential arrangement I may order today. Do you understand me?"

"Yes, Your Honor."

"Good. Then go talk again to your attorney and figure out if this clarification changes the logic of your decision to go forward with today's hearing."

***

Once the judge learned that McCabe was still choosing to proceed with today's hearing, she surprised all of us by declaring that she wanted an evidentiary hearing to produce a written record in case the nonprevailing party wanted to go up on appeal without delay. And then she added, "While I will be ruling on temporary physical custody from the bench today, I am entirely open to scheduling a second day for this hearing if any party so requests because of a missing witness, or if I determine to do that on my own. Mr. Miller, would you like to give a brief opening argument?"

Miller did as good a job as anyone could possibly do with what he had to work with—and with just one day's preparation. His principal argument was that all homes, and all parenting styles, are different. Arguably, he said, the only way to determine if a given parenting philosophy is successful is whether or not the child or children of that home turn out well. "And, Your Honor," he cleverly argued, "I don't doubt that in the long personal interview that you held with Michael today, you found him intact, articulate, intelligent, and even charming. The credit for that, Judge, has to go to Mr. McCabe—it was he who raised the child essentially single-handedly from age two to today." Miller shrewdly went on to admit that there were clear irregularities in the McCabe household and parenting style. "There's plenty of room for improvement in Mr. McCabe's parenting skills," he admitted. "Mr. McCabe would have no problem at all with the court ordering him to obtain professional counseling to improve these skills. And above and beyond the parenting advice," Miller continued, "Mr. McCabe is entirely open to receiving treatment to begin to work on his PTSD issues." Finally, Miller added that "if the court thinks Mickey could benefit from counseling, well, that too would make perfect sense. And the homeschooling will be brought into line with requirements—or ceased in favor of enrolling the child in public school." All in all, it was a brief and skillfully argued opening.

When Attorney Miller had finished, Judge McGovern looked my way. "Your opening, Counselor."

Since the judge knew where I was heading with my position, I decided to save my powder.

"Judge, with the court's permission, I'd like to reserve my opening until after the close of the respondent's case."

"Allowed. Mr. Miller, you may call your first witness," the judge ruled in a stern tone of voice. She clearly was upset that the hearing was being held today—despite her clear preference that both sides take the time to properly prepare for trial. I could only assume that she held this against Mr. McCabe and his intransigence—or his impatience to move on in life, whichever it was. From my point of view, I had to figure that all this accrued to Mickey's advantage, since by this point, I knew for certain that he unambiguously wanted to move on in life and away from Steven McCabe. The image of seeing him adopted in the future by a real family began to play before my mind, and I was ready to go to battle to help make this happen. Just then, Attorney Miller's voice brought me back to the present reality.

"The respondent calls Steven McCabe." McCabe was sworn in, and Attorney Miller proceeded to elicit the story of how the two-year-old Mickey was dropped off at the house by a woman McCabe had dated years before, but barely knew. He testified how he raised and educated the boy as best he could considering his agoraphobia, and how he had made use of the Children's Hospital emergency room for both Mickey's minor childhood illnesses and the accidentally broken arm. McCabe exhibited remorse at how he hadn't done an adequate job of allowing Mickey to play with other children—and how he was entirely open to counseling to improve in this and other spheres of parenting. The only part of McCabe's direct testimony that seems to merit direct quotation from the hearing transcript is his take on the domestic violence he visited on Goodwin and Mickey; his wording sheds light on how a dangerous connection operates in the mind of an abusive spouse:

Attorney Miller: Mr. McCabe, was there anything out of the ordinary about your marriage?

Mr. McCabe: Yes. This is not easy to admit, Your Honor. But sometimes I beat my wife. It's not that I intended to, or planned to, or wanted to. It's this damn PTSD I got from soldiering. It just boils up inside me from time to time, and it strikes out wildly—sometimes at those I love the most. As soon as the boiling would stop, I'd come back into my mind and apologize a hundred times over, and we'd be fine for months and months. I was a great husband during those periods. And then, all of a sudden one day, it would come boiling back up again, and I would strike out at my lovely Audrey and hit her yet another time. I hated that part of myself so much for doing this; you can't imagine. Sometimes I thought about ending it all. But I couldn't, because of Mickey.

Attorney Miller: Mr. McCabe, did you ever, in any way, hit, push, or even yell at Mickey during one of these PTSD eruptions?

Mr. McCabe: Maybe a few times, but nothing serious. I don't know why, really. I just never went after the boy—or not very often. It was almost always Audrey who took the brunt of the PTSD shit . . . Oops. sorry, Your Honor, I mean the PTSD violence. I don't blame her in the least for leaving me. I have no trouble saying that. I pray she'll come back and give me another chance, but I don't even know where to reach her or send a letter. Weird how you can live every day of the year with someone for years and years, and then suddenly they're gone from your life.

Attorney Miller: Mr. McCabe, what are your feelings toward your wife and your son?

Mr. McCabe: I love them both, even if that is hard for you to under-stand given what I've just told you. The violence that erupts out of me has nothing to do with love or lack of love; it's not even me doing it: it's the PTSD. It has a life of its own. I can't control it. Having PTSD is like finding yourself to be a real-life Mr. Hyde. I know that now, and I'm ready to seek help. I know Audrey is gone, and I understand that: Who would want to run into Mr. Hyde from time to time? No one. But Mickey is different: he's all I have. I love him so much. He's what my life is all about—I don't work, I don't have friends, I don't go out much because of my agoraphobia. And now I don't have Audrey. And Mickey's broken arm was an acci-dent: I just grabbed him as he ran by, and snap.

By the end of his testimony, McCabe was sobbing and sniffling. I sat there, only fifteen or twenty feet from the witness stand, trying my best to figure out if this was an act, or if he was legitimately and deeply torn apart by the upending of his life. I had no way to tell. Did he actually *love* these two people whom he beat and battered and iso-lated? And even if we assume that the psychology of a battering spouse is so complex, so multilayered, that they can repetitively strike out with great violence and still "love" their victims, from the law's point of view, do we care that they have such affection for those they assault? In Massachusetts and most other US jurisdictions, it only takes one spouse to file for divorce—the fact that the other spouse is "still in love" is legally irrelevant. I wondered if I dared argue to the court that McCabe's expressed love for his battered wife and abused child was also legally irrelevant.

My ponderings were interrupted at this point by the judge. "Your witness, Mr. Freiberg." I was trying to discern from the judge's voice—unsuccessfully, I might add—her reaction to the witness. I had just a few more moments of stall time to think through the tone of my cross-examination strategy when the massive courtroom door slammed shut, brazenly announcing the entrance of someone who obviously had not bothered to read the neatly typed three-by-five card that was taped on the door: Do Not Let Door Slam Behind You When Court Is in Session. Like everyone else in the courtroom, I turned to see what poor soul had committed this sin of sins—and found myself staring at my star witness, Dr. Evan Newsom. Understandably, Dr. Newsom was frozen in absolute stillness by the circumstances of his explosive entrance.

Someone had to break the silence, and that clearly had to be me, given that the intruder was my expert—no doubt delivered by my able associate. "Good afternoon, Dr. Newsom," I called out. "You're just on time. Please come forward so I may introduce you to Her Honor. Judge McGovern, this is Dr. Evan Newsom, head of pediatrics at Children's Hospital. Dr. Newsom is the co-petitioners' proposed expert witness, may it please the court."

Once Attorney Miller had assented to my motion that Dr. Newsom be permitted to testify out of order, which the court allowed, I expressly reserved my right to cross-examine Mr. McCabe later in the trial. I then called Dr. Newsom to the stand to be sworn in by the judge's trial clerk. In order to qualify him to testify as an expert witness, I asked a series of questions that elicited testimony about his training and professional accomplishments, including how he had treated hundreds of abused children, and how he had published scores of articles and numerous books dealing directly with the effects on children of growing up in households rife with domestic violence. These included one entitled *Unhappy Families: Clinical and Research Perspectives on Family Violence*, and another called *Treating Child Abuse and Family Violence Victims in Hospitals: A Program for Training and Services*.

Given that Dr. Newsom is a renowned expert on intra-family violence—the archetype of a dangerous connection—it seems well worthwhile to closely examine a number of passages of his testimony from the hearing transcript:

Attorney Freiberg: Doctor, can you please tell the court the general story of the current case as I have relayed it to you in the telephone conference we had about Michael, the child in question in this care and protection petition proceeding.

Dr. Newsom: As I understand this child's background from you, he is the son of a past girlfriend of Mr. McCabe. Mr. McCabe had unprotected sexual relations with Michael's mother, whose last name he does not recall or never knew. He also understands that other men had access to her during the relevant time frame. The child told you, Attorney Freiberg, that Mr. McCabe often told him that he was not the boy's biological father.

I understood from you that Mr. McCabe suffers from serious post-traumatic stress disorder incident to military service in violent war zones, and is today a fully disabled person who receives Medicaid benefits. One manifestation of Mr. McCabe's PTSD is an extreme case of agoraphobia, which causes him to leave his residence only very occasionally. A second manifestation of his PTSD are his periodic, out-of-control, explosive bouts of violent behavior, followed by periods of great remorse and repetitive apologies to those harmed during the outbreaks.

You also reported to me that Mr. McCabe has chosen to homeschool Michael but does so with zero compliance with Massachusetts General Laws Chapter 76, Section 1, or Chapter 71, Sections 1, 2, and 3. Mr. McCabe, you told me, failed to submit an annual notice form to his school district, failed to receive written approval of proposed textbooks and workbooks that were to be used, failed to deliver notice of the proposed curriculum and subjects to be covered, failed to submit notice of and receive approval of the methods of assessment that were to be used, and failed to submit the child on a periodic basis for required standardized testing.

With respect to family violence, you told me that there has been a pattern of repetitive spousal violence toward Mr. McCabe's spouse, Ms. Audrey Goodwin. You also told me that you saw the boy with a broken arm, and that Ms. Goodwin told a Ms. Maria Becker, a licensed independent social worker, that the arm had been broken by Mr. McCabe. You gave me the date of the child's appearance at the emergency room of Boston Children's Hospital, and as I am chief of staff of the hospital's child protection services, I was able to locate the child's medical record. The child's name was given that day as Michael Goodwin, and the cause of the broken ulna and radius—the forearm bones—was listed as "a fall while horsing around at home." Audrey Goodwin has submitted an affidavit, you told me, in which she states that the cause of the double arm bone fracture was, in fact, not an accidental fall but occurred incident to Mr. McCabe grabbing the arm of the child who was running past him in the household.

Attorney Freiberg: Dr. Newsom, on the basis of the information you have just described, and assuming it to be accurate for purposes of this question, are you able to express an opinion, to a reasonable degree of medical certainty, as to whether or not it would be advisable for the child to remain in Mr. McCabe's home?

Dr. Newsom: I am, indeed, able, because I do not consider this to be anywhere near a close case. I hardly know where to start, but why don't I take the points that I made above in the same order:

First, the issue of the doubtful and doubted paternity is serious. Children need to grow up, if at all possible, securely embedded in a family lineage. The certainty of the connection a male child experiences with his father or father-substitute is partly a function of biological paternity, but it is even more powerfully a function of the expressed determination of the father/father-substitute to remain connected to the male child throughout the father's or father-substitute's life, whatever the future might bring. This is why I believe Michael when he told you that Mr. McCabe has often said to him, "I'm not really your father." After working in my field for many decades, I don't know of any more wounding remark a father or father-substitute can say to a son or stepson, and hence it is not a line children tend to fabricate. To the extent Mr. McCabe has made this remark to Michael, and to the extent Michael believes and processes this gut-wrenchingly hurtful remark, Mr. McCabe shows himself to be an inappropriate man to raise this boy.

Second, PTSD shows itself very differently in different victims. When I look at the behaviors of Mr. McCabe to assess the level of acuity of his particular case of PTSD, I am extremely pessimistic about his prognosis. The repeated, uncontrollable, spasmatic eruptions of family violence indicate a very serious level of acuity, as does the overlapping agoraphobia. The simultaneous appearance of these two indicia is even more pernicious: the latter keeps Mr. McCabe from seeking clinical treatment for the former. I would assess Mr. McCabe as being extremely dangerous to live with until and unless he succeeds in adequately treating his agoraphobia so that he can leave his home on a regular basis to commence and advance the clinical treatment he needs to work on his PTSD. In my view, the intensity of his disorder would require a considerable length of inpatient therapy to have any appreciable chance of success.

Third, even with the healthiest of family dynamics, I am professionally opposed to homeschooling. My lifetime of work in studying and writing about how boys grow into well-balanced and sensitive men indicates that a great deal of the socialization process must take place outside of the home. It's in school, on the playground, in sports clubs, on teams, and in hobby-centered groups where boys learn what they need to learn in order to grow into mature, well-centered men, including learning to respect authority figures, learning how to make connections with other children, and learning how to keep themselves safe from bullies and aggressive children. To attempt homeschooling in the evident pathology of the McCabe homestead is strongly counterindicated by all the research and clinical case studies of which I am aware.

Fourth, the level of repetitive spousal violence in the McCabe household is almost certainly far greater than you yet understand. Countless studies have shown that spousal violence is underreported not only as to how many women suffer at the hands of their significant other, but also as to how often and how severely an abused spouse is actually beaten. Research has uncovered a whole set of reasons why battered women tend to minimize what they are actually experiencing: the reasons range from embarrassment to denial to fear that an effort to escape can provoke even greater retaliatory attacks. It's a tip-of-the-iceberg-type phenomenon.

Now, with respect to Michael's broken arm. To begin with, I absolutely would apply the iceberg rule once again: there is *always* far more violence hidden than what is observed or admitted. It is my opinion that in a clinical setting where Michael feels free to speak openly about what he has experienced, he will be able to recall many more such incidents. The mind, and particularly the mind of a child, has an enormous capacity to repress traumatic memories if that is what promotes survival. Children attempt to remain connected to their parents or parent substitutes, including even parentified children who are forced to care for drug-addicted or alcoholic parents, and we also see this pattern in sexually, emotionally, and physically abused children. They find a host of reasons not to blame or report or run away from the dangerous relationship they have with their parent. So, the sum and substance of the broken arm incident, for me, is that I am very, very skeptical of reports of "accidental injuries" in circumstances where the parent is otherwise volatile and violent. Since the facts as reported to me are that Mr. McCabe repeatedly beat his wife, in all probability, he brutalized Michael on many other occasions than the one that resulted in the broken forearm bones.

Attorney Freiberg: So, Doctor, when you add up what you've testified to about the domestic violence in the McCabe household, do you have a basis on which to form an opinion, to a reasonable degree of medical certainty, about the propriety and wisdom of Michael remaining in the care and custody of Mr. McCabe?

Dr. Newsom: Yes.

Attorney Freiberg: What is your opinion, Doctor?

Dr. Newsom: For the foreseeable future, Michael should never again spend time in the McCabe household—supervised or unsupervised.

Not a single night. My opinion is that Michael should be permanently removed from the care and custody of Mr. McCabe. Above and beyond not being physically or psychologically safe, Michael would not be well served to continue to live with Mr. McCabe. Michael needs the stability of adults who understand that caring for a child involves a considerable degree of accommodating their needs, and Michael needs the presence of other children with whom he can play, laugh, and learn all the lessons of life that children teach one another.

Attorney Freiberg: No further questions, Your Honor.

Court: Thank you, Doctor. Let's take a brief break before the cross-examination of Dr. Newsom.

***

Dr. Harold Cummings, PhD, the expert witness on McCabe's side of the case, had one distinct advantage over Dr. Newsom: he had met with Mr. McCabe and could, therefore, if he chose, testify as to whatever positive traits of McCabe he had discerned—or could dream up. Cummings, who appeared to be in his early seventies, had been slightly bent and rounded by the passing of the years. His wore his silky, soft-looking snow-white hair in a simple bowl cut, which complemented the aura of gentleness and tranquility that surrounded the man. He smiled warmly at me as he slowly shuffled by the two counsel tables on his way to taking the witness stand. I liked the man at once, and a quick glance up at the judge confirmed that she did as well. Within minutes, Dr. Cummings had convinced me—and the judge, no doubt—that he was a kindhearted, well-intentioned professional whose point of view on the viability of McCabe's parenting of Mickey would merit careful consideration.

We learned from Dr. Cummings's responses that his education and academic life had been almost the polar opposite of Dr. Newsom's—who was all Yale and Harvard. Cummings, who held the position of emeritus professor of psychology at Boston University, had been raised on a milk farm in Vermont, and had been the first in his family to attend college. After filling us in on his career path and decades spent in child welfare research, he told the court: "My entire career has been to study, teach, and perform research in the sphere of child welfare. For many years now, I have served as a consultant to dozens of states thinking through how to reform their child welfare systems, both with respect to adjudicated delinquent youth, and with respect to social service children—like Mickey will be if you send him down that route. I am, Your Honor, an inveterate 'deinstitutionalizer,' if I can coin a word. I think that no kid should be institutionalized unless there is no alternative. It's that simple to me. And I'm here to explain why, in Mickey's case, there indeed is a viable alternative."

***

Once again, my reader, I want to share several key moments of testimony directly from the hearing transcript:

Attorney Miller: Dr. Cummings, you've been in this courtroom all day, and heard the testimony of Mr. McCabe as well as the testimony of Dr. Newsom. For purposes of answering the questions I am about to ask you, I would like you to assume a more or less worst-case-scenario set of facts about what has happened to date at the McCabe household. More precisely, I want you to assume that Mr. McCabe suffers from serious, untreated PTSD, which can precipitate uncontrollable, violent outbreaks. Second, assume that Mr. McCabe repeatedly battered his now-estranged wife. Third, assume that Mr. McCabe grabbed Michael's arm in an inappropriate manner leading to a fracture of both the ulna and radius bones. I even want you to assume that Mickey suffered numerous other violent incidents consistent with Dr. Newsom's "iceberg" concept of domestic violence. And fourth, please assume that the homeschooling of Michael was a function of Mr. McCabe's agoraphobia, just like the isolation of the child from other children, the shades-down household, and the absence of a telephone and television—assume all of these choices were driven by Mr. McCabe's psychological profile, not by his consideration of Mickey's best interests.

My question for you, Doctor, is as follows: If the judge were to issue findings completely consistent with the worst-case set of facts that I am asking you to assume, do you have an opinion, to a reasonable degree of scientific certainty, as to whether or not this court should remove Michael from the McCabe household and institutionalize the boy?

Dr. Cummings: Yes, I do.

Attorney Miller: And what is that opinion, sir?

Dr. Cummings: Let me begin by saying that, upon the facts you are asking me to assume, this is a case where reasonable persons could easily disagree as to which is the wisest of two possible routes for the judge to send Michael down. One path is down Social Service Avenue with its residential programs and foster homes. The other path is one where Michael stays at home while the Commonwealth floods the McCabe household with social services and clinical support. Dr. Newsom—a man for whom I have unlimited respect given the groundbreaking work he has accomplished in his decades of work for children and families—happens to counsel this court to take one side of the fork in the road, while I would counsel the other.

Attorney Miller: Unless Attorney Freiberg objects, or the court prefers otherwise, I would ask you, Dr. Cummings, to take whatever time you need to explain to the court why you would advise against removing Mickey from Mr. McCabe's household.

Attorney Freiberg: No objection, Your Honor.

Court: Allowed.

Dr. Cummings: I want to start by offering the court some statistics that show that the choice the court is forced to make today is between residential foster care, with all of its problems, and the McCabe household, with all of its problems. There is no easy path here, no easy solution to Michael's situation. In recent years, nationally, whereas there have been only about five thousand infants in foster care waiting for adoption, there have been about two hundred thousand children between one and five years of age, and about another two hundred thousand in the six-to-ten age bracket—all looking for a safe home. So Michael would join—and, in a sense, compete with—roughly four hundred thousand other children hoping to find an adoptive family. And here's the statistic that really counts: just under two-thirds of children in foster care spend two to five years institutionalized before being adopted. The other third never find a family. So, statistically, the court is really deciding in this case whether Michael would do better spending two to five years in residential or foster care, or whether he would do better being with his father in a reformed McCabe household. So let's look in more detail at each of these two settings, each of these two paths.

Most children in residential or foster care do not simply go to one setting and stay there. Typically, a child like Michael ends up being moved between a number of programs, for a host of different reasons—many of which have nothing to do with the particular child. Children who endure numerous placement changes do poorly when compared to those who don't. We also know that later, as adults, they fare far worse occupationally. The statistics documenting the negative effects on children of bouncing around between successive institutional placements have even prompted legislators to enact laws that call for shorter lengths of stay and more stable placements for children in foster care, such as the Adoption Assistance and Child Welfare Act of 1980, and the Adoption and Safe Families Act of 1997.

Even more noticeable, Your Honor, is the degree to which residential instability places a good deal of psychological stress on children. And this stress changes their lives. For instance, children who come from this background often have trouble later in life forming and keeping attachments. Many studies show how these children are also far more likely to exhibit substantial behavioral abnormalities. And let's not forget for a moment that residential changes for a child mean school changes. And school changes are both socially and educationally disruptive for children, particularly if there are multiple school changes. Studies have shown that children subjected to disruptive, multiple school changes require increased levels of medical attention and clinical counseling.

Your Honor, there is valid and reliable data in the literature—gathered on a national level—that makes it clear that children in residential or foster care programs are disproportionately in poor mental and physical health compared to other children. They are about twice as likely to have learning disabilities, developmental delays, asthma, obesity, and speech problems. They are about three times more likely to be afflicted with ADD/ADHD. They are about five times more likely to exhibit anxiety disorders. And they are about six times more likely to have behavioral problems, and they are seven times more likely to develop depression.

Now, Your Honor, it's fine for me to lay out the statistics that document the sadness of institutional upbringing—probably no one in this courtroom is particularly surprised about the general story these numbers tell us. So, that's the easy part of what I'm here today to testify about. Far more difficult—but incumbent on me—is to demonstrate to you how we could orchestrate a reconstruction of the McCabe family home so that Michael would be safe, well cared for, and nurtured by a father who looks forward to watching his boy grow up into a man who makes him proud. To my mind, here is the key question for you, Your Honor: Can Mr. McCabe get there with what he has to work with, if professional social services and other societal resources are made available to help him? The answer, I would suggest, is yes.

Your Honor, we live in an era when it is commonplace to see a dilapidated house be purchased for renovation. Architectural plans are drawn, demolition crews rid the property of rotten wood and broken glass. Only the foundation remains, and then the rebuilding begins: masons scrape out and replace the mortar that has turned to dust between the foundation stones, and then they apply fresh cement and straighten and solidify basement walls and weight-bearing columns. Carpenters arrive with the pitch-pine smell of fresh wood, and then with ten thousand hammer blows, they reframe the structure, followed by electricians who run new wiring and plumbers who lay new piping. Plasterers come next to cover the framing, only to give way to painters who bring the colors of the rainbow into play, and decorators who pick out the furniture that will provide comfort and a homelike atmosphere.

This is just a metaphor, Your Honor, and—like most metaphors—it is simultaneously instructive and inaccurate. So, on a practical level, how would we go about renovating the McCabe household? I am the first to admit that for my house-restoration metaphor to have any meaning in the context of this law case, it is incumbent on me to demonstrate to you how this would work.

First, I have been asked to assume that Dr. Newsom is correct that Mr. McCabe needs an initial period of inpatient hospitalization to begin to deal with his untreated PTSD. That can be readily arranged for, although we would need to find an appropriate, noninstitutional setting for Michael to be placed in during this time period. One potential resource for this would be Mr. McCabe's sister, who, I am told, has a perfectly normal household in Cincinnati, Ohio, and who has agreed to accept her nephew for this period. There might be other options as well.

Second, it sounds like the McCabe property needs some TLC. There is nothing wrong with the structure of the property, I am told. I should think some do-it-yourself work by father and son on some of these projects could have significant therapeutic value as they work together to renovate not just their house but also their family life together.

Third, the homeschooling needs to end, with Michael to be tested for grade level, and placed in the local public school upon his return from his respite placement, and Mr. McCabe's return from his inpatient treatment. The local public school bus system would pick him up at the corner, and take him to and from school—like any other child. Whether or not Michael could simply blend into the school population on his own, or whether he might need some remedial tutoring and/or counseling to help him in the transition, would need to be determined.

Fourth, both father and son would need family clinical counseling on how to recognize and deal with any subsequent PTSD-initiated angry outburst. Unlike earlier, classical psychiatry, today's trauma psychiatrists and clinicians know a great deal about how to spot the onset of such outbursts, and how those involved can take steps to stay safe.

Let me stop enumerating the tasks that, undertaken together, could renovate the dilapidated McCabe household. My point should be clear by now. Judge, the bottom line here is that we have a son who needs a father, and we have a father who needs a son. Why would we even think of sending both to navigate the seas of loneliness by permanently separating them? Why would we expose the child to the significant risks associated with institutionalizing him in a string of foster or institutional settings? Let's be more creative than that, Your Honor, let's come up with the imaginative planning and the marshalling of resources we need to renovate this family and give it a future.

When Dr. Cummings finished speaking, perfect silence settled over the courtroom. Attorney Miller, clever as a fox, had no intention of breaking it: every second that passed seemed to add to the gravitas of both the witness and the apparently sound logic of his testimony. Recognizing that I needed to break the spell, I was the first to speak. Again, from the court transcript:

Attorney Freiberg: Your Honor, I was wondering if we might take a break at this point, before the petitioners' cross-examination of Dr. Cummings.

Court: I think that's an excellent idea. Plus, I have two requests for all three counsel. I want you all to know that I have a trial scheduled for tomorrow morning that is scheduled for five days, and that after that, my schedule is packed dead solid for months. So, we are going to get our case resolved today—even if we have to stay to midnight. But, please, after you take some time to caucus on your respective sides, I want counsel for the department, the Italian Home, and the respondent to meet for ten minutes to see if there is any chance of your putting your heads together to work out a resolution that takes into account the sage advice we have all heard today from both Dr. Newsom and Dr. Cummings. Please try hard, gentlemen; you could take an enormous burden off my shoulders, and I would be eternally grateful. If you fail, order in pizza, because you're not going home until I hear from your witnesses what I need to hear to issue findings and an order on today's proceedings. The pizza should come from Three Aces on Massachusetts Avenue—they are in a league by themselves.

***

When we reported after the break that we had been entirely unable to advance settlement of the matter, the stoutly built judge seemed to somehow become even heavier in her chair. "Very well," she said, scrunching up her mouth like Charlie Brown in the Peanuts cartoons, "make mine pepperoni. And my courtroom personnel prefer that as well. Will there be a cross-examination of Dr. Cummings by the co-petitioners?" There was indeed. Once again, let's take a look at snippets from the trial transcript that show how little was left of Professor Cummings's testimony once DSS Attorney Jenkins gently raked him over the coals with what I experienced as a quietly intoned—but absolutely devastating—cross-examination:

Attorney Jenkins: Professor Cummings, once you completed your doctoral studies, you've never held a position other than being a university professor, isn't that correct?

Dr. Cummings: Yes, sir.

Attorney Jenkins: And, Professor, since you were involved with the team put together by Division of Youth Services Commissioner Jerome Miller back in the early 1970s to close the Massachusetts reform schools—you've never again worked with either the Department of Youth Services or the Department of Social Services, isn't that correct?

Dr. Cummings: That is correct.

Attorney Jenkins: So, it's fair to say, isn't it, Professor Cummings, that other than the fascinating involvement you had with Commissioner

Miller well over thirty years ago, you have no personal, firsthand knowledge of the inner workings of today's Department of Social Services?

Dr. Cummings: Yes. That's fair.

Attorney Jenkins: And it's also fair to say, isn't it, Professor, that you have no personal, firsthand knowledge about the details of the types of social services that the department is able to offer Mr. McCabe?

Dr. Cummings: Well, I have knowledge of the general panoply of services they offer, but as to the "details," no, probably not.

Attorney Jenkins: And, Professor, you also have no personal, firsthand knowledge of how the Department of Social Services deals with its internal budget constraints, appropriations, line item payment limitations for providers of services, and the like, true?

Dr. Cummings: Yes, that's true.

Attorney Jenkins: Alright, Professor, so in this framework, let's take a look at some of your earlier testimony. You testified that it might be advisable for Mr. McCabe to initiate the clinical treatment for his PTSD and agoraphobia in an inpatient hospital setting, did you not?

Dr. Cummings: Yes, I said it might prove advisable . . . but perhaps not necessary. Dr. Newsom testified that it probably is necessary, and he is a renowned expert, so, yes, it probably would be necessary.

Attorney Jenkins: Do you understand, sir, that the Department of Social Services does not have one single such inpatient mental health facility among its facilities?

Dr. Cummings: Well, then it could contract with any private inpatient facility—McLean Hospital, for example. That's a nationally respected psychiatric facility.

Attorney Jenkins: Do you know if the department has ever contracted with McLean Hospital—or any equivalent facility?

Dr. Cummings: Well, no, but they could.

Attorney Jenkins: And how do you know that, sir?

Dr. Cummings: Just by good sense, it's obvious.

Attorney Jenkins: And from what part of the DSS budget would this come?

Dr. Cummings: Well, that I don't know.

Attorney Jenkins: How about the Veterans Administration; do you think Mr. McCabe might be eligible for treatment in one of their facilities—his PTSD is, as I understand it, derived from his former military service.

Dr. Cummings: There you go! That's the type of creative thinking that's needed to piece together a way to keep this family connected.

Attorney Jenkins: What do you know, Professor, about the waiting period faced by a wounded warrior like Mr. McCabe before he would be able to enter an inpatient facility of the Veterans Administration for treatment of PTSD?

Dr. Cummings: Well, nothing actually . . . just what I've read in the press.

Attorney Jenkins: What if I told you that to even apply for such a program, Mr. McCabe would need to undergo a Veterans Administration psychiatric workup, and that the delay time to even begin such a workup would itself take over a year? Would you know if my statement was true—or false?

Dr. Cummings: No, I wouldn't. As I said, the little I know about the Department of Veterans Affairs hospitals is from the newspapers.

Attorney Jenkins: And it's true, isn't it, Professor, that most of the recent press coverage you're referring to is a string of stories and reports about the scandalously long waiting periods faced by our veterans for treatment and care, isn't that so?

Dr. Cummings: Well. Yes.

[...]

Attorney Jenkins: You testified that perhaps Michael could spend a family-based respite at Mr. McCabe's sister's very normal household in Cincinnati, Ohio; remember that?

Dr. Cummings: Yes.

Attorney Jenkins: Did you call the sister, or take any other steps to confirm what you had been told, or to inquire of her willingness to become involved in Michael's care?

Dr. Cummings: Well, no. That would be up to Mr. McCabe's attorney, not me.

Attorney Jenkins: Okay. Do you know if Mr. McCabe's attorney made that call at some point yesterday or today?

Dr. Cummings: Well, he might have, but to be honest, I believe he also was relying on a representation Mr. McCabe made to both of us when we met early this morning.

[...]

Attorney Jenkins: Now, Professor, the second aspect of your testimony about the advantages of keeping Michael with his father involved fixing up the McCabe household—turning it from a house into a home, as I believe you phrased it. You suggested fixing what's broken, opening up the shades, and painting the walls to bring light into the room, furnishing the household with comfortable soft furniture—remember your testimony?

Dr. Cummings: Yes, indeed.

Attorney Jenkins: Do you have any knowledge, sir, whether the department has the legal authority, the personnel, or the funds to undertake any such project on *a private dwelling*?

Dr. Cummings: Well, no, not really. But there is nothing expensive about a can of paint.

[. . .]

Attorney Jenkins: And, Professor, the third aspect of your testimony about the advantages of keeping Michael with his father involved getting Michael tested to determine his grade level, and then arranging for any remedial schoolwork that would be deemed necessary to allow him to enter public school, do you recall that testimony?

Dr. Cummings: Yes, of course.

Attorney Jenkins: Do you know if the department has the testing and remedial education capacities to do what you call for?

Dr. Cummings: Well, they must; they must see this all the time.

Attorney Jenkins: You're quite correct, sir, the department can and does deal all the time with children who need testing to determine their educational level and remedial classes to bring them up to the level of their age cohort. But what I don't believe you are familiar with, Professor—tell me if I'm wrong—is the nature of the programs the department has available to deal with its testing and remedial education responsibilities, or are you?

Dr. Cummings: Well, no; how could I be?

Attorney Jenkins: Professor, do you know that the department delivers these services in *only one way*: by funding residential treatment programs that are staffed with licensed professionals who are qualified to perform both the testing and the remedial educational components?

Dr. Cummings: Well, no, but why couldn't the department fund a private remedial education expert? They're certainly available.

Attorney Jenkins: And, Professor, it's fair to assume, isn't it, that Michael, who has never played with other children because of Mr. McCabe's agoraphobia, might need counseling to learn what we all learned from interacting in school with a mix of other children?

Dr. Cummings: Yes, that makes sense, of course.

Attorney Jenkins: And are you familiar, Professor, with the fact that the department's specialized residential treatment programs are designed to provide a range of supervised milieus where a previously isolated child such as Michael can learn, step by step, how to successfully play and interact with other children?

Dr. Cummings: I don't doubt that, sir. But there are so many downsides to being in one of those programs, as I described in my direct testimony.

[. . .]

Dr. Cummings: . . . My parents were normal parents. But what comprises normal parenting? Parents don't take parenting lessons; acceptable parenting varies widely: this is not, and it never was, a world of Ozzie and Harriet households.

Attorney Jenkins: Professor Cummings, I would suggest to you that the parenting in the McCabe household was beyond the pale—it was aberrant, it was unacceptable, and it was illegal. Surely, sir, it can't be your testimony that McCabe's parenting falls within what you called the "wide range of acceptable parenting styles." Or is it?

Dr. Cummings: I want to be clear about something. I certainly am *not* saying that the spousal abuse and the aberrant parenting in the McCabe house were acceptable or that they complied with the relevant social norms or, as your question points out, with the law. All I am saying is that the best way to get from where we are to a healthy, nurturing milieu for Michael to grow up in, is to work with both of them in a noninstitutionalized setting so that the two of them end up having each other for the future—so that they end up having a family for the future. This noninstitutionalized path is what would be best for Michael—if it's feasible.

Attorney Jenkins: But you don't know, do you, Professor, if what you suggest is or isn't feasible, do you?

Dr. Cummings: Um . . . well . . . no. Not really. But that's not my role; that's the role of the Department of Social Services.

Attorney Jenkins: Precisely. Thank you, Professor. I have no further questions, Your Honor.

***

Cummings's cross-examination made the perfect segue to the testimony of Case Supervisor Melonie O'Rourke and DSS Area Director Paul Phillips. Dr. Cummings had admitted that his keep-Michael-at-home philosophy was applicable only if doing so were feasible, and he had given us a jewel when he testified that the only party capable of determining what was or wasn't feasible was the Department of Social Services.

Our two witnesses testified that the Department of Social Services couldn't come anywhere near accomplishing what Cummings called for in his apple-pie-in-the-sky "renovation" of McCabe's life and home. In addition, both witnesses added an important additional point: the department is hugely in favor of "open adoptions." This meant that if Mr. McCabe successfully pursued treatment for his PTSD and his agoraphobia, and if his clinicians documented to the department that he had made significant progress in dealing with his issues, then the department could—and would—encourage his serving as a visiting resource for Mickey, even if Mickey lived elsewhere. This met what remained of Dr. Cummings's concerns: a renovated McCabe and a rescued Mickey could very well end up with involvement in each other's lives—if Mr. McCabe succeeded with the work he needed to do on his PTSD and agoraphobia.

**

Just at this point, the courtroom door slammed shut once again—and startled the hell out of all of us. I looked up at the judge and saw that she was about to yell at someone—and boy, did she ever. *"Pizza!"* she called out. "Good work, young man; bring those suckers right down to these tables."

"All rise. This honorable court is in recess" rang out in full volume—notwithstanding the fact that the ten of us in the courtroom were within a dozen feet of the bailiff.

If eating together connects people, what an amazing bond pizza can provide: the judge, the armed bailiff, the court stenographer, the three attorneys, the two DSS personnel, my witness Maria Becker, Dr. Cummings—we became as mixed in with one another as lettuce leaves in a salad. We all stood around the counsel tables gobbling pizza, guzzling soda, and chatting about complete nonsense. Everyone—and I do mean everyone—needed a break after nearly four hours of testimony about the grim business that had brought us all together.

"All right," the judge called out fifteen minutes into the pizza orgy—with red sauce dripping quite unjudicially down the left side of her chin. "I want the three attorneys to each bring a slice and their drink into my chambers with me." As we trundled after the judge into her chambers, I could hear those left behind performing higher math and making offers of great self-sacrifice as they divvied up what remained.

**

"Okay, Counsel, here is my big question for all three of you: Could someone explain to me why we don't have a perfect compromise position right in front of us? What if the boy goes into residential treatment for a period of time at the Italian Home, where he'll get the clinical therapy, educational assessment, and remedial education he needs. All of this takes a number of months, during which time Mr. McCabe can make an effort to get started on treatment for his problems. Then we mark up another hearing, and all of you come back before me again to report on Michael's progress on one hand, and on Mr. McCabe's progress on the other. Why doesn't that work?"

I grabbed the initiative just before Attorney Miller did. "It doesn't work, Your Honor, because it isn't fair to the boy."

The judge seemed startled by the hardness of the position I had taken. "Why do you say that, Counselor; what would your argument be?"

"Your Honor, it's not fair to Michael because it leads to the kind of prolonged presence in residential placement that Professor Cummings derided. This boy needs to move on in life—and he needs to begin forging new connections that will provide him security going forward. And that's what he unambiguously—and to my mind, wisely—wants to do. Mr. McCabe didn't gingerly step over the line of unacceptable parenting—he vaulted over it. The broken arm—however exactly it happened—would for certain be substantiated by the DSS as child abuse. And there has been a prodigious amount of neglect. What we have here, Judge, is serious abuse, and monumental neglect by a very sick man. I can respect Dr. Cummings's point that children are better off in life when linked to their biological family, if that's at all feasible. But Dr. Cummings expressly didn't want the child lingering for years in an institutionalized setting, and I fear that's exactly what will happen if we sit around waiting for Mr. McCabe to change from a caterpillar into a butterfly. And it's certainly not clear that McCabe is Michael's biological father. I don't believe Mr. McCabe can pull off a metamorphosis in anything like the time frame that Dr. Cummings would consider acceptable, and even if he did, Judge, some caterpillars never become butterflies—they're just moths."

The judge let out a long, exhausted lungful of air. "So, what would you have me do, Counselor?"

"I totally agree with what you said earlier about the value of Mickey spending a spell in a specialized institution such as the Italian Home. But from my perspective, that should happen simultaneously with a vigorous search for the right adoptive home. There is every reason to be optimistic about quickly finding Mickey a really good adoptive home. In my opinion, his chances in life will be far better in a multichild adoptive home setting than they would be in a McCabe setting—even if Mr. McCabe somehow pulls off a miraculous transformation."

After a full thirty or forty seconds of thought, the judge turned to DSS Attorney Jenkins. "And your thoughts?"

"Nothing to add to what Attorney Freiberg said; the DSS has precisely the same point of view."

Again, the sound of silence was thick in the judge's chambers. For some reason, I could hear my heart pulsing away; I even wondered if others could. Then, she turned to Attorney Miller: "And counsel for Mr. McCabe, the floor is yours."

"Your Honor, we all agree that my client requires major clinical treatment. Clearly he's not ready to parent Michael next week just because we spruce up his house this week and put up those damn window shades that are making my case so hard to argue." Laughs all around. "I'd be the first to admit that it's probably unknowable if and when Mr. McCabe will have made enough documented progress to be trusted with Michael. But there's no reason to believe it's impossible. So why close the door on him permanently?"

Miller continued. "And, Your Honor, I also agree with Attorney Freiberg that we're not here to look out for my client's best interest—we're here to provide you evidence and argument about how Michael's best interests can best be served. So the real question that presents itself is just how much Mr. McCabe to leave in Mickey's life. Obviously, it can't be a hundred percent—both son and father need some time apart. But Dr. Cummings was compelling in his argument that it also shouldn't be zero percent. This is a vibrant eight-year-old who knows his father full well—both the ugly parts and, in all likelihood, a basketful of beautiful parts that none of us are familiar with or discussing. My client is due some credit for his role in turning out such a great kid, no?"

Attorney Miller continued: "Your Honor, I can get behind the idea you expressed earlier. Let's figure out the right-length respite period at the Italian Home, as the DSS suggests. During this period, McCabe would contact the Department of Veterans Affairs and get actively involved in working on his issues, with a goal of impressing you with his advances. Simultaneously, the DSS can search for an adoptive home. Then we come right back into your chambers—say, three months from now—and think through together whatever plan seems best for the boy. It would probably be clear by that point. If not, we litigate the matter with a lot more evidence and insight than we have at this point."

The judge was actually smiling when Miller finished. Talk about hitting the ball out of the ballpark. "All right, then. I think I want to go in just that direction. Why don't counsel for the DSS and counsel for the co-petitioners take a few minutes to confer on the details you want included. I'll come out on the bench in ten minutes, and either you three have a deal to put before me, or I'll come up with one along the lines Attorney Miller just expressed. Thank you, gentlemen."

***

Back in the courtroom, Attorney Jenkins and I huddled with Area Director Phillips and Melonie O'Rourke, the DSS social worker, while Attorney Miller went out in the hallway with Mr. McCabe. Phillips, aware that I was also general counsel to The Home for Little Wanderers, confirmed what O'Rourke had told me earlier: the adoption placement work for Michael would be assigned to The Home. As Phillips phrased it, "That way, Terry, you personally can deal with the complexities of searching for an adoptive home for a child who is not yet legally freed for adoption. Good luck with that." On the way back into the courtroom, Attorney Miller gave a thumbs-up to Attorney Jenkins and me, and we were ready to rock and roll—we had a deal.

"*Court! All rise. This court is in session, the Honorable Chief Judge Sheila McGovern presiding. You may be seated.*"

Turning again to the transcript:

Court: Would one of the attorneys like to make a motion to which the others will assent?

Attorney Jenkins: Yes, Your Honor. The Department of Social Services moves that this court approve a consent agreement which the three attorneys to this action will draft in the coming three days. The thrust of the agreement is that Michael's legal and physical custody shall remain in the Department of Social Services. Michael shall be placed by the department in residential treatment at the Italian Home for Children, which shall provide clinical treatment, educational assessment, and remedial classes. In addition, the department shall immediately contract with the adoption department of The Home for Little Wanderers to locate an appropriate adoptive home. During the same three-month period, Mr. McCabe shall seek inpatient clinical treatment for his mental health issues. Michael's institutional treatment shall end three months from now, with this court to determine at that time whether Michael would be best served by going back home with Mr. McCabe or by moving ahead with adoption placement and proceedings.

Court: Mr. Freiberg?

Attorney Freiberg: The petitioner Italian Home for Children assents to the motion, Your Honor.

Attorney Miller: The respondent assents to the motion, Your Honor.

Court: Anything else we need to do this evening, gentlemen?

Attorney Freiberg: Your Honor, my witness Ms. Maria Becker is in court to testify today. She has been here all day, Judge. Given the late hour, rather than examine her, may I make an offer of proof as to what her testimony would have been, the agreement between the parties being that if the matter needs to be litigated at the end of the three month period, and if Ms. Baker is for some reason unavailable, the offer of proof shall be admitted in evidence.

Attorney Miller: No objection, Your Honor.

With that I had Ms. Becker come forward and stand next to me. I then described to the court Ms. Becker's professional qualifications as a licensed independent social worker, and explained for the record that in a series of sessions, Ms. Goodwin had relayed to Ms. Becker the details of approximately ten incidents of violent spousal abuse leading to black eyes, bruises, and contusions about the face, shoulders, chest, vaginal area, and arms. Furthermore, I stated for the record that Ms. Becker had the professional practice of chronicling after each such session what Ms. Goodwin had disclosed to her, and she was prepared to offer a copy of her written chronicles in evidence. I then moved that a notarized, certified true copy of Ms. Becker's chronicle be entered in evidence, which the court allowed after both Attorneys Miller and Jenkins assented. And that was the end of one very, very long and draining day in court. Or so I thought.

As I began to pack up my briefcase, a female observer who had spent the entire afternoon and evening in court called out from her seat: "Your Honor. May I speak on this case?" Again, to quote from the hearing transcript:

Court: Can you please identify yourself to the court.

Spectator: Yes, Your Honor. My name is Leslie Flanagan. I work for Audrey Goodwin at her bakery. She is the wife of Mr. McCabe, and she is in hiding, Your Honor. She is afraid of Mr. McCabe because he threatened her—for years—about what he'd do if she left, if she talked. Over and over and over again, she would come to work at the bakery all beaten up, bruises all over, tons of cover-up that hid nothing, big sunglasses to hide her black eyes. Each time after she was beaten, she was depressed, in fear, and so terribly trapped—he wouldn't even allow a phone line to the house. And she was never permitted to leave the home alone other than to commute between home and work. Then things would get fine between them, and during these periods between beatings, we made the best French bread in Boston—wonderful types of breads and pastries from all the regions of France. Ask him [Spectator points at Attorney Freiberg] ... he was a regular customer, and it was he who first figured out about the beatings because, once, when he was paying for his bread, he asked me if Audrey was safe at home. Can you please order Mr. McCabe to stay away from Audrey and the bakery shop? He came by the bakery this morning and grabbed her arm when she was just arriving for the day. It scared her so bad.

I wouldn't say what followed was chaotic, but it was more or less the courtroom version of chaos. Attorney Miller signaled Mr. McCabe to stand up and come with him. "Bring your coat," he called out. "We're done here for today." As soon as they were together, Miller whispered something to McCabe, and they started to leave the courtroom. Since the court stenographer was still typing away, we can go back to the transcript for this:

Court: Hold on right there, Attorney Miller. I need to speak to your client. Apparently, we're not quite done for the evening.

Attorney Miller: Well, *we* are done, Judge. The business we came here to deal with today is finished; we can handle other matters on another day, with proper notice.

Court: Mr. Miller, either you and your client come down into the docket, or I will have the bailiff arrest your client. You have five seconds to make a decision.

I was pretty sure I could see McCabe sizing up his chances of getting beyond the football-player-size bailiff, who had positioned himself by the courtroom door with his arms crossed against his chest—and then think the better of it. McCabe and Attorney Miller went down into the well, standing below the judge's bench, no more than ten feet from her.

Court: Good decision, gentlemen. Mr. McCabe, as I understand where we stand, there is no dispute in this case about the fact that you battered your wife; you admitted that in open court, and several others have testified and spoken to that effect as well. Am I correct?

Attorney Miller: Objection, Your Honor. I am advising Mr. McCabe to assert his Fifth Amendment rights with respect to your insistence that he testify against himself as to a potentially criminal matter.

Court: It's a little late for that, Mr. Miller. Your client admitted in open court during his direct testimony that he regretted battering his wife. Let's put it this way: Does Mr. McCabe wish to take the stand and change his testimony?

Attorney Miller: No, Your Honor. Mr. McCabe has finished his testimony for the day.

Attorney Freiberg: Actually, Your Honor, if I may. I haven't had an opportunity to cross-examine Mr. McCabe; I reserved my cross until my case in chief. Would it be procedurally helpful to the court if I called Mr. McCabe back to the stand at this time for a very limited cross-examination?

Court: Good thinking, Counselor. Yes, and then call Ms. Flanagan. Everyone else, sit down; this court is still in session. Mr. Freiberg, the briefer you are, the happier I will be.

Attorney Freiberg: The petitioner calls Steven McCabe to the stand.

Court: Mr. McCabe, you are still sworn in from earlier today; I want you to concentrate on the pledge you made to "tell only the truth, the whole truth, and nothing but the truth." Do you remember swearing to that?

Mr. McCabe: Yeah.

Court: Mr. McCabe, it's not "yeah," it's "yes, Your Honor" or "yes, Judge." Do you understand?

Mr. McCabe: Yeah, Your Honor.

Court: Proceed, Mr. Freiberg.

Attorney Freiberg: Mr. McCabe, I'm going to examine you this evening on only one issue, reserving my right to recall you for further cross-examination at a later date if that proves necessary. Sir, do you remember your testimony this morning in which you showed considerable remorse for the spousal abuse you visited on your wife, and the fact that you did not blame her for leaving you? Do you remember that?

Mr. McCabe: Well, yeah, I'm sorry I pushed her a few times, and hit her a few times, but it was nothing serious; this is all being blown out of proportion.

Attorney Freiberg: Mr. McCabe, I want you to think carefully before answering my questions, because the judge just admonished you to remember the oath you took this morning. Ms. Leslie Flanagan just told the court that there were approximately ten days when Ms. Goodwin went into her bakery beaten and bruised—and wearing oversize sunglasses to hide her black eyes. Was it you who struck her, causing those black eyes and bruises?

Mr. McCabe: Maybe twice, maybe three times, we've been over this. Why are you torturing me over this? I'm a soldier returned from war with horrific nightmares, cold sweats, flashbacks to when platoon mates of mine stepped on an IED and were blown into pieces no bigger than a . . . than a . . . coffee cup. You can't even begin to understand what I've been through.

Attorney Freiberg: I'm sure that's true, sir. And I am truly sorry for the suffering you describe. But all we're concerned with at the moment is whether this court should issue a temporary restraining order ordering you to stay away from your wife and her bakery shop. Were you near the bakery this morning?

Attorney Miller: Objection, Your Honor, he's badgering the witness, and I—

Court: Overruled. Sit down, Mr. Miller. Proceed, Attorney Freiberg.

Attorney Freiberg: Did you see her this morning, or try to, or have you been near her bakery? Remember, sir, you are under oath.

Mr. McCabe: [Hesitant to respond; delays his response] Yeah, I went first thing this morning, hoping Audrey would talk to me and work things out like we always did. I very politely tried to start a conversation. But she wouldn't even look at me—she just tried to enter the bakery without talking to me.

Attorney Freiberg: And you reached out and touched her?

Mr. McCabe: I just grabbed her lightly by the arm so she wouldn't go inside. I just wanted to say that I knew I had been wrong to strike her, and that I would go get help, and that I needed her—and that I still loved her.

Attorney Freiberg: I have no further questions, Your Honor. At this point, I move that this court issue an injunction pursuant to Massachusetts General Laws, Chapter 209A, barring Mr. McCabe from coming within one thousand feet of Ms. Goodwin, or one thousand feet of her bakery, and also barring him from directly contacting Ms. Goodwin by any other means.

Attorney Miller: I object, Your Honor. Such an order is not needed. The respondent is quite capable of keeping his distance from Ms. Goodwin, and will do so voluntarily.

Court: Your objection is noted for the record, Attorney Miller. Attorney Freiberg, will you have your office draft an appropriate Chapter 209A restraining order and bring it in tomorrow to my trial clerk?

Attorney Freiberg: Yes, Judge.

Court: Mr. McCabe, I am ordering you to stay at all times at least a thousand feet away from your wife, from her bakery, from the Italian Home for Children, and from Michael. If you go nearer than that to her, or to her bakery, or to the Italian Home, or to Michael,

I will have you arrested. Am I perfectly clear?

Mr. McCabe. Yeah. No problem. I don't really want to be near the bitch anymore anyways.

Judge McGovern's mouth dropped wide open, and she just stared at McCabe. It took her the better part of half a minute to determine what she wanted to do next.

Court: Ms. Flanagan, would you please tell Ms. Goodwin that she is perfectly safe to return to work at her bakery. Please tell her that if she has the slightest reason to believe that Mr. McCabe is approaching her in any way, or stalking her, or spying on her, or trying to contact her—anything—she, or you now that we know each other, should immediately come right back to this courtroom with any details, and I will deal with the matter forthwith. Also, I will have a copy of the restraining order delivered to the bakery tomorrow.

Next, I called Ms. Leslie Flanagan to the stand, and she proceeded to describe on the record what she had earlier told the judge. And then, finally, we were done for the day. I stood up and started once again to pack my briefcase with the case folders, looking forward to heading home. But no such luck. The judge called out, "I want all three counsel in my chambers, *now*."

***

While I obviously don't have a courtroom transcript to quote from, I can easily reconstruct the conversation that ensued in the judge's chambers from memory: what was said remains vividly present in my mind—no doubt because my license to practice law was at stake. The judge was in a stern and businesslike mood from her very first words:

"Okay, first things first. The consent agreement we talked about earlier this evening is now null and void. In its place, I will be issuing findings and an order as soon as I can write them up, and I can tell you right now that they will grant permanent legal and physical custody of Michael to the Department of Social Services. I will also invite the department to proceed, whenever it determines it appropriate, to file under Massachusetts General Laws Chapter 210, Section 3, a petition to this court to commence proceedings for the involuntary termination of parental rights. Obviously, Attorney Miller, your client will have the opportunity at that time to contest the petition. If, at that time, he can demonstrate that he is indeed the biological father of the boy, and also that he has made significant—very significant—progress in his mental status and parenting capacities, who knows what the outcome may be? Is everybody clear on what I've just said?"

The three of us simultaneously said, "Yes, Your Honor."

"Now, Attorney Freiberg, as to you. What the hell is going on in this case? Ms. Flanagan said you were a regular customer at the bakery, that you had noticed Ms. Goodwin's bruises, and that you had even asked her if Ms. Goodwin was safe at home. Is all this true?"

Oh boy, where was this heading? "Yes, Your Honor."

"So, I'm going to assume it is not a coincidence that you appear in this case as counsel for the Italian Home. For how many years have you brought cases before me for the Italian Home, The Home for Little Wanderers, Carney Hospital, and the others?"

"Let's say twenty years; at least that, Your Honor."

"And you have always been a perfectly honorable attorney, and never once did I have reason to question anything you said or did. But this case is different. I need to know *exactly* what you did, so that I can determine if there was an ethical violation involved that would require me to file a report with the Board of Bar Overseers."

And so, with no option to do otherwise, I launched into my story, commencing—why not, the judge obviously liked to eat—with the bread. "Judge, this bakery changed our neighborhood; it's an incredible French bakery with stupendous baguettes with thick, crunchy crusts that have a sourdough-like flavor—they're as good as you can find in France. The bakery makes a dozen other types of French bread and pastries—all because Ms. Goodwin took herself with no family money, just her own ingenuity, and apprenticed in all sorts of different regions throughout France.

"Then one day, Judge, the quality of the bread sunk like a stone in water—there was no crunch to the crust, no flavor to the baguette. The atmosphere in the shop went from exuberance and joyfulness to the most depressive atmosphere you can imagine. A month or so later, the quality of the bakery and its bread had returned, only to plunge back down a few months later. It took me three cycles of this to realize that, when the bakery was in the dumps, Ms. Goodwin was wearing huge sunglasses to cover up black eyes and tons of makeup to try to hide bruises on her cheeks and neck."

"But, Counselor," the judge interrupted, "what if the woman just had mental issues, you know, been a depressive or something? What if your theory of her being a battered wife had been entirely wrong? Did you ever think of that?"

"I did, Your Honor; I thought a lot about that. So, knowing that she was a graduate of the Johnson and Wales baking program, I sent my private eye down to speak to one of her professors. She was described by her professor as having a consistently optimistic, sunshiny personality; he said she was the bright light of her class. The more I read about how spousal abuse operates, and the more I spoke to college professor ex-colleagues of mine who are knowledgeable about 'battered wife syndrome,' the more convinced I became that she was trapped in an abusive home life."

I then detailed how I got Ms. Becker, a licensed independent clinical social worker, involved and what she was told by Ms. Goodwin. "After yet another pair of black eyes, Ms. Goodwin approached Ms. Becker saying that she wanted to make an effort at fleeing the McCabe household while she still had enough strength to do so. Ms. Becker told her that she knew an attorney who would be helpful. And, sure enough, a few hours after that idea was first mentioned between the two of them, they were in my law office."

"Ah, so Ms. Goodwin did consult with you?" the judge interjected.

"Yes, Judge, that one time. I gave her the name of an attorney whose practice is specialized in working with domestic abuse victims. She took the name, thanked me, dictated and signed the affidavit that was submitted to you today as Exhibit One to the petition, and that was the last time I ever saw the woman. It was at the very end of that one meeting, Judge, that she shocked the hell out of me when she said something like, 'I'll be okay, but I'm very worried about the boy.' My investigator, who had staked out the McCabe house to learn what he could, had not picked up a single hint of a child living in the home. As soon as the two women left my office, I called Area Director Paul Phillips and told him what I'd heard, and he asked me to call my client, the Italian Home, to see if they had a bed for an eight-year-old boy. And here we are."

I stood there with shaking knees, in abject fear that I was about to be soundly rebuked—and possibly even formally headed into disciplinary proceedings—by one of the Commonwealth's most respected judges. Only once before in my life had I ever been so overwhelmed with foreboding: I was ten years old, and I stood, with the same two shaking knees, awaiting the judgment of my grammar school principal as to whether or not I was the pupil who had set off the hallway fire alarm.

The judge looked up and stared straight into my eyes, and said in that particularly serious tone of voice reserved for judges, "I want you to tell me precisely what motivated you to launch your offensive. And I mean I want to hear *precisely* what was in your heart."

Talk about a soft pitch over the heart of the plate. "Bread, Your Honor. Bread."

She paused just a touch before saying, "Ah, the bakery. It was that good?"

"It was *that* good."

At this point, the judge sat silently with her arms on the edge of her desk, her interlocked fingers joining her two hands. She stared down at her hands for at least half a minute and then turned to face the two other attorneys. "Gentlemen, please tell me if you have any objection whatsoever—or any friendly amendment—to what I'm about to say. As I see it, Attorney Freiberg's surveillance of the McCabe house is neither illegal nor unethical. Neither is his setting up the social worker confidante in the commuter train car, because Ms. Goodwin's speech to Ms. Becker was voluntary, and because it was not secretly recorded. In fact, it sounds like whatever Ms. Goodwin said was treated as privileged under the Commonwealth's social worker privilege statute. The two women subsequently went to see Mr. Freiberg as an attorney—no problem there—and in that visit, he first learned about the boy's plight and immediately reported what he learned to DSS. So, while his little crusade to save a battered woman is unusual—*highly unusual*—that doesn't necessarily make it either illegal or unethical, unless I'm missing something in my analysis. Am I?"

DSS Attorney Jenkins played his cards perfectly: he remained stone silent. Attorney Miller, as Jenkins hoped, felt compelled to speak into the vacuum. "If Your Honor has no problem with it, then neither do I. My only job here is to present arguments aimed at preserving Mr. McCabe's rights to enjoy the company of his son. Mr. McCabe needs counseling, and it's indisputable that the boy needs educational testing and remedial schoolwork. So everyone's better off precisely because the abuse came out into the open—whatever Your Honor ends up ordering. But I say kudos to my adversary—he helped the wife escape what sounds like pure hell, he helped Mickey get going in his life, and he even helped bring my client to the point where he admits to himself that he needs to go seek professional clinical help for his PTSD."

"I agree, Judge," Attorney Jenkins chimed in. "No one except the McCabes—*no one*—even knew of this boy's existence. He doesn't even have a last name. As an attorney for the Department of Social Services, I work on case after case of child abuse and child neglect—and the idea that a child without a name, whose existence is completely unknown to the outside world, is being raised by a mentally ill person in an isolated, dark, locked-down house is abhorrent to me. I find that absolutely terrifying. Was the boy taken for regular medical checkups with a pediatrician? No. Has he ever played with another child? No. Can he read, can he write, can he spell, can he do age-appropriate math, can he draw, can he do any sport or exercise activity, does he know anything about the world outside his house? Who knows? There's only three things we *do* know at this point: First, this child is way better off being out of McCabe's personal prison. Second, so is the wife. And third, so—in all probability—is Mr. McCabe. Everybody wins, Judge. I think it's that simple. Everybody is better off because this has all come out into the light."

Again, the judge went silent, with her left elbow on her desk, and her chin perched in her left hand, calmly and quietly thinking this all through. Finally, she spoke, looking over at me. "I want two things from you, Counselor, and we'll call ourselves square. First, I don't want to ever hear about any more Don Quixote legal adventures from you.

Everything fell your way this time, but it could easily have blown up in your face. Do you agree?"

"Absolutely."

The judge nodded her assent. Then, looking at me square in the eyes, she added: "And here's what else I need from you. I grew up one of eight kids, mostly boys. Stuff got broken—all the time. So my dad finally made a sign, framed it, and hung it up on the hallway wall. It read—in typed red letters—You Break It—You Fix It." McGovern paused to let her story sink in. "I can see that you meant well and that you even ended up doing well: your concern for your favorite baker precipitated the end of a pathological situation. God knows what would have happened in that household over time. So what you did, ended up being a good thing. *But you've created an orphan.* Now go find me just the right family for him—so that I can finalize his adoption. And do it soon—for the reasons Dr. Cummings articulated. You're counsel to half the adoption agencies in Boston—go pull strings. Tell them I told you to. *You broke it—you fix it.*"

And then, sage jurist that she was, the judge looked over at Attorney Miller and added: "And you, Counselor, as for Mr. McCabe, please tell him that I wish him well. Please tell him that partial credit counts in my classroom. While he will have neither legal nor physical custody of the boy so long as I sit on this bench, I will gladly work with you to create a plan for a healthy Mr. McCabe to have visitation with Michael—supervised at first, but perhaps later as a visiting resource. Mr. Miller, you bring me a healthy Mr. McCabe, and I'll see to it that he will have significant involvement with the boy. All right, then," the judge concluded. "We're done here. Everybody go home."

We were just about out her door when Her Honor let out a loud, "Hey, guys." All three of us jerked our heads around simultaneously. "Thanks for the pizza . . . Three Aces does it like nobody else, don't you agree?" We let ourselves out of the locked front door of the courthouse at almost exactly 10:30 p.m.—nearly nine hours after we'd first entered.

***

As you might imagine, I got to know Mickey better as I worked on his adoption quest—per Judge McGovern's directive—to "fix what I had broken." And, frankly, this was a first for me: I had never before taken an active role on behalf of a particular child to promote their prompt adoption. But a promise is a promise.

I continued to deal directly with Marilyn Morningstar, the adoption program director at The Home for Little Wanderers. At our first meeting after the hearing, she flashed me a collegial smile as I entered and crossed the room—and gestured for me to take a seat in one of the visitors' chairs facing her desk. Even as I sat down, I was flooded with an awareness of how *desperately I needed* to earn full vindication from Judge McGovern. I felt almost like a naughty child working hard to get back in the good graces of his parent. And it also dawned on me at this moment that a successful and accelerated adoption search was entirely dependent on whether or not I could convince Morningstar to remain fully committed to my project.

For a good half hour, I expanded upon what I had previously told her about Mickey. I also told her the full story about my ethically borderline quixotic undertaking to save my neighborhood baker, and about everything that Longfellow had done and learned. I relayed how DSS would file its petition to terminate McCabe's parental rights in the coming weeks, and why I was now certain that I could guarantee a rapid court judgment on the petition—especially if I could tell the judge that we had located a family that was, as I poetically phrased it, at least a "nine on a scale of ten." And finally, for good measure, I told Morningstar about the family motto of Judge McGovern's father, and about her judicial order to me to fix what I had broken.

During my entire monologue, Morningstar had not said a word. And then she surprised the hell out of me with her response, which, as always, cut right to the heart of the matter.

"Oh stop looking so pitifully worried. Of course, we can work together to find this boy a good home! That's what I do! And, personally, I don't give a hoot about the legal fine points involved. You saw someone in distress, and you did something about it. I say, bravo. Full stop. Now, let's get to work and find a 'nine,' maybe even a 'ten,' for your Mickey. How long do we have?"

It took me a moment to accept that we had just bounded over what I had seen as a potentially troublesome hurdle—we were going to cut the queue. "Up to three months, I should think," I responded. "The boy is at the Italian Home for Children; they're working with him on what he's been through—and on the transition he faces."

"Okay," Morningstar said. "I need about two weeks, maybe a touch more, to select and contact two or three potential adoptive families. We're going to have some great options, I can assure you. In fact, I've recently taken a look at two families who might be ideal placements for this eight-year-old—I'm not sure I'd know how to choose between them. They are really each just about perfect. But I'm getting way ahead of myself. In the meantime, since you're both our counsel and also counsel to the Italian Home, go see how much you can learn about Mickey. It would help me enormously in my selection process to know about his academic achievement level, especially what grade equivalency he has obtained. What are his hobbies? What does *he* want in a family? How is his health? The more information you can gather about who he really is, what he really likes to do, what triggers him, what soothes him, what excites him—and so on—the better job I can do in matching him with a family. Keep in mind, this boy lost his mother at age two years, not age two days. That leaves a mark. Then he lost half his childhood by not being allowed to play with other kids, from what you said. Then he lost his stepmother—even though you said they both told you that they weren't allowed to grow that close to one another. But it's still a loss, even if he experienced her more as a fellow victim than as a nurturing stepparent. And now he's losing his father figure. 'Snow on snow on snow'—do you know the old hymn? Here we have 'loss on loss on loss.'"

***

About two weeks passed before Morningstar called, and three days later, Mickey and I found ourselves climbing the stairs to the adoption department at The Home for Little Wanderers. Mickey gazed openmouthed at the nineteenth-century floor-to-ceiling built-in oak cabinets that held what, to him, were undoubtedly the most valuable items in all the world: files packed with the names of families seeking to adopt lost children. Morningstar explained how the process would work: there would be an initial meeting here at The Home where Mickey would meet a prospective adoptive family. If both parties reported a willingness to go on to the next step, there would be a day visit to the home of the family. If that went well for everyone, an overnight visit would then be arranged. And, finally, if everyone was in favor of proceeding, Mickey would move into the pre-adoptive house and begin his future life with his new family. The law, Morningstar described, required at least six months together in this interim status before the adoption could be finalized by a judge of the Probate and Family Court. (And I certainly knew exactly which judge that would be.)

Morningstar had barely completed her sentence when Mickey broke in, seemingly at ease with the unfamiliar surroundings. "That all makes sense to me, Mrs. Morningstar. But can I ask you two questions?"

"Of course, dear," Morningstar declared with grandmotherly warmth.

"Terry told me you've already located two fabulous families, and there might be others as well. Terry said they're both great, only really different. Can I learn about both of them?"

Morningstar was caught. On one hand, that wasn't how the process worked, at least in her many decades of practicing adoption social work. After all, abandoning an interested family in favor of its competition had potential negative consequences on the likelihood the rejected family would again be interested in reinitiating the adoption process with another child. "Let's think about that, Mickey. It would be highly unusual. What's your second question?"

Mickey paused, seemingly to find just the right words. "Well, Mrs. Morningstar, you see, I have the first name 'Michael,' but I don't have any last name at all because of my background. And I'm going to need one now that I'll be out in the world. And yours is the most beautiful name I've ever heard. So, I was wondering if you would possibly agree to share it with me. 'Michael Morningstar'—wouldn't that be a beautiful name?"

Morningstar actually blushed—there was no question about it. All I could do was look down to hide my smile. Morningstar even had to clear her throat a bit before she could respond. "Well, Mickey, when an adoption is finalized, the judge files papers to change the adopted child's last name to that of his new adoptive family. And that seems like a really good idea, doesn't it, if everybody is going to be in the same family? Don't you agree?"

"That makes sense, of course, Mrs. Morningstar. But that's at least six months away, if I understood what you just said, and I'm still going to need a last name between now and then, don't you think?"

Damn, this kid was good. "I suppose you're right, Mickey. So what if I said yes on the condition that, when we do put together a finalized adoption for you, you'll have the judge change your name to your new family's last name? What do you say?"

There is no way I can put into words the grin that spread across Mickey's young face—mirrored at once by an equally beaming smile on Morningstar's senior visage. And they just froze that way for a bit, intoxicated by their mutual fascination. Imagine what this meant to Mickey: it was his first last name—*ever*—even if it was only being borrowed. And as to what it all meant to Morningstar, that became clear at once. "Mickey, why don't we make this a team effort? Terry here can be the attorney who legalizes the finalization, and in the interim, we'll all coordinate our efforts to find you just the right family. Any family will be very lucky to have you join it; if I were young and married and had other kids for you to play with, I'd adopt you in a heartbeat."

"Really?"

"Really!"

"Cool. So when can we meet the two families and think through which one would work best for me? And Terry said, if neither seems right, we can start over and find new ones."

Morningstar looked over at me with the exact look people give when their opponent unexpectedly calls out "checkmate." "I think this is a great idea," Morningstar responded. "The three of us will meet both families, take a look at both homes, and . . . we'll . . . vote. It will take three yeses to make it a go. What do you say, Counselor; will you join us throughout the search process?"

Okay, then. This never-ending labyrinth of a non-case had just added an entirely new wing to the maze.

***

Roughly ten days later, Mickey and I found ourselves back in Morningstar's oaken office. "All right, gentlemen," she began, "I've been back through the files, and I continue to think that the two families I told Terry about a while back remain our best prospects. Let me summarize, if I might, what I see to be the contrast between the two of them." Mickey politely interrupted Morningstar at this point to ask if she had a pad of paper and a pencil he could borrow to take notes. And boy, did he ever take notes. McCabe's homeschooling, I had to admit, had not been entirely ineffective.

"Now, Mickey Morningstar, I'm going to give you a copy of the files on these two families. It's very confidential information—and you have to treat it that way. The names in the file, and what we discuss between the three of us, cannot be shared with anyone. However, if you leave the names off, and just call them 'Family Number One' and 'Family Number Two,' then you can talk about the two options with your clinical social worker over at the Italian Home, do you understand?" Mickey replied with a vigorously affirmative shake of his head. "And we'll keep your copy of the file here in my office, if that's all right with you." Another nod followed from Mickey.

"Okay, then, let's talk first about Family Number One—the Thompson household." She began by describing the parents: the father was a surgeon at Massachusetts General Hospital, with quite a distinguished career. The mother was a sculptor—an artist—not famous or anything, but quite accomplished. Both had attended Ivy League schools, and Morningstar even provided a little sociology lesson for Mickey by telling him that highly educated, high-achieving parents are often able to pass along to their children the advantages that flow from their accomplishments.

Morningstar next described how the family had previously adopted two children, a girl, now twelve, and a boy, who is ten. She mentioned that she had been told that the ten-year-old desperately wanted to have a little brother. Mickey—in silence—broke out in a huge smile and vigorously scribbled the word "brother" on his notepad. Morningstar went on to describe how the Thompsons also served as emergency care providers, and that many babies and children had received good and loving emergency respite care from them for a day or a week before being more permanently placed for foster care with another family. "So, Mickey, one thing for you to take note of is that we have over ten years of experience with the Thompsons, and we have every reason to believe that they would welcome you into their family. We also know that they have a lot of experience with what adoptive parents need to do to help a child catch up with their schoolwork and so on. So, that's a good thing, right?"

When Mickey finally finished his note-taking and looked up, Morningstar added: "Now, you have quite a few photographs in the file I gave you. Shall we look at them together?" Mickey nodded, and off the three of us went on a visual tour of the stately Thompson family home on its manicured grounds, including eight-by-eleven photographs of a huge swing set/climbing apparatus in the side yard, an in-ground pool in the backyard, the dining room with the table set for a formal-looking dinner, the large bedroom Mickey would share with the ten-year-old, and the boy's closet with his clothes arranged in perfect order. There were also half a dozen photos depicting the two children, the parents, and even the grandparents. These family photographs were almost Victorian: everyone—even the children—seemed formally posed, and there was only an occasional smile. Mickey took his own sweet time looking through the photographs, and when he finished, he went right through the entire pile again. Only then did he look up at Morningstar.

"Any questions about the Thompson household, or shall we turn to Maria and Giuseppe Colombaro, and their home?"

Mickey's head jerked up quickly from his note-taking. "What beautiful names!"

"Aren't they?" Morningstar confirmed. "Italian names, Mickey. And you'll need a beautiful name after borrowing 'Morningstar' for the interim, don't you think?" The two of them shared the sweetest little smile at this remark. There is no way I can adequately describe how different Mickey already was, only about two months from when I'd first met him. It was like watching a flower bud develop and open in time-lapse photography.

"The Colombaros live in a section of Boston called the North End," Morningstar began. "It's a major tourist attraction in the city because it seems like you're in Italy. It's very near Boston Harbor, so with a ten-minute walk, you can look out over the water."

"Wow," Mickey asserted loudly without looking up from his note-taking.

Morningstar smiled, and then continued her description. "They live in what's called a 'triple-decker,' Mickey. That means a three-story residential building that has three apartments, one on each floor. Some of the children—I think the boys—live on the top floor, the Colombaros and their daughters live on the middle level, and the bottom floor belongs to Mr. Colombaro's parents, and Mrs. Colombaro's mother lives there as well, I think."

"The boys have their own place?" Mickey asked in wonder.

"Yes, if I remember correctly," Morningstar replied. "If I am not mistaken, the upper floor serves as a dormitory for the boys, since there are nine children in the family. Four of the children are birth children of the Colombaros, with the remaining five having been adopted over the years. The Colombaros are what I like to call 'the more the merrier' kind of people. Whether you're talking about a weekend party or taking in more kids, that's just who they are. I've been to their house four or five times to complete the postplacement visitation reports that I have to do for an adoption, so I've seen their lifestyle up close and personal. Maria—Mrs. Colombaro—is happiest when cooking. And when you're feeding that many people, shopping for food and cooking never ends. The kids help with the cooking, and they were all singing as they chopped and stirred—it was quite something to hear. And to smell! Such wonderful odors. And there was no end to the laughter at the table that night. It was just another meal, but it sounded and seemed like a party."

I glanced over at Mickey's notepad as he spiritedly underlined the word "laughter" three or four times.

Morningstar then described how the Colombaros make their living: "The family owns and runs the oldest and most famous Italian bakery in the North End."

It was suddenly apparent to me that Mickey had stopped taking notes. He was frozen—just sitting perfectly still—with his mouth hanging wide open—mesmerized by what Morningstar had just said. When she, too, noticed this, she smiled and asked, "What is it, Mickey?"

Mickey's face glazed over; some trigger within him had been activated. He was silent for quite a few moments, and then, in a breathy voice, he told us what was on his mind. "I love bread, Mrs. Morningstar. I mean, everybody loves to eat bread. And pastry. But for me, bread's more special than pastry . . . for me, bread's even more special than bread."

That remark brought complete silence upon all three of us. For some reason, I found myself almost whispering to Mickey when I asked, "What do you mean by that, Mickey; can you find some other words to say that?"

"Because bread's warm. Really warm. Audrey is a baker. Every day, she'd bring home breads that she'd taken out of her bakery's oven before they were fully done. Then, at home, she'd finish them in our oven just before we were going to eat. To me, that hot bread was like hugs. Does that sound crazy? Steve didn't hug me because he wasn't my dad, and Audrey didn't hug me because Steve didn't want her to. But the warm bread hugged me—I mean—in its own way. Not really, of course, but in its own way."

Mickey fell silent after this almost cathartic outburst; he looked off into space and went somewhere else. It seemed to me that he had never thought about this before, and you could sense his mind churning away, trying to understand. Morningstar got prepared to speak, but I signaled her not to, and then the two of us just sat there, allowing Mickey to go inside himself and explore his feelings. A full minute or more passed before he smiled broadly and shared with us a remarkable memory:

"I just remembered something, or reheard it in my mind's ear." (I've never forgotten that phrase; I wonder if it's the only time it has ever been formed.) "The only times Steve allowed Audrey to hug me was after he had beaten her up. I would cry and cry and cry at the sound of his fists hitting her body. And I couldn't breathe right. And she never cried out; she just took the hitting as if . . . as if she thought she deserved it. Then—when it was finally, finally all out of him—Steve would go into their room and cry like a baby. For hours and hours. I could hear him through the wall. And Audrey would come into my little room and sit on the side of my bed and hug me and comfort me—or maybe we were comforting each other." After he finished saying this, there was another long, long silence where Mickey just sat perfectly still in the golden glow of the oaken walls of Morningstar's office, not blinking, not caring that his mouth hung half open. These were some of the quietest moments I've ever lived. And then came a voice from deep, deep inside him—and I knew the voice: some involuntary part of Mickey's mind was emulating Audrey's voice. "So, Mickey, the last two steps in making the croissants involve adding the final slab of butter, and then the rolling. The dough that has been resting in a ball for hours in the refrigerator already has butter in it, but this step adds more—lots more. Mickey, after we let the dough ball warm, we take a rolling pin and roll it out into a rectangle—about eighteen inches by about fourteen inches. Then we lay on top of it a butter slab—about twelve inches by about eight inches by about three-eighths of an inch thick. We roll the butter in with our rolling pin, and then we fold the dough down to half its size. Then flour it lightly and flour your rolling pin, and roll the dough out until it's once again about eighteen by fourteen. We repeat the folding and rolling over and over and over. This is what makes the flaky layers, Mickey." Tears were streaming down the boy's face and dripping onto his lap—to which he paid absolutely no attention. "Then comes the fun part, Mickey. We cut the final roll out of the dough in strips about six inches high, and then we cut each strip into triangles, one this way, one that way, one this way, one that way. Then you just roll up each dough triangle from the bottom, and bend down the ends a touch if it is a butter croissant or not if it is a margarine croissant. Oh, Mickey, if only I could take you to the bakery: you'd be so good at rolling up the triangles. Then into the oven they go, and out they come when they're golden brown—to rest. As they rest, Mickey, they get better and better and better. Now, you rest, too, my boy, you go to sleep, and you'll feel better and better and better when you wake up."

Again, Mickey's mouth dropped open and he sat in perfect silence, his tears slowly abating. We three just sat there, silently, without the slightest movement, waiting. And then something inside Mickey resolved. You could see his blinking return, and then, at peace with his tears, he turned toward me and said, now in his own voice, "That's how bread hugged me."

***

And so on a Saturday two weeks later, Marilyn Morningstar, Mickey "Morningstar," and I all arrived at The Home for Little Wanderers just a bit before nine in the morning. We met in a special room decorated like a living room, intended to put children and families at ease in such meetings. There was also a one-way mirror on the wall, through which clandestine monitoring could be effectuated if called for.

At nine sharp, in came the Thompsons with their two children, each impeccably dressed. Dr. Thompson was a tall, lean man whose posture was well north of perfect; he was dressed in a suit and tie. Mrs. Thompson, equally trim and attractive, wore her brunette hair in a bouffant style; she had on an expensive-looking gray tweed suit. The boy had on a starched, button-down madras shirt and khaki slacks, while his sister sported a navy-blue dress accented with white lace at the sleeves. The two Thompson children sat remarkably still, and it took Morningstar's many years of experience to coax occasional conversation from them. Looking back, I would estimate that Dr. Thompson spoke about two-thirds of the time, leaving the remaining third to be divided between Morningstar's questions and the occasional contributions made by Mrs. Thompson and the three children.

Mickey took his behavioral cues from the Thompson children, matching their submission to Dr. Thompson's somewhat overbearing, but probably entirely accurate, presentation of what life was like in "my" household, as he phrased it. Dr. and Mrs. Thompson, quite appropriately, asked Mickey about his expectations, hobbies, interests, likes, dislikes, and so on. Mickey was utterly honest in his responses, in no way trying to hide that in many, perhaps most, spheres of life, his shut-in childhood meant that he had not yet developed all the skills and abilities of children raised in a normal manner. He never once tried to hide what he'd been through, and he openly and honestly answered every question Dr. Thompson posed.

At the end of the two-hour-long session, Morningstar asked if the Thompson children would like Mickey to give them a tour of The Home's facility and playgrounds, and the three of them walked out, leaving the adults to discuss the next step in the process. It was quickly decided that, if Mickey agreed, there would be a home visit the following Saturday, which, to my surprise, Morningstar said we would all attend. And that was pretty much the sum and substance of the morning meeting.

Lunch was a treat and a half. Mickey and I were invited to join Morningstar and The Home's children in their dining room. There must have been about seventy or eighty children in the room, and there was that glorious din of children's voices and laughter—a sound that is absolutely universal, no matter what language children are speaking. I first noticed this when I had the opportunity to travel to China on a law case for a collection of US adoption agencies: I visited three large orphanages, and was struck by how a playground full of children chattering and yelling in Mandarin sounded exactly like a playground in the States. As you might imagine, after the dry and formal meeting with the Thompsons, the uplifting sound of children's laughter felt like a plunge in the sea on a hot summer day.

After lunch and a brief walk around the grounds to stretch our legs, we found ourselves back in the "living room" waiting for the Colombaros, who arrived more than half an hour late. Their entrance reminded me of the famous act in the circuses of my youth, when clown after clown after clown after clown exited from the door of the tiniest little car. There were, after all, fourteen Colombaros to meet and greet, given that the three grandparents also attended.

I guess I would describe the scene as controlled bedlam, and what few constraints there were on dress, conversation, or laughter—or anything else—were self-imposed. Each child had dressed as he or she preferred, and Mr. Colombaro had a visible amount of flour on the left shoulder of his short-sleeved, dark-blue polo shirt. He apologized for being late, explaining that all of them had wanted to come to meet Mickey, and the morning had been crazy because the bakery had to remain open in the afternoon while we were meeting. That meant they had had to commence baking earlier than usual, and then welcome friends who had offered to help augment the professional baking staff for the busy afternoon retailing process.

The description of home life was left mostly to Mrs. Colombaro, with frequent interjections from the children, many of which caused peals of laughter, while others led to vibrant and good-spirited debate. Mickey was able to be Mickey this time around. I could see him creating tenuous new connections with many of the children by sharing a look, or a smile or a laugh, or when one of them spoke up or interrupted the adults with a one-liner. And he didn't for a moment hesitate to connect with the parents. At one appropriate moment after Mrs. Colombaro had noticed and had worked on patting the flour off her husband's shoulder, Mickey took the initiative to tell Mr. Colombaro about his fascination with baking. He briefly described how his "sort-of stepmother," as he phrased it, was a master baker in her own right, and then he pointed at me. "My attorney knows her bakery—that's how he got involved with us. It's good baking, isn't it, Terry?"

Needless to say, I had no trouble confirming the quite extraordinary bread and pastry the shop produced.

Mickey spoke right up. "I know the recipes by heart; Audrey taught them to me. I know how to bake—even the croissants. Sometimes Audrey would show me how in the kitchen. Maybe one day I could show you French baking, and you could teach me Italian baking." Mr. Colombaro was stunned into silence, the way a bull is stunned into stillness by the efforts of a master matador. Mickey then turned to Mrs. Colombaro and announced, "Mrs. Morningstar said she had dinner at your house one night and that the odors and flavors were amazing. He looked over at Morningstar, who nodded with a smile. Mrs. Colombaro blushed, and then Mickey came in with the coup de grâce: "Would you ever teach cooking lessons to a boy?"

When I asked toward the end of the meeting if the children wanted Mickey to take them on a tour around The Home, they all ran whooping out the door with him in a matter of seconds, and I do mean *with* him.

In the ten remaining minutes that the adults spent together, it was agreed that there would be a home visit two Saturdays hence, and that it would be at dinnertime so that the complex arrangements of running the bakery in the absence of the family could be avoided. With that, we walked outside together to gather the children—which Mr. Colombaro accomplished with the single best whistle I've ever heard. It wasn't just that his fingers-in-the-mouth whistling was loud: it was because his gather-the-children whistle was Mozart's incalculably beautiful Queen of the Night theme from his opera *The Magic Flute*. Opera, I was to learn, was at the heart and soul of Colombaro family culture, and it turned out that it was arias from Italian opera that were being sung in the kitchen when the children helped with the cooking.

Once the family had driven off in their commercial-size family van—which sported the words "Modern Day Bakery" on both sides, while the front was festooned with a hand-painted, almost childlike version of a smiling cannoli—we were joined by Mickey's clinical social worker, who had come over from the Italian Home for Children, and who had spent both sessions on the other side of the one-way mirror. Once we got down to business, the line the social worker opened with immediately sprang to the very top of my personal list of the most perceptive summations I've ever heard:

"Do I need to say *anything*?"

***

More than twenty-five years have somehow passed since Mickey chose—surprise, surprise—that baking was his life's passion. You can find him in the afternoons in Boston's North End behind the sales counter or, in the early mornings, down in the basement extracting baked goods from the ovens with a ten-foot-long wooden spatula that looks like it was the same implement used nearly a century ago by his adoptive grandfather. He's married now, the father of two little children of his own, and so far as I know, he's thrilled with the life path he chose.

And five miles to the south, you'll find Audrey Goodwin, although she's asked that I not reveal the town where her new bakery and coffee shop is located. She's also doing just fine in her work life—because while some media-generated food fads come and go, if you bake good bread— really good bread—the world will still beat a path to your door. This was true a hundred years ago, and it's true today, and—I'll go out on a limb and make a prediction—it will still be true a century from now.

***

It's time to conclude my story about this non-case that was so unlike any other in which I was ever involved. I want to share with you, my reader, just a few final thoughts about Audrey Goodwin.

I never learned anything about Goodwin's experiences in the safe house, or how she was supported emotionally during the successful transition that she made—a transition that so many women find so entirely daunting. I continue to patronize her bakery, of course, and there are times when Goodwin spots me at the cash register and comes forward from the back of the shop to convert my proposed purchase into yet another thank-you gift. Being paid in quality bread for helping out a baker in duress . . . if only I could figure out a way to get that news to my childhood idol, Margaret the cook.

There were two lessons I learned from Goodwin's case, for which I remain enormously grateful. First, it was only through working on Goodwin's case that my eyes were finally opened to both the shameful history and current status of domestic violence that so many women suffer.

As for the shameful history, one horrifying thing that I learned was that our laws against wife beating date back only a little over a century. Before that, a wife was essentially chattel, and in many jurisdictions, there were few restrictions on what a husband could do to his wife. It was almost universally the case, for example, that it was impossible for a husband to rape his wife—*as a matter of law*. And even in those American jurisdictions that were early in the movement to correct this deficiency, of which Massachusetts was one, police and courts often failed to enforce the new laws.[18] Until very recently, there actually was greater legal enforcement to prevent and punish cruelty to animals than to wives: the American Society for the Prevention of Cruelty to Animals was around many years before statutory regimes were passed to protect American wives. Even today, there are still many countries in the world where there is no statutory protection of women whatsoever,[19] and, of course, Putin's Russia made headlines in 2017 when it decriminalized any domestic violence that does not result in serious bodily injury.[20]

---

18. *History of Domestic Violence: A Timeline of the Battered Women's Movement*, Minnesota Center Against Violence and Abuse; *Safety Network: California's Domestic Violence Resource*, 1999. Also see Barbara Mantel, "Domestic Violence: Are Federal Programs Helping to Curb Abuse?" *CQ Researcher* 23, no. 41 (2013) and Elizabeth Pleck, *Domestic Tyranny: The Making of American Social Policy Against Family Violence from Colonial Times to the Present* (Champaign, Illinois: University of Illinois Press, 1987).

19. Vivian Achieng, "15 Countries Where Domestic Violence Is Legal," *The Clever*, May 26, 2017, https://www.theclever.com/15-countries-where-domestic-violence-is-legal/.

20. Anastasia Manuilova, "Nine Months After New Domestic Violence Law, Russian Women Still Struggle," *The Moscow Times*, November 25, 2017, https://www.themoscowtimes.com/2017/11/24/nine-months-on-russian-women-grapple-with-new-domestic-violence-laws-a59686.

In the United States, it was fully 1984 before Congress passed a federal law to protect women and children who were victims of domestic abuse. Known as the Family Violence Prevention and Services Act, it provided funds to encourage the formation of shelters and other resources for victims of family violence. Then, thanks in part to the remarkable amount of publicity surrounding the O. J. Simpson case and his trial for the murder of Nicole Brown Simpson (and Ron Goldman), Congress enacted the Violence Against Women Act (VAWA) in 1994. With the new act, it appeared that American society was finally going to get serious about protecting women and children from domestic violence. Thanks to VAWA, cities and towns throughout the country would receive federal funding to deal with the crisis of domestic violence that so many faced. The problem, however, is that VAWA requires reauthorization every five years, and this was held up by Republicans in 2013 before finally being passed. In 2018, however, while the next required reauthorization passed in the House (with 1 Democrat and 157 Republicans voting against it), it has completely stalled in the Senate. Republican senators, apparently, will not support the House version, which extends the existing ban on weapon possession by domestic violence perpetrators to other men convicted of dating violence or stalking. How sad that this has developed into such an intractable partisan matter.

And just a brief word about the second lesson I learned from dealing with Audrey Goodwin's non-case: it taught me about the psychological cost to women who are victims of domestic violence. Goodwin called me about half a year after her escape from McCabe's little private hell to ask for a referral to a competent trauma psychiatrist. I gave her the name of a superb and highly specialized clinician and also asked if she would mind signing a release allowing the clinical psychiatrist I was recommending to speak with me about her case. What I hoped to learn, I explained, was more about the level and specifics of psychological damage done by batterers to their victims. She willingly agreed, and also permitted me to publish an account of what I was told—using a pseudonym, of course.

Accordingly, over nearly four years, I was able to consult with Dr. Janet Young, the psychiatrist to whom I referred Ms. Goodwin. Over that period of time, Dr. Young and I discussed a goodly number of fascinating subtopics about how Audrey Goodwin's persona was affected by being subjected for eight years to McCabe's repeated beatings, reign of fear, and imposed isolation. Here, however, I want to report about only one such subtopic: whether or not the psychological effects of McCabe's spousal abuse of Goodwin left her with post-traumatic stress disorder (PTSD)—the same reaction to trauma from which McCabe suffered from his terrifying experiences as a soldier. Why is this important? Because, if a battered wife—and, in about 85 percent of domestic violence cases, it is the woman who is dominated and beaten—can be so injured by domestic abuse that she can validly be given the diagnosis of PTSD, then she is suffering a level of psychic injury *equivalent to what a soldier experiences from the horrors of battlefield killing.*

Let's take a brief technical look at whether or not the diagnosis of PTSD that Audrey Goodwin received from Dr. Young was justified. The diagnosis requires at least one "intrusion symptom," where the traumatic event is persistently reexperienced in upsetting memories, nightmares, flashbacks, or emotional distress (or physical reactivity) after exposure to traumatic reminders. Dr. Young relayed details to me that made it clear that Goodwin suffered from *all* these intrusion symptoms.

There is also a requirement of a consistent "avoidance of trauma-related stimuli" reaction by the victim, either by dissociating themselves from thoughts or feelings related to their trauma or by avoiding external reminders of the trauma in their everyday lives. Like many beaten wives, Ms. Goodwin had been sexually submissive to an extreme extent. Dr. Young doubted that Goodwin would ever again recover from her total revulsion to sexuality: the sexualized element of McCabe's brutal dominance was so terrorizing, and the body's role in trauma memories is so central, that Dr. Young doubted that Goodwin would ever be able to separate the sexual suffering she endured from McCabe from her sexuality in general.

So, it was clear to Dr. Young that Audrey Goodwin was indeed fully qualified to receive a diagnosis of PTSD. She didn't even consider it a close case. In other words, Audrey Goodwin was suffering the same level of full-blown PTSD as was her battlefield-scarred husband. *That's how serious domestic violence is.* And on top of this, Dr. Young emphasized, trauma treatment for domestic violence victims is even less likely to be effective than trauma treatment for soldiers, because the person who hurt them was not the enemy—it was the person they slept with and the person who, between bouts of violent abuse, was gentle and loving to the extreme. It was the person they felt most connected to, and the person from whom they accepted soothing. As Dr. Young phrased it in one call, "When the person who tenderly nurtures your wounds is the person who wounded you, the psychological scar tissue will change your life."

***

Cervantes, the author of the great Spanish-language classic *Don Quixote de la Mancha*, wrote in the early 1600s: "All sorrows are less with bread." When I first ran across that line, I scribbled it down on a piece of paper and crammed the note into my wallet. And, sure enough, the next time I found myself at the Modern Day Bakery, I remembered it, pulled it out, and read it to Mickey—Mickey Colombaro. He just smiled, held up his finger for me to wait a moment, and three minutes later came back up from the basement ovens with a sign that someone had made his adoptive grandfather many, many years earlier. It had a picture of Mahatma Gandhi glued on it, and it quoted the great man: "There are people in the world so hungry that God cannot appear to them except in the form of bread." I just smiled back, tried without success to pay for my purchases, and left to get home before the bread cooled off. Now that I think about it, only about a month after that, I read the same Cervantes quote to Goodwin when I stopped by her new bakery to purchase one of her still extraordinarily sourdough-like *épi*-shaped baguettes, and she responded with a quote that she had memorized—this one from the indomitable Julia Child—who reportedly once dared say: "How can a nation be called great if its bread tastes like Kleenex?"

***

Sometimes, these days, when I wait for my train in Boston's storied subway system, I glance over at a recently appended security sign that reads When You See Something, Say Something. It's a good motto, and a powerful reminder that the safety of each of us is the concern of all of us. Once in my life, I actually lived up to that motto, and how wonderfully it has paid off: lots and lots of both Italian and French bread—none of which tastes like Kleenex.

EPILOGUE

Without a doubt, we humans are social animals. We always have been. And when we are alone—when we are chronically alone, or when we feel chronically alone—we don't do very well.

So many clients, through so many years, tried to say this to me in so many ways. But it was often hard for me to identify the loneliness lurking in their background as I dealt with the specifics of whatever their particular legal matter was. These days, in contrast, we are all aware of the public health threat posed by chronic loneliness. It's headline news, and fully out in the open: "Theresa May Appoints . . . Minister for the Lonely Millions," "How Social Isolation Is Killing Us," or, as phrased by a former United States surgeon general, "America Is in the Midst of a Loneliness Epidemic."[21]

So, what are the facts? About a third of us self-identify as chronically lonely,[22] and the self-reporting questionnaire from which these statistics were derived has repeatedly been shown to be both valid and reliable.[23] And here's another sad fact: in the United States, in 2012, 28

---

21. *London Times*, January 17, 2018; *New York Times*, December 22, 2016; Vivek H. Murthy, *This Morning Newsletter*, October 10, 2017.
22. Brad Edmondson, "All the Lonely People," *AARP*, November/December 2010.
23. Daniel W. Russell, "UCLA Loneliness Scale (Version 3): Reliability, Validity, and Factor Structure," *Journal of Personality Assessment* 66, no. 3 (1996): 20–40. A copy of the scale is included as the appendix to *Four Seasons of Loneliness: A Lawyer's Case Stories* by J. W. Freiberg.

percent of adult households were single-person households,[24] and that number has surely grown in the past eight years. But there's yet a third statistical reality about loneliness that underlies the logic of the book you've just read: it's not the same third. In other words, only about half of chronically lonely people actually live alone,[25] and, correspondingly, only about half of those who live alone see themselves as chronically lonely.[26] So what's going on here?

These findings tell us that about half of all chronically lonely people live enmeshed in what appears from the outside to be a normal network of connections. So being *misconnected* with others is just as likely to lead to chronic loneliness as being *disconnected* from others.

Why is any of this important? Because chronic loneliness—objective or subjective—causes excruciating pain, and then it destroys your health and hastens your death.[27] And if you think the term "excruciating pain" seems a bit exaggerated, ask yourself which hurts more—breaking a bone in your body or having someone you love walk out on you? People commit suicide over severed love; they don't over broken bones.

So, let's pause a moment to examine why chronic loneliness is so enormously painful. What is it about us humans that makes us ache so profoundly when we feel lonely?

To my mind, the difference between us and our fellow mammals can be seen in how we humans raise our children. Just like other mammals, and many other animals as well, we provide shelter and sustenance in raising our young. But by orders of magnitude, we do much, much more than that—and we do so for many more years. And as we nurse, soothe, calm, coddle, caress, embrace, nurture, and teach our children all that needs to be learned over all those years, we engender the development of neural pathways in their brains—biochemical pathways that will both prepare and impel these children to seek connection with others as they set out in life on their own.[28] In other words,

24. Jonathan Vespa, Jamie M. Lewis, and Rose M. Kreider, *America's Families and Living Arrangements: 2012* (Washington DC: US Census Bureau Report, 2013).
25. John T. Cacioppo and William Patrick, *Loneliness: Human Nature and the Need for Social Connection* (New York: W. W. Norton, 2008).
26. Cacioppo and Patrick, *Loneliness*.
27. Cacioppo and Patrick, *Loneliness*.
28. Amy Banks and Leigh Ann Hirschman, *Wired to Connect: The Surprising Link*

human children raised by well-functioning parents are both neurologically formed and psychologically configured to become functioning social beings—that is, to connect, to befriend, to love, to mate, and to parent.

Now, in this context of thinking about adult humans as quintessentially social beings, consider the implications of a recent study that reported that the neural pathway for the sensation of feeling *excluded* is exactly the same neural pathway in the brain that interprets incoming signals of pain.[29] In the opinion of some neuropsychiatrists, the fair interpretation of this finding is that, evolutionarily, it was advantageous for human physiology to handle separation from the group with the same top-of-the-line neuronal wiring that was otherwise reserved for transmitting signals of injury.[30] And this makes sense: in the ancient world, a human separated from its family or community would have been in grave danger. This is precisely why those deviants and criminals in the ancient world who didn't receive the death penalty for their offenses were given the second-worst punishment conceivable at the time: banishment from their village or locality—and thereby loss of connection with everyone they knew.[31]

I learned this lesson, you may recall, not from scholarly books but from the unruly teenage boys whom I overheard on that swimming float as reported in the story "Three Souls Caught in a Spider's Web." Their conspiracy to exclude—*to banish*—some poor, overweight, slow-running schoolmate was a powerful clue as to why Herbert Britton treated his criminal defendant clients as if he were a spider—ensnaring them in the silken threads of his delusions of friendship. In the end, it was thanks to those boys that I came to understand why my client was satisfied with living alone, working alone, and surviving

Between Brain Science and Strong, Healthy Relationships (New York: Tarcher/Penguin, 2016).

29. Naomi I. Eisenberger and Matthew D. Lieberman, "Why Rejection Hurts: A Common Neural Alarm System for Physical and Social Pain," *Trends in Cognitive Science* 8, no. 7 (2004): 294–300. See Amy Banks, "Loneliness and the Power of Permanency," in *Growing Up Lonely: Disconnection and Misconnection in the Lives of Our Children*, ed. J. W. Freiberg (Boston: Philia Books, 2019).

30. Banks and Hirschman, *Wired to Connect*.

31. E. M. C. van Houts, ed., *Exile in the Middle Ages*, International Medieval Research (IMR 13); *Selected Proceedings from the International Medieval Congress* (University of Leeds, July 2002).

on the thin emotional soup of his fantasy that his law clients were his personal friends. Britton, I came to see, had decided to avoid the risk and pain of rejection that are part and parcel of striking out to make new connections. For him, it was safer to concentrate entirely on those who were forced into a relationship with him on the basis of a judicial order of appointment of public counsel.

But, of course, the pain of loneliness can also torture the lives of those who come upon it by happenstance, despite having been raised by a family that neuronally and psychologically equipped them to seek connection, friendship, and love. And here I think of poor Bernard Boursicot in "The Woman Who Was Never There." I am confident in reporting that Boursicot was seeking a true connection with Shi Pei-Pu when the lovers shared their first kiss on the grounds of the French embassy in Beijing. But that's not at all what he received in return: we now know that Shi Pei-Pu was busy setting a "honeypot" trap to ensnare the young diplomat.[32] This is why I never located any credible evidence that corroborated my client's insistence that Boursicot was the "love of my life." On the contrary, the evidence seemed to say that their relationship was a textbook example of a fraudulently induced misconnection.

The Shi Pei-Pu story reminds us that there is always risk and exposure when we set out to make a new connection with someone we've recently met—precisely because we are vulnerable to being deceived, as Boursicot was. In the traditional world, this risk must have been markedly lower than today: people available to stand in as potential friends or mates were from the same village, or town or neighborhood, and most of the families involved probably either knew each other or knew of each other. So, up to a few hundred years ago, one presumably didn't often make connections with strangers—and fraudulently induced relationships must have been rare indeed. But today, how different everything is, especially in the dating game. About half of the US population consists of unmarried single adults, and about 40 percent of them use online dating.[33] And people do find mates: about 20

32. Roger Faligot and Rémi Kauffer, *Kang Sheng: Le maître espion de Mao* (Paris: Perrin, 2014).

33. Isabel Thottain, "10 Online Dating Statistics You Should Know," *Eharmony*. https://www.eharmony.com/online-dating-statistics/.

percent of current committed relationships began online.[34] But what is relevant for our discussion here is that other studies have shown that just over half of the people who use a dating app lie in their online dating profile.[35] While exaggerating details of their work life or personal accomplishments probably doesn't often rise to the level of misrepresenting their gender like Shi Pei-Pu did, by all odds, elements of significant fraudulent inducement must exist in the substructure of a great many of today's relationships. These little insertions of dishonesty in the presentation of self at the beginning of an affiliation are like diminutive, undetonated land mines buried just beneath the topography of a relationship: they silently and patiently await detonation.

Loneliness, of course, does not come only to those who make a poor selection of a potential new connection. It can also sneak up on those who are firmly connected and flourishing in a network of family and friends, as was young Victoria in "The Girl Who Inherited France." In some sense, of course, even our most stable and solid linkages to others always remain vulnerable, even doomed: nearly all of us live through the deaths of our grandparents, then our parents, and then, later in life, friend after friend after friend. But imagine coming home from the first grade to learn that your mother had died and was forever gone—and realizing, over the days and weeks that followed, just what those words really meant: that you would never, ever see her again. But Victoria had her father, his family, and all her school friends and neighborhood friends—until she almost didn't.

Sometimes I used to ask myself what would have happened to Victoria if Dr. Dagnaud and Sophie Bernard had not been so incredibly openhearted and willing to accept Victoria into their lives. What would it have been like for Victoria if the judge had sent her to live with her grandmother in small-town Texas, severing every connection and sense of place that she had known in her young life? While I had other cases where children survived such total transplants, their success in doing so was always, if memory serves, a function of their being able to admit to themselves that they had not been safe at home. Mickey Colombaro from "Bread Should Not Taste like Kleenex" was a perfect

---

34. Thottain, "10 Online Dating Statistics."
35. Thottain, "10 Online Dating Statistics."

example of this. Once he sensed that moving to a new home with a new family would mean a monumental increase in his personal safety, he sloughed off the man who had stood in as his father the way a chick breaks free of its shell and moves on. So far as I know, he has seldom thought back about Steven McCabe, nor, for that matter, has he sought out his onetime ally in the household, Audrey Goodwin. He's moved on in life. In contrast, Victoria would have been going in the opposite direction: from a safe and loving family setting in a vibrant community to older, unknown grandparents who were religious zealots in a tiny town on the outskirts of nowhere. Victoria would have found herself in an unaccustomed setting, without a single familiar face, and it is hard to imagine that she would have had the strength of character, at six years of age, to survive so much loss and remain the intact, optimistic, bright-eyed child I came to know.

Many clients—certainly the majority—did not perceive how chronic loneliness was waiting just beyond the horizon. But a few particularly perceptive individuals were indeed very much aware of the threat that misconnection represented to their well-being. Certainly the most dedicated and determined warrior against loneliness was Billy Denver, whom you met in "The Boy Who Was Older Than His Parents." Billy fought loneliness head-on. Unwilling to settle for even the relatively subtle form of misconnection that he experienced in the limited ability of each of his parents to fully emote and connect with him, he "hired" me as his attorney to deal with the issue—just the way others seek an attorney when their neighbor's new driveway encroaches on their yard. I found great courage in his determination to insist upon a better-quality connection with his parents, and sometimes I even wondered if what he had had in mind was another project altogether: improving the relationship between his two parents before his time ran out. I don't believe I've ever been more moved by being present as a client met his fate. Let me put it this way: the coins in that cigar box would have fully paid my lawman bill. Well, actually, to be perfectly honest, it would have taken the coins *and* the pen that could write in five colors—not four. It's in my desk drawer even now.

There were other cases where those who sought connection found only terror, and never again dared subject themselves to the risks involved in heading back out into the world to connect with new others. Audrey Goodwin, the baker from "Bread Should Not Taste like Kleenex," deserves a medal for the courage she exhibited in breaking free from the domestic violence that her abusive husband visited upon her in that dark, gloomy house that was her prison. I learned from the literature on spousal abuse that I plunged into when Goodwin's non-case first came my way, how enormously difficult escape is for the vast majority of battered spouses. But it wasn't just courage that saved Goodwin. According to Dr. Young—the psychiatrist who worked with Goodwin after her escape to help her adjust to a normal life—Goodwin might never have been able to garner the strength it took to escape had she not been a master baker. On a practical level, her skills provided the finances she needed to escape—in contrast to so many other victims of abusive relationships who remain at home with their abuser simply because they do not have the funds that would be needed to leave and live on their own. But far more important, in Dr. Young's opinion, was what her mastery of baking did for Goodwin on a psychological level. However successful her abusive husband might have been in diminishing her self-worth in general, there was no way he could belittle her baking skills. As Dr. Young phrased it, "She was a *master* of her trade. When you are a master tradesperson or craftsperson or artist or musician—or anything else—you are simply not subject to domination by degradation. You know what really saved her? It was those same baguettes that got you involved in the first place."

Tragically, Goodwin has never again been able to venture out into the world of new and uncertain relationships. At least not yet. But while Goodwin may end up forever withdrawn, her erstwhile stepson bolted forward into his new life with total determination—which, at his age, was all about connecting with his new adoptive family. And did he ever. Today, Mickey plies the Colombaro family trade in Boston's North End. About half a dozen years ago, I stopped by his family's bakery, and when I was waiting in line to pay for a loaf of Italian country bread (all right, all right—and a box of cannoli—I admit it), I found myself queued up directly behind a very senior citizen. When this lady went to take her cash purse out of her pocketbook, her three-footed cane slipped out from under the crook of her arm and clanged to the floor. Naturally, I scooped it up for her, and as she turned to retrieve it and thank me, I remet Marilyn Morningstar—the retired head of the adoption program with whom I had worked to help Mickey Colombaro find a safe life. I hadn't seen her in nearly a decade, and, indeed, it would prove to be the last time I would ever see her. Fortunately, we took the time to have a coffee at the Caffé Vittoria just down the street from the bakery.

As you might imagine, our conversation began with mutual exclamations of how magnificently well Mickey's adoption had turned out for him. Even at eight years of age—or perhaps nine, by then, neither of us could remember—he had wanted with all his heart and soul to find a "real family" and to dive into it the way one dives in for a swim on a hot summer day. But then we turned to talking about adoption in general, and about what a psychologically complex phenomenon of reconnection it proves to be for many—perhaps most—children adopted over the age of five or six. I'd been involved in the legal work for dozens of older-child adoptions, while Morningstar had been involved in the adoptive placement of hundreds and hundreds of these children in her half century of work, first as an employee and then as the head of one of Boston's largest adoption agencies. So I was fascinated by her answer to a question I posed about what it was in Mickey's background or character that allowed him to so successfully move on from Mickey X to Mickey Morningstar to Mickey Colombaro.

Morningstar took her own sweet time to think through her answer; clearly, she was savoring our little tea party—and one after another of my cannoli. Finally, in a voice as soft as alpaca wool, she spoke, and as nearly as I can remember, this is how she replied: "It was easy for Mickey to move on, because Mr. McCabe had expressly and repeatedly told the boy that he didn't believe that Mickey was actually his son. I remember that he said those words even after all these years, because I found them so shocking. Children—and adults as well—need to be and to feel securely and safely connected with those they live with. Otherwise they move on. And that's precisely what Mickey did, and why he was able to bond so effectively with his adoptive family. When Mr. McCabe said to him, 'I'm not really your dad,' he was, in effect, also saying, 'We're not really connected, not in a forever way, so feel free to leave and find something better.' And Mickey did just that. Who wouldn't. Because it's all about connections, Terry. It's all about connections."

***

So here, my reader, our paths do part. I'm honored, frankly, that you've trusted me to guide you on this journey, some of it through thorny pathways. Loneliness is not a pleasant topic, for sure, but it's worth recognizing that the connections we establish with one another as we live out our lives are as important to our health as whether we eat properly, exercise adequately, control our alcohol and substance intake, and reject tobacco. These comparisons are not mere hyperbole: many studies have shown that being chronically lonely is as deleterious to our health as heavy cigarette smoking, morbid obesity, or a totally sedentary lifestyle.[36]

And while we all recognize that total or near-total isolation can lead to devastating loneliness—save for the few among us who are equipped to find peace in solitude—it is perhaps harder to admit that we can find ourselves equally lonely even though we are enmeshed in a network of connections. The single goal of this collection of case stories has been to take a look at some of the different ways in which what appear from the outside to be viable and functioning interpersonal connections may, upon closer inspection, prove to be misconnections.

And let's not forget that misconnections, at times, can be additionally pernicious in that they all too often act to mask the presence of chronic loneliness: one can believe oneself to be involved in significant affective networks that, in fact, don't really exist. Herbert Britton in "Three Souls Caught in a Spider's Web" was the poster child for this type of doubly dangerous misconnection. He was both entirely alone in the world and also completely unaware of his loneliness because of how he misconstrued the nature of his relationships with his law clients. I suppose to some extent we all are subject to misrepresenting to ourselves the quality of our relationships—*perhaps especially we men.* We men all too often settle for friendships that are far from what they

---

36. The late John T. Cacioppo and his colleagues at the University of Chicago have produced an amazing body of work on the lethality of loneliness. See B. N. Uchino, J. T. Cacioppo, and J. K. Kiecolt-Glazer, "The Relationship Between Social Support and Physiological Processes: A Review with Emphasis on Underlying Mechanisms and Implications for Health," *Psychological Bulletin* 119 (1996): 488–531. A good summary is found in Cacioppo and Patrick, *Loneliness.*

potentially could be: if only we could stop talking about sports and speak more often and more openly with one another about how we feel about our relationships, and what we could do to get more out of them.

***

And finally, in closing, permit me to say just a very few last words about Billy Denver, "The Boy Who Was Older Than His Parents." If Billy had not left this life so early, so prematurely, I would most assuredly have asked him to take a look at an early draft of this manuscript to give me feedback and critique. The boy was a child prodigy with respect to interpersonal relationships; he understood as well as anybody I've ever met the importance of being emotionally and experientially present for your relationships with others. If your mind is elsewhere, he would have said, so, too, will be your heart.

ABOUT THE AUTHOR

J. W. Freiberg holds a PhD from UCLA and a JD from Harvard Law School. He was formerly assistant professor and director of graduate studies in the Department of Sociology at Boston University, where he taught courses on social psychology and the sociology of law. In addition to having been a long-standing member of the Centre d'étude des Mouvements Sociaux in Paris, Freiberg has held positions at several of Boston's oldest law firms and is the author or editor of four previous books: *Growing Up Lonely: Disconnection and Misconnection in the Lives of Our Children*; *Four Seasons of Loneliness: A Lawyer's Case Stories*; *Critical Sociology: European Perspectives*; and *The French Press: Class, State, and Ideology*. He has also published over thirty-five articles, book introductions, and other scholarly works on social psychology and legal issues. His writings have been translated into French, Italian, and Japanese. During his career, Freiberg was awarded a Woodrow Wilson Dissertation Fellowship, a National Science Foundation Research Fellowship, and a Centre National de la Recherche Scientifique Fellowship. Largely retired from the active practice of law, he serves as a justice of the peace for the Commonwealth of Massachusetts, and lives in Boston with his wife, near their children.

CPSIA information can be obtained
at www.ICGtesting.com
Printed in the USA
LVHW040246021020
667743LV00003B/931